CLYMER®

BMW

F650 • 1994-2000

D1709627

The world's finest publisher of mechanical how-to manuals

PRIMEDIA
Business Magazines & Media

P.O. Box 12901, Overland Park, Kansas 66282-2901

11/27/02

Copyright ©2002 PRIMEDIA Business Magazines & Media Inc.

FIRST EDITION
First Printing July, 2002

Printed in U.S.A.

CLYMER and colophon are registered trademarks of PRIMEDIA Business Magazines & Media Inc.

ISBN: 0-89287-802-9

Library of Congress: 2002107947

AUTHOR: Ed Scott.

TECHNICAL PHOTOGRAPHY: Ed Scott with technical assistance from Jordan Engineering, Oceanside California. F650 courtesy of Brattin Motors BMW, San Diego, California. U.K. technical assistance courtesy David Gath of Motohaus Marketing.

TECHNICAL ILLUSTRATIONS: Errol and Mitzi McCarthy.

WIRING DIAGRAMS: Robert Caldwell.

EDITOR: James Grooms.

PRODUCTION: Susan Hartington.

TOOLS AND EQUIPMENT: Moto-Bins Ltd at www.motobins.co.uk and K & L Supply at www.klsupply.com

COVER: Mark Clifford Photography, Los Angeles, California. F650 courtesy of Harry Haus with assistance from West Valley Cycle Sales, Inc., Winnetka, California.

Chapter One
General Information   1

Chapter Two
Troubleshooting   2

Chapter Three
Lubrication, Maintenance and Tune-up   3

Chapter Four
Engine Top End   4

Chapter Five
Engine Lower End   5

Chapter Six
Clutch   6

Chapter Seven
Transmission and Gearshift Mechanism   7

Chapter Eight
Fuel, Exhaust and Emission Control Systems   8

Chapter Nine
Electrical System   9

Chapter Ten
Cooling System   10

Chapter Eleven
Wheels, Hubs, Tires and Drive Chain   11

Chapter Twelve
Front Suspension and Steering   12

Chapter Thirteen
Rear Suspension   13

Chapter Fourteen
Brakes   14

Chapter Fifteen
Body   15

Index   16

Wiring Diagram   17

CLYMER PUBLICATIONS
PRIMEDIA Business Magazines & Media
Chief Executive Officer Timothy M. Andrews
President Ron Wall

EDITORIAL	MARKETING/SALES AND ADMINISTRATION
Editor James Grooms	**Vice President,** **PRIMEDIA Business Directories & Books** Rich Hathaway
Technical Writers Ron Wright Ed Scott George Parise Mark Rolling Michael Morlan Jay Bogart	**Marketing Manager** Elda Starke **Advertising & Promotions Coordinator** Melissa Abbott **Associate Art Directors** Chris Paxton Tony Barmann
Production Supervisor Dylan Goodwin	**Sales Manager/Marine** Dutch Sadler
Lead Editorial Production Coordinator Shirley Renicker	**Sales Manager/Motorcycles** Matt Tusken
Editorial Production Coordinators Greg Araujo Shara Pierceall	**Operations Manager** Patricia Kowalczewski **Sales Manager/Manuals** Ted Metzger
Editorial Production Assistants Susan Hartington Holly Messinger Darin Watson	**Customer Service Manager** Terri Cannon **Customer Service Supervisor** Ed McCarty
Technical Illustrators Steve Amos Robert Caldwell Mitzi McCarthy Bob Meyer Mike Rose	**Customer Service Representatives** Susan Kohlmeyer April LeBlond Courtney Hollars Jennifer Lassiter Ernesto Suarez **Warehouse & Inventory Manager** Leah Hicks

The following books and guides are published by PRIMEDIA Business Directories & Books.

 The Electronics Source Book

More information available at *primediabooks.com*

CONTENTS

QUICK REFERENCE DATA IX

CHAPTER ONE
GENERAL INFORMATION 1
Manual organization
Warnings, cautions and notes
Safety
Serial numbers
Fasteners
Shop supplies

Basic tools
Precision measuring tools
Electrical system fundamentals
Special tools
Basic service methods
Storage

CHAPTER TWO
TROUBLESHOOTING 36
Operating requirements
Starting the engine
Engine performance
Starting system
Charging system
Ignition system
Fuel system
Engine noises

Engine lubrication
Clutch
Transmission
Lighting system
Excessive vibration
Front suspension and steering
Brake system

CHAPTER THREE
LUBRICATION, MAINTENANCE AND TUNE-UP 47

Pre-ride checklist
Tires and wheels
Battery
Engine lubrication
Fork oil
Control cables
Periodic lubrication

Air filter
Brakes
Drive chain and sprockets
Cooling system
Rear suspenion
Fasteners
Tune-up

CHAPTER FOUR
ENGINE TOP END 82

Service precautions
Cylinder head cover
Camshafts
Camshaft chain tensioner and guide rails
Camshaft drive chain

Cylinder head
Valve lifters and shims
Valves and valve components
Cylinder
Pistons and piston rings

CHAPTER FIVE
ENGINE LOWER END 129

Servicing engine in frame
Engine
Crankcase right side cover
Crankcase left side cover
Tachometer drive mechanism
Oil pumps
Primary drive gear and camshaft
  drive chain

Starter clutch and gears
Crankcase, crankshaft and balancer
  shaft
Engine oil circuit bleeding
Engine break-in

CHAPTER SIX
CLUTCH 169

Clutch release lever and bearings
Clutch

Clutch service
Clutch cable replacement

CHAPTER SEVEN
TRANSMISSION AND GEARSHIFT MECHANISM 183

Transmission operation
Transmission
Transmission overhaul

Transmission inspection
Internal shift mechanism

CHAPTER EIGHT
FUEL, EXHAUST AND EMISSION CONTROL SYSTEMS. 200

Carburetor operation
Carburetor
Throttle cable
Starting enrichment valve (choke)
  cable replacment
Fuel tank
Fuel shutoff valve
Air filter air box

Exhaust system
Crankcase breather system
Evaporative emission control system
  (California models)
Evaporative emission control
  system service
Secondary air system
  (U.S. and Switzerland models)

CHAPTER NINE
ELECTRICAL SYSTEM 226

Preliminary inspections
Battery box
Charging system
Alternator
Voltage regulator
Capacitor discharge ignition
Starting system

Starter relay replacement
Lighting system
Switches
Horn
Instruments
Fuses
Wiring diagram

CHAPTER TEN
COOLING SYSTEM 255

Safety precautions
Hoses and hose clamps
Cooling system inspection
Radiator and cooling fan

Cooling fan
Thermostat
Water pump

CHAPTER ELEVEN
WHEELS, HUBS, TIRES AND DRIVE CHAIN 265

Bike stands
Front wheel
Rear wheel
Driven sprocket and driven
  flange
Front and rear hubs

Wheel runout
Wheel service
Wheel balance
Tires
Tire changing
Drive sprocket and chain

CHAPTER TWELVE
FRONT SUSPENSION AND STEERING. 289

Handlebar
Steering head

Front fork

CHAPTER THIRTEEN
REAR SUSPENSION **313**

Shock absorber
Rear swing arm
Swing arm service

Shock linkage
Bearing replacement

CHAPTER FOURTEEN
BRAKES **330**

Brake fluid selection
Brake service
Front brake pad replacement
Front brake caliper
Front master cylinder
Rear brake pad replacement

Rear brake caliper
Rear master cylinder
Rear brake pedal
Brake hose replacement
Brake disc
Bleeding the system

CHAPTER FIFTEEN
BODY **353**

Seat
Front fender
Rear mudguard
Cylinder head side cover
Side cover

Engine lower cover
Windshield and front fairing
Fuel tank cover
Saddlebags
Footpegs

INDEX **362**

WIRING DIAGRAM **368**

QUICK REFERENCE DATA

MOTORCYCLE INFORMATION

MODEL:_____ YEAR:_____

VIN NUMBER:_____

ENGINE SERIAL NUMBER:_____

CARBURETOR SERIAL NUMBER OR I.D. MARK:_____

TIRE INFLATION PRESSURE (COLD)*

Model	kPa	PSI
Front wheels		
Rider only	186	27
Full load	228	33
Rear wheels		
Rider only		
F 650, Funduro,		
Strada, SE	196	28.5
F 650 ST	228	33
Full load	245	35.5

*Tire pressure for original equipment tires. Aftermarket tires may require different inflation pressure.

RECOMMENDED LUBRICANTS AND FLUIDS

Item	Quantity	Recommended type
Engine oil		
Oil and filter change	22.1 L (2.21 U.S. qts./3.70 Imp. pts.)	API SF, SG or SH
Viscosity	–	SAE 20W/50*
Front fork oil (at oil change)		
Regular suspension	600 cc (20 U.S. oz./16.8 Imp. oz.)	BMW 7.5 wt. fork oil
Lowered suspension	650 cc (22 U.S. oz./18 Imp. oz.)	
Brake fluid	–	DOT4
Coolant		
Cooling system	1.2 L (1.27 U.S. qt./2.11 Imp. pts.)	BMW anti-freeze
Recovery tank	200 cc (6.7 U.S. oz./5.6 Imp. oz.)	
Coolant mixing ratio	50% anti-freeze/50% distilled water	–
Battery water	–	Distilled or purified water
Miscellaneous lubricants		
High-performance lubricating		
paste grease	–	Optimoly MP 3
High performance assembly		
paste grease	–	Optimoly TA
Roller bearing grease	–	Retinax EP2

*See Chapter Three, Figure 12 for recommended viscosity ratings for various ambient temperatures.

FORK OIL CAPACITY

	cc	U.S. oz.	Imp. oz.
Regular suspension	600	20	16.8
Lowered suspension	650	22	18

MAINTENANCE AND TUNE-UP SPECIFICATIONS

Item	Specification
Engine compression	NA
Spark plugs	NGK D8EA
Gap	0.6-0.7 mm (0.024-0.028 in.)
Idle speed	1300-1400 rpm
Valve clearance	
Intake and exhaust	0.10-0.15 mm (0.004-0.006 in.)
Ignition timing	Non-adjustable
Brake pad minimum thickness	
Front and back	1.5 mm (0.06 in.)
Drive chain slack	20-30 mm (0.8-1.20 in.)
Clutch cable free play at hand lever	1.5-2.5 mm (0.06-0.10 in.)

MAINTENANCE AND TUNE-UP TORQUE SPECIFICATIONS

Item	N•m	in.-lb.	ft.-lb.
Camshaft mount bolts	10	88	–
Coolant drain screw	10	88	–
Engine oil drain plug	40	–	29
Front fork			
Cap bolt	25	–	18
Drain screw	6	53	–
Handlebar clamp screws	25	–	18
Oil filter cover screw	10	88	–
Oil tank drain plug	10	88	–
Rear axle nut	100	–	74
Steering stem locknut	100	–	74
Upper fork bridge bolts	25	–	18
Valve cover bolts	10	88	–

REPLACEMENT BULBS

Item	Size	Type
Headlamp	12V 60/55	H4 halogen
Parking lamp	12V 4W	T8/4
Brake/tail lamp	12V 21/5	WP25-2
Turn signal lamp	12V 10W	P25-1

INTRODUCTION

The F650, introduced in Europe in 1994, brings back BMW's single-cylinder motorcycle tradition after a 27-year hiatus. This extremely successful bike was the result of a joint venture between BMW and Italian manufacturer Aprilla. It was so successful, approximately one-quarter of BMW's annual sales in the U.K. were F650 models.

The U.S. model was introduced in 1997 as the F650ST. The 18 in. front rim (one inch smaller than the F650), road tires, narrower handlebars and lower seat height make the F650ST a more street-oriented model.

The engine, a liquid-cooled, dual overhead camshaft, four-valve single, is built by Austrian engine manufacture Bombardier-Rotax. The large displacement single is equipped with a constant-vacuum carburetor for each intake port and a stainless steel dual exhaust header to feed and scavenge the four valve head. The muffler incorporates a catalytic converter; this converter, combined with a dual plug cylinder head, ensures that exhaust emissions are kept to a minimum.

Departing from BMW's tradition of shaft drive machines, power is transmitted to the rear wheel via an O-ring chain and a constant mesh five-speed transmission controlled by a wet clutch.

The chassis' excellent ground clearance for off-road riding and quick, predictable handling, a rear shock with rebound and spring preload adaptable for various riding conditions and loads, combined with its overall light weight, make this bike an excellent commuter and trail rider.

CHAPTER ONE

GENERAL INFORMATION

This detailed and comprehensive manual covers the BMW F650 Single from 1994-2000 in the United Kingdom and from 1997-2000 for U.S. models.

The text provides complete maintenance, tune-up, repair and overhaul information. Hundreds of photos and drawings guide the reader through every job.

A shop manual is a reference tool and, as in all Clymer manuals, the chapters are thumb tabbed for easy reference. Important items are indexed at the end of the manual. All procedures, tables and figures are designed for the reader who may be working on the motorcycle for the first time. Frequently used specifications and capacities from individual chapters are summarized in the *Quick Reference Data* at the front of the book.

Tables 1-8 are at the end of this chapter.

MANUAL ORGANIZATION

All dimensions and capacities are expressed in metric and U.S. standard units of measurement.

This chapter provides general information on shop safety, tool use, service fundamentals and shop supplies. The tables at the end of the chapter include general vehicle information.

Chapter Two provides methods for quick and accurate diagnosis of problems. Troubleshooting procedures present typical symptoms and logical methods to pinpoint and repair the problem.

Chapter Three explains all routine maintenance necessary to keep the vehicle running well. Chapter Three also includes recommended tune-up procedures, eliminating the need to constantly consult the chapters on the various assemblies.

Subsequent chapters describe specific systems such as engine, transmission, clutch, drive system, fuel and exhaust systems, suspension and brakes. Each disassembly, repair and assembly procedure is discussed in step-by-step form.

Some of the procedures in this manual specify special tools. In most cases, the tool is illustrated in use. Well-equipped mechanics may be able to substitute similar tools or fabricate a suitable replacement. However, in some cases, the specialized equipment or necessary expertise may make it impractical for the home mechanic to attempt the procedure. When necessary, such operations are identified in the text with the recommendation to have a dealership or specialist perform the task. It may be less expensive to have a professional perform these jobs, especially when considering the cost of the equipment.

WARNINGS, CAUTIONS AND NOTES

The terms WARNING, CAUTION and NOTE have specific meanings in this manual.

A WARNING emphasizes areas where injury or even death could result from negligence. Mechanical damage may also occur. WARNINGS *are to be taken seriously*.

A CAUTION emphasizes areas where equipment damage could result. Disregarding a CAUTION could cause permanent mechanical damage, though injury is unlikely.

A NOTE provides additional information to make a step or procedure easier or clearer. Disregarding a NOTE could cause inconvenience, but would not cause equipment damage or personal injury.

SAFETY

Professional mechanics can work for years and never sustain a serious injury or mishap. Follow these guidelines and practice common sense to safely service the vehicle.

1. Do not operate the vehicle in an enclosed area. The exhaust gasses contain carbon monoxide, an odorless, colorless, and tasteless poisonous gas. Carbon monoxide levels build quickly in small enclosed areas and can cause unconsciousness and death in a short time. Make sure the work area is properly ventilated, or operate the vehicle outside.

2. *Never* use gasoline or any extremely flammable liquid to clean parts. Refer to *Cleaning Parts* and *Handling Gasoline Safely* in this chapter.

3. *Never* smoke or use a torch in the vicinity of flammable liquids such as gasoline or cleaning solvent.

4. If welding or brazing on the vehicle, remove the fuel tank, carburetor and shocks to a safe distance, at least 50 ft. (15 m) away.

5. Use the correct type and size of tools to avoid damaging fasteners.

6. Keep tools clean and in good condition. Replace or repair any worn or damaged equipment.

7. When loosening a tight fastener, be guided by what could happen if the tool slips.

8. When replacing fasteners, make sure the new fasteners are of the same size and strength as the original ones.

9. Keep the work area clean and organized.

10. Wear eye protection *anytime* the safety of your eyes is in question. This includes procedures involving drilling, grinding, hammering, compressed air and chemicals.

11. Wear the correct clothing for the job. Tie up or cover long hair so it cannot get caught in moving equipment.

12. Do not carry sharp tools in clothing pockets.

13. Always have an approved fire extinguisher available. Make sure it is rated for gasoline (Class B) and electrical (Class C) fires.

14. Do not use compressed air to clean clothes, the vehicle or the work area. Debris may be blown into the eyes or skin. *Never* direct compressed air at yourself or someone else. Do not allow children to use or play with any compressed air equipment.

15. When using compressed air to dry rotating parts, hold the part so it cannot rotate. Do not allow the force of the air to spin the part. The air jet is capable of rotating parts at extremely high speed. The part may be damaged or disintegrate, causing serious injury.

16. Do not inhale the dust created by brake pad and clutch wear. These particles may contain asbestos. In addition, some types of insulating materials and gaskets may also contain asbestos. Inhaling asbestos particles is hazardous to people's health.

17. Never work on the vehicle while someone is working under it.

18. When placing the vehicle on a stand, make sure it is secure before walking away.

Handling Gasoline Safely

Gasoline is a volatile, flammable liquid and is one of the most dangerous items in the shop.

Because gasoline is used so often, many people forget that it is hazardous. Only use gasoline as fuel for gasoline internal combustion engines. Keep in mind when working on a vehicle that gasoline is always present in the fuel tank, fuel line and carbure-

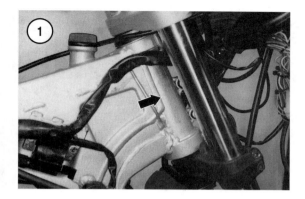

tors. To avoid a disastrous accident when working around the fuel system, carefully observe the following precautions:

1. *Never* use gasoline to clean parts. See *Cleaning Parts* in this chapter.
2. When working on the fuel system, work outside or in a well-ventilated area.
3. Do not add fuel to the fuel tank or service the fuel system while the vehicle is near open flames, sparks or where someone is smoking. Gasoline vapor is heavier than air and it collects in low areas. Gasoline vapor is more easily ignited than liquid gasoline.
4. Allow the engine to cool completely before working on any fuel system component.
5. When draining the carburetors, catch the fuel in a plastic container and pour it into an approved gasoline storage device.
6. Do not store gasoline in glass containers. If the glass breaks, a serious explosion or fire may occur.
7. Immediately wipe up spilled gasoline with rags. Store the rags in a metal container with a lid until they can be properly disposed of, or place them outside in a safe place for the fuel to evaporate.
8. Do not pour water on a gasoline fire. Water spreads the fire and makes it more difficult to put out. Use a class B, BC or ABC fire extinguisher to extinguish the fire.
9. Always turn off the engine before refueling. Do not spill fuel onto the engine or exhaust system. Do not overfill the fuel tank. Leave an air space at the top of the tank to allow room for the fuel to expand due to temperature fluctuations.

Cleaning Parts

Cleaning parts is one of the more tedious and difficult service jobs performed in the home garage.

There are many types of chemical cleaners and solvents available for shop use. Most are poisonous and extremely flammable. To prevent chemical exposure, vapor buildup, fire or serious injury, observe each product warning label and note the following:

1. Read and adhere to the entire product label before using any chemical. Always know what type of chemical is being used and whether it is poisonous or flammable.
2. Do not use more than one type of cleaning solvent at a time. If mixing chemicals is called for, measure the proper amounts according to the manufacturer.
3. Work in a well-ventilated area.
4. Wear chemical-resistant gloves.
5. Wear safety glasses.
6. Wear a vapor respirator if the instructions call for it.
7. Wash hands and arms thoroughly after cleaning parts.
8. Keep chemical products away from children and pets.
9. Thoroughly clean all oil, grease and cleaner residue from any part that must be heated.
10. Use a nylon brush when cleaning parts. Metal brushes may cause a spark.
11. When using a parts washer, only use the solvent recommended by the manufacturer. Make sure the parts washer is equipped with a metal lid that will lower in case of fire.

Warning Labels

Most manufacturers attach information and warning labels to the vehicle. These labels contain instructions that are important to personal safety when operating, servicing, transporting and storing the vehicle. Refer to the owner's manual for the description and location of labels. Order replacement labels from the manufacturer if they are missing or damaged.

SERIAL NUMBERS

Serial numbers are stamped on various locations on the frame, engine, transmission and carburetor. Record these numbers in the *Quick Reference Data* section in the front of the book. Have these numbers available when ordering parts.

The frame serial number (**Figure 1**) is stamped on the right side of the frame steering head.

The VIN number label (**Figure 2**) is located on the top frame cross member under the seat.

Engine serial number (**Figure 3**) is stamped on a top rear portion of the crankcase next to the rear swing arm pivot shaft area.

The carburetor serial number (**Figure 4**) is located on the side of the carburetor body above the float bowl.

FASTENERS

Proper fastener selection and installation is important to ensure that the vehicle operates as designed and can be serviced efficiently. The choice of original equipment fasteners is not arrived at by chance. Make sure that replacement fasteners meet all the same requirements as the originals.

Threaded Fasteners

Threaded fasteners secure most of the components on the vehicle. Most are tightened by turning them clockwise (right-hand threads). If the normal rotation of the component being tightened would loosen the fastener, it may have left-hand threads. If a left-hand threaded fastener is used, it is noted in the text.

Two dimensions are required to match the threads of the fastener: the number of threads in a given distance and the outside diameter of the threads.

Two systems are currently used to specify threaded fastener dimensions: the U.S. Standard system and the metric system. Although fasteners may appear similar, close inspection shows that the thread designs are not the same (**Figure 5**).

Pay particular attention when working with unidentified fasteners; mismatching thread types can damage threads.

NOTE
To ensure that the fastener threads are not mismatched or cross-threaded, start all fasteners by hand. If a fastener is hard to start or turn, determine the cause before tightening with a wrench.

The length (L, **Figure 6**), diameter (D) and distance between thread crests (pitch) (T) classify metric screws and bolts. A typical bolt may be identified by the numbers, 8 × 1.25 × 130. This indi-

cates the bolt has diameter of 8 mm, the distance between thread crests is 1.25 mm and the length is 130 mm. Always measure bolt length as shown in **Figure 6** to avoid purchasing replacements of the wrong length.

The numbers located on the top of the fastener (**Figure 6**) indicate the strength of metric screws and bolts. The higher the number, the stronger the fastener is. Unnumbered fasteners are the weakest.

Many screws, bolts and studs are combined with nuts to secure particular components. To indicate

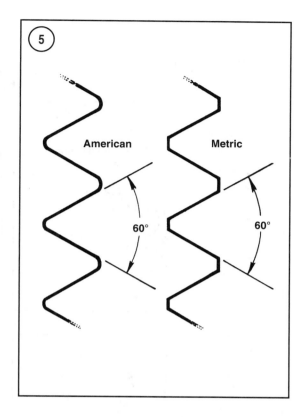

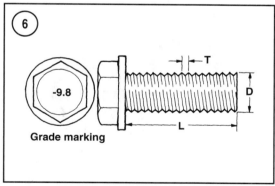

Torque Specifications

The materials used in the manufacture of the vehicle may be subjected to uneven stresses if the fasteners of the various subassemblies are not installed and tightened correctly. Fasteners that are improperly installed or work loose can cause extensive damage. It is essential to use an accurate torque wrench, described in this chapter, with the torque specifications in this manual.

Specifications for torque are provided in Newton-meters (N•m), foot-pounds (ft.-lb.) and inch-pounds (in.-lb.). Refer to **Table 5** for general torque specifications. To use **Table 5**, first determine the size of the fastener as described in *Fasteners* in this chapter. Torque specifications for specific components are at the end of the appropriate chapters. Torque wrenches are covered in the *Basic Tools* section.

Self-Locking Fasteners

Several types of bolts, screws and nuts incorporate a system that creates interference between the two fasteners. Interference is achieved in various ways. The most common type is the nylon insert nut and a dry adhesive coating on the threads of a new bolt.

Self-locking fasteners offer greater holding strength than standard fasteners, which improves their resistance to vibration. Most self-locking fasteners cannot be reused. The materials used to form the lock become distorted after the initial installation and removal. It is a good practice to discard and replace self-locking fasteners after their removal. Do not replace self-locking fasteners with standard fasteners.

the size of a nut, manufacturers specify the internal diameter and the thread pitch.

The measurement across two flats on a nut or bolt indicates the wrench size.

> *WARNING*
> *Do not install fasteners with a strength classification lower than what was originally installed by the manufacturer. Doing so may cause equipment failure and/or damage.*

Washers

There are two basic types of washers: flat washers and lockwashers. Flat washers are simple discs with a hole to fit a screw or bolt. Lockwashers are used to prevent a fastener from working loose. Washers can be used as spacers and seals, or to help distribute fastener load and to prevent the fastener from damaging the component.

As with fasteners, when replacing washers make sure the replacements are of the same design and quality.

Cotter Pins

A cotter pin is a split metal pin inserted into a hole or slot to prevent a fastener from loosening. In certain applications, such as the rear axle on some motorcycles, the fastener must be secured in this way. For these applications, a cotter pin and castellated (slotted) nut is used.

To use a cotter pin, first make sure the diameter is correct for the hole in the fastener. After correctly tightening the fastener and aligning the holes, insert the cotter pin through the hole and bend the ends over the fastener (**Figure 7**). Unless instructed to do so, never loosen a torqued fastener to align the holes. If the holes do not align, tighten the fastener just enough to achieve alignment.

Cotter pins are available in various diameters and lengths. Measure length from the bottom of the head to the tip of the shortest pin.

Snap rings and E-clips

Snap rings (**Figure 8**) are circular-shaped metal retaining clips. They are required to secure parts and gears in place on parts such as shafts, pins or rods. External-type snap rings are used to retain items on shafts. Internal-type snap rings secure parts within housing bores. In some applications, snap rings of varying thickness determine endplay in addition to securing the component(s). These are usually called selective snap rings.

Two basic types of snap rings are used: machined and stamped. Machined snap rings (**Figure 9**) can be installed in either direction, since both faces have sharp edges. Stamped snap rings (**Figure 10**) are manufactured with a sharp edge and a round edge. When installing a stamped snap ring in a thrust application, install the sharp edge facing away from the part producing the thrust.

E-clips and circlips are used when it is not practical to use a snap ring. Remove E-clips with a flat blade screwdriver by prying between the shaft and E-clip. To install an E-clip, center it over the shaft groove and push or tap it into place.

Observe the following when installing snap rings:

1. Remove and install snap rings with snap ring pliers. See *Snap Ring Pliers* in this chapter.

2. In some applications, it may be necessary to replace snap rings after removing them.

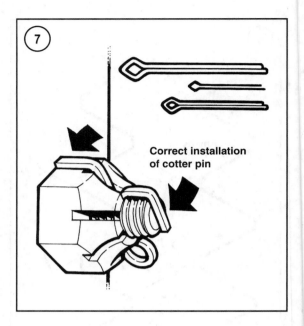

Correct installation
of cotter pin

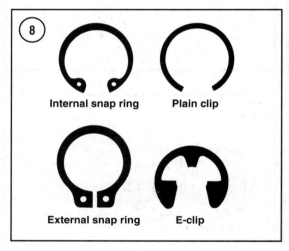

Internal snap ring   Plain clip

External snap ring   E-clip

3. Compress or expand snap rings only enough to install them. If overly expanded, they lose their retaining ability.

4. After installing a snap ring, make sure it seats completely.

5. Wear eye protection when removing and installing snap rings.

SHOP SUPPLIES

Lubricants and Fluids

Periodic lubrication helps ensure a long service life for any type of equipment. Using the correct

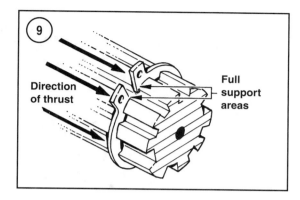

Direction of thrust
Full support areas

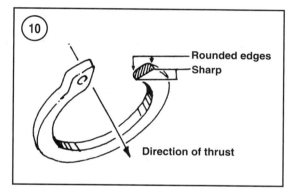

Rounded edges
Sharp
Direction of thrust

type of lubricant is as important as performing the lubrication service, although in an emergency, the wrong type is better than none. The following section describes the types of lubricants most often required. Make sure to follow the manufacturer's recommendations for lubricant types.

Engine oils

Engine oil is classified by two standards: the American Petroleum Institute (API) service classification and the Society of Automotive Engineers (SAE) viscosity rating. This information is on the oil container label. Two letters indicate the API service classification. The number or sequence of numbers and letter (10W-40 for example) is the oil's viscosity rating. The API service classification and the SAE viscosity index are not indications of oil quality.

The service classification indicates that the oil meets specific lubrication standards. The first letter in the classification (S) indicates that the oil is for gasoline engines. The second letter indicates the standard the oil satisfies. The classification started with the letter A and is currently at the letter J.

Always use an oil with a classification recommended by the manufacturer. Using an oil with a different classification can cause engine damage.

Viscosity is an indication of the oil's thickness. Thin oils have a lower number while thick oils have a higher number. Engine oils fall into the 5- to 50-weight range for single-grade oils.

Most manufacturers recommend multigrade oil. These oils perform efficiently across a wide range of operating conditions. Multigrade oils are identified by a W after the first number, which indicates the low-temperature viscosity.

Engine oils are most commonly mineral (petroleum) based; however, synthetic and semi-synthetic types are used more frequently. When selecting engine oil, follow the manufacturer's recommendation for type, classification and viscosity when selecting engine oil.

Greases

Grease is lubricating oil with thickening agents added to it. The National Lubricating Grease Institute (NLGI) grades grease. Grades range from No. 000 to No. 6, with No. 6 being the thickest. Typical multipurpose grease is NLGI No. 2. For specific applications, manufacturers may recommend water-resistant type grease or one with an additive such as molybdenum disulfide (MoS_2).

Brake fluid

Brake fluid is the hydraulic fluid used to transmit hydraulic pressure (force) to the wheel brakes. Brake fluid is classified by the Department of Transportation (DOT). Current designations for brake fluid are DOT 3, DOT 4 and DOT 5. This classification appears on the fluid container.

Each type of brake fluid has its own definite characteristics. Do not intermix different types of brake fluid. DOT 5 fluid is silicone-based. DOT 5 brake fluid is not compatible with other brake fluids or in systems for which it is not designed. Mixing DOT 5 fluid with other fluids may cause brake failure. When adding brake fluid, *only* use the fluid recommended by the manufacturer.

Brake fluid will damage any plastic, painted or plated surface it contacts. Use extreme care when working with brake fluid and remove any spills immediately with soap and water.

Hydraulic brake systems require clean and moisture-free brake fluid. Never reuse brake fluid. Keep containers and reservoirs properly sealed.

> *WARNING*
> *Never put a mineral-based (petroleum) oil into the brake system. Mineral oil will cause rubber parts in the system to swell and break apart, resulting in complete brake failure.*

Cleaners, Degreasers and Solvents

Many chemicals are available to remove oil, grease and other residue from the vehicle. Before using cleaning solvents, consider how they will be used and disposed of, particularly if they are not water-soluble. Local ordinances may require special procedures for the disposal of many types of cleaning chemicals. Refer to *Safety and Cleaning Parts* in this chapter for more information on their use.

Use brake parts cleaner to clean brake system components when contact with petroleum-based products will damage seals. Brake parts cleaner leaves no residue. Use electrical contact cleaner to clean electrical connections and components without leaving any residue. Carburetor cleaner is a powerful solvent used to remove fuel deposits and varnish from fuel system components. Use this cleaner carefully, as it may damage finishes.

Generally, degreasers are strong cleaners used to remove heavy accumulations of grease from engine and frame components.

Most solvents are designed to be used in a parts washing cabinet for individual component cleaning. For safety, use only nonflammable or high flash point solvents.

Gasket Sealant

Sealants are used in combination with a gasket or seal and are occasionally used alone. Follow the manufacturer's recommendation when using sealants. Use extreme care when choosing a sealant different from the type originally recommended. Choose sealants based on their resistance to heat, various fluids and their sealing capabilities.

One of the most common sealants is RTV, or room temperature vulcanizing sealant. This sealant cures at room temperature over a specific time pe-

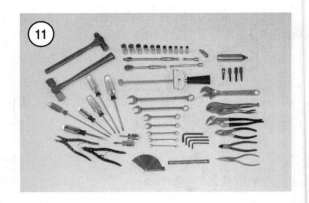

riod. This allows the repositioning of components without damaging gaskets.

Moisture in the air causes the RTV sealant to cure. Always install the tube cap as soon as possible after applying RTV sealant. RTV sealant has a limited shelf life and will not cure properly if the shelf life has expired. Keep partial tubes sealed and discard them if they have surpassed the expiration date.

Applying RTV sealant

Clean all old gasket residue from the mating surfaces. Remove all gasket material from blind threaded holes; it can cause inaccurate bolt torque. Spray the mating surfaces with aerosol parts cleaner and then wipe with a lint-free cloth. The area must be clean for the sealant to adhere.

Apply RTV sealant in a continuous bead 2-3 mm (0.08-0.12 in.) thick. Circle all the fastener holes unless otherwise specified. Do not allow any sealant to enter these holes. Assemble and tighten the fasteners to the specified torque within the time frame recommended by the RTV sealant manufacturer.

Gasket Remover

Aerosol gasket remover can help remove stubborn gaskets. This product can speed up the removal process and prevent damage to the mating surface that may be caused by using a scraping tool. Most of these types of products are very caustic. Follow the gasket remover manufacturer's instructions for use.

Threadlocking Compound

A threadlocking compound is a fluid applied to the threads of fasteners. After tightening the fas-

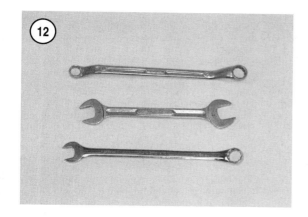

tener, the fluid dries and becomes a solid filler between the threads. This makes it difficult for the fastener to work loose from vibration, or heat expansion and contraction. Some threadlocking compounds also provide a seal against fluid leakage.

Before applying threadlocking compound, remove any old compound from both thread areas and clean them with aerosol parts cleaner. Use the compound sparingly. Excess fluid can run into adjoining parts.

Threadlocking compounds are available in different strengths. Follow the particular manufacturer's recommendations regarding compound selection. Manufacturers of threadlocking compound offer a wide range of compounds for various strength, temperature and repair applications.

BASIC TOOLS

Most of the procedures in this manual can be carried out with simple hand tools and test equipment familiar to the home mechanic. Always use the correct tools for the job at hand. Keep tools organized and clean. Store them in a tool chest with related tools organized together.

Quality tools are essential. The best are constructed of high-strength alloy steel. These tools are light, easy to use and resistant to wear. Their working surface has no sharp edges and the tool is carefully polished. They have an easy-to-clean finish and are comfortable to use. Quality tools are a good investment.

When purchasing tools to perform the procedures covered in this manual, consider the tool's potential frequency of use. If a tool kit is just now being started, consider purchasing a basic tool set (**Figure 11**) from a large tool supplier. These sets are available in many tool combinations and offer substantial savings when compared to individually purchased tools. As work experience grows and tasks become more complicated, specialized tools can be added.

Screwdrivers

Screwdrivers of various lengths and types are mandatory for the simplest tool kit. The two basic types are the slotted tip (flat blade) and the Phillips tip. These are available in sets that often include an assortment of tip sizes and shaft lengths.

As with all tools, use a screwdriver designed for the job. Make sure the size of the tip conforms to the size and shape of the fastener. Use them only for driving screws. Never use a screwdriver for prying or chiseling metal. Repair or replace worn or damaged screwdrivers. A worn tip may damage the fastener, making it difficult to remove.

Wrenches

Open-end, box-end and combination wrenches (**Figure 12**) are available in a variety of types and sizes.

The number stamped on the wrench refers to the distance between the work areas. This size must match the size of the fastener head.

The box-end wrench is an excellent tool because it grips the fastener on all sides. This reduces the chance of the tool slipping. The box-end wrench is designed with either a 6- or 12-point opening. For stubborn or damaged fasteners, the 6-point provides superior holding ability by contacting the fastener across a wider area at all six edges. For general use, the 12-point works well. It allows the wrench to be removed and reinstalled without moving the handle over such a wide arc.

An open-end wrench is fast and works best in areas with limited overhead access. It contacts the fastener at only two points, and is subject to slipping under heavy force, or if the tool or fastener is worn. A box-end wrench is preferred in most instances, especially when breaking loose and applying the final tightness to a fastener.

The combination wrench has a box-end on one end, and an open-end on the other. This combination makes it a very convenient tool.

Adjustable Wrenches

An adjustable wrench or Crescent wrench (**Figure 13**) can fit nearly any nut or bolt head that has clear access around its entire perimeter. Adjustable wrenches are best used as a backup wrench to keep a large nut or bolt from turning while the other end is being loosened or tightened with a box-end or socket wrench.

Adjustable wrenches contact the fastener at only two points, which makes them more subject to slipping off the fastener. The fact that one jaw is adjustable and may loosen only aggravates this shortcoming. Make certain the solid jaw is the one transmitting the force.

Socket Wrenches, Ratchets and Handles

Sockets that attach to a ratchet handle (**Figure 14**) are available with 6-point (A, **Figure 15**) or 12-point (B) openings and different drive sizes. The drive size indicates the size of the square hole that accepts the ratchet handle. The number stamped on the socket is the size of the work area and must match the fastener head.

As with wrenches, a 6-point socket provides superior-holding ability, while a 12-point socket needs to be moved only half as far to reposition it on the fastener.

Sockets are designated for either hand or impact use. Impact sockets are made of thicker material for more durability. Compare the size and wall thickness of a 19-mm hand socket (A, **Figure 16**) and the 19-mm impact socket (B). Use impact sockets when using an impact driver or air tools. Use hand sockets with hand-driven attachments.

> *WARNING*
> *Do not use hand sockets with air or impact tools, as they may shatter and cause injury. Always wear eye protection when using impact or air tools.*

Various handles are available for sockets. The speed handle is used for fast operation. Flexible ratchet heads in varying lengths allow the socket to be turned with varying force, and at odd angles. Extension bars allow the socket setup to reach difficult areas. The ratchet is the most versatile. It allows the user to install or remove the nut without removing the socket.

Sockets combined with any number of drivers make them undoubtedly the fastest, safest and most convenient tool for fastener removal and installation.

Impact Driver

An impact driver provides extra force for removing fasteners by converting the impact of a hammer

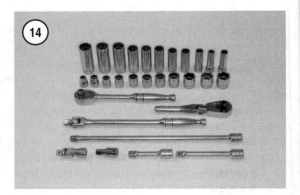

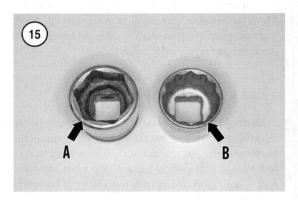

A   B

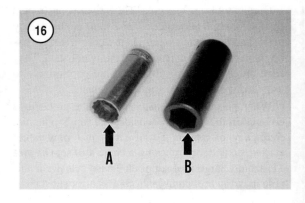

A   B

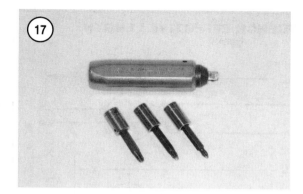

into a turning motion. This makes it possible to re-move stubborn fasteners without damaging them. Impact drivers and interchangeable bits (**Figure 17**) are available from most tool suppliers. When using a socket with an impact driver make sure the socket is designed for impact use. Refer to *Socket Wrenches, Ratchets and Handles* in this section.

WARNING
Do not use hand sockets with air or impact tools, as they may shatter and cause injury. Always wear eye protec-tion when using impact or air tools.

Allen Wrenches

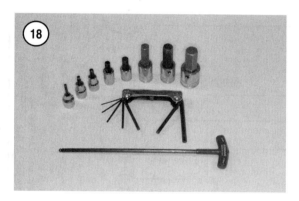

Allen or setscrew wrenches (**Figure 18**) are used on fasteners with hexagonal recesses in the fastener head. These wrenches are available in L-shaped bar, socket and T-handle types. A metric set is required when working on most vehicles. Allen bolts are sometimes called socket bolts.

Torque Wrenches

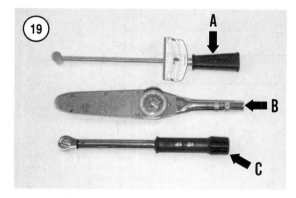

A torque wrench is used with a socket, torque adapter or similar extension to tighten a fastener o a measured torque. Torque wrenches come in sev-eral drive sizes (1/4, 3/8, 1/2 and 3/4) and have various methods of reading the torque value. The drive size in-dicates the size of the square drive that accepts the socket, adapter or extension. Common methods of reading the torque value are the deflecting beam (A, **Figure 19**), the dial indicator (B) and the audible click (C). When choosing a torque wrench, consider the torque range, drive size and accuracy. The torque specifications in this manual provide an indication of the range required. A torque wrench is a precision tool that must be properly cared for to remain accurate. Store torque wrenches in cases or separate padded drawers within a toolbox. Follow the manufacturer's instructions for their care and calibration.

Torque Adapters

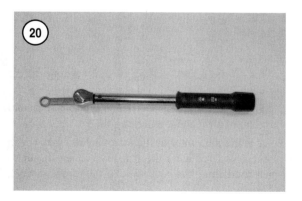

Torque adapters or extensions extend or reduce the reach of a torque wrench. The torque adapter shown in **Figure 20** is used to tighten a fastener that cannot be reached due to the size of the torque wrench head, drive, and socket. If a torque adapter

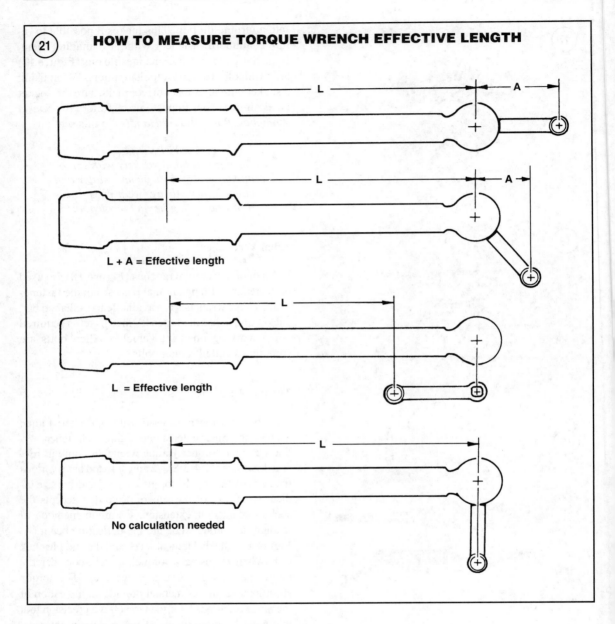

(21) **HOW TO MEASURE TORQUE WRENCH EFFECTIVE LENGTH**

L + A = Effective length

L = Effective length

No calculation needed

changes the effective lever length (**Figure 21**), the torque reading on the wrench will not equal the actual torque applied to the fastener. It is necessary to recalibrate the torque setting on the wrench to compensate for the change of lever length. When a torque adapter is used at a right angle to the drive head, calibration is not required, since the effective length has not changed.

To recalculate a torque reading when using a torque adapter, use the following formula, and refer to **Figure 21**.

$$TW = \frac{TA \times L}{L + A}$$

TW is the torque setting or dial reading on the wrench.

TA is the torque specification and the actual amount of torque that will be applied to the fastener.

A is the amount that the adapter increases (or in some cases reduces) the effective lever length as measured along the centerline of the torque wrench (**Figure 21**).

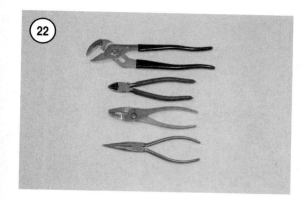

In this example, the torque wrench would be set to the recalculated torque value (TW = 16.5 ft.-lb.). When using a beam-type wrench, tighten the fastener until the pointer aligns with 16.5 ft.-lb. In this example, although the torque wrench is preset to 16.5 ft.-lb., the actual torque is 20 ft.-lb.

Pliers

Pliers come in a wide range of types and sizes. Pliers are useful for holding, cutting, bending, and crimping. Do not use them to turn fasteners. **Figure 22** and **Figure 23** show several types of useful pliers. Each design has a specialized function. Slip-joint pliers are general-purpose pliers used for gripping and bending. Diagonal cutting pliers are needed to cut wire and can be used to remove cotter pins. Needlenose pliers are used to hold or bend small objects. Locking pliers (**Figure 23**), sometimes called Vise grips, are used to hold objects very tightly. They have many uses, ranging from holding two parts together to gripping the end of a broken stud. Use caution when using locking pliers, as the sharp jaws will damage the objects they hold.

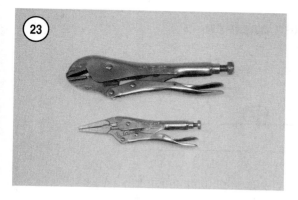

Snap Ring Pliers

Snap ring pliers are specialized pliers with tips that fit into the ends of snap rings to remove and install them.

Snap ring pliers are available with a fixed action (either internal or external) or convertible (one tool works on both internal and external snaprings). They may have fixed tips or interchangeable ones of various sizes and angles. For general use, select a convertible-type pliers with interchangeable tips.

> *WARNING*
> *Snap rings can slip and fly off when removing and installing them. Also, the snap ring pliers tips may break. Always wear eye protection when using snap ring pliers.*

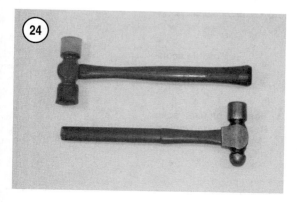

L is the lever length of the wrench as measured from the center of the drive to the center of the grip.

The effective length is the sum of L and A (**Figure 21**).

Example:
TA = 20 ft.-lb.
A = 3 in.
L = 14 in.

$$TW = \frac{20 \times 14}{14 + 3} = \frac{280}{17} = 16.5 \text{ ft. lb.}$$

Hammers

Various types of hammers (**Figure 24**) are available to fit a number of applications. A ball-peen hammer is used to strike another tool, such as a

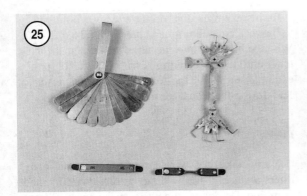

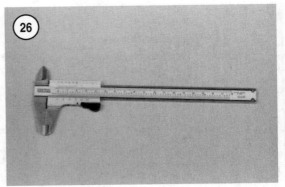

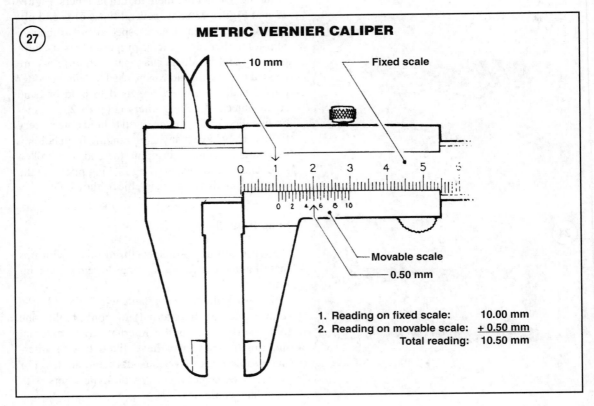

METRIC VERNIER CALIPER

10 mm

Fixed scale

Movable scale

0.50 mm

1. Reading on fixed scale:	10.00 mm
2. Reading on movable scale:	+ 0.50 mm
Total reading:	10.50 mm

punch or chisel. Soft-faced hammers are required when a metal object must be struck without damaging it. *Never* use a metal-faced hammer on engine and suspension components, as damage will occur in most cases.

Always wear eye protection when using hammers. Make sure the hammer face is in good condition and the handle is not cracked. Select the correct hammer for the job and make sure to strike the object squarely. Do not use the handle or the side of the hammer to strike an object.

PRECISION MEASURING TOOLS

The ability to accurately measure components is essential to successfully rebuild an engine. Equipment is manufactured to close tolerances, and obtaining consistently accurate measurements is essential to determining which components require replacement or further service.

Each type of measuring instrument is designed to measure a dimension with a certain degree of accuracy and within a certain range. When selecting the measuring tool, make sure it is applicable to the task.

(28)

DECIMAL PLACE VALUES*

0.1	Indicates 1/10 (one tenth of an inch or millimeter)
0.010	Indicates 1/100 (one one-hundreth of an inch or millimeter)
0.001	Indicates 1/1,000 (one one-thousandth of an inch or millimeter)

*This chart represents the values of figures placed to the right of the decimal point. Use it when reading decimals from one-tenth to one one-thousandth of an inch or millimeter. It is not a conversion chart (for example: 0.001 in. is not equal to 0.001 mm).

As with all tools, measuring tools provide the best results if cared for properly. Improper use can damage the tool and result in inaccurate results. If any measurement is questionable, verify the measurement using another tool. A standard gauge is usually provided with measuring tools to check accuracy and calibrate the tool if necessary.

Precision measurements can vary according to the experience of the person performing the procedure. Accurate results are only possible if the mechanic possesses a feel for using the tool. Heavy-handed use of measuring tools will produce less accurate results. Hold the tool gently by the fingertips so the point at which the tool contacts the object is easily felt. This feel for the equipment will produce more accurate measurements and reduce the risk of damaging the tool or component. Refer to the following sections for specific measuring tools.

Feeler Gauge

The feeler or thickness gauge (**Figure 25**) is used for measuring the distance between two surfaces.

A feeler gauge set consists of an assortment of steel strips of graduated thicknesses. Each blade is marked with its thickness. Blades can be of various lengths and angles for different procedures.

A common use for a feeler gauge is to measure valve clearance. Wire (round) type gauges are used to measure spark plug gap.

Calipers

Calipers (**Figure 26**) are excellent tools for obtaining inside, outside and depth measurements. Although not as precise as a micrometer, they allow reasonable

precision, typically to within 0.05 mm (0.001 in.). Most calipers have a range up to 150 mm (6 in.).

Calipers are available in dial, vernier or digital versions. Dial calipers have a dial readout that provides convenient reading. Vernier calipers have marked scales that must be compared to determine the measurement. The digital caliper uses an LCD to show the measurement.

Properly maintain the measuring surfaces of the caliper. There must not be any dirt or burrs between the tool and the object being measured. Never force the caliper closed around an object; close the caliper around the highest point so it can be removed with a slight drag. Some calipers require calibration. Always refer to the manufacturer's instructions when using a new or unfamiliar caliper.

To read a vernier caliper, refer to **Figure 27**. The fixed scale is marked in 1-mm increments. Ten individual lines on the fixed scale equal 1 cm. The moveable scale is marked in 0.05 mm (hundredth) increments. To obtain a reading, establish the first number by the location of the 0 line on the movable scale in relation to the first line to the left on the fixed scale. In this example, the number is 10 mm. To determine the next number, note which of the lines on the movable scale align with a mark on the fixed scale. A number of lines will seem close, but only one will align exactly. In this case, 0.50 mm is the reading to add to the first number. The result of adding 10 mm and 0.50 mm is a measurement of 10.50 mm.

Micrometers

A micrometer is an instrument designed for linear measurement using the decimal divisions of the inch or meter (**Figure 28**). While there are many types and styles of micrometers, most of the procedures in this manual call for an outside micrometer. The outside micrometer is used to measure the outside diameter of cylindrical forms and the thickness of materials.

A micrometer's size indicates the minimum and maximum size of a part that it can measure. The usual sizes (**Figure 29**) are 0-1 in. (0-25 mm), 1-2 in. (25-50 mm), 2-3 in. (50-75 mm) and 3-4 in. (75-100 mm).

Micrometers that cover a wider range of measurements are available. These use a large frame with interchangeable anvils of various lengths. This type of micrometer offers a cost savings; however, its overall size may make it less convenient.

Reading a Micrometer

When reading a micrometer, numbers are taken from different scales and added together. The following sections describe how to read the measurements of various types of outside micrometers.

For accurate results, properly maintain the measuring surfaces of the micrometer. There cannot be any dirt or burrs between the tool and the measured object. Never force the micrometer closed around an object. Close the micrometer around the highest point so it can be removed with a slight drag. **Figure 30** shows the markings and parts of a standard inch micrometer. Be familiar with these terms before using a micrometer in the following sections.

Standard inch micrometer

The standard inch micrometer is accurate to one-thousandth of an inch (0.001). The sleeve is marked in 0.025 in. increments. Every fourth sleeve mark is numbered 1, 2, 3, 4, 5, 6, 7, 8, 9. These numbers indicate 0.100, 0.200, 0.300, and so on.

The tapered end of the thimble has twenty-five lines marked around it. Each mark equals 0.001 in. One complete turn of the thimble will align its zero mark with the first mark on the sleeve or 0.025 in.

When reading a standard inch micrometer, perform the following steps while referring to **Figure 31**.
1. Read the sleeve and find the largest number visible. Each sleeve number equals 0.100 in.
2. Count the number of lines between the numbered sleeve mark and the edge of the thimble. Each sleeve mark equals 0.025 in.

3. Read the thimble mark that aligns with the sleeve line. Each thimble mark equals 0.001 in.

NOTE
If a thimble mark does not align exactly with the sleeve line, estimate the amount between the lines. For accurate readings in ten-thousandths of an inch (0.0001 in.), use a vernier inch micrometer.

4. Add the readings from Steps 1-3.

Vernier inch micrometer

A vernier inch micrometer is accurate to one ten-thousandth of an inch or 0.0001 in. It has the same marking as a standard inch micrometer with an additional vernier scale on the sleeve (**Figure 32**).

The vernier scale consists of 11 lines marked 1-9 with a 0 on each end. These lines run parallel to the thimble lines and represent 0.0001 in. increments.

When reading a vernier inch micrometer, perform the following steps while referring to **Figure 33**.

1. Read the micrometer in the same way as a standard micrometer. This is the initial reading.

2. If a thimble mark aligns exactly with the sleeve line, reading the vernier scale is not necessary. If they do not align, read the vernier scale in Step 3.

3. Determine which vernier scale mark aligns with one thimble mark. The vernier scale number is the amount in ten-thousandths of an inch to add to the initial reading from Step 1.

(30)

STANDARD INCH MICROMETER

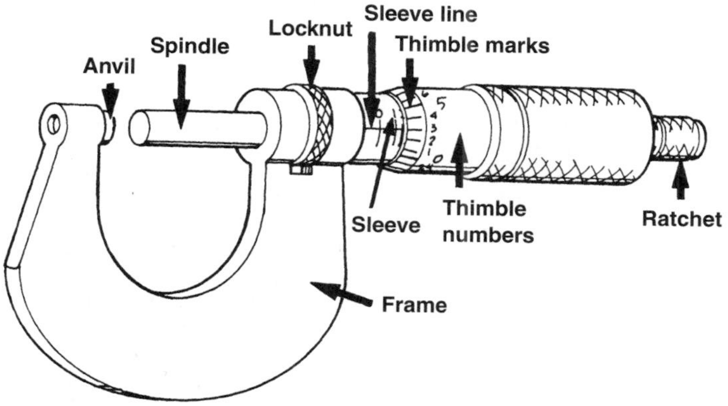

(31)

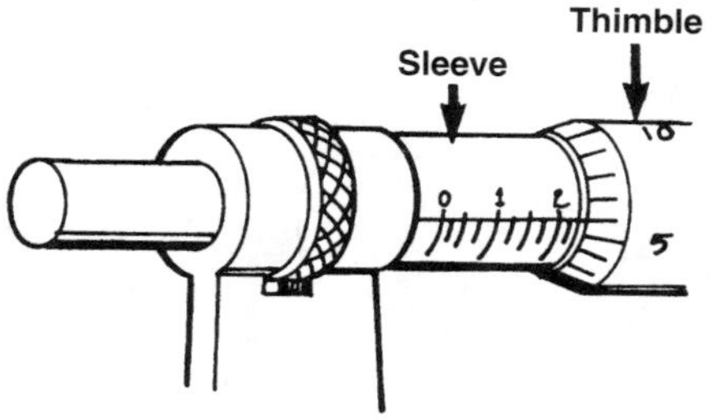

1. Largest number visible on the sleeve line	0.200 in.
2. Number on sleeve marks visible on the sleeve line and the thimble edge	0.025 in.
3. Thimble mark that aligns with sleeve line	0.006 in.
Total reading	0.231 in.

(32)

VERNIER INCH MICROMETER

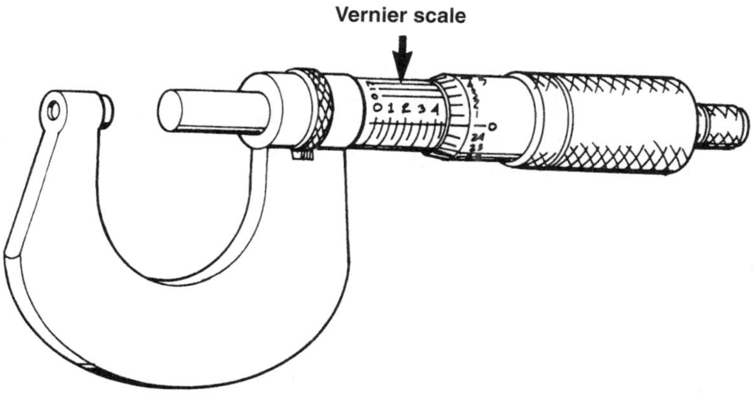

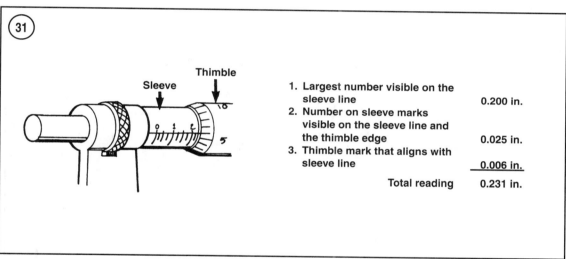

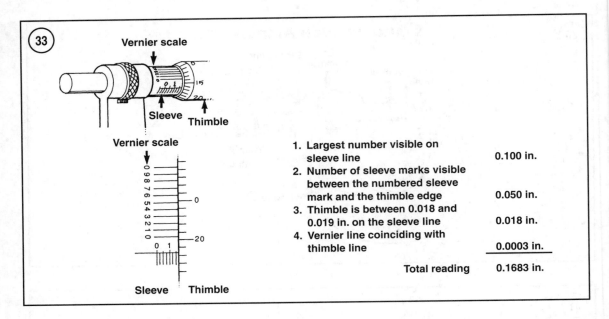

(33)

Vernier scale

Sleeve Thimble

Vernier scale

Sleeve Thimble

1. Largest number visible on
   sleeve line — 0.100 in.
2. Number of sleeve marks visible
   between the numbered sleeve
   mark and the thimble edge — 0.050 in.
3. Thimble is between 0.018 and
   0.019 in. on the sleeve line — 0.018 in.
4. Vernier line coinciding with
   thimble line — 0.0003 in.

   Total reading — 0.1683 in.

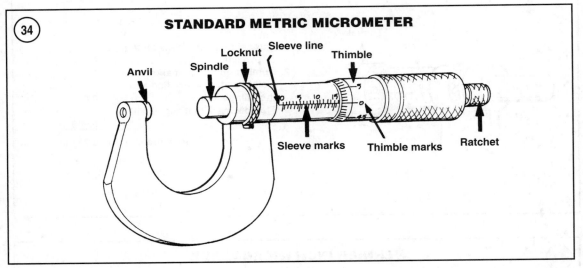

(34)

STANDARD METRIC MICROMETER

Anvil   Spindle   Locknut   Sleeve line   Thimble

Sleeve marks   Thimble marks   Ratchet

Metric micrometer

The standard metric micrometer (**Figure 34**) is accurate to one one-hundredth of a millimeter (0.01 mm). The sleeve line is graduated in millimeter and half millimeter increments. The marks on the upper half of the sleeve line equal 1.00 mm. Every fifth mark above the sleeve line is identified with a number. The number sequence depends on the size of the micrometer. A 0-25 mm micrometer, for example, will have sleeve marks numbered 0 through 25 in 5 mm increments. This numbering sequence continues with larger micrometers. On all metric mi-

crometers, each mark on the lower half of the sleeve equals 0.50 mm.

The tapered end of the thimble has fifty lines marked around it. Each mark equals 0.01 mm. One complete turn of the thimble aligns its 0 mark with the first line on the lower half of the sleeve line or 0.50 mm.

When reading a metric micrometer, add the number of millimeters and half-millimeters on the sleeve line to the number of one one-hundredth millimeters on the thimble. Perform the following steps while referring to **Figure 35**.

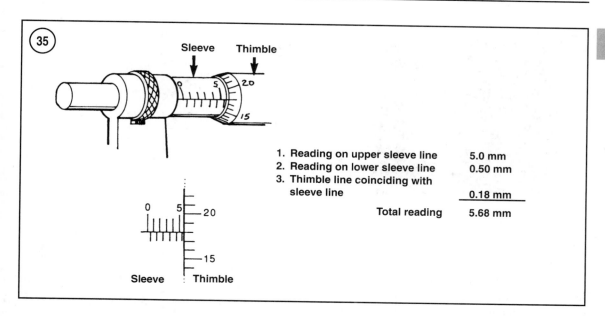

1. Reading on upper sleeve line   5.0 mm
2. Reading on lower sleeve line   0.50 mm
3. Thimble line coinciding with
   sleeve line   0.18 mm

   Total reading   5.68 mm

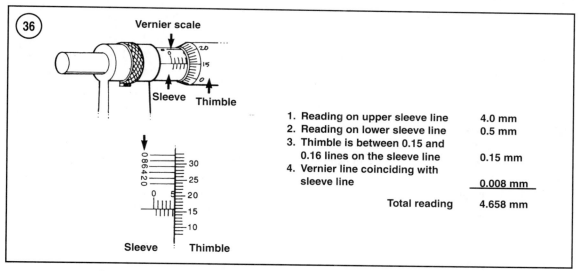

1. Reading on upper sleeve line   4.0 mm
2. Reading on lower sleeve line   0.5 mm
3. Thimble is between 0.15 and
   0.16 lines on the sleeve line   0.15 mm
4. Vernier line coinciding with
   sleeve line   0.008 mm

   Total reading   4.658 mm

1. Read the upper half of the sleeve line and count the number of lines visible. Each upper line equals 1 mm.

2. See if the half-millimeter line is visible on the lower sleeve line. If so, add 0.50 mm to the reading in Step 1.

3. Read the thimble mark that aligns with the sleeve line. Each thimble mark equals 0.01 mm.

> *NOTE*
> *If a thimble mark does not align exactly with the sleeve line, estimate the amount between the lines. For accurate readings in two-thousandths of a millimeter (0.002 mm), use a metric vernier micrometer.*

4. Add the readings from Steps 1-3.

Metric vernier micrometer

A metric vernier micrometer is accurate to two-thousandths of a millimeter (0.002 mm). It has the same markings as a standard metric micrometer with the addition of a vernier scale on the sleeve. The vernier scale consists of five lines marked 0, 2, 4, 6, and 8. These lines run parallel to the thimble lines and represent 0.002 mm increments.

When reading a metric vernier micrometer, refer to **Figure 36** and perform the following steps.

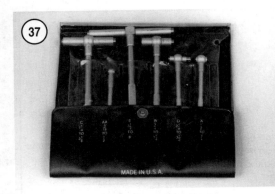

1. Read the micrometer in the same way as a standard metric micrometer. This is the initial reading.

2. If a thimble mark aligns exactly with the sleeve line, reading the vernier scale is not necessary. If they do not align, read the vernier scale in Step 3.

3. Determine which vernier scale mark aligns exactly with one thimble mark. The vernier scale number is the amount in two-thousandths of a millimeter to add to the initial reading from Step 1.

Micrometer Adjustment

Before using a micrometer, check its adjustment as follows.

1. Clean the anvil and spindle faces.

2A. To check a 0-1 in. or 0-25 mm micrometer:
   a. Turn the thimble until the spindle contacts the anvil. If the micrometer has a ratchet stop, use it to ensure that the proper amount of pressure is applied.
   b. If the adjustment is correct, the 0 mark on the thimble will align exactly with the 0 mark on the sleeve line. If the marks do not align, the micrometer is out of adjustment.
   c. Follow the manufacturer's instructions to adjust the micrometer.

2B. To check a micrometer larger than 1 in. or 25 mm, use the standard gauge supplied by the manufacturer. A standard gauge is a steel block, disc or rod that is machined to an exact size.
   a. Place the standard gauge between the spindle and anvil and measure its outside diameter or length. If the micrometer has a ratchet stop,

use it to ensure that the proper amount of pressure is applied.
   b. If the adjustment is correct, the 0 mark on the thimble will align exactly with the 0 mark on the sleeve line. If the marks do not align, the micrometer is out of adjustment.
   c. Follow the manufacturer's instructions to adjust the micrometer.

Micrometer Care

Micrometers are precision instruments. They must be used and maintained with great care. Note the following:

1. Store micrometers in protective cases or separate padded drawers in a toolbox.

2. When in storage, make sure the spindle and anvil faces do not contact each other or an other object. If they do, temperature changes and corrosion may damage the contact faces.

3. Do not clean a micrometer with compressed air. Dirt forced into the tool will cause wear.

4. Lubricate micrometers with WD-40 to prevent corrosion.

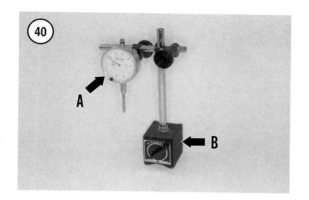

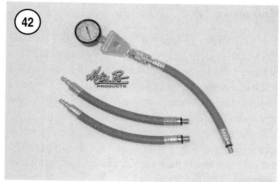

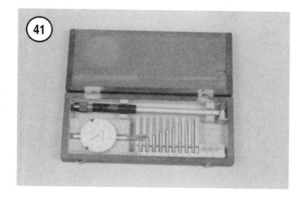

Dial Indicator

A dial indicator (A, **Figure 40**) is a gauge with a dial face and needle used to measure variations in dimensions and movements. Measuring brake rotor runout is a typical use for a dial indicator.

Dial indicators are available in various ranges and graduations and with three basic types of mounting bases: magnetic, clamp, or screw-in stud. When purchasing a dial indicator, select the magnetic stand type (B, **Figure 40**) with a continuous dial.

Cylinder Bore Gauge

A cylinder bore gauge is similar to a dial indicator. The gauge set shown in **Figure 41** consists of a dial indicator, handle, and different length adapters (anvils) to fit the gauge to various bore sizes. The bore gauge is used to measure bore size, taper and out-of-round. When using a bore gauge, follow the manufacturer's instructions.

Telescoping and Small Bore Gauges

Use telescoping gauges (**Figure 37**) and small hole gauges (**Figure 38**) to measure bores. Neither gauge has a scale for direct readings. An outside micrometer must be used to determine the reading.

To use a telescoping gauge, select the correct size gauge for the bore. Compress the movable post and carefully insert the gauge into the bore. Carefully move the gauge in the bore to make sure it is centered. Tighten the knurled end of the gauge to hold the movable post in position. Remove the gauge and measure the length of the posts. Telescoping gauges are typically used to measure cylinder bores.

To use a small-bore gauge, select the correct size gauge for the bore. Carefully insert the gauge into the bore. Tighten the knurled end of the gauge to carefully expand the gauge fingers to the limit within the bore. Do not overtighten the gauge, as there is no built-in release. Excessive tightening can damage the bore surface and damage the tool. Remove the gauge and measure the outside dimension (**Figure 39**). Small hole gauges are typically used to measure valve guides.

Compression Gauge

A compression gauge (**Figure 42**) measures combustion chamber (cylinder) pressure, usually in psi or kg/cm^2. The gauge adapter is either inserted or screwed into the spark plug hole to obtain the reading. Disable the engine so it will not start and hold the throttle in the wide-open position when performing a compression test. An engine that does not have adequate compression cannot be properly tuned. See Chapter Three.

Multimeter

A multimeter (**Figure 43**) is an essential tool for electrical system diagnosis. The voltage function indicates the voltage applied or available to various electrical components. The ohmmeter function tests circuits for continuity, or lack of continuity, and measures the resistance of a circuit.

Some manufacturers' specifications for electrical components are based on results using a specific test meter. Results may vary if using a meter not recommended by the manufacturer. Such requirements are noted when applicable.

Ohmmeter (analog) calibration

Each time an analog ohmmeter is used or if the scale is changed, the ohmmeter must be calibrated.

Digital ohmmeters do not require calibration.
1. Make sure the meter battery is in good condition.
2. Make sure the meter probes are in good condition.
3. Touch the two probes together and observe the needle location on the ohms scale. The needle must align with the 0 mark to obtain accurate measurements.
4. If necessary, rotate the meter ohms adjust knob until the needle and 0 mark align.

ELECTRICAL SYSTEM FUNDAMENTALS

A thorough study of the many types of electrical systems used in today's vehicles is beyond the scope of this manual. However, an understanding of electrical basics is necessary to perform simple diagnostic tests.

Voltage

Voltage is the electrical potential or pressure in an electrical circuit and is expressed in volts. The more pressure (voltage) in a circuit, the more work that can be performed.

Direct current (DC) voltage means the electricity flows in one direction. All circuits powered by a battery are DC circuits.

Alternating current (AC) means that the electricity flows in one direction momentarily then switches to the opposite direction. Alternator output

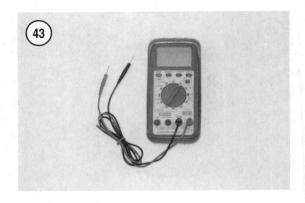

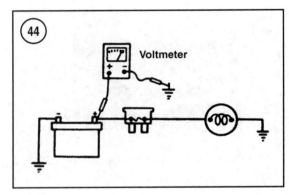

is an example of AC voltage. This voltage must be changed or rectified to direct current to operate in a battery-powered system.

Measuring voltage

Unless otherwise specified, perform all voltage tests with the electrical connectors attached.

When measuring voltage, select the meter range that is one scale higher than the expected voltage of the circuit to prevent damaging the meter. To determine the actual voltage in a circuit, use a voltmeter. To simply check if voltage is present, use a test light.

> *NOTE*
> *When using a test light, either lead can be attached to ground.*

1. Attach the negative meter test lead to a good ground (bare metal). Make sure the ground is not insulated with a rubber gasket or grommet.
2. Attach the positive meter test lead to the point being checked for voltage (**Figure 44**).

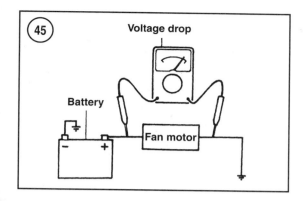

45

Voltage drop

Battery

Fan motor

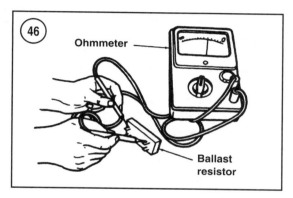

46

Ohmmeter

Ballast resistor

3. Turn on the ignition switch. The test light should light or the meter should display a reading. The reading should be within one volt of battery voltage. If the voltage is less, there is a problem in the circuit.

Voltage drop test

Resistance causes voltage to drop. This resistance can be measured in an active circuit by using a voltmeter to perform a voltage drop test. A voltage drop test compares the difference between the voltage available at the start of a circuit to the voltage at the end of the circuit while the circuit is operational. If the circuit has no resistance, there will be no voltage drop. The greater the resistance, the greater the voltage drop will be. A voltage drop of one volt or more indicates excessive resistance in the circuit.

1. Connect the positive meter test lead to the electrical source (where electricity is coming from).

2. Connect the negative meter test lead to the electrical load (where electricity is going). See **Figure 45**.

3. If necessary, activate the component(s) in the circuit.

4. A voltage reading of 1 volt or more indicates excessive resistance in the circuit. A reading equal to battery voltage indicates an open circuit.

Resistance

Resistance is the opposition to the flow of electricity within a circuit or component and is measured in ohms. Resistance causes a reduction in available current and voltage.

Resistance is measured in a inactive circuit with an ohmmeter. The ohmmeter sends a small amount of current into the circuit and measures how difficult it is to push the current through the circuit.

An ohmmeter, although useful, is not always a good indicator of a circuit's actual ability under operating conditions. This is due to the low voltage (6-9 volts) that the meter uses to test the circuit. The voltage in an ignition coil secondary winding can be several thousand volts. Such high voltage can cause the coil to malfunction, even though it tests acceptable during a resistance test.

Resistance generally increases with temperature. Perform all testing with the component or circuit at room temperature. Resistance tests performed at high temperatures may indicate high resistance readings and result in the unnecessary replacement of a working component.

Measuring resistance and continuity testing

CAUTION
*Only use an ohmmeter on a circuit that has no voltage present. The meter will be damaged if it is connected to a live circuit. An analog meter must be calibrated each time it is used or the scale is changed. See **Multimeter** in this chapter.*

A continuity test can determine if the circuit is complete. This type of test is performed with an ohmmeter or a self-powered test lamp.

1. Disconnect the negative battery cable.

2. Attach one test lead (ohmmeter or test light) to one end of the component or circuit.

3. Attach the other test lead to the opposite end of the component or circuit (**Figure 46**).

4. A self-powered test light will come on if the circuit has continuity or is complete. An ohmmeter will indicate either low or no resistance if the circuit has continuity. An open circuit is indicated if the meter displays infinite resistance.

Amperage

Amperage is the unit of measure for the amount of current within a circuit. Current is the actual flow of electricity. The higher the current, the more work that can be performed up to a given point. If the current flow exceeds the circuit or component capacity, the system will be damaged.

Measuring amps

An ammeter measures the current flow or amps of a circuit (**Figure 47**). Amperage measurement requires that the circuit be disconnected and the ammeter be connected in series to the circuit. Always use an ammeter that can read higher than the anticipated current flow to prevent damage to the meter. Connect the red test lead to the electrical source and the black test lead to the electrical load.

SPECIAL TOOLS

Some of the procedures in this manual require special tools. These are described in the appropriate chapter and are available from either the manufacturer or a tool supplier.

In many cases, an acceptable substitute may be found in an existing tool kit. Another alternative is to make the tool. Many schools with a machine shop curriculum welcome outside work that can be used as practical shop applications for students.

BASIC SERVICE METHODS

Most of the procedures in this manual are straightforward and can be performed by anyone reasonably competent with tools. However, consider personal capabilities carefully before attempting any operation involving major engine disassembly.

1. Front, in this manual, refers to the front of the vehicle. The front of any component is the end closest to the front of the vehicle. The left and right sides re-

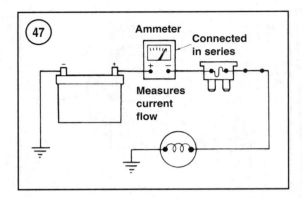

fer to the position of the parts as viewed by the rider sitting on the seat facing forward.

2. Whenever servicing an engine or suspension component, secure the vehicle in a safe manner.

3. Tag all similar parts for location and mark all mating parts for position. Record the number and thickness of any shims as they are removed. Identify parts by placing them in sealed and labeled plastic sandwich bags.

4. Tag disconnected wires and connectors with masking tape and a marking pen. Do not rely on memory alone.

5. Protect finished surfaces from physical damage or corrosion. Keep gasoline and other chemicals off painted surfaces.

6. Use penetrating oil on frozen or tight bolts. Avoid using heat where possible. Heat can warp, melt or affect the temper of parts. Heat also damages the finish of paint and plastics.

7. When a part is a press fit or requires a special tool for removal, the information or type of tool is identified in the text. Otherwise, if a part is difficult to remove or install, determine the cause before proceeding.

8. To prevent objects or debris from falling into the engine, cover all openings.

9. Read each procedure thoroughly and compare the illustrations to the actual components before starting the procedure. Perform the procedure in sequence.

10. Recommendations are occasionally made to refer service to a dealership or specialist. In these cases, the work can be performed more economically by the specialist than by the home mechanic.

11. The term *replace* means to discard a defective part and replace it with a new part. *Overhaul* means to remove, disassemble, inspect, measure, repair

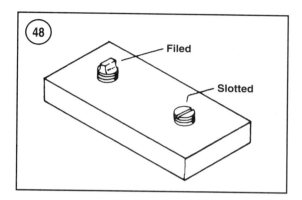

and/or replace parts as required to recondition an assembly.

12. Some operations require the use of a hydraulic press. If a press is not available, have these operations performed by a shop equipped with the necessary equipment. Do not use makeshift equipment that may damage the vehicle.

13. Repairs are much faster and easier if the vehicle is clean before starting work. Degrease the vehicle with a commercial degreaser; follow the directions on the container for the best results. Clean all parts with cleaning solvent while removing them.

CAUTION
Do not apply a chemical degreaser to an O-ring chain. These chemicals damage the O-rings. Use kerosene to clean O-ring type chains.

CAUTION
Do not direct high-pressure water at steering bearings, carburetor hoses, wheel bearings, suspension and electrical components. The water will force the grease out of the bearings and possibly damage the seals.

14. If special tools are required, have them available before starting the procedure. When special tools are required, they will be described at the beginning of the procedure.

15. Make diagrams of similar-appearing parts. For instance, crankcase bolts are often not the same lengths. Do not rely on memory alone. It is possible that carefully laid out parts will become disturbed, making it difficult to reassemble the components correctly without a diagram.

16. Make sure all shims and washers are reinstalled in the same location and position.

17. Whenever rotating parts contact a stationary part, look for a shim or washer.

18. Use new gaskets if there is any doubt about the condition of old ones.

19. If self-locking fasteners are used, replace them with new ones. Do not install standard fasteners in place of self-locking ones.

20. Use grease to hold small parts in place if they tend to fall out during assembly. Do not apply grease to electrical or brake components.

Removing Frozen Fasteners

If a fastener cannot be removed, several methods may be used to loosen it. First, apply penetrating oil such as Liquid Wrench or WD-40. Apply it liberally and let it penetrate for 10-15 minutes. Rap the fastener several times with a small hammer. Do not hit it hard enough to cause damage. Reapply the penetrating oil if necessary.

For frozen screws, apply penetrating oil as described, then insert a screwdriver in the slot and rap the top of the screwdriver with a hammer. This loosens the rust so the screw can be removed normally. If the screw head is too damaged to use this method, grip the head with locking pliers and twist the screw out.

Avoid applying heat unless specifically instructed, as it may melt, warp or remove the temper from parts.

Removing Broken Fasteners

If the head breaks off a screw or bolt, several methods are available for removing the remaining portion. If a large portion of the remainder projects out, try gripping it with locking pliers. If the projecting portion is too small, file it to fit a wrench or cut a slot in it to fit a screwdriver (**Figure 48**).

If the head breaks off flush, use a screw extractor. To do this, centerpunch the exact center of the remaining portion of the screw or bolt. Drill a small hole in the screw and tap the extractor into the hole. Back the screw out with a wrench on the extractor (**Figure 49**).

Repairing Damaged Threads

Occasionally, threads are stripped through carelessness or impact damage. Often the threads can be

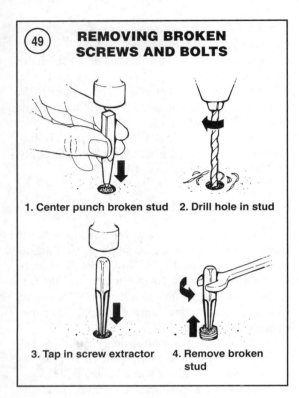

REMOVING BROKEN SCREWS AND BOLTS

1. Center punch broken stud   2. Drill hole in stud

3. Tap in screw extractor   4. Remove broken stud

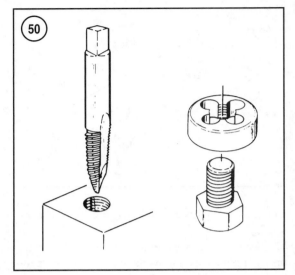

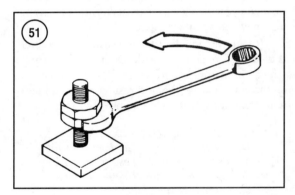

repaired by running a tap (for internal threads on nuts) or die (for external threads on bolts) through the threads (**Figure 50**). To clean or repair spark plug threads, use a spark plug tap.

If an internal thread is damaged, it may be necessary to install a Helicoil or some other type of thread insert. Follow the manufacturer's instructions when installing their insert.

If it is necessary to drill and tap a hole, refer to **Table 8** for metric tap and drill sizes.

Stud Removal/Installation

A stud removal tool is available from most tool suppliers. This tool makes the removal and installation of studs easier. If one is not available, thread two nuts onto the stud and tighten them against each other. Remove the stud by turning the lower nut (**Figure 51**).

1. Measure the height of the stud above the surface.

2. Thread the stud removal tool onto the stud and tighten it, or thread two nuts onto the stud.

3. Remove the stud by turning the stud remover or the lower nut.

4. Remove any threadlocking compound from the threaded hole. Clean the threads with an aerosol parts cleaner.

5. Install the stud removal tool onto the new stud or thread two nuts onto the stud.

6. Apply threadlocking compound to the threads of the stud.

7. Install the stud and tighten with the stud removal tool or the top nut.

8. Install the stud to the height noted in Step 1 or its torque specification.

9. Remove the stud removal tool or the two nuts.

Removing Hoses

When removing stubborn hoses, do not exert excessive force on the hose or fitting. Remove the hose clamp and carefully insert a small screwdriver or pick tool between the fitting and hose. Apply a

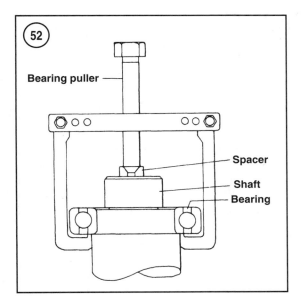

Bearing puller

Spacer
Shaft
Bearing

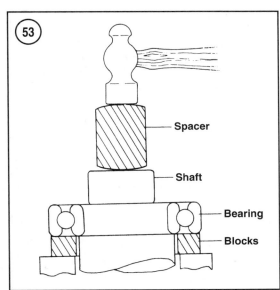

Spacer

Shaft

Bearing

Blocks

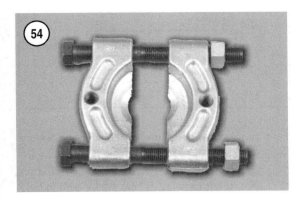

spray lubricant under the hose and carefully twist the hose off the fitting. Clean the fitting of any corrosion or rubber hose material with a wire brush. Clean the inside of the hose thoroughly. Do not use any lubricant when installing the hose (new or old). The lubricant may allow the hose to come off the fitting, even with the clamp secure.

Bearings

Bearings are used in the engine and transmission assembly to reduce power loss, heat and noise resulting from friction. Because bearings are precision parts, they must be maintained by proper lubrication and maintenance. If a bearing is damaged, replace it immediately. When installing a new bearing, take care to prevent damaging it. Bearing replacement procedures are included in the individual chapters where applicable. Use the following sections as a guideline.

NOTE
Unless otherwise specified, install bearings with the manufacturer's mark or number facing outward.

Removal

While bearings are normally removed only when damaged, there may be times when it is necessary to remove a bearing that is in good condition. However, improper bearing removal will damage the bearing and maybe the shaft or case half. Note the following when removing bearings.
1. When using a puller to remove a bearing from a shaft, take care that the shaft is not damaged. Always place a piece of metal between the end of the shaft and the puller screw. In addition, place the puller arms next to the inner bearing race. See **Figure 52**.
2. When using a hammer to remove a bearing from a shaft, do not strike the hammer directly against the shaft. Instead, use a brass or aluminum rod between the hammer and shaft (**Figure 53**) and make sure to support both bearing races with wooden blocks as shown.
3. The ideal method of bearing removal is with a hydraulic press. Note the following when using a press:
   a. Always support the inner and outer bearing races with a suitable size wooden or aluminum spacer ring (**Figure 54**). If only the outer

race is supported, pressure applied against the balls and/or the inner race will damage them.

b. Always make sure the press ram (**Figure 55**) aligns with the center of the shaft. If the ram is not centered, it may damage the bearing and/or shaft.

c. The moment the shaft is free of the bearing, it will drop to the floor. Secure or hold the shaft to prevent it from falling.

Installation

1. When installing a bearing in a housing, apply pressure to the *outer* bearing race (**Figure 56**). When installing a bearing on a shaft, apply pressure to the *inner* bearing race (**Figure 57**).

2. When installing a bearing as described in Step 1, some type of driver is required. Never strike the bearing directly with a hammer or the bearing will be damaged. When installing a bearing, use a piece of pipe or a driver with a diameter that matches the bearing inner race. **Figure 58** shows the correct way to use a driver and hammer to install a bearing.

3. Step 1 describes how to install a bearing in a case half or over a shaft. However, when installing a bearing over a shaft and into a housing at the same time, a tight fit will be required for both outer and inner bearing races. In this situation, install a spacer underneath the driver tool so that pressure is applied evenly across both races. See **Figure 59**. If the outer race is not supported as shown in **Figure 59**, the balls will push against the outer bearing race and damage it.

Interference fit

1. Follow this procedure when installing a bearing over a shaft. When a tight fit is required, the bearing inside diameter will be smaller than the shaft. In this case, driving the bearing on the shaft using normal methods may cause bearing damage. Instead, heat the bearing before installation. Note the following:

a. Secure the shaft so it is ready for bearing installation.

b. Clean all residue from the bearing surface of the shaft. Remove burrs with a file or sandpaper.

c. Fill a suitable pot or beaker with clean mineral oil. Place a thermometer rated above 120° C (248° F) in the oil. Support the ther-

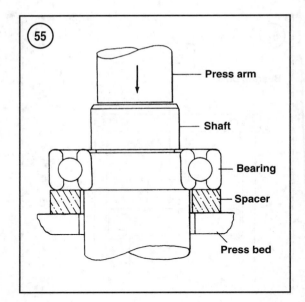

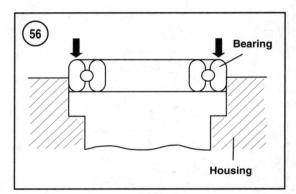

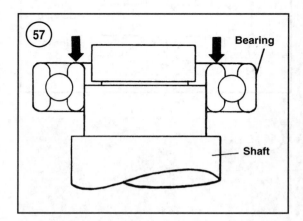

mometer so that it does not rest on the bottom or side of the pot.

d. Remove the bearing from its wrapper and secure it with a piece of heavy wire bent to hold

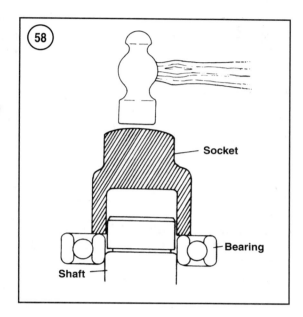

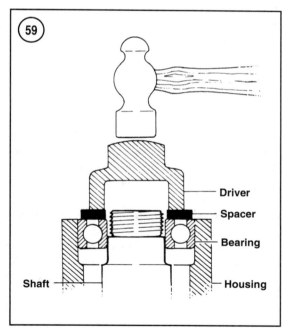

tion must be done quickly. Make sure the bearing is installed completely.

2. Follow this step when installing a bearing in a housing. Bearings are generally installed in a housing with a slight interference fit. Driving the bearing into the housing using normal methods may damage the housing or cause bearing damage. Instead, heat the housing before the bearing is installed. Note the following:

CAUTION
Before heating the housing in this procedure, wash the housing thoroughly with detergent and water. Rinse and rewash the cases as required to remove all traces of oil and other chemical deposits.

a. Heat the housing to approximately 212° F (100° C) in an oven or on a hot plate. An easy way to check that it is the proper temperature is to place tiny drops of water on the housing; if they sizzle and evaporate immediately, the temperature is correct. Heat only one housing at a time.

CAUTION
Do not heat the housing with a propane or acetylene torch. Never bring a flame into contact with the bearing or housing. The direct heat will destroy the case hardening of the bearing and will likely warp the housing.

b. Remove the housing from the oven or hot plate, and hold onto the housing with a kitchen potholder, heavy gloves or heavy shop cloth. It is hot!

NOTE
Remove and install the bearings with a suitable size socket and extension.

c. Hold the housing with the bearing side down and tap the bearing out. Repeat for all bearings in the housing.

d. Before heating the bearing housing, place the new bearing in a freezer if possible. Chilling a bearing slightly reduces its outside diameter while the heated bearing housing assembly is slightly larger due to heat

it in the pot. Hang the bearing in the pot so it does not touch the bottom or sides of the pot.

e. Turn the heat on and monitor the thermometer. When the oil temperature rises to approximately 120° C (248° F), remove the bearing from the pot and quickly install it. If necessary, place a socket on the inner bearing race and tap the bearing into place. As the bearing chills, it will tighten on the shaft, so installa-

expansion. This will make bearing installation easier.

NOTE
Always install bearings with the manufacturer's mark or number facing outward.

e. While the housing is still hot, install the new bearing(s) into the housing. Install the bearings by hand, if possible. If necessary, lightly tap the bearing(s) into the housing with a socket placed on the outer bearing race (**Figure 56**). Do not install new bearings by driving on the inner-bearing race. Install the bearing(s) until it seats completely.

Seal Replacement

Seals (**Figure 60**) are used to contain oil, water, grease or combustion gasses in a housing or shaft. Improper removal of a seal can damage the housing or shaft. Improper installation of the seal can damage the seal. Note the following:

1. Prying is generally the easiest and most effective method of removing a seal from a housing. However, always place a rag underneath the pry tool (**Figure 61**) to prevent damage to the housing.
2. Pack waterproof grease in the seal lips before the seal is installed.
3. In most cases, install seals with the manufacturer's numbers or marks face out.
4. Install seals with a socket placed on the outside of the seal as shown in **Figure 62**. Drive the seal squarely into the housing. Never install a seal by hitting against the top of the seal with a hammer.

STORAGE

Several months of non-use can cause a general deterioration of the vehicle. This is especially true in areas of extreme temperature variations. This deterioration can be minimized with careful preparation for storage. A properly stored vehicle will be much easier to return to service.

Storage Area Selection

When selecting a storage area, consider the following:

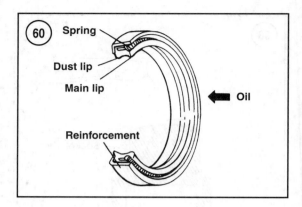

1. The storage area must be dry. A heated area is best, but not necessary. It should be insulated to minimize extreme temperature variations.
2. If the building has large window areas, mask them to keep sunlight off the vehicle.
3. Avoid buildings in industrial areas where corrosive emissions may be present. Avoid areas close to saltwater.
4. Consider the area's risk of fire, theft or vandalism. Check with an insurer regarding vehicle coverage while in storage.

Preparing the Vehicle for Storage

The amount of preparation a vehicle should undergo before storage depends on the expected length of non-use, storage area conditions and personal preference. Consider the following list the minimum requirement:

1. Wash the vehicle thoroughly. Make sure all dirt, mud and road debris is removed.
2. Start the engine and allow it to reach operating temperature. Drain the engine oil regardless of the riding time since the last service. Fill the engine with the recommended type of oil.
3. Drain all fuel from the fuel tank, run the engine until all the fuel is consumed from the lines and carburetors.
4. Remove the spark plugs and pour a teaspoon of engine oil into the cylinder. Place a rag over the openings and slowly turn the engine over to distribute the oil. Reinstall the spark plugs.
5. Remove the battery. Store the battery in a cool and dry location.
6. Cover the exhaust and intake openings.
7. Reduce the normal tire pressure by 20%.
8. Apply a protective substance to the plastic and rubber components, including the tires. Make sure

to follow the manufacturer's instructions for each type of product being used.

9. Place the vehicle on a stand or wooden blocks, so the wheels are off the ground. If this is not possible, place a piece of plywood between the tires and the ground. Inflate the tires to the recommended pressure if the vehicle cannot be elevated.

10. Cover the vehicle with old bed sheets or something similar. Do not cover it with any plastic material that will trap moisture.

Returning the Vehicle to Service

The amount of service required when returning a vehicle to service after storage depends on the length of non-use and storage conditions. In addition to performing the reverse of the above procedure, make sure the brakes, clutch, throttle and engine stop switch work properly before operating the vehicle. Refer to Chapter Three and evaluate the service intervals to determine which areas require service.

Table 1 MODEL YEAR COVERAGE

Model	Year
F 650 (U.S. and U.K.)	1997-2000
F 650 ST (U.S.)	1997
F650 Funduro (U.K.)	1994-1996
F650 Strada (U.K.)	1997-1999
F650 Strada SE (U.K.)	2000

Table 2 GENERAL SPECIFICATIONS

Item/model	mm	in.
Wheelbase		
F 650, Funduro, Strada, SE	1480	58.3
F 650 ST	1470	57.9
Overall length		
F 650 Funduro, Strada, SE	2180	85.8
F 650 ST	2160	85.0
Overall width (over mirrors)		
F 650, Funduro, Strada, SE	880	34.6
F 650 ST	880	34.6
Overall height		
F 650, Funduro, Strada, SE	1220	48.0
F 650 ST	1190	46.9
Seat height		
F 650, Funduro, Strada, SE	810	31.9
F 650 ST	785	30.9

Table 3 VEHICLE WEIGHT

Model	kg	lbs.
Weight[1]		
F 650, Funduro, Strada SE	189	417
F 650 ST	191	421
Gross weight limit[2]	371	818
Maximum payload		
F 650, Funduro, Strada, SE	182	401
F 650 ST	180	397
Axle load distribution		
front/rear ratio	48/52	

1. Road ready with full fuel tank, engine oil and fork oil.
2. GVWL is the maximum allowable vehicle weight. This includes combined vehicle, rider(s) and accessory weight.

Table 4 CONVERSION TABLES

Multiply:	By:	To get the equivalent of:
Length		
Inches	25.4	Millimeter
Inches	2.54	Centimeter
Miles	1.609	Kilometer
Feet	0.3048	Meter
Millimeter	0.03937	Inches
Centimeter	0.3937	Inches
Kilometer	0.6214	Mile
Meter	3.281	Mile
Fluid volume		
U.S. quarts	0.9463	Liters
U.S. gallons	3.785	Liters
U.S. ounces	29.573529	Milliliters
Imperial gallons	4.54609	Liters
Imperial quarts	1.1365	Liters
Liters	0.2641721	U.S. gallons
Liters	1.0566882	U.S. quarts
Liters	33.814023	U.S. ounces
Liters	0.22	Imperial gallons
Liters	0.8799	Imperial quarts
Milliliters	0.033814	U.S. ounces
Milliliters	1.0	Cubic centimeters
Milliliters	0.001	Liters
Torque		
Foot-pounds	1.3558	Newton-meters
Foot-pounds	0.138255	Meters-kilograms
Inch-pounds	0.11299	Newton-meters
Newton-meters	0.7375622	Foot-pounds
Newton-meters	8.8507	Inch-pounds
Meters-kilograms	7.2330139	Foot-pounds
Volume		
Cubic inches	16.387064	Cubic centimeters
Cubic centimeters	0.0610237	Cubic inches

(continued)

Table 4 CONVERSION TABLES (continued)

Multiply:	By:	To get the equivalent of:
Temperature		
Fahrenheit	(F − 32°) × 0.556	Centigrade
Centigrade	(C × 1.8) + 32	Fahrenheit
Weight		
Ounces	28.3495	Grams
Pounds	0.4535924	Kilograms
Grams	0.035274	Ounces
Kilograms	2.2046224	Pounds
Pressure		
Pounds per square inch	0.070307	Kilograms per square centimeter
Kilograms per square centimeter	14.223343	Pounds per square inch
Kilopascals	0.1450	Pounds per square inch
Pounds per square inch	6.895	Kilopascals
Speed		
Miles per hour	1.609344	Kilometers per hour
Kilometers per hour	0.6213712	Miles per hour

Table 5 GENERAL TORQUE SPECIFICATIONS

Thread diameter	N•m	ft.-lb.
5 mm		
Bolt and nut	5	4
Screw	4	3
6 mm		
Bolt and nut	10	8
Screw	9	7
6 mm flange bolt and nut	12	9
6 mm bolt with 8 mm head	9	7
8 mm		
Bolt and nut	22	16
Flange bolt and nut	27	20
10 mm		
Bolt and nut	35	25
Flange bolt and nut	40	29
12 mm		
Bolt and nut	55	40

* Use the torque specifications in this table for tightening non-critical fasteners. Always refer to the tightening torque table listed at the end of the respective chapter(s) for torque specifications for critical applications. If a torque specification is not included in the tightening torque table, use the specifications in this table.

Table 6 TECHNICAL ABBREVIATIONS

ABDC	After bottom dead center
ATDC	After top dead center
BBDC	Before bottom dead center
BDC	Bottom dead center
BTDC	Before top dead center

(continued)

Table 6 TECHNICAL ABBREVIATIONS (continued)

C	Celsius (Centigrade)
cc	Cubic centimeters
cid	Cubic inch displacement
CDI	Capacitor discharge ignition
cu. in.	Cubic inches
F	Fahrenheit
ft.	Feet
ft.-lb.	Foot-pounds
gal.	Gallons
H/A	High altitude
hp	Horsepower
ICU	Ignition control unit
in.	Inches
in.-lb.	Inch-pounds
I.D.	Inside diameter
kg	Kilograms
kgm	Kilogram meters
km	Kilometer
kPa	Kilopascals
L	Liter
m	Meter
MAG	Magneto
ml	Milliliter
mm	Millimeter
N•m	Newton-meters
O.D.	Outside diameter
OE	Original equipment
oz.	Ounces
psi	Pounds per square inch
PTO	Power take off
pt.	Pint
qt.	Quart
rpm	Revolutions per minute

Table 7 METRIC TAP AND DRILL SIZES

Metric size	Drill equivalent	Decimal fraction	Nearest fraction
3 × 0.50	No. 39	0.0995	3/32
3 × 0.60	3/32	0.0937	3/32
4 × 0.70	No. 30	0.1285	1/8
4 × 0.75	1/8	0.125	1/8
5 × 0.80	No. 19	0.166	11/64
5 × 0.90	No. 20	0.161	5/32
6 × 1.00	No. 9	0.196	13/64
7 × 1.00	16/64	0.234	15/64
8 × 1.00	J	0.277	9/32
8 × 1.25	17/64	0.265	17/64
9 × 1.00	5/16	0.3125	5/16
9 × 1.25	5/16	0.3125	5/16
10 × 1.25	11/32	0.3437	11/32
10 × 1.50	R	0.339	11/32
11 × 1.50	3/8	0.375	3/8
12 × 1.50	13/32	0.406	13/32
12 × 1.75	13/32	0.406	13/32

Table 8 DECIMAL AND METRIC EQUIVALENTS

Fractions	Decimal in.	Metric mm	Fractions	Decimal in.	Metric mm
1/64	0.015625	0.39688	33/64	0.515625	13.09687
1/32	0.03125	0.79375	17/32	0.53125	13.49375
3/64	0.046875	1.19062	35/64	0.546875	13.89062
1/16	0.0625	1.58750	9/16	0.5625	14.28750
5/64	0.078125	1.98437	37/64	0.578125	14.68437
3/32	0.09375	2.38125	19/32	0.59375	15.08125
7/64	0.109375	2.77812	39/64	0.609375	15.47812
1/8	0.125	3.1750	5/8	0.625	15.87500
9/64	0.140625	3.57187	41/64	0.640625	16.27187
5/32	0.15625	3.96875	21/32	0.65625	16.66875
11/64	0.171875	4.36562	43/64	0.671875	17.06562
3/16	0.1875	4.76250	11/16	0.6875	17.46250
13/64	0.203125	5.15937	45/64	0.703125	17.85937
7/32	0.21875	5.55625	23/32	0.71875	18.25625
15/64	0.234375	5.95312	47/64	0.734375	18.65312
1/4	0.250	6.35000	3/4	0.750	19.05000
17/64	0.265625	6.74687	49/64	0.765625	19.44687
9/32	0.28125	7.14375	25/32	0.78125	19.84375
19/64	0.296875	7.54062	51/64	0.796875	20.24062
5/16	0.3125	7.93750	13/16	0.8125	20.63750
21/64	0.328125	8.33437	53/64	0.828125	21.03437
11/32	0.34375	8.73125	27/32	0.84375	21.43125
23/64	0.359375	9.12812	55/64	0.859375	22.82812
3/8	0.375	9.52500	7/8	0.875	22.22500
25/64	0.390625	9.92187	57/64	0.890625	22.62187
13/32	0.40625	10.31875	29/32	0.90625	23.01875
27/64	0.421875	10.71562	59/64	0.921875	23.41562
7/16	0.4375	11.11250	15/16	0.9375	23.81250
29/64	0.453125	11.50937	61/64	0.953125	24.20937
15/32	0.46875	11.90625	31/32	0.96875	24.60625
31/64	0.484375	12.30312	63/64	0.984375	25.00312
1/2	0.500	12.70000	1	1.00	25.40000

CHAPTER TWO

TROUBLESHOOTING

The troubleshooting procedures described in this chapter provide typical symptoms and logical methods for isolating the cause(s). There may be several ways to solve a problem, but only a systematic approach will be successful in avoiding wasted time and possibly unnecessary parts replacement.

Gather as much information as possible to aid in diagnosis. Never assume anything and do not overlook the obvious. Make sure there is fuel in the tank and the fuel shutoff valve (**Figure 1**) is in the ON position. Learning to recognize symptoms will make troubleshooting easier. In most cases, expensive and complicated test equipment is not needed to determine whether repairs can be performed at home. On the other hand, be realistic and do not start procedures that are beyond the experience and equipment on hand. Many service departments will not take work that involves the reassembly of damaged or abused equipment, if they do, expect the cost to be high. If the motorcycle does require the

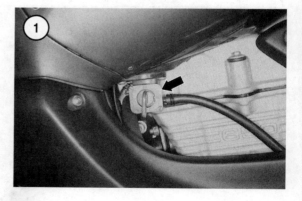

attention of a professional, describe symptoms and conditions accurately and fully. The more information a technician has available, the easier it will be to diagnose the problem.

Proper lubrication, maintenance and periodic tune-ups reduce the chance that problems will occur. However, even with the best of care the motorcycle may require troubleshooting.

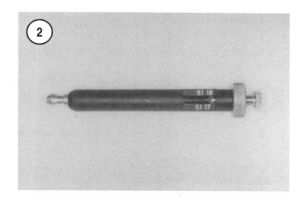

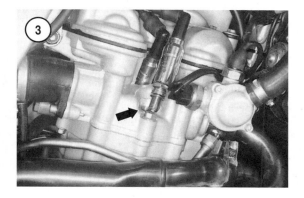

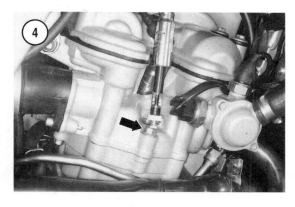

OPERATING REQUIREMENTS

An engine needs three basic elements to run properly: correct air/fuel mixture, compression and a spark at the correct time. If any one element is missing, the engine will not run. Four-stroke engine operating principles are described in Chapter Four.

If the machine has been sitting for any length of time and refuses to start, check and clean the spark plugs and then inspect the fuel delivery system. This includes the fuel tank, fuel valve and fuel lines to the carburetor. Gasoline deposits may have gummed up

the carburetor jets and air passages. Gasoline tends to lose its potency after standing for long periods. Condensation may contaminate the fuel with water. Drain the old fuel (fuel tank, fuel lines and carburetors) and start with fresh fuel.

STARTING THE ENGINE

Engine Fails to Start (Spark Test)

Perform the following spark test to determine if the ignition system is operating properly.

> *CAUTION*
> *Before removing the spark plugs in Step 1, clean all dirt and debris away from the plug base. Dirt that falls into the cylinder will cause rapid engine wear.*

1. Refer to Chapter Three and disconnect the spark plug wire and remove the spark plug.

> *NOTE*
> *A spark tester is a useful tool for testing spark output.* **Figure 2** *shows the Motion Pro Ignition System Tester (part No. 08-0122). This tool is inserted in the spark plug cap and its base is grounded against the cylinder head. The tool's air gap is adjustable and it allows the visual inspection of the spark while testing the intensity of the spark. This tool is available through motorcycle repair shops.*

2. Cover the spark plug hole with a clean shop cloth to lessen the chance of gasoline vapors being emitted from the hole.

3. Insert the spark plug (**Figure 3**), or spark tester (**Figure 4**), into its plug cap and ground the spark plug base against the cylinder head. Position the spark plug so the electrode is visible.

> *WARNING*
> *Mount the spark plug, or tester, away from the spark plug hole in the cylinder so that the spark or tester cannot ignite the gasoline vapors in the cylinder. If the engine is flooded, do not perform this test. The firing of the spark plug can ig-*

nite fuel that is ejected through the spark plug hole.

> NOTE
> *If a spark plug is used, perform this test with a new spark plug.*

4. Turn the ignition switch to the ON position.

> WARNING
> *Do **not** hold the spark plug, wire or connector, or a serious electrical shock may result.*

5. Turn the engine over with the electric starter. A crisp blue spark should be evident across the spark plug electrode or spark tester terminals. If there is strong sunlight on the plug, shade the plug by hand to better see the spark.

6. If the spark is good, check for one or more of the following possible malfunctions:
   a. Obstructed fuel line or fuel filter.
   b. Low compression or engine damage.
   c. Flooded engine.

7. If the spark is weak or if there is no spark, refer to *Engine is Difficult to Start* in this chapter.

> NOTE
> *If the engine backfires during starting, the ignition timing may be incorrect due to a defective ignition component.*

Engine is Difficult to Start

Check for one or more of the following possible malfunctions:
1. Fouled spark plug(s).
2. Improperly adjusted enrichener valve.
3. Intake manifold air leak.
4. Plugged fuel tank filler cap.
5. Clogged fuel line.
6. Contaminated fuel system.
7. Improperly adjusted carburetor(s).
8. Defective ignition control unit.
9. Defective ignition coil(s).
10. Damaged ignition coil primary and secondary wires.
11. Incorrect ignition timing.
12. Low engine compression.
13. Engine oil too heavy for winter temperatures.
14. Discharged battery.

15. Defective starter motor.
16. Loose or corroded starter and/or battery cables.
17. Loose ignition sensor and control unit electrical connector.

Engine Will Not Crank

Check for one or more of the following possible malfunctions:
1. Ignition switch turned OFF.
2. Faulty ignition switch.
3. Engine run switch in OFF position.
4. Defective engine run switch.
5. Loose or corroded starter and battery cables.
6. Discharged or defective battery.
7. Defective starter motor.
8. Defective starter solenoid.
9. Slipping starter clutch assembly.
10. Seized piston.
11. Seized crankshaft bearings.
12. Broken connecting rod.

ENGINE PERFORMANCE

In the following check list, it is assumed that the engine runs, but is not operating at peak performance. This will serve as a starting point from which to isolate a performance malfunction.

Fouled Spark Plugs

If the spark plugs continually foul, check for the following:
1. Severely contaminated air filter element.
2. Incorrect spark plug heat range. See Chapter Three.
3. Rich fuel mixture.
4. Worn or damaged piston rings.
5. Worn or damaged valve guide oil seals.
6. Excessive valve stem-to-valve guide clearance.
7. Incorrect carburetor float level.

Engine Runs but Misfires

1. Fouled or improperly gapped spark plugs.
2. Damaged spark plug cables.
3. Incorrect ignition timing.
4. Defective ignition components.
5. An obstructed fuel line or fuel shutoff valve.

2

6. Obstructed fuel filter.
7. Clogged carburetor jets.
8. Loose battery connection.
9. Wiring or connector damage.
10. Water or other contaminates in the fuel.
11. Weak or damaged valve springs.
12. Incorrect camshaft/valve timing.
13. Damaged valve(s).
14. Dirty electrical connections.
15. Intake manifold or carburetor air leak.
16. Plugged carburetor vent hose.
17. Plugged fuel tank vent system.

Engine Overheating

1. Incorrect carburetor adjustment or jet selection.
2. Incorrect ignition timing or defective ignition system components.
3. Improper spark plug heat range.
4. Faulty cooling system:
   a. Faulty radiator cap.
   b. Defective water pump.
   c. Clogged radiator and engine cooling passages.
   d. Collapsed coolant hoses.
   e. Coolant contaminated or deteriorated.
   f. Defective cooling fan and/or fan control switch.
5. Low oil level.
6. Oil not circulating properly.
7. Leaking valves.
8. Heavy engine carbon deposits.

Engine Runs Rough with Excessive Exhaust Smoke

1. Clogged air filter element.
2. Rich carburetor adjustment.
3. Enrichener valve not operating correctly.
4. Water or other fuel contaminants.
5. Clogged fuel line and/or filter.
6. Spark plug(s) fouled.
7. Defective ignition coil(s).
8. Defective ignition control unit or pickup coil.
9. Loose or defective ignition circuit wire.
10. Short circuits from damaged wire insulation.
11. Loose battery cable connections.
12. Incorrect camshaft/valve timing.
13. Intake manifold or air filter air leaks.

Engine Loses Power

1. Incorrect carburetor adjustment.
2. Engine overheating.
3. Incorrect ignition timing.
4. Incorrectly gapped spark plug(s).
5. Obstructed muffler.
6. Dragging brake(s).

Engine Lacks Acceleration

1. Incorrect carburetor adjustment.
2. Clogged fuel line.
3. Incorrect ignition timing.
4. Dragging brake(s).

Valve Train Noise

1. Bent valve.
2. Worn or damaged camshaft bearing(s).
3. Worn or damaged camshaft gear(s).

STARTING SYSTEM

The starting system consists of the battery, starter motor, starter relay, start switch and related wiring.

When the ignition switch is turned on and the start button is pushed in, current is transmitted from the battery to the solenoid coil. This causes the coil contacts to close, allowing electricity to flow from the battery to the starter motor.

Refer to Chapter Nine for starter motor service.

Troubleshooting Preparation

Before troubleshooting the starting system, check the following:
1. Make sure the battery is fully charged.
2. Battery cables must be the proper size and length. Replace damaged or undersized cables.
3. All electrical connections are clean and tight. High resistance caused from dirty or loose connectors can affect voltage and current levels.
4. The wiring harness is in good condition, with no worn or frayed insulation or loose harness sockets.
5. The fuel tank is filled with an adequate supply of fresh gasoline.
6. The spark plugs are in good condition and properly gapped.
7. The ignition system is working correctly.

Troubleshooting

The basic starter related troubles are:
1. Starter motor does not spin.
2. Starter motor spins but does not engage.
3. The starter motor will not disengage after the start button is released.
4. Loud grinding noises when starter motor turns.
5. Starter motor stalls or spins too slowly.

CAUTION
Never operate the starter motor for more than 30 seconds at a time. Allow the starter to cool before reusing it. Failing to allow the starter motor to cool after continuous starting attempts can damage the starter.

Starter motor does not spin

1. Turn the ignition switch ON and push the starter button (**Figure 5**) while listening for a click at the starter relay. Turn the ignition switch OFF and note the following:
   a. If the starter relay clicks, test the starter relay as described in Chapter Nine. If the starter relay test readings are correct, continue with Step 2.
   b. If the solenoid clicks, go to Step 3.
   c. If there was no click, go to Step 6.
2. Check the wiring connectors between the starter relay and solenoid. Note the following:
   a. Repair any dirty, loose fitting or damaged connectors or wiring.
   b. If the wiring is good, remove the starter motor as described in Chapter Nine. Perform the solenoid and starter motor bench tests described in this section.
3. Perform a voltage drop test between the battery and solenoid terminals. The normal voltage drop is less than 2 volts. Note the following:
   a. If the voltage drop is less than 2 volts, perform Step 4.
   b. If the voltage drop is more than 2 volts, check the solenoid and battery wires and connections for dirty or loose fitting terminals; clean and repair as required.
4. Remove the starter motor as described in Chapter Nine. Momentarily connect a fully charged 12-volt battery to the starter motor. If the starter motor is operational, it will turn when connected to the battery.

Disconnect the battery and note the following. If the starter motor does not turn, disassemble the starter motor as described in Chapter Nine, and check it for opens, shorts and grounds.

5. If there is no click when performing Step 1, measure voltage between the starter button and the starter relay. The voltmeter must read battery voltage. Note the following:
   a. If battery voltage is noted, continue with Step 7.
   b. If there is no voltage, go to Step 8.
6. Check for voltage at the starter button. Note the following:
   a. If there is voltage at the starter button, test the starter relay as described in this section.
   b. If there is no voltage at the starter button, check continuity across the starter button. If there is voltage leading to the starter button but no voltage leaving the starter button, replace the button switch and retest. If there is no voltage leading to the starter button, check the starter button wiring for dirty or loose-fitting terminals or damaged wiring; clean and/or repair as required.

CHARGING SYSTEM

The charging system consists of the battery, alternator and a solid state voltage regulator/rectifier.

The alternator generates alternating current (AC) which the rectifier converts to direct current (DC). The regulator maintains the voltage to the battery and load (lights, ignition and accessories) at a constant voltage despite variations in engine speed and load.

A malfunction in the charging system generally causes the battery to remain undercharged.

Service Precautions

Before servicing the charging system, observe the following precautions to prevent damaging any charging system component.

1. Never reverse battery connections. Damage will occur to the motorcycle's electrical systems.
2. Do not short across any connection.
3. Never start the engine with the alternator disconnected from the voltage regulator/rectifier, unless instructed to do so during testing.
4. Never attempt to start or run the engine with the battery disconnected.
5. Never attempt to use a high-output battery charger to help start the engine.
6. Before charging the battery, remove it from the motorcycle as described in Chapter Nine.
7. Never disconnect the voltage regulator/rectifier connector with the engine running. The voltage regulator/rectifier (**Figure 6**) is mounted on top of the rear fender under the seat.
8. Make sure the negative battery cable is connected to the engine and frame.

Troubleshooting

Before testing the charging system, visually check the following.

1. Check the battery connections at the battery. If polarity is reversed, check for a damaged regulator/rectifier.
2. Check for loose or corroded battery cable connectors.
3. Inspect all wiring between the battery and the alternator stator for worn or cracked insulation or loose connections. Replace wiring or clean and tighten connections as required.

4. Check the battery condition. Clean and recharge as described in Chapter Three.

IGNITION SYSTEM

The transistorized ignition system uses no breaker points to trigger the primary ignition. Problems with the solid-state system are rare due to the lack of moving parts that wear out or require adjustment.

If a problem does occur, it generally causes a weak spark or no spark. An ignition system in this state is easier to troubleshoot than one that only malfunctions at a specific engine load or temperature.

Refer to the wiring diagram at the back of the manual when troubleshooting and Chapter Nine for component replacement procedures.

Ignition System Precautions

Certain measures must be taken to protect the ignition system.

1. Never disconnect any of the electrical connectors while the engine is running.
2. Apply dielectric grease to all electrical connectors prior to reconnecting them. This will help seal out moisture.
3. Make sure all electrical connectors are free of corrosion and are completely coupled to each other.
4. The ignition control unit must always be mounted securely to the top of the rear fender under the seat.

Troubleshooting Preparation

1. Refer to the wiring diagrams at the back of this manual for the specific model.
2. Check the wiring harness for visible signs of damage.
3. Make sure all connectors are properly attached to each other and locked in place.
4. Check all electrical components for a good ground to the engine.
5. Check all wiring for short circuits or open circuits.
6. Remove the seat as described in Chapter Fifteen.
7. Make sure the fuel tank has an adequate supply of fresh gasoline.

8. Check spark plug cable routing and their connections at the spark plugs. If there is no spark or only a weak one, repeat the test with new spark plugs. If the condition remains the same with new spark plugs and if all external wiring connections are good, the problem is most likely in the ignition system. If a strong spark is present, the problem is probably not in the ignition system. Check the fuel system.

9. Remove the spark plugs and examine them as described in Chapter Three.

Ignition Control Unit
Testing and Replacement

There are no test procedures from the manufacturer for the ignition control unit (ICU). If the ignition control unit is suspect, have a BMW dealership check it out by replacing the ICU with a test ICU. Make sure that nothing has been overlooked before purchasing a new ICU. Most parts suppliers will not accept returns on electrical components.

Ignition Coil Cables and Caps Inspection

All models are equipped with resistor- or suppression-type spark plug cables. These cables reduce radio interference. The cable's conductor consists of a carbon-impregnated fabric core material instead of solid wire.

If a plug cable becomes damaged, either due to corrosion or conductor breaks, its resistance increases. Excessive cable resistance will cause engine misfire and other ignition or driveability problems.

When troubleshooting the ignition system, inspect the spark plug cables (**Figure 7**) for:

1. Corroded or damaged connector ends.
2. Breaks in the cable insulation that could allow arcing.
3. Split or damaged plug caps that could allow arcing to the cylinder head.

Replace a damaged or questionable spark plug cable assembly.

FUEL SYSTEM

Many riders automatically assume that the carburetors are at fault if the engine does not run properly. While fuel system problems are not uncommon, carburetor adjustment is seldom the answer. In

many cases, adjusting will only compound the problem by making the engine run worse.

Begin fuel system troubleshooting with the fuel tank and work through the system, reserving the carburetors as the final point. Most fuel system problems result from an empty fuel tank, a plugged fuel filter or fuel valve, old fuel, a dirty air filter or clogged carburetor jets.

Identifying Carburetor Conditions

Refer to the following conditions to identify whether the engine is running lean or rich.

Rich

1. Fouled spark plugs.
2. Engine misfires and runs rough under load.
3. Excessive exhaust smoke as the throttle is increased.
4. An extreme rich condition results in a choked or dull sound from the exhaust and an inability to clear the exhaust with the throttle held wide open.

Lean

1. Blistered or very white spark plug electrodes.
2. Engine overheats.
3. Slow acceleration, engine power is reduced.
4. Flat spots on acceleration that are similar in feel to when the engine starts to run out of gas.
5. Engine speed fluctuates at full throttle.

Troubleshooting

Isolate fuel system problems to the fuel tank, fuel shutoff valve and filter, fuel hoses, external fuel filter

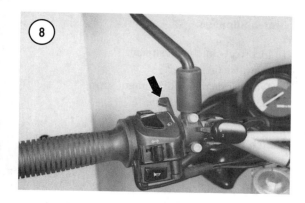

(if used) or carburetors. The following procedures assume that the ignition system is working properly and is correctly adjusted.

Fuel Level System

Proper carburetor operation depends on a constant and correct carburetor fuel level. As fuel is drawn from the float bowl during engine operation, the float level in the bowl drops. As the float drops, the fuel valve moves away from its seat and allows fuel to flow through the seat into the float bowl. Fuel entering the float bowl will cause the float to rise and push against the fuel valve. When the fuel level reaches a predetermined level, the fuel valve is pushed against the seat to prevent the float bowl from overfilling.

If the fuel valve fails to close, the engine will run too rich or flood with fuel. Symptoms of this problem are rough running, excessive black smoke and poor acceleration. This condition will sometimes clear up when the engine is run at wide-open throttle, as the fuel is being drawn into the engine before the float bowl can overfill. As the engine speed is reduced, however, the rich running condition returns.

Several things can cause fuel overflow. In most instances, it can be as simple a small piece of dirt trapped between the fuel valve and seat or an incorrect float level. If fuel is flowing out of the overflow tube connected to the bottom of the float bowl, the fuel valve inside the carburetor is being held open. First check the position of the fuel shutoff valve lever. Turn the fuel shutoff valve OFF. Then lightly tap on the carburetor float bowl and turn the fuel shutoff valve ON. If the fuel flow stops running out of the overflow tube, whatever was holding the fuel valve off of its seat now has been dislodged. If fuel contin-

ues to flow from the overflow tube, remove and service the carburetor. See Chapter Eight.

Starting Enrichment (Choke) System

A cold engine requires a rich mixture to start and run properly. A cable-actuated starter enrichment lever (**Figure 8**) on the handlebar and the valve on the carburetor are used for cold starting.

If the engine is difficult to start when cold, check the starting enrichment (choke) cable adjustment as described in Chapter Three.

ENGINE NOISES

1. A knocking or pinging noise during acceleration can be caused by using a lower octane fuel than recommended or a poor grade of fuel. Incorrect carburetor jetting and an incorrect (hot) spark plug heat range can cause pinging. Refer to *Spark Plug Heat Range* in Chapter Three. Also check for excessive carbon buildup in the combustion chamber or a defective ignition module.
2. A slapping or rattling noise at low speed or during acceleration can be caused by excessive piston-to-cylinder wall clearance. Check also for a bent connecting rod or worn piston pin and/or piston pin hole in the piston.
3. A knocking or rapping noise while decelerating is usually caused by excessive rod bearing clearance.
4. A persistent knocking is usually caused by worn main bearings. If the main bearings are in good condition, consider the following:
   a. Loose engine mounts.
   b. Cracked frame.
   c. Leaking cylinder head gasket.
   d. Exhaust pipe leakage at cylinder head ports.
   e. Stuck piston ring(s).
   f. Broken piston ring(s).
   g. Partial engine seizure.
   h. Excessive connecting rod bearing clearance.
   i. Excessive connecting rod side clearance.
   j. Excessive crankshaft runout.
   k. Incorrect balancer shaft-to-crankshaft alignment.
5. A rapid on-off squeal indicates a compression leak around the cylinder head gasket or spark plugs.

6. Excessive valve train noise can be caused by a valve sticking in a guide. Also check for worn cam gears and/or cams.

ENGINE LUBRICATION

An improperly operating engine lubrication system will quickly lead to serious engine damage. Check the engine oil level weekly as described in Chapter Three. Oil pump service is covered in Chapter Five.

Excessive Oil Consumption or Engine Smoke

1. Worn valve guides and/or seals.
2. Worn or damaged piston rings.
3. Oil tank overfilled.
4. Oil tank filter restricted.
5. Oil filter restricted.
6. Leaking cylinder head surfaces.

Oil Fails to Return to Oil Tank

1. Oil lines or fittings restricted or damaged.
2. Oil pump damaged or operating incorrectly.
3. Oil tank empty.
4. Oil filter restricted.
5. Damaged oil feed pump.

Engine Oil Leaks

1. Restricted or damaged oil return line to oil tank.
2. Loose engine parts.
3. Damaged gasket sealing surfaces.
4. Oil tank overfilled.
5. Restricted oil filter.

CLUTCH

All clutch troubles, except adjustments, require partial clutch disassembly to identify and cure the problem. Refer to Chapter Six for clutch service procedures.

Clutch Chatter or Noise

This problem is usually caused by worn or warped friction and steel plates.

Clutch Slippage

1. Incorrect clutch adjustment.
2. Worn friction plates.
3. Weak or damaged diaphragm spring.
4. Damaged pressure plate.

Clutch Dragging

1. Incorrect clutch adjustment.
2. Warped clutch plates.
3. Worn or damaged clutch shell or clutch hub.
4. Worn or incorrectly assembled clutch ball and ramp mechanism.
5. Incorrect primary chain alignment.

TRANSMISSION

Transmission symptoms are sometimes hard to distinguish from clutch symptoms. Refer to Chapter Seven for transmission service procedures.

Jumping Out of Gear

1. Worn or damaged gear shifter parts.
2. Severely worn or damaged gears and/or shift forks.

Difficult Shifting

1. Worn or damaged shift forks.
2. Worn or damaged shift fork dogs.
3. Weak or damaged shift lever return spring.
4. Clutch drag.

Excessive Gear Noise

1. Worn or damaged bearings.
2. Worn or damaged gears.
3. Excessive gear backlash.

LIGHTING SYSTEM

If bulbs burn out frequently, check for excessive vibration, loose connections that permit sudden current surges, or the installation of the wrong type of bulb.

Most light and ignition problems are caused by loose or corroded ground connections. Check these prior to replacing a bulb or electrical component.

EXCESSIVE VIBRATION

Excessive vibration is usually caused by loose engine mounting hardware. A bent axle shaft or loose suspension component will cause high-speed vibration problems. Vibration can also be caused by the following conditions:

1. Engine balance shaft incorrectly aligned with the crankshaft.
2. Cracked or broken frame.
3. Loose or damaged engine mounts.
4. Improperly balanced wheel(s).
5. Defective or damaged wheel(s).
6. Defective or damaged tire(s).
7. Internal engine wear or damage.
8. Loose or worn steering head bearings.
9. Loose swing arm pivot shaft nut.

FRONT SUSPENSION AND STEERING

Poor handling may be caused by improper tire inflation pressure, a damaged or bent frame or front steering components, worn wheel bearings or dragging brakes. Possible causes for suspension and steering malfunctions are listed below.

Irregular or Wobbly Steering

1. Loose wheel axle nut(s).
2. Loose or worn steering head bearings.
3. Excessive wheel bearing play.
4. Wheel out of alignment.
5. Unbalanced wheel assembly.
6. Bent or damaged steering stem or frame at steering neck.
7. Tire incorrectly seated on rim.

Stiff Steering

1. Low front tire air pressure.
2. Bent or damaged steering stem or frame.
3. Loose or worn steering head bearings.

Stiff or Heavy Fork Operation

1. Incorrect fork springs.
2. Incorrect fork oil viscosity.
3. Excessive amount of fork oil.
4. Bent fork tubes.

Poor Fork Operation

1. Worn or damage fork tubes.
2. Fork oil capacity low due to leaking fork seals.
3. Bent or damaged fork tubes.
4. Contaminated fork oil.
5. Incorrect fork springs.

Poor Rear Shock Absorber Operation

1. Weak or worn spring.
2. Damper unit leaking.
3. Shock shaft worn or bent.
4. Incorrect rear shock spring.
5. Rear shock adjusted incorrectly.

BRAKE SYSTEM

All models are equipped with front and rear disc brakes. Good brakes are vital to the safe operation of any vehicle. Perform the maintenance specified in Chapter Three to minimize brake system problems. Brake system service is covered in Chapter Fourteen. When refilling the front and rear master cylinders, use only DOT 4 brake fluid.

Insufficient Braking Power

Worn brake pads or disc, air in the hydraulic system, glazed or contaminated pads, low brake fluid level, or a leaking brake line or hose can cause this problem. Visually check for leaks. Check for worn brake pads. Check also for a leaking seal in the caliper(s). Bleed and adjust the brakes. Replace a leaking master cylinder or brake caliper. Brake drag will result in excessive heat and brake fade. See *Brake Drag* in this section.

Spongy Brake Feel

This problem is generally caused by air in the hydraulic system. Bleed the brakes as described in Chapter Fourteen

Brake Drag

Check for worn, loose or missing parts in the brake calipers. Check the brake discs for excessive runout.

Brakes Squeal or Chatter

Check brake pad thickness and disc condition. Check that the caliper anti-rattle springs are properly installed and in good condition. Clean off any dirt on the pads. Loose components can also cause this. Check for:

1. Warped brake disc
2. Loose brake disc.
3. Loose caliper mounting bolts.
4. Loose front axle nut.
5. Worn wheel bearings.
6. Damaged hub.

CHAPTER THREE

LUBRICATION, MAINTENANCE AND TUNE-UP

This chapter covers lubrication, maintenance and tune-up procedures. A schedule, specifications, lubricants and capacities are listed in **Tables 1-6** at the end of the chapter.

To maximize the service life of the motorcycle and gain the utmost in safety and performance, it is necessary to perform periodic inspections and maintenance. Minor problems found during routine service can be corrected before they develop into major ones.

Perform the pre-ride checklist before the first ride of the day. Refer to the maintenance schedule and perform the items listed at the appropriate mileage intervals. If the motorcycle is continually operated in extreme conditions, including partial water submersion or exposure to mud, blowing dirt and debris, shorten the maintenance intervals accordingly.

All of the items listed in the maintenance schedule are listed in this chapter; however, the procedures, if they require more than minor disassembly, are covered in the appropriate subsequent chapter.

PRE-RIDE CHECKLIST

General Inspection

1. Check tire condition and inflation pressure. Refer to *Tires and Wheels* in this chapter.
2. Check wheel rim condition. Inspect the front and rear suspension. Make sure they have a good solid feel with no looseness.
3. Check the engine oil level as described in this chapter. Inspect the engine, oil tank and lines for leakage.
4. Check the coolant level as described in this chapter.
5. Check the front and rear brake operation. Make sure the fluid level in both reservoirs is above the low level line. Add DOT 4 brake fluid as required.
6. Check the throttle operation. The throttle must move smoothly and snap back when released. Adjust throttle free play, if necessary, as described in this chapter.

7. Check clutch operation. If necessary adjust the clutch as described in this chapter.

8. Inspect the fuel lines and fittings for leakage.

9. Inspect the exhaust system for leakage or damage.

10. Check the drive chain condition and tension as described in this chapter.

11. Check the fuel level in the tank. Top off, if required.

Lights and Horn

With the engine running, check the following.

1. Pull the front brake lever and check that the brake light comes on.

2. Push the rear brake pedal down and check that the brake light comes on soon after the pedal has been depressed.

3. Make sure the headlight and taillight are on.

4. Move the dimmer switch up and down between the high and low positions, and make sure both headlight elements are working.

5. Push the turn signal switch to the left and right positions and make sure all four turn signal lights are working.

6. Check the horn button operation.

7. If the horn or any light fails to work properly, refer to Chapter Nine.

TIRES AND WHEELS

Tire Pressure

Check the tire pressure often to maintain tire profile, traction, and handling, as well as to get the maximum life out of the tire. Carry a tire gauge in the motorcycle's tool kit. **Table 2** lists the cold tire pressures for the OE tires.

NOTE
After checking and adjusting the air pressure, reinstall the air valve caps. These caps prevent small debris from collecting in the valve stems and causing air leakage or incorrect tire pressure readings.

Tire Inspection

The tires take a lot of punishment, so inspect them periodically for excessive wear, deep cuts and em-

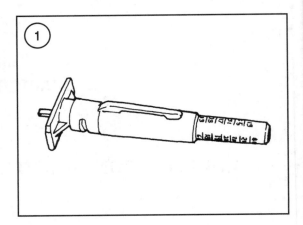

bedded objects such as stones or nails. If a nail or other object is found in a tire, mark its location with a light crayon prior to removing it. This will help locate the hole for repair.

Refer to Chapter Nine for tire changing and repair information. Measure with a tread depth gauge (**Figure 1**) or a small ruler. Refer to the minimum tread depth specification located on the tire sidewall. Replace the tire when the tread is worn to the specified dimension.

Spoke Tension

Check the wheels for loose or damaged spokes. Refer to Chapter Eleven for wheel service.

Rim Inspection

Check the wheel rims for cracks and other damage. If damaged, a rim can make the bike handle poorly. Refer to Chapter Eleven for wheel service.

BATTERY

The battery is an important component in the motorcycle's electrical system, yet most electrical system troubles result from battery neglect. Clean and inspect the battery at periodic intervals.

On all models covered in this manual, the negative side is the ground. When removing the battery, disconnect the negative (–) cable first, then the positive (+) cable. This minimizes the chance of a tool shorting to ground when disconnecting the positive battery cable.

Negative Battery Cable

Some of the component replacement procedures and some of the test procedures in this chapter require disconnecting the negative battery cable as a safety precaution.

1. Remove the seat as described in Chapter Fifteen.
2. Remove the left side cover as described in Chapter Fifteen.
3. Remove the bolt (A, **Figure 2**) securing the negative battery cable. Move the cable away from the

battery to avoid making accidental contact with the battery post.
4. Reverse the previous procedures to connect the negative battery cable. Make sure the bolt (A, **Figure 2**) is tight.

Battery Cable Service

To ensure good electrical contact between the battery and the electrical cables, the cables must be clean and free of corrosion.

1. If the battery cable terminals are badly corroded, disconnect them from the motorcycle's electrical system.
2. Thoroughly clean each terminal and the battery posts with a wire brush and then with a baking soda solution. Rinse thoroughly with clean water and wipe dry with a clean cloth.
3. After cleaning, apply a thin layer of dielectric grease to the battery posts before reattaching the cables.
4. After connecting the battery cables, apply another light coat of dielectric grease to them to retard corrosion.

Battery Removal/Installation

1. Remove the seat as described in Chapter Fifteen.
2. Remove the left side cover as described in Chapter Fifteen.
3. Remove the bolt and disconnect the negative battery cable (A, **Figure 2**).
4. Remove the bolt (B, **Figure 2**) securing the battery holder and remove the holder (C).
5. Disconnect the vent tube (**Figure 3**) from the battery. Leave the tube routed through the frame.
6. Remove the bolt and disconnect the positive battery cable (A, **Figure 4**).
7. Carefully slide the battery (B, **Figure 4**) out of the battery box.
8. Inspect the battery box (**Figure 5**) for corrosion or damage. Replace if necessary.
9. Position the battery with the negative cable terminal toward the front of the frame.
10. Reinstall the battery onto the battery box in the frame.
11. Install the battery holder and tighten the bolt securely.
12. Connect the vent tube (**Figure 3**) onto the battery.
13. Connect the positive cable (A, **Figure 4**). Tighten the bolt securely.

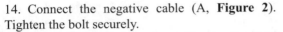

14. Connect the negative cable (A, **Figure 2**). Tighten the bolt securely.

15. After connecting the battery cables, apply a light coating of dielectric grease to them to retard corrosion.

16. Install the left side cover and seat as described in Chapter Fifteen.

Electrolyte Level Check

1. Maintain the electrolyte level between the two marks on the battery case (**Figure 6**).

2. If the electrolyte level must be adjusted, remove the battery from the frame as described in this section. Do not add water while the battery is installed in the frame. If the electrolyte overflows onto the rear portion of the frame, corrosion will result.

3. Make sure all cell caps are in place and are tight; tighten if necessary.

4. If the electrolyte level is correct, reinstall the battery.

Cleaning, Inspection and Adding Water

1. Remove the battery.

2. Inspect the battery tray for contamination or damage. Clean with a solution of baking soda and water.

3. Check the entire battery case for cracks or other damage. If the battery case is warped, discolored or has a raised top, the battery has overheated due to overcharging.

4. Check the battery terminal bolts, spacers and nuts for corrosion, deterioration or damage. Clean parts thoroughly with a solution of baking soda and water. Replace severely corroded or damaged parts.

> *CAUTION*
> *Keep cleaning solution out of the battery cells. Baking soda will neutralize*

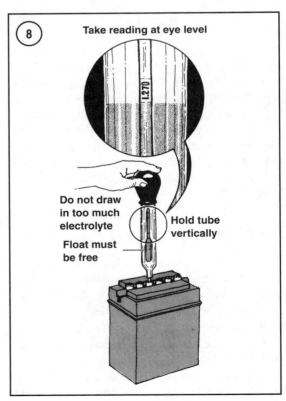

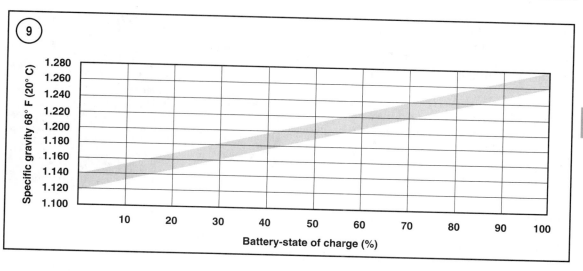

the electrolyte and seriously weaken the battery.

5. Clean the top of the battery with a stiff bristle brush using the baking soda and water solution. Thoroughly rinse off all baking soda residue with freshwater.

6. Check the battery cable terminals for corrosion and damage. If corrosion is minor, clean the battery cable terminals with a stiff wire brush. Replace severely worn or damaged cables.

CAUTION
Do not overfill the battery cells in Step 7. The electrolyte will expand during charging and may overflow if the level is above the upper level line.

7. Remove the fill caps (**Figure 7**) from the battery cells and check the electrolyte level in each cell. Add distilled water, if necessary, to bring the level within the upper and lower level lines on the battery case (**Figure 6**). Install the caps and tighten securely.

CAUTION
Adding water to the cells will dilute the electrolyte. The diluted electrolyte can freeze and destroy the battery during sub-freezing temperatures. Therefore, during cold weather, charge the battery after adding water to the cells.

Battery Testing

Checking the specific gravity of the battery electrolyte is the best way to check the battery's state of charge. Specific gravity is the density of the electrolyte as compared to pure water. To check the specific gravity, use a hydrometer with numbered graduations from 1.100 to 1.300 rather than one with just color-coded bands. To use the hydrometer, squeeze the rubber ball, insert the tip into the cell and release the ball (**Figure 8**).

NOTE
Adding water to the cells will lower the specific gravity (density) of the electrolyte. After adding water, charge the battery for 15-20 minutes at a rate high enough to cause vigorous gassing.

Draw sufficient electrolyte to float the weighted float inside the hydrometer. When using a temperature-compensated hydrometer, release the electrolyte and repeat this process several times to make sure the thermometer has had time to adjust to the electrolyte temperature before taking the reading.

Hold the hydrometer vertically and note the number in line with the surface of the electrolyte (**Figure 8**). This is the specific gravity for this cell. Return the electrolyte to the cell from which it came. The specific gravity of the electrolyte in each battery cell is an excellent indication of that cell's condition. Refer to **Figure 9**. A fully charged cell will read 1.260-1.280 while a cell in good condition reads from 1.230-1.250 and anything below 1.140

is discharged. Charging is also necessary if the specific gravity varies more than 0.050 from cell to cell. After charging, if the specific gravity still varies more than 0.050, the battery has failed.

> *NOTE*
> *If a temperature-compensated hydrometer is not used, add 0.004 to the specific gravity reading for every 10° above 80° F (25° C). For every 10° below 80° F (25° C), subtract 0.004.*

Charging

As the battery charges, the electrolyte begins to bubble. This is called gassing. If one cell does not bubble, it is probably defective. Also, if the specific gravity of the cell is considerably lower than the other cells (0.050 points or more) after the battery is charged, the cell is defective.

If a battery not in use loses its charge within a week after charging or if the specific gravity drops quickly, the battery is defective. A good battery should only self-discharge approximately 1% each day.

> *WARNING*
> *During charging, highly explosive hydrogen gas is released from the battery. Charge the battery only in a well-ventilated area, and away from open flames (including pilot lights on some gas home appliances). Do not allow any smoking in the area. Never check the charge of the battery by arcing across the terminals; the resulting spark can ignite the hydrogen gas.*

> *CAUTION*
> *Always remove the battery from the motorcycle before connecting the charging equipment.*

1. Remove the battery from the motorcycle as described in this chapter.
2. Set the battery on a stack of newspapers or shop cloths to protect the workbench surface.
3. Make sure the battery charger is turned to the OFF position, prior to attaching the charger leads to the battery.
4. Connect the positive charger lead to the positive battery terminal and the negative charger lead to the negative battery terminal.

5. Remove all fill/vent caps (**Figure 7**) from the battery, set the charger at 12 volts, and switch it on. Normally, a battery should be charged at 1/10 its capacity.

> *CAUTION*
> *Maintain the electrolyte level at the upper level during the charging cycle; check and refill with distilled water as necessary.*

6. The charging time depends on the discharged condition of the battery.
7. After the battery has been charged for the predetermined time, turn the charger OFF, disconnect the leads and check the specific gravity. It should be within the limits specified in **Figure 9**. If it is within specification and remains stable for one hour, the battery is charged.

Battery Initialization

A new battery must be *fully* charged to a specific gravity of 1.260-1.280 before installation. To bring the battery to a full charge, give it an initial full charge. Using a new battery without an initial full charge will cause permanent battery damage. That is, the battery will never be able to hold more than

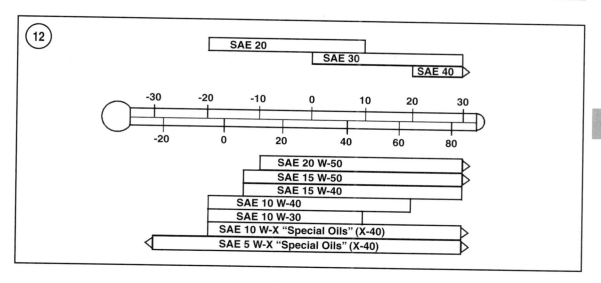

3

an 80% charge. Charging a new battery after it has been used will not bring its charge to 100%. When purchasing a new battery, verify its charge status.

> *NOTE*
> *Recycle the old battery. When a new battery is purchased, turn in the old one for recycling. Most motorcycle dealerships will accept the old battery in trade when purchasing a new one. Never place an old battery in the household trash since it is illegal, in most states, to place any acid or lead (heavy metal) contents in landfills.*

ENGINE LUBRICATION

Engine Oil Level Check

The F650 engine is a dry-sump design. The majority of the oil is stored in the frame oil tank, while the remaining oil is stored in the crankcase. Check the engine oil level with the dipstick/oil filler cap (**Figure 10**) located on top of the frame backbone between the steering head and the fuel tank.

1. Start and run the engine for approximately 10 minutes or until the engine has reached normal operating temperature. Then turn the engine off and allow the oil to settle in the oil tank.
2. Place the bike on a level surface and park it on the centerstand.
3. Wipe the area around the dipstick/oil filler cap with a clean rag. Then unscrew and remove the dipstick/oil filler cap (**Figure 10**) from the oil tank.

Wipe the dipstick off with a clean rag and screw the dipstick/oil filler cap all the way into the oil tank until it bottoms. Unscrew and remove the dipstick/oil filler cap again and check the oil level on the dipstick. The oil level should be at the MAX mark on the dipstick (**Figure 11**). If the oil level is below the MAX mark, continue with Step 4. If the oil level is correct, go to Step 4.

4. To correct the oil level, add an engine oil with the correct viscosity (**Figure 12**) and service classification (**Table 4**).

> *CAUTION*
> *Never add oil above the MAX mark.*

> *NOTE*
> *Special oils are approved individually by BMW AG and are available from an authorized BMW motorcycle dealership.*

5. Check the oil filler cap O-ring (**Figure 13**) for cracks or other damage. Replace the O-ring if necessary.
6. Reinstall the dipstick/oil filler cap.

Engine Oil and Filter Change

Regular oil and filter changes will contribute more to engine longevity than any other maintenance performed. **Table 1** lists the recommended oil and filter change interval. This assumes that the motorcycle is operated in moderate climates. If the motorcycle is not operated often, refer to the time interval because

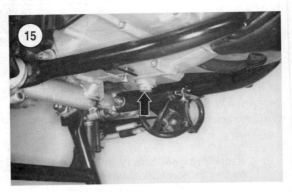

combustion acids, formed by gasoline and water vapor, contaminate the oil even if the motorcycle is not run for several months. If the motorcycle is operated in dusty conditions, the oil will become contaminated more quickly and should be changed more frequently than recommended.

Use a motorcycle oil with an API service classification of *SF*, *SG* or *SH*. The classification is printed on the container. It is suggested that the oil manufactured and sold by BMW dealerships should be used in this engine. A substitute brand of oil may be used, but first confer with a BMW dealership regarding which types are compatible. Always try to use the same brand of oil at each change. Using oil additives is not recommended, as they may cause clutch slippage.

WARNING
Contact with oil may cause skin cancer. Wash oil from hands with soap and water as soon as possible.

NOTE
*The engine oil tank is an integral part of the frame upper backbone and is connected to the engine with two hoses. The dipstick/oil filler cap is located on top of the frame backbone oil tank in front of the fuel tank (**Figure 10**).*

NOTE
Never dispose of motor oil in the trash, on the ground or down a storm drain. Many service stations and oil retailers will accept used oil for recycling. Do not combine other fluids with motor oil to be recycled. To locate a recycler, contact the American Petroleum Institute (API) at www.recycleoil.org.

1. Start and run the engine until it has reached normal operating temperature. Then turn the engine off and allow the oil to settle in the oil tank and crankcase. Support the bike on the centerstand so the oil can drain completely.

NOTE
Before removing the dipstick/oil filler cap, clean off all debris around it.

2. Remove the dipstick/oil filler cap (**Figure 10**), as this will speed up the flow of oil.
3. Remove the skid plate.
4. Remove both cylinder head side covers as described in Chapter Fifteen.

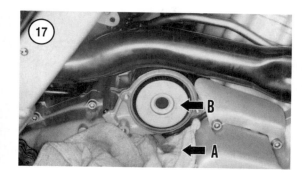

case cavity. Remove the screws and the cover and O-ring.

d. Quickly remove the oil filter (B, **Figure 17**), as oil will begin to run out.

e. Hold the filter over the drain pan and pour out the remaining oil. Place the filter in a plastic bag, seal it and dispose of it properly.

f. Thoroughly clean the crankcase oil filter cavity (**Figure 18**) with a shop cloth moistened in solvent. Wipe off any spilled oil from the drive sprocket cover and/or the right crankcase side cover.

g. Coat the cover O-ring seal with clean oil.

h. Position the new oil filter so the end with the large opening (**Figure 19**) goes in first.

i. Install the new oil filter and the oil filter cover. Install the cover screws and tighten to the specification in **Table 6**.

10. Remove and clean the engine oil tank filter as described in this chapter.

11. Clean the threads of both drain plug receptacles. Inspect the threads for damage. Install both drain plugs and tighten them to the specifications in **Table 6**.

CAUTION
Do not overtighten the crankcase drain plug; it is easy to strip the threads in the crankcase. If minor damage has occurred, the plug can be replaced with a K-series Allen head type that will engage a larger number of crankcase threads. If necessary, install the Helicoil sump plug repair kit (BMW part No. 11 11 2 343 436).

12. Remove the aluminum foil from the exhaust pipe and clean off any spilled oil with an aerosol parts cleaner. The pipe will smoke if any oil residue remains.

13. Insert a funnel into the oil tank opening and add the correct viscosity and quantity of oil into the oil tank. Insert the dipstick/oil filler cap into the frame oil tank and screw it on until it is tight.

NOTE
After oil has been added, the oil level will register above the MAX dipstick/oil filler cap mark (Figure 11) until the engine runs and the engine and oil filter fills with oil. To obtain a correct reading after adding oil and in-

5. Wrap aluminum foil over the exhaust pipe (B, **Figure 14**) to keep oil off the pipe in the following procedure.

6. Place a drain pan underneath the frame oil tank and remove the drain plug (A, **Figure 14**).

7. Place another drain pan underneath the crankcase and remove the drain plug (**Figure 15**).

8. Allow the oil to drain completely.

9. To replace the oil filter perform the following:

a. Move the drain pan underneath the crankcase adjacent to the oil filter.

b. Loosen the two screws securing the oil filter cover (**Figure 16**).

c. Place a shop cloth (A, **Figure 17**) under the oil filter cover to catch residual oil in the crank-

*stalling a new oil filter, follow the pro-
cedure in Step 13.*

14. After changing the engine oil and filter, check
the oil level as follows:
  a. Start and run the engine for 1 minute, then shut
  it off.
  b. Check the oil level on the dipstick/oil filler cap
  as described in this chapter.
  c. If the oil level is correct, it will register in the
  dipstick's safe operating level range. If so, *do
  not* top off or add oil to bring it to the MAX
  level on the dipstick.
15. Check the oil filter and both drain plugs for
leaks.
16. Dispose of the used oil properly.
17. Install the skid plate.
18. Install both cylinder head side covers as described in Chapter Fifteen.

Engine Oil Tank Filter Cleaning

Clean the engine oil tank filter during engine oil
and filter changes.
1. Remove the front fairing as described in Chapter
Fifteen.
2. Remove the fuel tank as described in Chapter
Eight.
3. Place a shop cloth under the oil hose fitting (A,
Figure 20). Loosen the hose clamp and disconnect
the oil hose fitting (B, **Figure 20**) from the filter.
4. Unscrew the oil filter element assembly (**Figure
21**) from the oil tank on the frame down tube.
5. Clean the filter in solvent and dry with compressed air.
6. Inspect the filter (A, **Figure 22**) for damage. Replace as necessary.
7. Inspect the O-ring seal (B, **Figure 22**) for hardness or deterioration. Replace if necessary.
8. Screw the oil filter (**Figure 21**) into place on the
frame down tube and tighten securely.
9. Connect the oil hose onto the filter stub pipe (B,
Figure 20). Make sure it is securely connected.
Tighten the hose clamp.
10. Remove the shop cloths and discard if necessary.
11. Install the fuel tank as described in Chapter
Eight.
12. Install the front fairing as described in Chapter
Fifteen.

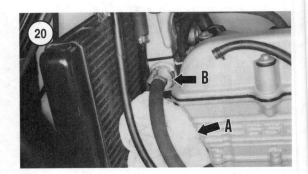

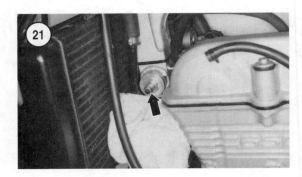

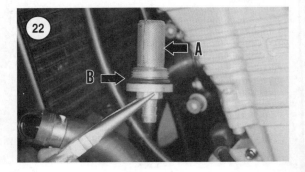

FORK OIL

Change the fork oil at the interval in **Table 1**.

1. Support the bike on a stand or floor jack with the
front wheel off the ground. See *Bike Stands* in
Chapter Twelve.

2. On the left fork leg, remove the screws securing
the front brake caliper cover (**Figure 23**) and remove the cover.

3. On models with a lowered suspension, remove
the handlebar as described in Chapter Twelve.

4. Place a drain pan beside one fork slider, then remove the drain plug and washer (**Figure 24**) from
the slider.

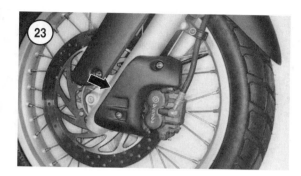

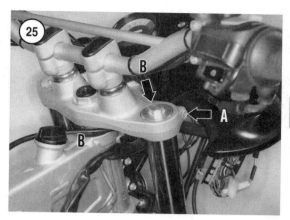

3

12. Install the fork cap bolt (B, **Figure 25**) and tighten to the specification in **Table 6**.

13. Tighten the upper fork bridge pinch bolts (A, **Figure 25**) to the specification in **Table 6**.

14. Install the front brake caliper cover (**Figure 23**) and tighten the screws securely.

15. On models with a lowered suspension, install the handlebar as described in Chapter Twelve.

16. Road test the bike and check for leaks.

CONTROL CABLES

Inspection

Inspect the control cables at the intervals specified in **Table 1** or when they become stiff or sluggish. Inspect each cable for fraying and cable sheath damage. Cables are relatively inexpensive and should be replaced if faulty. Do not lubricate the OE nylon-lined cables with cable lubricant.

CAUTION
Oil and most cable lubricants will cause the cable liner to expand, pushing the liner against the cable sheath. Nylon-lined cables are normally used dry. If the original equipment type cables have been replaced, lubricate them as described in this procedure.

CAUTION
Do not use chain lube to lubricate control cables.

CAUTION
The starting enrichment valve (choke) cable is designed to operate with some

WARNING
The fork cap bolts are under spring pressure. Protect yourself accordingly.

NOTE
Step 5 is shown with the front fairing removed to better illustrate the steps.

5. Loosen the upper fork bridge pinch bolts (A, **Figure 25**).

6. Remove the fork cap bolt (B, **Figure 25**).

CAUTION
Do not allow the fork oil to come in contact with any of the brake components.

7. Replace the drain screw washer if damaged.

8. After the fork oil has thoroughly drained, install the drain plug and washer into the fork slider. Tighten the drain plug to the specification in **Table 6**.

9. Repeat Steps 2-8 for the opposite fork leg.

10. Refill each fork leg with the correct viscosity and quantity of fork oil. Refer to **Table 4**.

11. Repeat for the opposite fork leg.

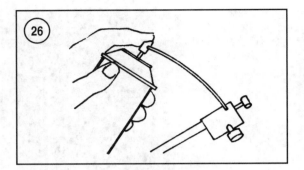

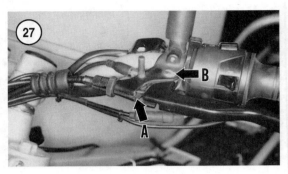

*cable resistance. Do **not** lubricate the enrichener cable or its conduit.*

NOTE
The major cause of cable breakage or cable stiffness is improper lubrication. Maintaining the cables as described in this section will ensure long service life.

1A. Disconnect the clutch cable ends as described under *Clutch Cable Replacement* in Chapter Six.

1B. Disconnect the throttle cable end as described under *Throttle Cable Replacement* in Chapter Eight.

2. Attach a lubricator tool to the cable following its manufacturer's instructions (**Figure 26**).

NOTE
Place a shop cloth at the end of the cable to catch all excess lubricant.

3. Insert the lubricant nozzle tube into the lubricator, press the button on the can and hold it down until the lubricant begins to flow out of the other end of the cable. If the lubricant squirts out from around the lubricator, it is not clamped to the cable properly. Loosen and reposition the cable lubricator.

NOTE
If the lubricant does not flow out of the other end of the cable, check the cable for fraying, bending or other damage. Replace damaged cables.

4. Remove the lubricator tool and wipe off both ends of the cable.

5A. Reconnect the clutch cable ends as described under *Clutch Cable Replacement* in Chapter Six.

5B. Reconnect the throttle cable end as described under *Throttle Cable Replacement* in Chapter Eight.

6. Adjust the cables as described in this chapter.

Clutch Cable Adjustment

1. Pull the clutch lever toward the handlebar until resistance is felt and measure the free play between the clutch lever and the clutch lever support (A, **Figure 27**). The correct free play measurement is 1.5-2.5 mm (0.06-0.10 in.). If resistance is felt as soon as the clutch lever is pulled, there is no cable free play.

2. At the clutch lever, slide the rubber boot (A, **Figure 28**) off the cable adjuster.

3. Loosen the adjuster locknut (B, **Figure 28**) and turn the adjuster (C) in or out to obtain the correct amount of free play. Tighten the locknut (B).

4. If this procedure cannot correct the amount of free play, either the cable has stretched to the point that it needs to be replaced or the clutch friction discs are worn and need replacing. Refer to Chapter Six for clutch cable and clutch service.

5. Slide the rubber boot back over the cable adjuster.

6. Start the engine and check the clutch operation.

Throttle Cable Operation and Adjustment

1. Open and release the throttle grip with the handlebar pointed in various positions. In each position, the throttle must open and close smoothly. If the throttle cable binds or moves roughly, inspect the cable for

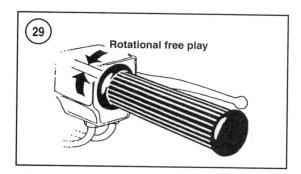

Rotational free play

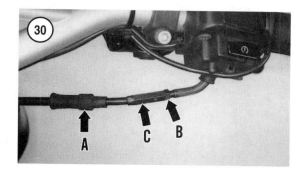

A C B

kinks, bends or other damage. Replace a damaged cable. If the cable moves smoothly and is not damaged, continue to Step 2.

2. Slowly open the throttle and measure the free play at the throttle grip flange (**Figure 29**) until resistance is felt. If resistance is felt as soon as the throttle grip is turned, there is no cable free play.

3. If adjustment is necessary, slide the rubber boot (A, **Figure 30**) off the cable adjuster.

4. Loosen the adjuster locknut (B, **Figure 30**) and turn the adjuster (C) in or out to obtain the correct amount of free play. Tighten the locknut (B).

5. If this procedure cannot correct the amount of free play, either the cable has stretched to the point that it needs to be replaced. Refer to Chapter Eight for throttle cable replacement.

6. Slide the rubber boot back over the cable adjuster.

7. Start the engine and check the throttle operation.

WARNING
Do not ride the motorcycle until the throttle cable is properly adjusted. Likewise, the cable must not catch or pull when the handlebar is turned from side to side. Improper cable routing and adjustment can cause the throttle to stick open. This could cause loss of control and a possible crash. Recheck this adjustment before riding the motorcycle.

PERIODIC LUBRICATION

Throttle Control Grip

Lubricate the throttle control grip at the intervals in **Table 1**. To remove and install the throttle grip, refer to *Throttle Cable Replacement* in Chapter Eight. Lubricate the throttle control grip (where it contacts the handlebar) with Shell Retinax EP2 grease.

Steering Head Bearing

Lubricate the steering head bearings at the interval in **Table 1**. Complete lubrication requires removing the steering head assembly. Refer to Chapter Eleven.

Swing Arm Bearings

Lubricate the swing arm bearings and pivot bolt at the interval in **Table 1**. Complete lubrication requires removing the swing arm assembly. Refer to Chapter Thirteen.

Front Brake Lever Pivot Pin

Inspect the front brake lever pivot pin for lubrication at the intervals in **Table 1**. If the pin is dry, slide off the rubber boot (**Figure 31**) and lubricate the pivot pin (**Figure 32**) with a lightweight oil.

Clutch Lever Pivot Pin

Inspect the clutch lever pivot pin (B, **Figure 27**) at the intervals in **Table 1**. Lubricate the pin with a lightweight oil. To service the pivot pin, refer to *Clutch Cable Replacement* in Chapter Six.

Drive Chain Roller

Lubricate the drive chain roller at the intervals in **Table 1**.

AIR FILTER

Element Removal/Installation

Inspect the air filter at the interval in **Table 1**. Replace the element if it is excessively dirty, damaged or starts to deteriorate.

The air filter removes dust and abrasive particles before the air enters the carburetor and the engine. Without the air filter, particles will enter the engine and cause rapid wear of the piston rings, cylinder bores and bearings. They also might clog small passages in the carburetor. Never run the motorcycle without the element installed.

1. Remove the seat as described in Chapter Fifteen.

2. Remove the left side cover as described in Chapter Fifteen.

> *CAUTION*
> *The starter relay (A, **Figure 33**) is attached to the air filter housing cover. Do not damage the relay or wiring in the next step.*

3. Remove the bolts and carefully pull the air box cover (B, **Figure 33**) off and move it out of the way.

4. Remove the air filter element (**Figure 34**) and replace the element (**Figure 35**).

5. Wipe out the inside surfaces of the air box and cover with a damp rag.

6. Pull the end plug from the air box drain hose (**Figure 36**).

7. Drain out any accumulated oil.

8. Position a new air filter element with the tab (A, **Figure 37**) toward the rear of the housing and install it. Make sure it is properly seated.

9. Make sure the air box gasket (B, **Figure 37**) is in place.

10. Install the air box cover (B, **Figure 33**) and tighten the bolts securely.

11. Install the left side cover as described in Chapter Fifteen.

12. Install the seat as described in Chapter Fifteen.

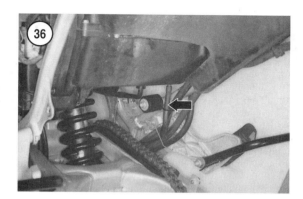

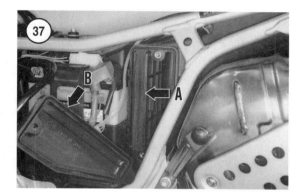

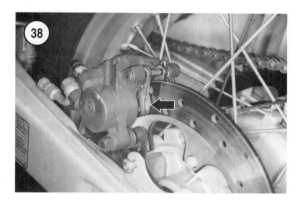

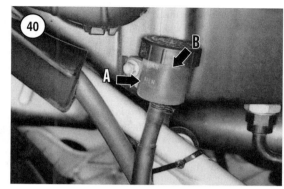

3

BRAKES

Brake Pad Inspection

Without removing the front or rear brake calipers, inspect the brake pads (**Figure 38**) for damage.

Measure the thickness of each brake pad lining with a ruler. Replace the brake pad if its thickness is worn past the minimum thickness in **Table 5**. Replace the brake pads as described in Chapter Fourteen.

Disc Brake Fluid Level

1. To check the front master cylinder, perform the following:
    a. Turn the handlebar straight ahead so the master cylinder is level.
    b. Observe the brake fluid level through the inspection window (**Figure 39**) on the master cylinder reservoir. The brake fluid should be above the lower level line.
2. To check the rear master cylinder, perform the following:
    a. Support the bike so that the rear master cylinder is level.
    b. Remove the frame right side cover as described in Chapter Fifteen.
    c. Make sure the brake fluid level is above the lower level mark on the reservoir (A, **Figure 40**).

> *CAUTION*
> *Be careful when handling brake fluid. Do not spill it on painted or plastic surfaces, as it damages them. Wash the area immediately with*

soap and water and thoroughly rinse it.

> *NOTE*
> *To control the flow of brake fluid from a new container, punch a small hole in the seal next to the edge of the pour spout. This helps eliminate the fluid spillage, especially while adding fluid to the small reservoir.*

3. If the brake fluid level is low, perform the following:

   a. Clean any dirt from the master cylinder cover prior to removing it.
   b. Remove the top cover and lift the diaphragm out of the reservoir. Refer to **Figure 41** for the front master cylinder and B, **Figure 40** for the rear master cylinder.
   c. Add fresh DOT 4 brake fluid to correct the level.
   d. Reinstall the diaphragm and top cover. Tighten the screws securely on the front master cylinder.

> *NOTE*
> *If the brake fluid level is low enough to allow air in the hydraulic system, bleed the brakes as described in Chapter Twelve.*

Front and Rear Brake Disc Inspection

Visually inspect the front and rear brake discs (**Figure 42**) for scoring, cracks or other damage. Measure the brake disc thickness, and if necessary, service the brake discs as described in Chapter Fourteen.

Disc Brake Lines and Seals

Check the brake lines between each master cylinder and each brake caliper. If there is any leakage, tighten the connections and bleed the brakes as described in Chapter Twelve.

Disc Brake Fluid Change

Every time the reservoir cover is removed, a small amount of dirt and moisture enters the brake fluid. The same thing happens if a leak occurs or if any part of the hydraulic system is loosened or disconnected.

Dirt can clog the system and cause unnecessary wear. Water in the fluid vaporizes at high temperatures, impairing the hydraulic action and reducing brake performance.

To change brake fluid, follow the brake bleeding procedure in Chapter Fourteen. Continue adding new fluid to the master cylinder until the fluid leaving the caliper is clean and free of contaminants and air bubbles.

DRIVE CHAIN AND SPROCKETS

Inspect the drive chain and sprockets at the interval in **Table 1**.

Drive Chain Cleaning

There is no maintenance interval for cleaning the drive chain. Clean the chain when it becomes dirty, caked with mud and other debris.

> *NOTE*
> *The rear swing arm must be removed to remove the drive chain. If the drive chain is not too dirty, clean it off sev-*

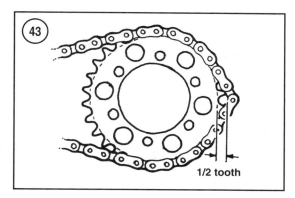

1/2 tooth

eral times with a shop rag soaked in
kerosene. Clean the entire chain and
let dry, then lubricate it as described
in the following procedure.

1. Remove the drive chain as described in Chapter
Thirteen.
2. Clean the drive chain in a plastic pan partially
filled with kerosene. If necessary, remove dirt from
the chain with a soft nylon brush. Do not use a metal
bristle or similar hard brush, as its bristles will damage the O-rings.

CAUTION
Do not clean an O-ring drive chain
with anything but kerosene. Most sol-
vents and gasoline will cause the
O-rings to swell and deteriorate, per-
manently damaging the chain.

3. After the chain is clean, hang it up to allow the
cleaning solution to drip off. Then lubricate the
chain as described in this chapter.
4. Lubricate the chain roller.
5. Reinstall the chain on the motorcycle as described in Chapter Thirteen.

Drive Chain Lubrication (Non-O-ring Chain)

Lubricate the drive chain before each ride. A
properly maintained chain will provide maximum
service life and reliability.
1. Support the bike on the centerstand or a work
stand with the rear wheel off the ground.
2. Shift the transmission into NEUTRAL.
3. Turn the rear wheel and lubricate the chain with
a commercial-type chain spray. Do not over-lubri-
cate the drive chain, as this will cause dirt to collect
on the chain and sprockets.

4. Wipe off all excess oil from the rear hub, wheel
and tire.

Drive Chain Lubrication (O-Ring Chain)

NOTE
If the O-ring chain was previously lu-
bricated with a tacky chain lubricant,
clean the chain (and sprockets) to re-
move all residue, dirt and grit. Clean
the chain as described in this chapter.

1. Support the bike on the centerstand or on a stand
or floor jack with the rear wheel off the ground. See
Bike Stands in Chapter Twelve.
2. Shift the transmission into NEUTRAL.
3. Externally lubricate the chain with a SAE 30-50
weight motor oil, WD-40, or a good grade of chain
lubricant (non-tacky) specifically formulated for
O-ring chains.

CAUTION
Do not use a tacky chain lubricant on
O-ring chains. Dirt and other abra-
sive materials that stick to the lubri-
cant will stick against the O-rings and
damage them. An O-ring chain is
pre-lubricated during its assembly.
External oiling is only required to pre-
vent chain rust and to keep the
O-rings pliable.

4. Wipe off all excess oil from the rear hub, wheel
and tire.

Drive Chain/Sprocket Wear Inspection

Check the drive chain, both sprockets and the
chain roller for wear frequently and replace the
parts when excessively worn or damaged.
A quick check will give an indication of when to
actually measure chain wear. At the rear sprocket,
pull one of the links away from the sprocket. If the
link pulls away more than 1/2 the height of a
sprocket tooth, the chain is excessively worn (**Figure 43**).
To measure chain wear, perform the following:
1. Check the inner plate chain links. They must be
lightly polished on both sides. If the chain shows
considerable uneven wear on one side, the sprockets are not aligned. Excessive wear requires the
drive chain and both sprockets to be replaced.

2. If the drive chain is worn, inspect the drive and driven sprockets for the following defects:

    a. Undercutting or sharp teeth (**Figure 44**).

    b. Broken teeth (**Figure 45**).

3. If excessive wear or damage is evident, replace the drive chain and both sprockets as a set. Rapid drive chain wear occurs if a new drive chain is installed on worn sprockets.

Drive Chain Adjustment

The drive chain must have adequate slack so the chain is not strung tight when the swing arm is horizontal. On the other hand, too much slack may cause the chain to jump off the sprockets with potentially disastrous results.

Off-road riding in mud and sand will make the chain tighter. Under these conditions, stop and recheck chain slack. If necessary, loosen the chain adjustment so that it is not too tight.

Check the drive chain free play slack before riding the bike. **Table 5** lists drive chain slack specifications.

1. Support the bike on the centerstand or a stand or floor jack with the rear wheel off the ground. See *Bike Stands* in Chapter Twelve.

2. Spin the wheel and check the chain for tightness at several spots. Check and adjust the chain at its tightest point (the chain wears unevenly).

3. At the bottom rung of the drive chain (**Figure 46**), move the chain up and then down and measure the total distance the chain moves (**Figure 47**).

4. Compare the drive chain slack with the specifications in **Table 5**. If necessary, adjust the drive chain as follows.

> *NOTE*
> *When adjusting the drive chain, maintain rear wheel alignment. A misaligned rear wheel can cause poor handling and pulling to one side or the other, as well as increased chain and sprocket wear. Wheel alignment marks are on the swing arm and chain adjusters.*

    a. Loosen the axle nut (A, **Figure 48**).

    b. Turn the rear axle adjuster screw (B, **Figure 48**) on each side. Turn both adjuster screws so the chain adjuster plate index marks align with the same marks on each side of the swing arm (**Figure 49**). Recheck chain slack.

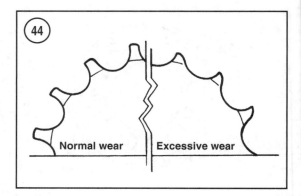

Normal wear | Excessive wear

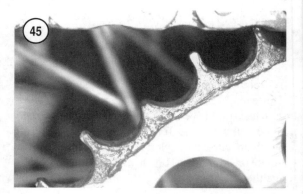

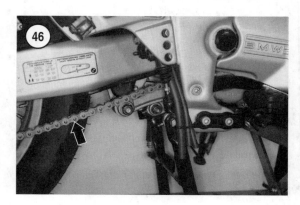

5. When the chain slack is correct, check wheel alignment by sighting along the chain from the rear sprocket. The chain must leave the sprocket in a straight line (A, **Figure 50**). If it is turned to one side or the other (B and C, **Figure 50**), perform the following:

    a. Adjust the wheel alignment by turning one adjuster or the other. Recheck chain play.

    b. Confirm swing arm accuracy by measuring from the center of the swing arm pivot shaft to the center of the rear axle. If necessary, make a tool like the one shown in **Figure 51** to accurately check chain alignment.

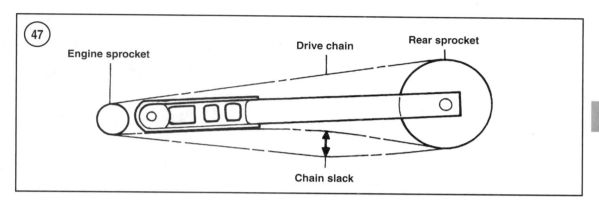

Engine sprocket

Drive chain

Rear sprocket

Chain slack

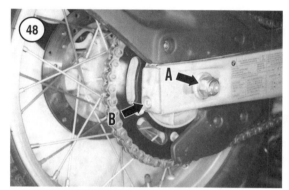

A

B

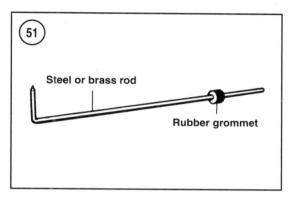

Steel or brass rod

Rubber grommet

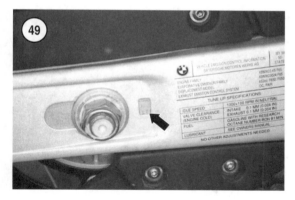

A   B   C

6. Tighten the rear axle nut (A, **Figure 48**) to the specification in **Table 6**.

7. Spin the wheel several times and recheck the free play at its tightest point once again. Make sure the free play is within specification.

Inspection

NOTE
The following photographs are shown with the swing arm removed to better illustrate the steps.

Inspect the drive chain slider (**Figure 52**) and roller (**Figure 53**). Replace if excessively worn or damaged as described in Chapter Thirteen.

Lubricate the roller at the intervals in **Table 1**.

COOLING SYSTEM

Cooling System Inspection

Once a year, or whenever troubleshooting the cooling system, check the following items. If the test equipment is not available, refer testing to a BMW dealership.

> *WARNING*
> *Never remove the radiator cap, coolant drain screw or disconnect any hose while the engine and radiator is hot. Scalding fluid and steam may be blown out under pressure and cause serious injury.*

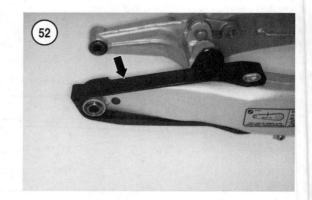

1. Remove the seat as described in Chapter Fifteen.
2. Remove the front fairing and the fuel tank cover as described in Chapter Fifteen.
3. With the engine cold, remove the radiator cap (**Figure 54**).
4. Check the rubber washers on the radiator cap (**Figure 55**). Replace the cap if the washers show signs of deterioration, cracking or other damage.

> *CAUTION*
> *Do not exceed the cooling system pressure specified in Step 5, or the cooling system components will be damaged.*

5. Pressure test (**Figure 56**) the cooling system to 98 kPa (14.23 psi). If the system fails to hold this pressure, check for the following conditions:
   a. Leaking or damaged hoses.
   b. Leaking water pump seal.
   c. Loose water pump mounting bolts.
   d. Warped water pump sealing surface.
   e. Warped cylinder head or cylinder mating surfaces.

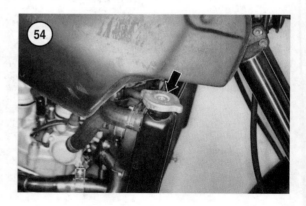

6. Check all cooling system hoses for damage or deterioration. Refer to **Figure 57** and **Figure 58**. Replace any questionable hose. Make sure all hose clamps are tight.
7. Carefully clean the radiator core. Use a whisk broom, compressed air or low-pressure water. Straighten bent radiator fins with a screwdriver.

Coolant Check

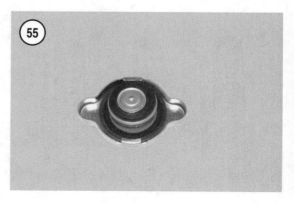

> *WARNING*
> *Never remove the radiator cap, coolant drain screw or disconnect any hose while the engine and radiator are hot. Scalding fluid and steam may be blown out under pressure and cause serious injury.*

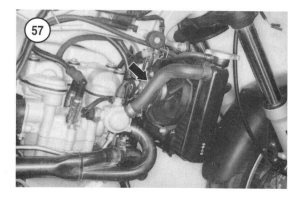

3

Before starting the bike, check the coolant level in the remote reservoir as follows.

1. Remove the seat as described in Chapter Fifteen.

2. Remove the right side cover as described in Chapter Fifteen.

3. The coolant level must be up to the MAX mark on the coolant remote reservoir (A, **Figure 59**).

4. If the level is low, remove the fill cap (B, **Figure 59**), add a sufficient amount of antifreeze and water (in a 50:50 ratio) as described under *Coolant*. Reinstall the fill cap.

5. Install the right side cover and seat as described in Chapter Fifteen.

Coolant

Use only a high quality, nitrite-free long life antifreeze compounded for aluminum engines.

Mix the antifreeze with water in a 50:50 ratio. **Table 4** lists coolant capacity. When mixing antifreeze with water, make sure to use only distilled (or purified) water. Never use tap or salt water, as this will damage engine parts. Purchase distilled water at supermarkets or drug stores in gallon containers.

Coolant Change

Completely drain and refill the cooling system at the interval in **Table 1**.

It is sometimes necessary to drain the coolant from the system to perform a service procedure on some part of the engine. If the coolant is still in good condition (not time to replace the coolant), the coolant can be reused if it is kept clean. Drain the coolant into a *clean* drain pan and then pour the coolant into a *clean* sealable container like a plastic milk or bleach bottle and screw on the cap. This coolant can then be reused.

> *WARNING*
> *Antifreeze is classified as an environmental toxic waste by the EPA and cannot legally be disposed of by flushing down a drain or pouring it onto the ground. Place antifreeze in a suitable container and dispose of it according to local EPA regulations. Do*

not store coolant where it is accessible to children or animals.

CAUTION
Use only a high-quality, nitrite-free long-life antifreeze compounded for aluminum engines.

CAUTION
Coolant will stain concrete and will damage or kill plants. Do not drain the coolant onto a driveway or allow it to drain into a planted area.

CAUTION
Be careful not to spill antifreeze on painted surfaces, as it will destroy the finish. Wash immediately with soapy water and rinse thoroughly with clean water.

Perform the following procedure when the engine is *cold*.

1. Remove the seat as described in Chapter Fifteen.
2. Remove the front fairing and the fuel tank cover as described in Chapter Fifteen.
3. With the engine cold, remove the radiator cap (**Figure 54**). This will speed up the draining process.
4. Place a clean container under the water pump.

WARNING
When draining the coolant in this section, never remove the radiator cap, coolant drain screw or disconnect any hose while the engine and radiators are hot. Scalding fluid and steam may be blown out under pressure and cause serious injury.

5. Remove the coolant drain screw and washer (**Figure 60**) on the water pump and drain the coolant into a clean container.
6. Flush the cooling system with clean tap water directed through the radiator filler neck. Allow this water to drain completely.

NOTE
If any type of colored residue drains out with the coolant, flush the cooling system for at least 10 minutes (Step 4).

7. Install a new washer on the drain screw and apply Loctite No. 243, or an equivalent, to the screw threads.

8. Install the water pump coolant drain screw and washer (**Figure 60**) and tighten it to the specification in **Table 6**.
9. Refill the radiator by adding a 50:50 mixture of antifreeze and distilled water through the radiator filler neck. See **Table 4** for coolant capacity. Do not install the radiator cap at this time.
10. Lean the bike from side to side to bleed air trapped in the cooling system. When the bike is level, observe the coolant level in the radiator. Repeat this step until the coolant level stops dropping in the radiator.
11. Install and tighten the radiator cap (**Figure 54**).

WARNING
Never remove the radiator cap while the engine and radiators are hot. Scalding fluid and steam may be blown out under pressure and cause serious injury.

12. Start the engine and allow it to idle for a few minutes, then shut it off. After the engine cools down, remove the radiator cap and check the coolant level. Add coolant up to the filler neck, if necessary. Reinstall the radiator cap (**Figure 54**). Check the coolant drain screw for leaks.
13. Check the coolant level in the recovery tank. It must be up to the MAX mark on the coolant recovery tank (A, **Figure 59**).
14. Install the front fairing and the fuel tank cover as described in Chapter Fifteen.
15. Install the seat as described in Chapter Fifteen.

REAR SUSPENION

Rear Swing Arm Pivot Bolt

Check the rear swing arm pivot bolt tightness (Chapter Thirteen) at the intervals in **Table 1**.

Lubricate the swing arm pivot bearings (Chapter Thirteen) at the interval in **Table 1**.

Rear Shock Absorber and Linkage

Check the rear shock absorber for oil leakage or damaged bushings. Check the shock absorber and linkage mounting bolts and nuts for tightness. Refer to Chapter Thirteen for service procedures.

FASTENERS

Constant vibration can loosen many fasteners on a motorcycle. Check the tightness of all fasteners, especially those on:

1. Engine mounting hardware.
2. Engine side covers.
3. Handlebar and front fork.
4. Gearshift lever.
5. Sprocket bolts and nuts.
6. Brake pedal and lever.
7. Exhaust system.
8. Lighting equipment.

TUNE-UP

A complete tune-up restores performance and power lost due to normal wear and deterioration of engine parts. Because engine wear occurs over a combined period of time and mileage, perform the engine tune-up procedures at the intervals specified in **Table 1**. More frequent tune-ups may be required if the motorcycle is operated primarily in stop-and-go traffic.

Replace the spark plugs at every other tune-up or if the electrodes show signs of wear, fouling or erosion.

Perform the procedures in the following order and refer to **Table 5** for specifications.

1. Clean or replace the air filter element.
2. Check engine compression.
3. Check or replace the spark plugs.
4. Check and adjust the valve clearance.
5. Adjust carburetor idle speed.

Air Filter

Inspect and if necessaary replace the air filter element before performing other tune-up procedures. Refer to *Air Filter* in this chapter.

Compression Test

A compression check is one of the most effective ways to check the condition of the engine. If possible, check the compression at each tune-up, record and compare it with the readings at subsequent tune-ups. This may help spot any developing problems.

1. Prior to starting the compression test, make sure the following is correct:
    a. The cylinder head and cylinder bolts and nuts are torqued to specification. Refer to Chapter Four.
    b. The battery is fully charged to ensure proper engine cranking speed.
2. Warm the engine to normal operating temperature. Shut off the engine.
3. Remove one of the spark plugs and reinstall it in its cap. Place the spark plug against the cylinder head to ground it.
4. Connect the compression tester to the cylinder, following its manufacturer's instructions (**Figure 61**).
5. Place the throttle in the wide-open position.
6. Make sure the starting enrichment (choke) lever (**Figure 62**) is pushed forward to the fully OFF position.

7. Crank the engine over until there is no further rise in pressure.

8. Record the reading and remove the tester.

9. Reinstall the spark plug and reconnect the cap.

Results

The manufacturer does not provide a specified compression pressure. At the first tune-up, perform this test and record the compression pressure. At the next compression test, compare the results against those from the first test.

If the reading differs significantly from the first, this indicates worn or broken rings, leaky or sticky valves, a blown head gasket or a combination of all.

If compression readings do not differ by more than 10 percent, the rings and valves are in good condition. A low reading (10 percent or more) indicates valve or ring trouble. To determine which, pour about a teaspoon of engine oil into the spark plug hole. Turn the engine over once to distribute the oil, then take another compression test and record the reading. If the compression increases significantly, the valves are good but the rings are defective on that cylinder. If compression does not increase, the valves require servicing.

> *NOTE*
> *An engine cannot be tuned to maxi-mum performance with low compres-sion.*

Spark Plug Removal

1. Refer to Chapter Fifteen and remove the follow-ing:
   a. Remove the seat.
   b. Remove left cylinder head side cover.
   c. Remove the fuel tank cover

> *CAUTION*
> *Whenever the spark plugs are re-moved, dirt around them can fall into the plug holes. This can cause serious engine damage.*

2. Blow away any loose dirt or debris that may have accumulated around the base of the spark plugs.

3. Grasp the spark plug lead (**Figure 63**), and twist from side to side to break the seal loose. Then pull

the cap off the spark plug. If the cap is stuck to the plug, twist it slightly to break it loose.

4. Install the spark plug socket onto the spark plug. Make sure it is correctly seated and install an open-end wrench or socket handle and remove the spark plug. Mark the spark plug with the cylinder number from which it was removed.

5. Repeat for the remaining spark plug.

6. Thoroughly inspect each plug. Look for broken center porcelain, excessively eroded electrodes and excessive carbon or oil fouling.

> *CAUTION*
> *Spark plug cleaning with a sand-blasting device is not recommended. The plug must be completely free of all abrasive cleaning material when done. If not, the abrasive material will fall into the cylinder during operation and cause damage.*

7. Inspect the spark plug caps and secondary wires for damage, or hardness. If any portion is damaged, the cap and secondary wire must be replaced as an assembly.

Spark Plug Gap and Installation

Carefully gap the spark plugs to ensure a reliable, consistent spark with a spark plug gap gauge.

1. Remove the new spark plugs from the boxes. In-stall the small adapter onto the end of the spark plug.

2. Insert the wire gap gauge between the center and side electrode of the plug (**Figure 64**). The correct gap is listed in **Table 5**. If the gap is correct, a slight drag will be felt as the wire gauge is pulled through. If there is no drag or the gauge will not pass through,

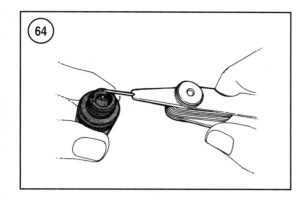

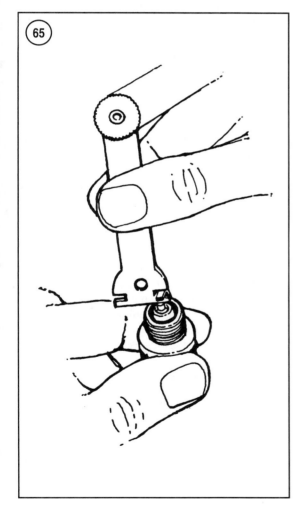

CAUTION
The cylinder head is aluminum and the spark plug hole is easily damaged.

4. Slowly screw the spark plug into the cylinder head by hand until it seats. Very little effort is required. If force is necessary, the plug is cross-threaded; unscrew it and try again.

NOTE
Do not overtighten. This will only squash the gasket and destroy its sealing ability.

5. Hand-tighten the plug until it seats against the cylinder head, then tighten an additional 1/4 to 1/2 turn after the gasket makes contact with the cylinder head.

6. Install the spark plug cap and lead on the correct spark plug. Rotate the cap slightly in both directions and make sure it is attached to the spark plug.

7. Repeat for the other spark plug.

Spark Plug Heat Range

Plugs with heat ranges that are either hotter or colder than the original plugs are available. However, in most cases the heat range of the spark plugs originally installed by the manufacturer (**Table 5**) will perform adequately under most conditions. Do not change the spark plug heat range to compensate for adverse engine or carburetion conditions. This will only compound the problem.

In general, use a hot plug for low speeds and low temperatures. Use a cold plug for high speeds and high temperatures. The plugs should operate hot enough to burn off unwanted deposits, but not so hot that it becomes damaged or causes preignition. Determine if plug heat range is correct by examining the insulator as described in *Spark Plug Reading*.

When replacing plugs with another type, make sure the reach or thread length is correct. The thread length of any replacement spark plug must be the same as the original, which matches the length of the threads in the cylinder head. A longer than standard plug could interfere with the piston, causing engine damage. A short plug will provide poor ignition.

bend the side electrode with the gapping tool (**Figure 65**) to adjust the gap.

3. Apply a *light coat* of antiseize lubricant to the threads of the spark plug before installing it. Do *not* use engine oil on the plug threads.

Spark Plug Reading

Reading the spark plugs can provide a significant amount of information regarding engine performance. Reading plugs that have been in use gives an indication of spark plug operation, air/fuel mixture composition and engine conditions (such as oil consumption or pistons). Before checking the spark plugs, operate the motorcycle under a medium load for approximately six miles (10 km). Avoid prolonged idling before shutting off the engine. Remove the spark plugs as described in this chapter. Examine each plug and compare it to those in **Figure 66** while referring to the following sections to determine the operating conditions.

If the plugs are being read to determine if carburetor jetting is correct, start with new plugs and operate the bike at the load that corresponds to the jetting information desired. For example, if the main jet is in question, operate the bike at full throttle and shut the engine off and coast to a stop.

Normal condition

If the plug has a light tan- or gray-colored deposit and no abnormal gap wear or erosion, good engine, air/fuel mixture and ignition conditions are indicated. The plug in use is of the proper heat range and may be serviced and returned to use.

Carbon fouled

Soft, dry, sooty deposits covering the entire firing end of the plug are evidence of incomplete combustion. Even though the firing end of the plug is dry, the plug's insulation decreases when in this condition. An electrical path is formed that bypasses the electrodes, resulting in a misfire condition. Carbon fouling can be caused by one or more of the following:

1. Rich fuel mixture.
2. Cold spark plug heat range.
3. Clogged air filter.
4. Improperly operating ignition component.
5. Ignition component failure.
6. Low engine compression.
7. Prolonged idling.

Oil fouled

The tip of an oil-fouled plug has a black insulator tip, a damp oily film over the firing end and a carbon layer over the entire nose. The electrodes are not worn. Oil-fouled spark plugs may be cleaned in an emergency, but it is better to replace them. It is important to correct the cause of fouling before the engine is returned to service. Common causes for this condition are:

1. Incorrect air/fuel mixture.
2. Low idle speed or prolonged idling.
3. Ignition component failure.
4. Cold spark plug heat range.
5. Engine still being broken in.
6. Valve guides worn.
7. Piston rings worn or broken.

Gap bridging

Plugs with this condition exhibit gaps shorted out by combustion deposits between the electrodes. If this condition is encountered, check for excessive carbon or oil in the combustion chamber. Be sure to locate and correct the cause of this condition.

Overheating

Badly worn electrodes and premature gap wear are signs of overheating, along with a gray or white blistered porcelain insulator surface. The most common cause for this condition is using a spark plug of the wrong heat range (too hot). If spark plug is the correct heat range and is overheated, consider the following causes:

1. Lean air/fuel mixture.
2. Improperly operating ignition component.
3. Engine lubrication system malfunction.
4. Cooling system malfunction.
5. Engine air leak.
6. Improper spark plug installation (overtightening).
7. No spark plug gasket.

Worn out

Corrosive gases formed by combustion and high-voltage sparks have eroded the electrodes. A spark plug in this condition requires more voltage to

66

SPARK PLUG CONDITION

3

NORMAL

GAP BRIDGED

CARBON FOULED

OVERHEATED

OIL FOULED

SUSTAINED PREIGNITION

fire under hard acceleration. Replace with a new spark plug.

Preignition

If the electrodes are melted, preignition is almost certainly the cause. Check for intake air leaks at the manifold and carburetor, or throttle body, and advanced ignition timing. It is also possible that a plug of the wrong heat range (too hot) is being used. Find the cause of the preignition before returning the engine into service. For additional information on preignition, refer to *Preignition* in Chapter Two.

Valve Clearance Measurement

Check and, if necessary, adjust the valve clearance (**Table 5**) at the intervals in **Table 1**. The exhaust valves are located at the front of the engine and the intake valves are located at the rear of the engine.

> *CAUTION*
> *For this procedure, the camshaft lobes must point away from the valve lifters. Clearance dimensions taken with the camshaft in any other position will give a false reading and lead to incorrect valve clearance adjustment and possible engine damage.*

> *NOTE*
> *Valve clearance measurement and adjustment must be performed with the engine cool, at room temperature (below 35° C/95° F).*

1. Refer to Chapter Fifteen and perform the following:
   a. Remove the seat.
   b. Remove both cylinder head side covers.
   c. Remove the fuel tank cover.
2. Remove the fuel tank as described in Chapter Eight.
3. Remove both spark plugs as described in this chapter. This will make it easier to turn the engine by hand.
4. Using a crisscross pattern, loosen and remove the special bolts securing the cylinder head cover (**Figure 67**) and remove the cover and gasket.

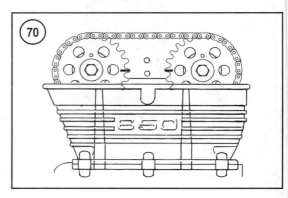

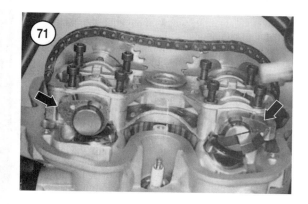

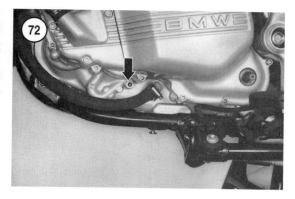

5. Remove the center plug (**Figure 68**) from the alternator cover.

6. Correctly position the camshafts as follows:

    a. Use a 6 mm Allen wrench on the alternator rotor. Rotate the engine in the normal *clockwise* direction, as viewed from the right-hand side of the engine, until both camshaft driven sprocket index marks (**Figure 69**) face each other (**Figure 70**).

    b. The camshaft lobes must point away from each other as shown in **Figure 71**.

    c. Also check that the piston is at TDC. Insert a scribe into the spark plug hole and touch the top of the piston. Slowly rotate the engine back and forth to ensure the piston is at TDC.

    d. If the camshaft lobes are not positioned correctly with the camshaft driven sprocket index marks aligned, rotate the engine 360° (one full revolution) until the camshaft lobes point away from each other. Recheck that the camshaft driven sprocket index marks (**Figure 69**) face each other (**Figure 70**).

7. On the lower left side of the crankcase, remove the Allen bolt (**Figure 72**).

NOTE
Some of the following photographs are shown with the crankshaft removed and some of the left side components removed to better illustrate the steps.

8. Direct a flashlight into the Allen bolt hole in the crankcase and check if the crankshaft counterbalance groove (**Figure 73**) is aligned with the hole. If necessary, slightly rotate the engine back and forth to ensure correct alignment of the groove with the bolt hole.

9. Install the BMW locking screw (part No. 11-6-570) (**Figure 74**) into the crankcase and index it into the crankshaft counterbalance groove. Tighten the locking screw securely.

10. With the engine in this position, check the valve clearance on all four valves.

NOTE
*Use a **metric feeler gauge** for measuring the valve clearance since the calculation used during the adjustment*

procedure are in metric rather than inch specifications.

NOTE
In the next step, start out with a feeler gauge of the specified clearance thickness. If this thickness is too large or small, change the gauge thickness until there is a drag on the feeler gauge when it is inserted and withdrawn.

11. Check the clearance by inserting a flat metric feeler gauge between the valve lifter and the camshaft lobe (**Figure 75**). When the correct gauge is selected, there will a slight resistance on the feeler gauge when it is inserted and withdrawn. Record the clearance and identify whether it is an intake or exhaust valve and on the right or left side of the cylinder head. This clearance dimension will be used during the following adjustment procedure, if necessary.

12. To adjust the clearance, replace the shim located on top of the valve lifter with a shim of different thickness. The shims are available from BMW dealerships in various thicknesses.

13. Measure the clearance of all valves prior to performing the *Valve Clearance Adjustment* in the following procedure.

14A. If the valves require adjustment, refer to *Valve Clearance Adjustment* in the following procedure.

14B. If valve clearance adjustment is not necessary, install all items removed.

Valve Clearance Adjustment

For calculations, use the midpoint of the specified clearance. For example, if the valve clearance is 0.10-0.15 mm, then the midpoint is 0.13 mm.

NOTE
*If working on a high-mileage engine, measure the thickness of the old shim with a micrometer (**Figure 76**) to make sure of the exact thickness of the shim. Also measure the new shim to make sure it is marked correctly.*

1. Remove both camshafts as described in Chapter Four.

2. To avoid confusion adjust one valve at a time.

3. Remove the shim (**Figure 77**) from the top of the valve lifter for the valve requiring adjustment.

4. Check the number on the bottom of the shim. If the number is no longer legible, measure it with a micrometer (**Figure 76**).

5. Using the measured valve clearance, the specified valve clearance listed in **Table 5**, and the old shim thickness, determine the new shim thickness with the following equation:

$a = (b-c) + d$

Where:

a equals the new shim thickness.

b equals the measured valve clearance.

c equals the specified valve clearance (mid-point of specification).

d equals the existing shim thickness.

NOTE
*The following numbers are for **examples only**. Use the numbers recorded during the **Valve Clearance Measurement** procedure.*

For example: If the measured valve clearance is 0.26 mm, the old shim thickness is 1.870 mm and

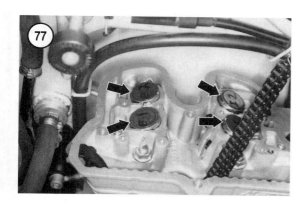

the specified valve clearance is 0.13 mm (midpoint of specification), then: a = (0.26 – 0.13) + 1.870. In this example the new shim thicknes equals 2.00 mm.

6. Apply clean engine oil to both sides of the new shim and to the receptacle on top of the valve lifter. Position the shim with the printed number side facing down and install the shim into the recess in the valve lifter.

7. Repeat this procedure for all valve assemblies that are out of specification.

8. Install the camshaft(s) as described in Chapter Four.

9. Use a 6-mm Allen wrench on the alternator rotor. Rotate the engine several complete revolutions in the normal *clockwise* direction, as viewed from the right-hand side of the engine, to seat the new shims and to squeeze out any excess oil between the shim, the spring retainer and the tappet.

10. Reinspect all valve clearances as described in the preceding procedure. If any of the clearances are still not within specification, repeat this procedure until all clearances are correct.

11. Make sure the O-ring is in place, then install the center plug (**Figure 68**) onto the alternator cover and tighten securely.

12. Install the cylinder head cover (**Figure 67**) and gasket. Using a crisscross pattern, tighten the special bolts securely.

13. Install both spark plugs as described in this chapter.

14. Install the fuel tank as described in Chapter Eight.

15. Refer to Chapter Fifteen and perform the following:
   a. Install the fuel tank cover.
   b. Install both cylinder head side covers.
   c. Install the seat.

Camshaft Chain Adjustment

An automatic cam chain tensioner assembly is attached to the backside of the cylinder head. No adjustment is possible nor required.

Ignition Timing

The ignition timing is controlled by the ignition control unit (ICU). There are no procedures for checking or adjusting the timing. If an ignition-related problem affecting the timing is suspected, inspect the ignition components as described in Chapter Nine.

Idle Speed Adjustment

1. Start the engine and warm it to normal operating temperature (cooling fan running). Shut OFF the engine.

2. Make sure the starting enrichment (choke) valve (**Figure 62**) is moved all the way forward to the OFF position.

3. Start the engine. With the engine idling, compare the tachometer reading to the idle speed specification in **Table 5**. If the tachometer reading is incorrect, adjust the idle speed as follows.

NOTE
The following photographs show the carburetor removed and partially disassembled to better illustrate the steps.

4. Remove the rubber plug (**Figure 78**) from the carburetor fitting.

5. Using a special angled screwdriver (BMW part No. 13 1 600), or an equivalent, turn the idle mixture

screw (**Figure 79**) in until it *lightly* seats, then back it out 3 1/2 turns.

6. Accelerate the engine a couple of times and release the throttle. The idle speed must return to the speed set in Step 3. If necessary, readjust the idle speed by turning the throttle stop screw (**Figure 80**). Shut off the engine.

7. Install the rubber plug (**Figure 78**).

Table 1 MAINTENANCE AND LUBRICATION SCHEDULE[1]

Pre-ride check
  Check tire condition and inflation pressure
  Check wheel rim condition
  Check engine oil level; add oil if necessary
  Check coolant level; add coolant if necessary
  Check brake fluid level and condition; add fluid if necessary
  Check brake lever operation and travel
  Check clutch operation
  Check choke (enrichener) cable operation
  Check fuel level in fuel tank; top off if necessary
  Check the fuel system for leakage
  Check the exhaust system for damage
  Check drive chain tension
  Check all lights and the horn

Initial 600 miles (1000 km)[2]
  Change engine oil and filter
  Check battery condition; clean cable connections if necessary
  Check the brake fluid level and condition; add fluid if necessary
  Check oil and brake lines for leakage
  Check front and rear brake pads and discs for wear
  Check tires for correct inflation pressure and for excessive wear or damage
  Check the drive chain tension; adjust if necessary
  Check the drive chain, drive sprocket and driven sprocket for wear or damage; replace as
   a set if necessary
  Check clutch lever operation; adjust if necessary
  Inspect spark plugs
  Inspect air filter element and air box
  Lubricate front brake and clutch lever pivot pin
  Check throttle cable operation
  Check enrichment valve (choke) cable operation
  Check engine idle speed; adjust if necessary
  Check fuel valve, fuel lines and all fittings for leaks or damage
  Check electrical switches and equipment for proper operation

(continued)

Table 1 MAINTENANCE AND LUBRICATION SCHEDULE[1] (continued)

Initial 600 miles (1000 km)[2] (continued)
  Check spoke nipple tightness; adjust if necessary
  Check all fasteners for tightness
  Road test the bike

Every 6000 miles (10,000 km)
  Check valve clearances; adjust if necessary
  Inspect spark plugs; replace if necessary
  Inspect air filter element and air box drain
  Check engine idle speed; adjust if necessary
  Check clutch free play; adjust if necessary
  Change engine oil and filter
  Clean oil tank filter
  Check the coolant level in remote reservoir; add coolant if necessary
  Clean fuel shutoff valve filters
  Adjust the CO value (U.S. and Switzerland models only[2])
  Check the brake fluid level and condition in both master cylinders; add fluid if necessary
  Check oil and brake lines for leakage
  Check front and rear brake pads and discs for wear
  Check electrical switches and equipment for proper operation
  Check spoke tension; adjust if necessary
  Check the drive chain and sprockets for wear or damage; replace as a set if necessary
  Lubricate the chain roller
  Lubricate stands and brake pedal pivot
  Lubricate throttle control
  Lubricate the brake and clutch lever pivots
  Check clutch cable operation
  Check throttle cable operation
  Check enrichment valve (choke) cable operation
  Check swing arm pivot bolt, and shock and linkage bolts for tightness
  Check all fasteners for tightness
  Road test bike

Every 12,000 miles (20,000 km)
  All items listed under 6000 miles (10,000 km)
  Replace front fork oil
  Inspect and lubricate the front and rear wheel bearings
  Inspect and lubricate the steering head bearings
  Inspect and lubricate the swing arm pivot bearings

Annual service (regardless of mileage)
  Replace engine coolant
  Replace brake fluid
  Check electrolyte level in battery
  Clean and grease battery terminals

1. Consider this maintenance schedule a guide to general maintenance and lubrication intervals. Harder than normal use and exposure to mud, water, high humidity indicates more frequent servicing to most of the maintenance items.
2. To be performed by a BMW dealership.

Table 2 TIRE INFLATION PRESSURE (COLD)*

Model	kPa	PSI
Front wheels		
Rider only	186	27
Full load	228	33

(continued)

Table 2 TIRE INFLATION PRESSURE (COLD)* (continued)

Rear wheels		
Rider only		
F 650, Funduro, Strada, SE	196	28.5
F 650 ST	228	33
Full load	245	35.5

*Tire pressure for original equipment tires. Aftermarket tires may require different inflation pressure.

Table 3 BATTERY STATE OF CHARGE

Specific gravity reading	Percentage of charge remaining
1.120-1.140	0
1.135-1.155	10
1.150-1.170	20
1.160-1.180	30
1.175-1.195	40
1.190-1.210	50
1.205-1.255	60
1.215-1.235	70
1.230-1.250	80
1.245-1.265	90
1.260-1.280	100

Table 4 RECOMMENDED LUBRICANTS AND FLUIDS

Item	Quantity	Recommended type
Engine oil		
Oil and filter change	22.1 L (2.21 U.S. qts/3.70 Imp. pts)	API SF, SG or SH
Viscosity	–	SAE 20W/50*
Front fork oil (at oil change)		
Regular suspension	600 cc (20 U.S. oz./16.8 Imp. oz.)/per leg	BMW 7.5 wt. fork oil
Lowered suspension	650 cc (22 U.S. oz./18 Imp. oz.)/per leg	
Brake fluid	–	DOT4
Coolant		
Cooling system	1.2 L (1.27 U.S. qt./2.11 Imp. pts.)	BMW antifreeze
Recovery tank	200 cc (6.7 U.S. oz./5.6 Imp. oz.)	
Coolant mixing ratio	50% antifreeze/50% distilled water	–
Battery water	–	Distilled or purified water
Miscellaneous lubricants		
High-performance lubricating		
paste grease	–	Optimoly MP 3
High performance assembly		
paste grease	–	Optimoly TA
Roller bearing grease	–	Retinax EP2

* See Figure 12 in this chapter for recommended viscosity ratings for various ambient temperatures.

Table 5 MAINTENANCE AND TUNE-UP SPECIFICATIONS

Item	Specification
Engine compression	NA
Spark plugs	NGK D8EA
Gap	0.6-0.7 mm (0.024-0.028 in.)
Idle speed	1300-1400 rpm
Idle mixture screw	3 1/2 turns out
Valve clearance	
Intake and exhaust	0.10-0.15 mm (0.004-0.006 in.)
Ignition timing	Non-adjustable
Brake pad minimum thickness	
Front and back	1.5 mm (0.06 in.)
Drive chain slack	20-30 mm (0.8-1.20 in.)
Clutch cable free play at hand lever	1.5-2.5 mm (0.06-0.10 in.)

Table 6 MAINTENANCE AND TUNE-UP TORQUE SPECIFICATIONS

Item	N•m	in.-lb.	ft.-lb.
Camshaft mount bolts	10	88	—
Coolant drain screw	10	88	—
Engine oil drain plug	40	—	29
Front fork			
Cap bolt	25	—	18
Drain screw	6	53	—
Handlebar clamp screws	25	—	18
Oil filter cover screw	10	88	—
Oil tank drain plug	10	88	—
Rear axle nut	100	—	74
Steering stem locknut	100	—	74
Upper fork bridge bolts	25	—	18
Valve cover bolts	10	88	—

CHAPTER FOUR

ENGINE TOP END

The engine is a liquid-cooled, dual overhead camshaft, four-valve single cylinder. The dual camshafts are driven by a single drive chain. **Figure 1** explains basic four-stroke engine operation.

This chapter provides complete service and overhaul procedures.

Tables 1-3 are at the end of the chapter.

SERVICE PRECAUTIONS

Before servicing the engine, note the following:

1. Review *Service Methods* and *Precision Measuring Tools* in Chapter One. Accurate measurements are critical to a successful engine rebuild.

2. Throughout the text, there are references to the left and right side of the engine. This refers to the engine as it is mounted in the frame, not how it may sit on the workbench.

3. Always replace worn or damaged fasteners with those of the same size, type and torque requirements.

Make sure to identify each bolt before replacing it. Lubricate bolt threads with engine oil, unless otherwise specified, before tightening. If a specific torque value is not provided, refer to the general torque specification table in Chapter One.

> *CAUTION*
> *The engine is assembled with hardened fasteners. Do not install fasteners with a lower strength grade classification.*

4. Use special tools where noted.

5. Store parts in boxes, plastic bags and containers (**Figure 2**). Use masking tape and a permanent waterproof marker to label parts.

6. Use a box of assorted size and color vacuum hose identifiers (**Figure 3**), Lisle (part No. 74600), to identify hoses and fittings during engine removal and disassembly.

7. Use a vise with protective jaws to hold parts.

① **FOUR-STROKE ENGINE PRINCIPLES**

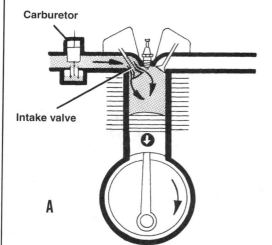

Carburetor

Intake valve

A

As the piston travels downward, the exhaust valve is closed and the intake valve opens, allowing the new air-fuel mixture from the carburetor to be drawn into the cylinder. When the piston reaches the bottom of its travel (BDC), the intake valve closes and remains closed for the next 1 1/2 revolutions of the crankshaft.

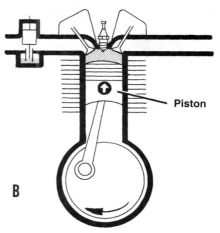

Piston

B

While the crankshaft continues to rotate, the piston moves upward, compressing the air-fuel mixture.

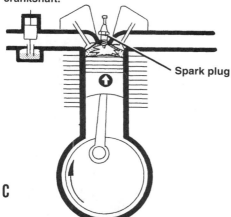

Spark plug

C

As the piston almost reaches the top of its travel, the spark plug fires, igniting the compresed air-fuel mixture. The piston continues to top dead center (TDC) and is pushed downward by the expanding gases.

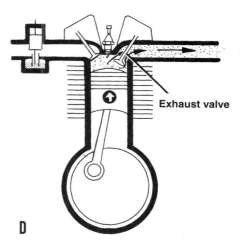

Exhaust valve

D

When the piston almost reaches BDC, the exhaust valve opens and remains open until the piston is near TDC. The upward travel of the piston forces the exhaust gases out of the cylinder. After the piston has reached TDC, the exhaust valve closes and the cycle repeats.

4

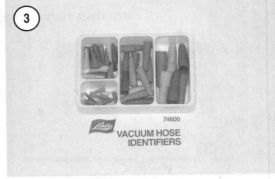

8. Use a press or special tools when force is required to remove and install parts. Do not try to pry, hammer or otherwise force them on or off.

9. Replace all O-rings and seals during reassembly. Apply a small amount of grease to the inner lips of each new seal to prevent damage when the engine is first started.

10. Record the location, position and thickness of all shims as they are removed.

11. Whenever any portion of the engine has been removed and the oil system drained, always bleed the oil circuit as described under *Engine Oil Circuit Bleeding* in Chapter Five.

CYLINDER HEAD COVER

Removal/Installation

1. Thoroughly clean all dirt and debris from the engine.

2. Refer to Chapter Fifteen and perform the following:

   a. Remove the seat.
   b. Remove both frame side covers.
   c. Remove both cylinder head covers.
   d. Remove the fuel tank cover.
   e. Remove the front fairing.

3. Remove the fuel tank as described in Chapter Eight.

4. Disconnect the spark plug leads.

5. Using a crisscross pattern, loosen and remove the special bolts securing the cylinder head cover (**Figure 4**).

6. Remove the cover and gasket.

7. Inspect the cylinder head cover (**Figure 5**) for damage. Replace it if necessary.

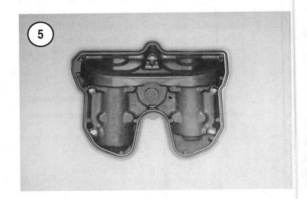

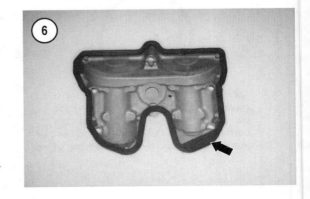

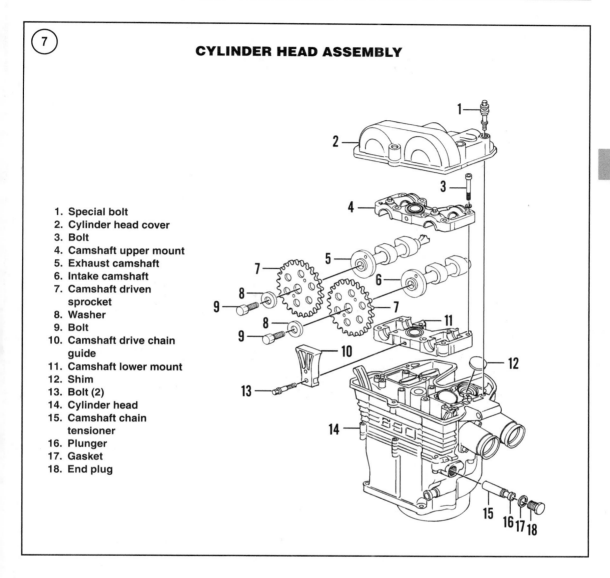

CYLINDER HEAD ASSEMBLY

1. Special bolt
2. Cylinder head cover
3. Bolt
4. Camshaft upper mount
5. Exhaust camshaft
6. Intake camshaft
7. Camshaft driven sprocket
8. Washer
9. Bolt
10. Camshaft drive chain guide
11. Camshaft lower mount
12. Shim
13. Bolt (2)
14. Cylinder head
15. Camshaft chain tensioner
16. Plunger
17. Gasket
18. End plug

8. Inspect the cylinder head cover gasket (**Figure 6**) for hardness or deterioration. Replace if necessary.

9. Thoroughly clean the cylinder head cover mating surface on the cylinder head.

10. Install the cylinder head cover and gasket.

11. Install the special bolts with integral rubber gaskets and tighten to the specification in **Table 3**.

12. Connect the spark plug leads.

13. Install the fuel tank as described in Chapter Eight.

14. Refer to Chapter Fifteen and perform the following:

   a. Install the front fairing.

b. Install the fuel tank cover.

c. Install both cylinder head covers.

d. Install both frame side covers.

e. Install the seat.

CAMSHAFTS

Refer to **Figure 7** and **Figure 8**.

Removal

1. Remove the cylinder head cover as described in this chapter.

CAMSHAFTS AND DRIVE CHAIN

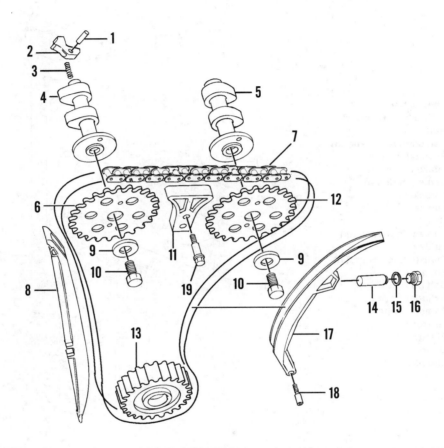

1. Pin
2. Centrifugal decompressor weight
3. Spring
4. Exhaust camshaft
5. Intake camshaft
6. Exhaust camshaft driven sprocket
7. Chain
8. Front guide rail
9. Washer
10. Bolt
11. Chain guide
12. Intake camshaft driven sprocket
13. Primary drive gear
14. Chain tensioner
15. Gasket
16. End plug
17. Rear tensioner guide rail
18. Bolt
19. Bolt (2)

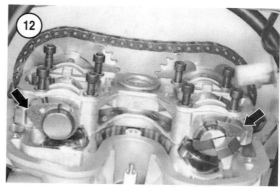

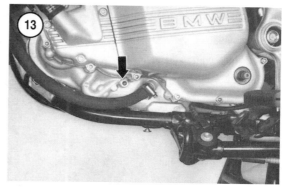

4

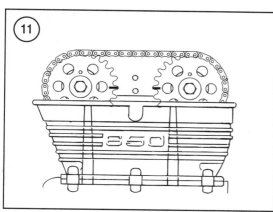

2. Remove the spark plugs as described in Chapter Three. This will make it easier to turn the engine by hand.

3. Remove the center plug (**Figure 9**) from the alternator cover.

4. Correctly position the camshafts as follows:

a. Use a 6 mm Allen wrench on the alternator rotor. Rotate the engine *clockwise*, as viewed from the right-hand side of the engine, until

both camshaft driven sprocket (**Figure 10**) index marks face each other (**Figure 11**).

b. The camshaft lobes must be facing away from each other as shown in **Figure 12**.

c. Also check that the piston is at TDC. Insert a scribe into the spark plug hole and touch the top of the piston. Slowly rotate the engine back and forth to ensure the piston is at TDC.

d. If the camshaft lobes are not positioned correctly with the camshaft driven sprocket index marks aligned, rotate the engine *clockwise* 360° (one full revolution) until the camshaft lobes face away from each other. Recheck that the camshaft driven sprocket (**Figure 10**) index marks face each other (**Figure 11**).

5. On the lower left side of the crankcase, remove the Allen bolt (**Figure 13**).

NOTE
Some of the following photographs show the crankshaft removed and some left side components removed to better illustrate the steps.

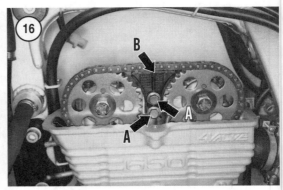

6. Shine a flashlight into the Allen bolt hole in the crankcase and check if the crankshaft counterbalance groove (**Figure 14**) is aligned with the hole. If necessary, slightly rotate the engine back and forth to ensure correct alignment of the groove with the bolt hole.

7. Install the locking screw (BMW part No. 11 6 570) (**Figure 15**) into the crankcase and index it into the crankshaft counterbalance groove. Tighten the locking screw securely.

8. Remove the camshaft drive chain tensioner as described in this chapter.

9. Remove the bolts (A, **Figure 16**) that secure the camshaft drive chain guide (B) and remove the guide from the chain.

10. Using a crisscross pattern, loosen then remove the bolts and washers securing the camshaft upper mount (**Figure 17**). Pull the upper mount straight up and off the camshafts.

11. Disengage the drive chain from the intake camshaft (**Figure 18**) and remove the camshaft.

12. Secure the camshaft drive chain (A, **Figure 19**) to the frame to prevent it from falling into the crankcase.

13. Disengage the drive chain from the exhaust camshaft (B, **Figure 19**) and remove the camshaft.

14. Pull the camshaft lower mount (**Figure 20**) straight up and off the cylinder head. Do not lose the locating dowels.

15. Inspect the camshafts as described in this chapter.

CAUTION
If the crankshaft must be rotated while the camshafts are removed, pull up on the camshaft drive chain to keep it

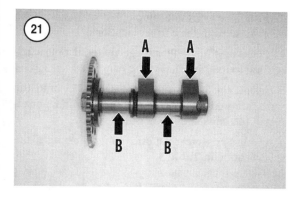

properly engaged on the crankshaft timing sprocket. Make certain that the drive chain is positioned correctly on the timing sprocket on the primary drive gear. If this is not done, the drive chain may become kinked and may damage the chain, the timing sprocket and the crankcase.

Inspection

When measuring the camshafts in this section, compare the actual measurements to the new and service wear limit specifications in **Table 2**. Replace parts that are out of specification or show damage as described in this section.

1. Check the camshaft lobes (A, **Figure 21**) for wear. The lobes should not be scored and the edges should be square.

2. Measure the height of each lobe (**Figure 22**) with a micrometer. Replace if it is out of specification.

3. Check each camshaft bearing journal (B, **Figure 21**) for wear and scoring.

4. Measure each camshaft bearing journal (**Figure 23**) with a micrometer. Replace if out of specification.

5. If the bearing journals are severely worn or damaged, check the bearing journals in the camshaft upper and lower mounts (**Figure 24**). They should not be scored or excessively worn. If any of the bearing surfaces are worn or scored, the upper and lower mounts must be replaced as a set.

6. Inspect the oil path (**Figure 25**) in the upper and lower mounts for blockage. Clean out if necessary.

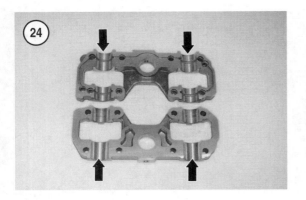

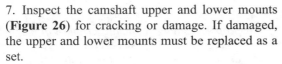

7. Inspect the camshaft upper and lower mounts (**Figure 26**) for cracking or damage. If damaged, the upper and lower mounts must be replaced as a set.

8. Inspect the camshaft driven sprockets (A, **Figure 27**) for broken or chipped teeth. Also check the teeth for cracking or rounding. If the camshaft driven sprockets are damaged or severely worn, replace the camshaft. Also, inspect the timing sprocket on the crankshaft primary drive gear as described in Chapter Five.

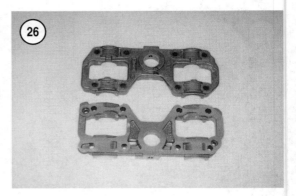

> *NOTE*
> *If the camshaft sprockets are worn, check the camshaft drive chain, chain guides and chain tensioner for damage.*

9. Check the tightness of each camshaft sprocket bolt (B, **Figure 27**). If necessary, tighten to the specification in **Table 3**.

10. Inspect the top surface of the camshaft drive chain guide (**Figure 28**) for wear or damage. Replace if necessary.

Camshaft Bearing Clearance Measurement

This procedure requires a Plastigage set. The camshafts must be installed into the cylinder head. Before installing the camshafts, clean all oil residue from the camshaft bearing journals and from the bearing surface of the camshaft upper and lower mounts.

1. Do not install the drive chain onto the camshafts for this procedure.

2. If removed, install the lower mount (**Figure 20**) onto the cylinder head.

3. Install the camshafts onto the lower mount in the cylinder head in the correct locations.

4. Place a strip of Plastigage material onto each bearing journal parallel to the camshaft.

5. Install the upper mount (**Figure 17**) onto the camshafts and the lower mount in the cylinder head. Install the bolts and washers.

6. Using a crisscross pattern, tighten the bolts to the specification in **Table 3**.

> *CAUTION*
> *Do not rotate the camshafts with the Plastigage material in place.*

7. Using a crisscross pattern, loosen and remove the bolts and washers that secure the camshaft upper mount (**Figure 17**). Pull the upper mount straight up and off the camshafts.

8. Measure the flattened Plastigage material (**Figure 29**) at the widest point of each bearing journal, according to the manufacturer's instructions. Compare to the specifications in **Table 2**.

9. Remove the camshafts.

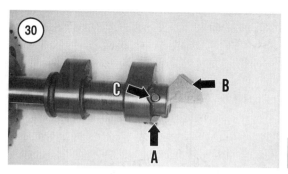

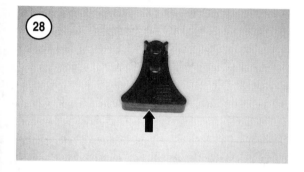

bearing surface is worn to the service limit, replace the camshaft. If the camshaft is within specification, replace the camshaft upper and lower mounts as a set.

Centrifugal Decompressor

The exhaust camshaft is equipped with a centrifugal lever decompressor. The small nib on the lever (A, **Figure 30**) touches the valve lifter to slightly open the exhaust valve when the engine is cranked for starting. After the engine has started, the camshaft rotation moves the centrifugal weight lever nib up and away from the valve lifter so there is no longer contact.

1. Move the centrifugal weight lever (B, **Figure 30**) back and forth to check for ease of movement and to make sure the spring returns the weight lever to the outward position.

> *CAUTION*
> *Do not remove and stretch the spring to achieve the correct dimension in Step 2. Doing so will alter the predetermined spring force and incorrectly alter the movement of the weight lever.*

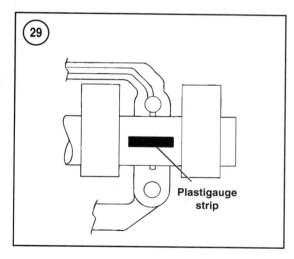

Plastigauge strip

> *CAUTION*
> *Be sure to remove all traces of Plastigage material from the bearing journals on the upper mount and from the camshaft bearing journal. Any material remaining in the engine can plug an oil control orifice and cause engine damage.*

10. If the bearing oil clearance is greater than specified in **Table 2**, refer to the camshaft bearing journal diameter recorded in *Inspection*, Step 4. If the

2. Hold the exhaust camshaft horizontal with the weight lever facing down. The spring must push the weight lever out 11.5 mm (0.45 in.) as shown in Dimension A in **Figure 31**. If the dimension is less than specified, replace the spring.

3. Hold the exhaust camshaft horizontal with the weight lever facing up. The weight lever nib must project beyond the camshaft by 0.6 mm (0.02 in.) as shown in Dimension B in **Figure 32**. If less than specified, replace the weight lever.

4. To replace the weight lever or spring, perform the following:

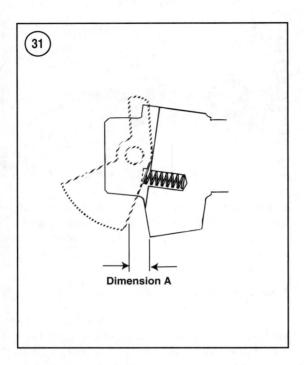

Dimension A

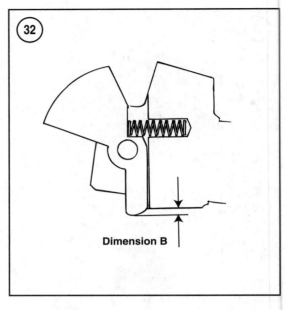

Dimension B

a. Use a suitable size drift and drive out the pin (C, **Figure 30**).
b. Remove the weight lever and spring (**Figure 33**).
c. Replace the weight and/or spring as necessary.
d. Install the pin and check for ease of movement.

Camshaft Installation

1. Pull up on the camshaft drive chain and make sure it is properly meshed with the timing sprocket on the primary drive gear.

> *NOTE*
> *If the crankshaft has not been moved since the camshafts were removed, the engine may still be at the correct position for camshaft installation. If the locking screw (BMW part No. 11 6 570) (Figure 34) is still in place in the crankcase, the engine is at TDC. Proceed with Step 3. If the piston is not at TDC, perform Step 2.*

2. If it is necessary to correctly position the piston at TDC, perform the following:

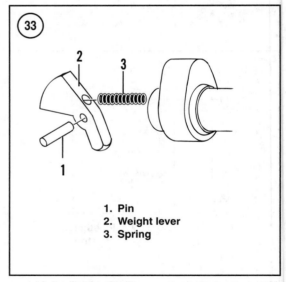

1. Pin
2. Weight lever
3. Spring

a. On the lower left side of the crankcase, remove the Allen bolt (**Figure 35**).

> *NOTE*
> *Some of the following photographs show the crankshaft removed and some left side components removed to better illustrate the steps.*

b. Shine a flashlight into the Allen bolt hole in the crankcase and check if the crankshaft counterbalance groove (**Figure 14**) is aligned

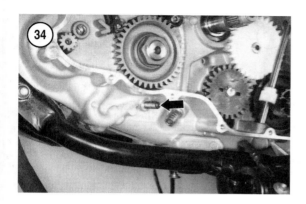

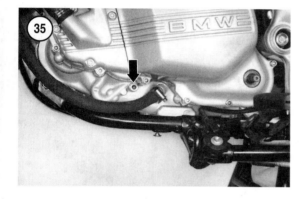

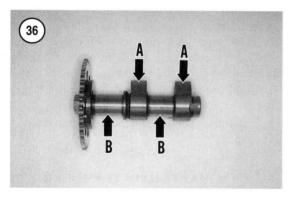

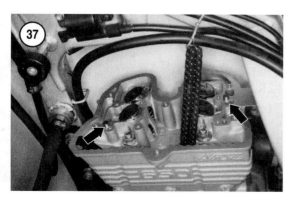

4

with the hole. If necessary, slightly rotate the engine back and forth to ensure correct alignment of the groove with the bolt hole.

c. Also check that the piston is at TDC. Insert a scribe into the spark plug hole and touch the top of the piston. Slowly rotate the engine back and forth to ensure the piston is at TDC.

d. Install the locking screw (BMW part No. 11 6 570) (**Figure 34**) into the crankcase and index it into the crankshaft counterbalance groove. Tighten the locking screw securely.

3. Apply a light complete coat of molybdenum disulfide grease to the each camshaft lobe (A, **Figure 36**) and bearing (B). Coat all bearing surfaces in the camshaft upper and lower mounts (**Figure 24**) with clean engine oil.

4. Make sure the locating dowels (**Figure 37**) are in place on the cylinder head.

5. Install the camshaft lower mount (**Figure 20**) onto the cylinder head. Push it down until it bottoms.

6. Install the exhaust camshaft (B, **Figure 19**) through the camshaft drive chain.

7. Lift up on the chain and rotate the exhaust camshaft until the index mark is facing toward the rear of the engine and is parallel with the top surface of the cylinder head. Properly index the camshaft into the lower mount and with the drive chain.

8. Install the intake camshaft (**Figure 18**) through the camshaft drive chain and onto the camshaft lower mount. Untie the camshaft drive chain.

9. Lift up on the drive chain and rotate the intake camshaft until the index mark is facing toward the front of the engine and is parallel with the top surface of the cylinder head. Properly index the camshaft into the lower mount and with the drive chain.

10. Insert your finger into the camshaft chain tensioner receptacle in the cylinder. Push on the camshaft drive chain to remove all slack. Check that both camshaft driven sprocket index marks (**Figure 38**) face each other (**Figure 39**). If necessary, readjust the camshaft(s) until this alignment is achieved.

11. Install the camshaft upper mount (**Figure 17**) onto both camshafts. Push it down until it bottoms.

12. Install the bolts and washers that secure the upper and lower mounts to the cylinder head.

13. Using a crisscross pattern, tighten the bolts securing the camshaft mounts. Tighten the bolts to the specification in **Table 3**.

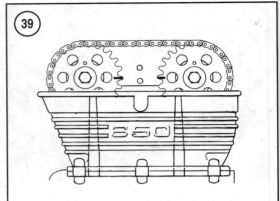

14. Install the camshaft drive chain guide (B, **Figure 16**) and bolts (A). Tighten the bolts securely.

> *CAUTION*
> *Engine damage could result from improper camshaft drive chain-to-camshaft installation and alignment. Recheck your work several times to be sure alignment is correct.*

15. Reinsert your finger into the tensioner receptacle in the cylinder and push hard on the chain to remove all slack. Recheck all of the timing marks to make sure all marks are still aligned properly. If incorrect, reposition the drive chain on the camshaft driven sprockets at this time.

16. Install the camshaft chain tensioner as described in this chapter.

17. After the tensioner is installed, recheck the alignment as shown in **Figure 39**. If any of the alignment points are incorrect, repeat this procedure until *all* are correct.

18. On the lower left side of the crankcase, unscrew and remove the BMW locking screw (**Figure 34**) from the crankcase.

19. Install the Allen bolt (**Figure 35**) and tighten securely.

> *CAUTION*
> *If there is any binding while rotating the crankshaft, **stop**. Determine the cause before proceeding.*

20. Use a 6 mm wrench on the alternator rotor. Rotate the engine *clockwise*, as viewed from the right side of the engine. Rotate the crankshaft several complete revolutions.

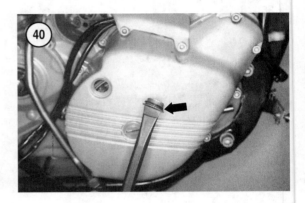

21. Make sure the O-ring seal (**Figure 40**) is in place on the center plug. Install the center plug onto the alternator cover and tighten securely.

22. Install the spark plugs as described in Chapter Three.

23. Install the cylinder head cover as described in this chapter.

CAMSHAFT CHAIN TENSIONER AND GUIDE RAILS

Camshaft Chain Tensioner and Guide Rails Preliminary Inspection

Refer to **Figure 41**.

1. Refer to Chapter Fifteen and perform the following:

   a. Remove the seat.

   b. Remove the frame left side cover.

   c. Remove the cylinder head left side cover.

2. Remove the cylinder head cover as described in this chapter.

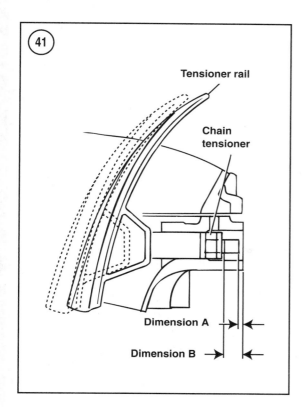

41

Tensioner rail

Chain
tensioner

Dimension A

Dimension B

42

3. Unscrew and remove the 22 mm end plug (**Figure 42**) and gasket from the end of the tensioner.

4. Push the end of the tensioner (**Figure 43**) against the rear tensioner rail until resistance is felt.

5. Measure the distance (Dimension A) from the sealing face of the cylinder to the end of the tensioner.

6. If the end of the tensioner moves in to, or past, the service limit of 9.5 mm (0.37 in.) Dimension B, inspect the tensioner rails and drive chain as described in this section.

43

7. Replace the worn parts and repeat this procedure to ensure correct drive chain tension.

8. Apply a light coat of ThreeBond TB1209, or equivalent to the end plug threads.

9. Install the 22 mm end plug (**Figure 42**) and *new* gasket onto the end of the tensioner. Tighten the end plug to the specification in **Table 3**.

10. Install the cylinder head cover as described in this chapter.

11. Refer to Chapter Fifteen and perform the following:

  a. Install the cylinder head left side cover.
  b. Install the frame left side cover.
  c. Install the seat.

**Camshaft Chain Tensioner
Removal/Inspection/Installation**

  Refer to **Figure 44**.

1. Refer to Chapter Fifteen and perform the following:

  a. Remove the seat.
  b. Remove the frame left side cover.
  c. Remove the cylinder head left side cover.

2. Unscrew and remove the 22 mm end plug (**Figure 42**) and gasket from the end of the tensioner.

3. Withdraw the tensioner assembly (**Figure 45**) from the cylinder receptacle.

4. Inspect the housing (A, **Figure 46**) for cracks or other damage. Replace the tensioner assembly if necessary.

5. Push the plunger in and out (**Figure 47**) and check for ease of movement.

6. Inspect the end plug (B, **Figure 46**) for thread damage. Repair if necessary.

7. Install a *new* gasket (C, **Figure 46**) onto the tensioner.

4

CAMSHAFTS AND DRIVE CHAIN

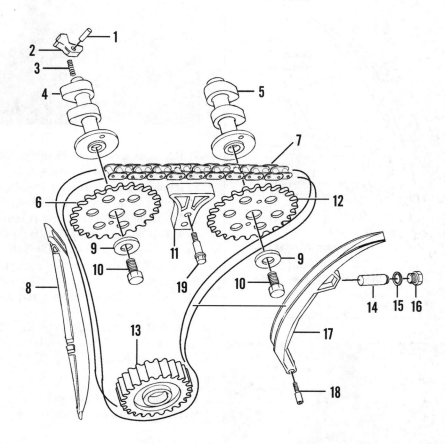

1. Pin
2. Centrifugal decompressor weight
3. Spring
4. Exhaust camshaft
5. Intake camshaft
6. Exhaust camshaft driven sprocket
7. Chain
8. Front guide rail
9. Washer
10. Bolt
11. Chain guide
12. Intake camshaft driven sprocket
13. Primary drive gear
14. Chain tensioner
15. Gasket
16. End plug
17. Rear tensioner guide rail
18. Bolt
19. Bolt (2)

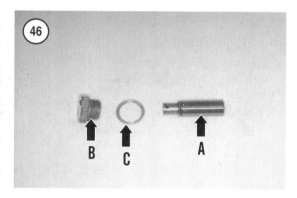

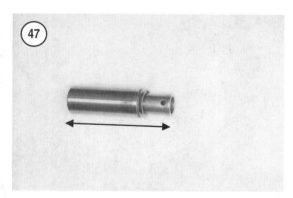

8. Apply a light coat of ThreeBond TB1209, or equivalent to the end plug threads prior to installation.

9. Slightly compress the tensioner assembly prior to installation.

10. Install the tensioner assembly (**Figure 43**) into the cylinder receptacle.

11. Install the 22 mm end plug and *new* gasket (**Figure 42**) onto the end of the tensioner. Tighten the end plug to the specification in **Table 3**.

12. Refer to Chapter Fifteen and perform the following:

   a. Install the cylinder head left side cover.

   b. Install the frame left side cover.

   c. Install the seat.

Camshaft Chain Tensioner Guide Rails Removal/Inspection/Installation

Refer to **Figure 44**.

1. Remove the cylinder head cover as described in this chapter.

2. Remove the camshafts as described in this chapter.

3. Remove the clutch assembly as described in Chapter Six.

4. Remove the bolt (**Figure 48**) securing the lower end of the rear tensioner guide rail to the crankcase.

5. Pull straight up and remove the rear tensioner guide rail (**Figure 49**) from the cylinder head.

6. Pull straight up and remove the front tensioner guide rail (**Figure 50**) from the cylinder head.

7. Inspect the wear surface of both guide rails (**Figure 51**) for wear or damage, replace as necessary.

8. Inspect the lower mounting portions of both guide rails (**Figure 52**) for wear or damage, replace as necessary.

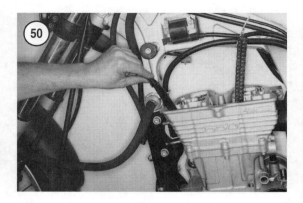

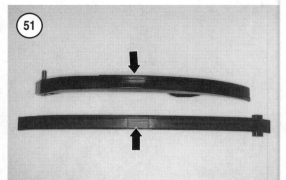

9. Make sure the camshaft drive chain is properly meshed with the sprocket (A, **Figure 53**) on the backside of the primary drive gear on the crankshaft.

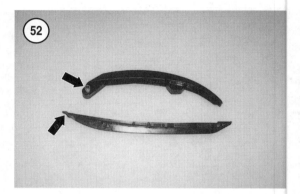

10. Install the front tensioner guide as follows:
   a. Position the front tensioner guide with the locating ears (**Figure 54**) at the top.
   b. Install the front tensioner guide and push it down until it seats on the crankcase lower receptacle (B, **Figure 53**).
   c. Ensure that the ears at the top are correctly located in the cylinder head (**Figure 55**).

11. Install the rear tensioner guide into position (**Figure 49**) and install the bolt (**Figure 48**). Tighten the bolt securely.

12. Install the clutch assembly as described in Chapter Six.

13. Install the camshafts as described in this chapter.

14. Install the cylinder head cover as described in this chapter.

CAMSHAFT DRIVE CHAIN

A continuous camshaft drive chain is used on all models. Do not cut the chain; replacement link components are not available.

Removal/Installation

Refer to **Figure 44**.

1. Remove the cylinder head cover as described in this chapter.

2. Remove the camshafts as described in this chapter.

3. Remove the clutch assembly as described in Chapter Six.

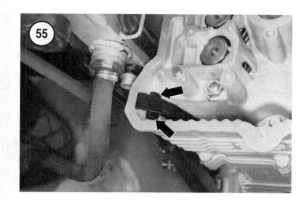

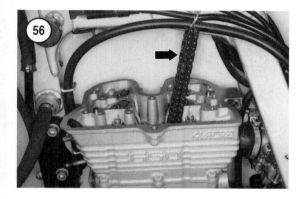

4. Remove the camshaft chain tensioner guide rails as described in this chapter.

5. Remove the primary drive gear as described in Chapter Five.

6. Pull the camshaft drive chain up through the chain tunnel in the cylinder head (**Figure 56**) and remove it.

7. Install by reversing these removal steps. Bleed the oil circuit as described under *Engine Oil Circuit Bleeding* in Chapter Five.

Inspection

If the following inspection shows that the cam chain is severely worn or damaged, the camshaft chain tensioner may not be tensioning the chain properly; refer to *Camshaft Chain Tensioner Inspection* in this chapter. Also, check the chain tensioner guides for excessive wear and damage.

1. Clean the camshaft chain in solvent. Dry the chain with compressed air.

2. Check the camshaft chain (**Figure 57**) for the following:

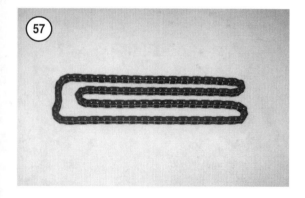

   a. Worn or damaged pins (A, **Figurre 58**) and rollers (B).

   b. Cracked or damaged side plates (C).

3. If the camshaft chain is severely worn or damaged, inspect both camshaft sprockets (**Figure 59**) and the primary drive gear sprocket (A, **Figure 60**) for the same wear conditions. If the camshaft sprockets show wear or damage, replace them at the same time. If the primary drive gear sprocket is worn, replace the primary drive gear (B, **Figure 60**).

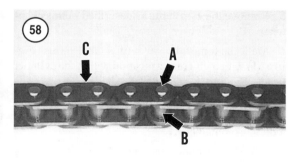

CAUTION
Do not run a new chain over severely
worn or damaged sprockets. Doing so

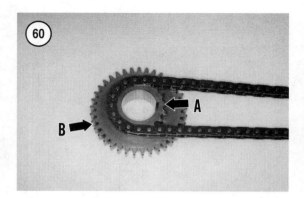

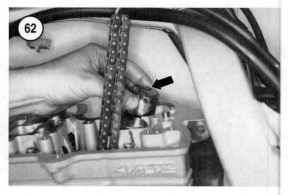

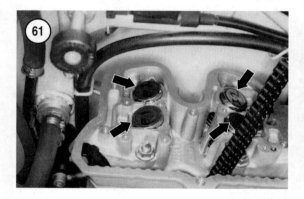

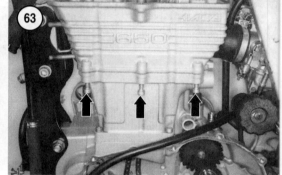

*may cause excessive chain wear after
only a short service period.*

CYLINDER HEAD

The cylinder head can be removed with the engine
in the frame, but does require the removal of the
crankcase studs. In some cases it may be possible to
remove the cylinder head with the studs in place depending on frame configuration and tolerances. First,
try to remove the cylinder head with the studs still in
place. If this is not possible, the studs must be removed.

Removal

1. Remove the exhaust pipe assembly as described
in Chapter Eight.

2. Drain the coolant as described in Chapter Three.

3. Remove the thermostat housing as described in
Chapter Ten.

4. Remove the cylinder head cover as described in
this chapter.

5. Remove the camshafts as described in this chapter.

6. Mark the top of the valve lifters and shims (**Figure 61**) with their correct location within the cylinder
head.

7. Remove each valve lifter and shim (**Figure 62**)
from the cylinder head receptacles and place them in
a divided container.

8. Loosen and remove the bolts and nuts securing
the cylinder head to the cylinder in the following order:

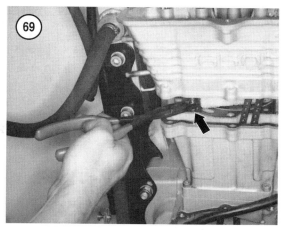

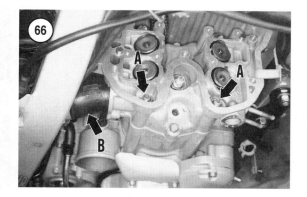

a. On the left side of the cylinder head, loosen and remove the three 6 mm Allen bolts (**Figure 63**).

b. On the right side of the cylinder head, loosen and remove the three 8 mm bolts. (**Figure 64**).

c. On the left side of the cylinder head, loosen and remove the single 8 mm bolt (A, **Figure 65**).

NOTE
Use a crisscross pattern to loosen the 10 mm nuts in the next two sub-steps.

d. On left side of the cylinder head, loosen and remove the two 10 flange nuts (B, **Figure 65**).

e. On right side of the cylinder head, loosen and remove the two 10 flange nuts (A, **Figure 66**).

9. Remove the bolts securing the carburetor intake tube (B, **Figure 66**) to the cylinder head. Leave the intake tube attached to the carburetors.

10. Tap the cylinder head with a rubber mallet to free it from the gasket and the cylinder.

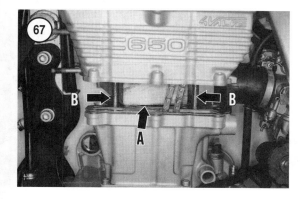

11. Raise the cylinder up, and place a wooden spacer (A, **Figure 67**) between the cylinder head and the cylinder to access the crankcase studs (B).

12. Use Vise Grip pliers (**Figure 68**) to loosen the two crankcase studs on each side.

13. After the studs are loose, completely unscrew them with pliers (**Figure 69**).

14. Withdraw the studs (A, **Figure 70**) out through the top of the cylinder head.

15. Work the camshaft drive chain (B, **Figure 70**) down through the chain cavity and remove the cylinder head from the cylinder.

16. Secure the camshaft drive chain to the frame.

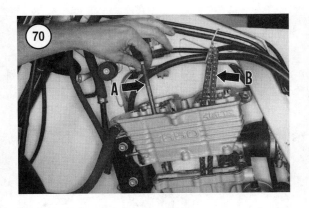

17. Remove the cylinder head gasket. Do not lose the two locating dowels in the cylinder.

Cylinder Head Inspection

1. If not already removed, remove the valve lifters and shims and keep them in order.
2. Thoroughly clean the outside of the cylinder head. Use a stiff brush, soap and water to remove all debris.
3. Remove all traces of gasket residue from the cylinder head and cylinder mating surfaces. Do not scratch the gasket surfaces.
4. *Without removing the valves*, use a wire brush to remove all carbon deposits from the combustion chamber (**Figure 71**). Use a fine wire brush dipped in solvent or make a scraper from hardwood. Take care not to damage the head, valves or spark plug threads.

> *CAUTION*
> *Cleaning the combustion chamber with the valves removed can damage the valve seat surfaces. A damaged or even slightly scratched valve seat will cause poor valve seating.*

5. Examine both spark plug threads in the cylinder head for damage. If damage is minor or if the threads are dirty or clogged with carbon, use a spark plug thread tap (**Figure 72**) and kerosene to clean the threads following the manufacturer's instructions. If thread damage is severe, restore the threads by installing a steel thread insert.

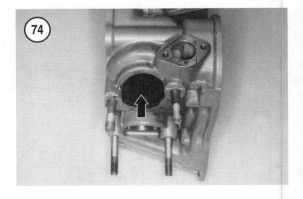

> *CAUTION*
> *Aluminum spark plug threads are commonly damaged due to galling, cross-threading and over-tightening.*

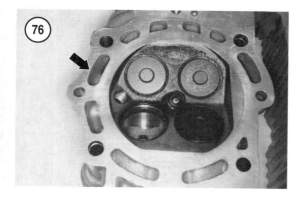

4

To prevent galling, apply an antiseize compound on the plug threads before installation and do not overtighten.

6. After all carbon is removed from combustion chambers and valve ports, and, if necessary, the spark plug thread hole is repaired, clean the entire head in solvent and dry with compressed air.

7. Examine the crown on the piston. The crown should show no signs of wear or damage. If the crown appears pecked or spongy-looking, also check the spark plug, valves and combustion chamber for aluminum deposits. If these deposits are found, the cylinder has overheated. Check for a lean fuel mixture or other conditions that could result in preignition.

8. Check for cracks in the combustion chamber, both intake ports (**Figure 73**), and both exhaust ports (**Figure 74**). Replace a cracked head if welding cannot repair it.

9. Inspect the threads (**Figure 75**) of the exhaust pipe studs for damage. Repair with a die if damaged.

CAUTION
If the cylinder head is bead-blasted, clean the head thoroughly with solvent and then with hot soapy water. Residual grit seats in small crevices and other areas and can be hard to get out. Also run a tap through each exposed thread to remove grit from the threads. Residue grit left in the engine will cause premature wear.

10. Thoroughly clean the inner portions of the cylinder head.

11. Make sure all coolant passageways (**Figure 76**) are clear. Clean out if necessary, then blow out with compressed air.

12. Check the cylinder head mounting boss (**Figure 77**) for cracks or damage.

13. Check the valves and valve guides (**Figure 78**) as described under *Valves and Valve Components* in this chapter.

14. Thoroughly clean the crankcase studs threads with a wire brush and solvent. Remove any threadlocking compound residue.

15. Inspect the crankcase studs (**Figure 79**) for straightness. Inspect the threads for damage. Repair with a die if damaged.

Installation

1. If removed, install the piston and cylinder as described in this chapter.
2. Make sure the cylinder head and cylinder gasket surfaces are clean.
3. If removed, install the locating dowels (**Figure 80**) into the cylinder.

> *CAUTION*
> *Do not use sealer on the cylinder head gasket. If using an aftermarket head gasket, follow the manufacturer's instructions for gasket installation.*

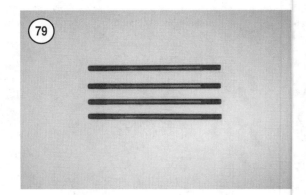

4. Install a *new* cylinder head gasket (**Figure 81**). Make sure all cylinder holes align with the gasket openings holes.
5. Carefully place a wooden spacer on top of the cylinder. Do not damage the cylinder head gasket.
6. Correctly position the cylinder head (A, **Figure 82**) over the cylinder and rest it on the wooden spacer (**Figure 83**). Run the camshaft drive chain up through the chain cavity. Secure the chain (B, **Figure 82**) up to the frame.
7. Apply a medium-strength threadlocking compound to the crankcase stud lower threads.
8. Install the studs (A, **Figure 70**) down through the top of the cylinder head and into the threaded receptacles in the crankcase. Thread the studs into the crankcase by hand or with pliers until tight.
9. Use Vise Grip pliers to securely tighten the two crankcase studs (**Figure 68**) on each side.
10. Raise the cylinder up and carefully remove the wooden spacer. Do not damage the cylinder head gasket.
11. Lower the cylinder head onto the cylinder gasket until it bottoms.
12. Loosely install the following cylinder head-to-cylinder mounting bolts and nuts:

   a. On the right side, install the two 10 flange nuts (A, **Figure 66**).
   b. On the left side, install the two 10 flange nuts (B, **Figure 65**).
   c. On the left side, install the single 8 mm bolt (A, **Figure 65**).
   d. On the right side, install the three 8 mm bolts (**Figure 64**).
   e. On the left side, install the three 6 mm Allen bolts (**Figure 63**).

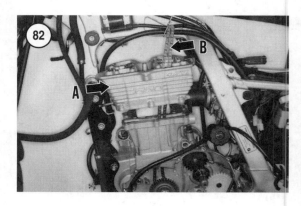

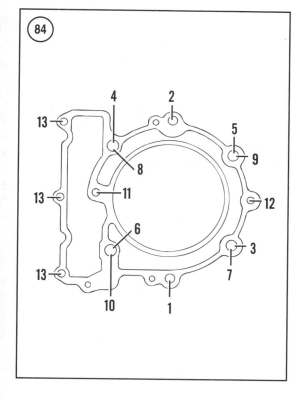

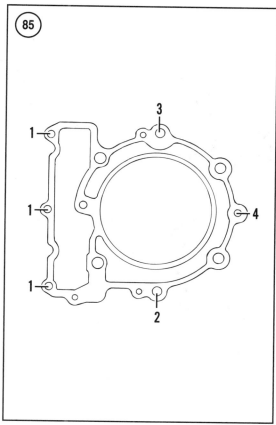

4

13. Follow the torque pattern (**Figure 84**) and tighten the fasteners to the specification in **Table 3**.

14. If, after the engine is completely assembled, there is coolant leakage between the cylinder head and the cylinder, perform the following:

    a. Loosen the bolts shown in **Figure 85**.

    b. Retighten the bolts to the specification in **Table 3** and in the torque pattern shown in **Figure 85**.

15. Move the carburetor intake tube into position on the cylinder head and install the bolts. Tighten the bolts securely.

16. Install the valve lifters and shims (**Figure 61**) into their recorded positions.

17. Install the camshafts as described in this chapter.

18. Install the cylinder head cover as described in this chapter.

19. Install the thermostat housing as described in Chapter Ten.

20. Refill the coolant as described in Chapter Three.

21. Install the exhaust pipe assembly as described in Chapter Eight.

22. Bleed oil circuit as described under *Engine Oil Circuit Bleeding* in Chapter Five.

VALVE LIFTERS AND SHIMS

Removal/Inspection/Installation

If the cylinder head is going to be inspected and/or serviced, remove the valve lifters and shims

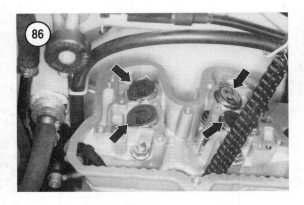

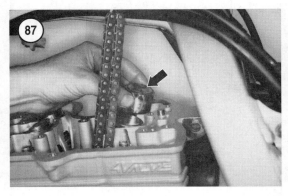

prior to removing the head. Do not intermix these parts as each one has its own wear pattern.

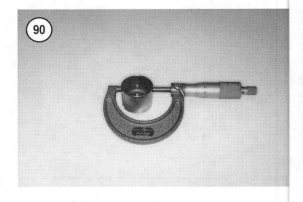

> *NOTE*
> *This procedure is shown with the engine removed to better illustrate the steps. It can be accomplished with the engine in the frame.*

1. Remove the camshafts as described in this chapter.

2. Mark the top of the valve lifters and shims (**Figure 86**) with their correct location within the cylinder head.

3. Remove each valve lifter and shim (**Figure 87**) from the cylinder head receptacles and place them in a divided container.

4. Remove the shim from the top of the lifter.

5. Clean the valve lifter and the lifter bore in the cylinder head with solvent and dry.

6. Inspect the outer surface of the valve lifter (**Figure 88**). If the side is scuffed or scratched, replace it.

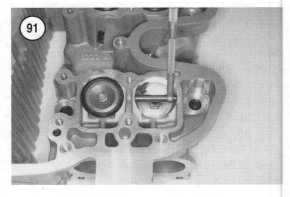

7. Inspect the inner surface of the lifter bore in the cylinder head (**Figure 89**) for wear or damage.

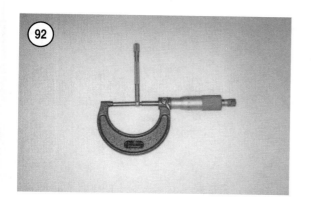

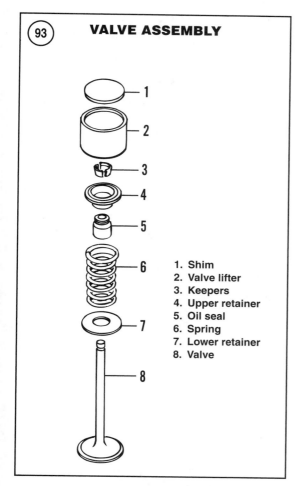

VALVE ASSEMBLY

1. Shim
2. Valve lifter
3. Keepers
4. Upper retainer
5. Oil seal
6. Spring
7. Lower retainer
8. Valve

8. Determine the lifter-to-bore clearance as follows:

   a. Measure the diameter of the lifter with a micrometer (**Figure 90**). Record the reading.

   b. Measure the diameter of the lifter bore in the cylinder head with a snap gauge (**Figure 91**).

Measure the snap gauge with a micrometer (**Figure 92**). Record the reading.

   c. Subtract the lifter diameter from the bore diameter. Refer to the service limit in **Table 2**. Replace any worn part(s).

9. Apply clean engine oil to the side of the valve lifter and install it.

10. After the valve lifters have been installed, rotate the lifters by hand to make sure they are seated correctly and rotate freely.

11. Install all shims onto the lifters.

12. Install the camshafts as described in this chapter.

VALVES AND VALVE COMPONENTS

Complete valve service requires a number of special tools, including a valve spring compressor, to remove and install the valves. The following procedures describe how to check for valve component wear and to determine what type of service is required.

Valve Removal

Refer to **Figure 93**.

1. Remove the cylinder head as described in this chapter.

2. Remove the valve lifters as described in this chapter.

3. Install the valve spring compressor over the valve spring upper retainer and against the valve head (**Figure 94**).

CAUTION
To avoid loss of spring tension, compress the spring only enough to remove the valve keepers.

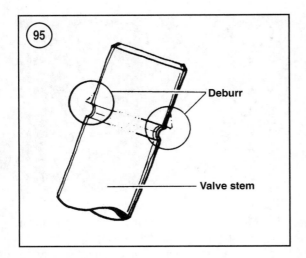

Deburr

Valve stem

4. Tighten the valve spring compressor until the valve keepers separate from the valve stem. Lift the valve keepers out through the valve spring compressor with a magnet or needlenose pliers.

5. Gradually loosen the valve spring compressor and remove it from the cylinder head.

6. Remove the spring upper retainer and the valve spring.

CAUTION
*Remove any burrs from the valve stem groove before removing the valve (**Figure 95**); otherwise the valve guide will be damaged as the valve stem passes through it.*

7. Remove the valve from the cylinder while rotating it slightly.

8. Remove the valve spring lower retainer.

9. Remove the valve guide oil seal.

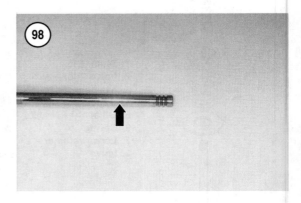

CAUTION
*Keep the components of each valve assembly together (**Figure 96**) by placing each set in a divided carton, or into separate small boxes or small reclosable plastic bags. Identify the components as either intake or exhaust. If both cylinders are disassembled, also label the components as front and rear. Do not intermix components from the valves or excessive wear may result.*

10. Repeat Steps 3-9 to remove the remaining valves.

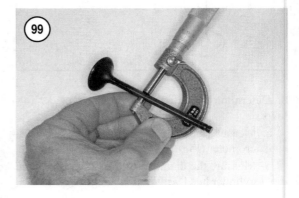

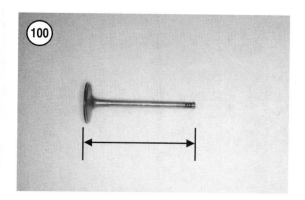

1. Clean valves in solvent. Do not gouge or damage the valve seating surface.

2. Inspect the valve face. Minor roughness and pitting (**Figure 97**) can be removed by lapping the valve as described in this chapter. Excessive unevenness to the contact surface is an indication that the valve is not serviceable.

3. Inspect the valve stem (**Figure 98**) for wear and roughness. Then measure the valve stem diameter with a micrometer (**Figure 99**).

4. Measure the length of each valve (**Figure 100**) with a vernier caliper.

5. Measure the outer diameter of the valve head with a micrometer.

6. Remove all carbon and varnish from the valve guides with a stiff spiral wire brush before measuring wear.

7. Measure the valve guide (**Figure 101**) diameter with a small hole gauge. Measure at the top, center and bottom positions. Then measure the small hole gauge.

8. Determine the valve stem-to-valve guide clearance by subtracting the valve stem diameter from the valve guide diameter.

9. If a small hole gauge is not available, insert each valve into its guide. Hold the valve just slightly off its seat and position a dial indicator next to the valve head. Rock the valve sideways as shown in **Figure 102**. If the valve rocks more than slightly, the guide is probably worn. However, as a final check, take the cylinder head to a BMW dealership or machine shop and have the valve guides measured.

10. Check the valve spring as follows:

    a. Check each of the valve springs for visual damage.

    b. Use a square to visually check the spring for distortion or tilt (**Figure 103**).

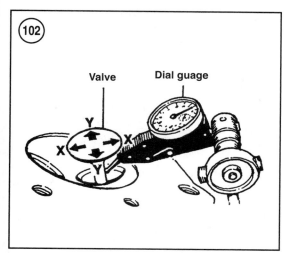

Valve   Dial guage

Valve Inspection

When measuring the valves and valve components in this section, compare the actual measurements to the new and/or wear limit specifications in **Table 2**. Replace parts that are out of specification or show damage as described in this section.

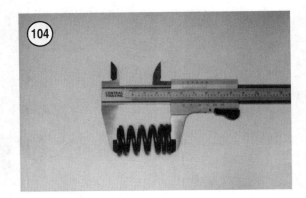

c. Measure the valve spring free length with a vernier caliper (**Figure 104**).

d. Repeat for each valve spring.

e. Replace defective springs.

11. Check the valve spring upper and lower retainers seats (**Figure 105**) for cracks or other damage.

12. Check the valve keepers and their fit onto the valve stem end (**Figure 106**). They must index tightly into the valve stem groove.

13. Inspect the valve seats (**Figure 107**) in the cylinder head. If worn or burned, they may be reconditioned as described in this chapter. Seats and valves in near-perfect condition can be reconditioned by lapping with fine carborundum paste as described in *Valve Seat Inspection*.

Valve Installation

1. Clean the end of the valve guide.

2. Install the spring lower retainer (**Figure 108**). Push it down until it is seated on the cylinder head surface (**Figure 109**).

3. Install the oil seal (**Figure 110**) and push it down until it bottoms on the lower retainer (**Figure 111**).

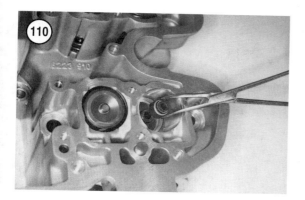

4

4. Coat a valve stem with molybdenum disulfide grease or an equivalent. Install the valve part way into the guide (**Figure 112**). Then, slowly turn the valve as it enters the oil seal and continue turning it until the valve is installed completely.

5. Work the valve back and forth in the valve guide to ensure the lubricant is distributed evenly within the valve guide.

6. Push the valve all the way into the cylinder head until it bottoms (**Figure 113**).

> *NOTE*
> *The valve spring is wound symmetrically and can be installed with either end in first.*

7. Install the valve spring (**Figure 114**) and make sure it is properly seated on the lower spring retainer (**Figure 115**).

8. Install the upper spring retainer (**Figure 116**) on top of the valve spring.

> *CAUTION*
> *To avoid loss of spring tension, compress the spring only enough to install the valve keepers.*

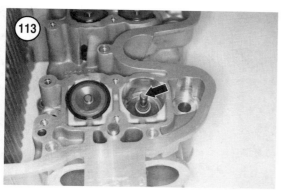

9. Compress the valve spring with a valve spring compressor until the keeper grooves are visible (**Figure 117**).

10. Apply a light coat of cold grease to the keepers and install both valve keepers (**Figure 118**).

11. Make sure both keepers are seated around the valve stem prior to releasing the compressor.

12. Slowly release tension from the compressor and remove it. After removing the compressor, inspect the valve keepers to make sure they are properly seated (**Figure 119**). Tap the end of the valve stem with a *soft-faced* hammer to ensure that the keepers are properly seated.

13. Repeat Steps 1-12 for the remaining valves.

14. Install the cylinder head as described in this chapter.

Valve Guide Replacement

> *CAUTION*
> *BMW does not recommend heating the cylinder head to replace the valve guides. The cylinder head must be at room temperature.*

1. Remove the valve assembly as described in this chapter.

2. Place the cylinder head on a wooden surface with the combustion chamber side facing down.

3. Prior to removing the valve guide, use a vernier caliper to measure the distance from the top of the valve guide to the cylinder head bore seat. Record this dimension.

4. Use a suitable size drift (A, **Figure 120**) and hammer to strike the valve guide at an oblique angle. Continue to strike the valve guide (B) until the upper portion breaks off at the circlip recess.

5. Remove the broken portion of the valve guide and the circlip. Discard the circlip.

> *CAUTION*
> *Use the correct size drift when removing the valve guide; otherwise, the tool may expand the end of the guide. An expanded guide will widen and damage the guide bore in the cylinder head as it passes through.*

6. Use a suitable size drift (**Figure 121**) and hammer to slowly tap the remaining portion of the valve guide out of the cylinder head.

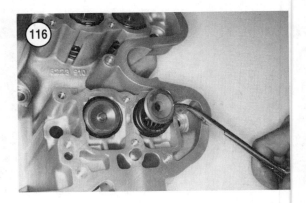

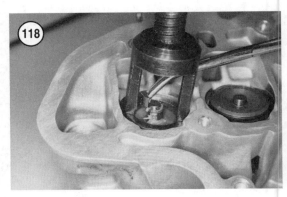

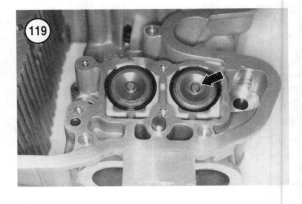

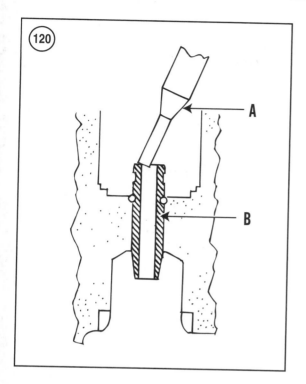

A

B

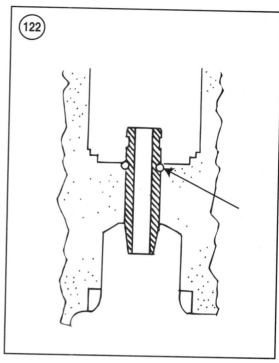

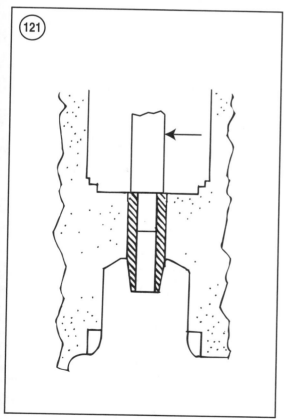

7. Inspect the valve guide bore in the cylinder head for damage or material sediment. If damage or sediment is present; replace the cylinder head.

8. Clean the valve guide bore in the cylinder head.

9. Apply a thin coating of molybdenum disulfide grease to the entire outer surface of the valve guide before installing it in the cylinder head.

10. Install the new guide using the drive tool (BMW part No. 11 6 590) and drive the guide into the cylinder head until the lower edge of the circlip groove is located at the base of the seat (**Figure 122**).

11. Install the valve guide to the same height recorded in Step 3 prior to removing the old valve guide. Refer to the height specification in **Table 2**.

NOTE
Replacement valve guides do not require a circlip.

NOTE
Replacement valve guides are sold with a smaller inside diameter than the valve stem, so the guide must be reamed to fit the valve stem.

12. Ream the new valve guide as follows:
   a. Apply a liberal amount of thread-cutting lubricant to the ream bit and to the valve guide bore.

b. Start the reamer tool (BMW part No. 6H 7) straight into the valve guide bore.

CAUTION
*Always rotate the tool **clockwise** when installing, cutting and withdrawing the tool from the new valve guide. If the tool is rotated in the opposite direction, the new valve guide will be damaged and must be replaced.*

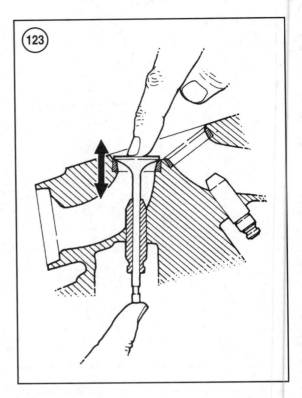

c. Apply light pressure to the end of the tool while rotating it *clockwise*. Only *light* pressure is required. Apply additional lubricant onto the reamer and into the valve guide while rotating the reamer.

d. Rotate the tool in the cutting direction and withdraw it from the valve guide. Clean off all cutting debris and reinsert the tool.

e. Continue to rotate the reamer until the entire tool has traveled through the valve guide and the shank of the reamer rotates freely.

f. Withdraw the reamer by rotating it *clockwise*.

g. Apply low-pressure compressed air to clean out the valve guide bore. Then clean the valve guide bore with the small spiral brush.

13. Repeat for any additional valve guides as necessary.

14. Soak the cylinder head in a container filled with hot, soapy water. Then clean the valve guides with a valve guide brush or an equivalent bristle brush—*do not use a steel brush*. Do not use cleaning solvent, kerosene or gasoline as these chemicals will not remove all of the abrasive particles produced during the honing operation. Repeat this step until all of the valve guides are thoroughly cleaned. Then rinse the cylinder head and valve guides in clear, cold water and dry them with compressed air.

15. After cleaning and drying the valve guides, apply clean engine oil to the guides to prevent rust.

16. Resurface the valve seats as described in *Valve Seat Reconditioning* in this chapter.

Valve Seat Inspection

1. Remove all carbon residue from each valve seat. Then, clean the cylinder head as described under *Valve Inspection* in this chapter.

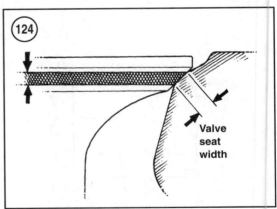

Valve seat width

NOTE
The most accurate method of checking the valve seat width and position is with machinist's dye.

2. Check the valve seats as follows:

a. Thoroughly clean the valve face and valve seat with contact cleaner.

b. Spread a thin layer of machinist's dye or Prussian blue evenly on the valve face.

c. Insert the valve into its guide.

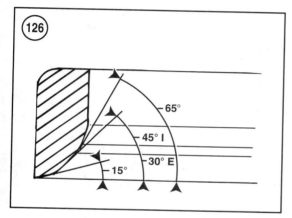

d. Support the valve by hand (**Figure 123**) and tap the valve up and down in the cylinder head. Do not rotate the valve, or a false reading will result.

e. Remove the valve and examine the impression left by the machinist's dye. The impressions on the valve and the seat must be even around their circumferences and the width (**Figure 124**) must be within the specifications in **Table 2**. If the width is beyond the specification or if the impression is uneven, recondition the valve seats.

3. Closely examine the valve seat in the cylinder head (**Figure 125**). It must be smooth and even with a polished seating surface.

4. Measure the valve seat width as shown in **Figure 124**. Compare it to the specification in **Table 2**.

5. If the valve seat is in good condition, install the valve as described in this chapter.

6. If the valve seat is not correct, recondition the valve seat as described in this chapter.

Valve Seat Reconditioning

Valve seat reconditioning requires considerable expertise and special tools to obtain the correct valve seat angles (**Figure 126**). In most cases it is more economical and practical to have these procedures performed by a BMW dealership or an experienced machinist.

If the equipment is available, perform the following procedure.

1. Clean the valve guides as described under *Valve Inspection* in this chapter.

2. Carefully rotate and insert the solid pilot into the valve guide. Make sure the pilot is correctly seated.

CAUTION
Valve seat accuracy depends on a correctly sized and installed pilot.

3. Using the 45-degree cutter, de-scale and clean the valve seat with one or two turns.

CAUTION
Measure the valve seat contact area in the cylinder head after each cut to make sure its size and area are correct. Over-grinding sinks the valves too far into the cylinder head, requiring replacement of the valve seat.

4. If the seat is still pitted or burned, turn the cutter until the surface is clean. Work slowly and carefully to avoid removing too much material from the valve seat.

5. Remove the pilot from the valve guide.

6. Apply a small amount of valve lapping compound to the valve face and install the valve. Rotate the valve against the valve seat using a valve lapping tool. Remove the valve.

7. Measure the valve seat width (**Figures 124**) with a vernier caliper. Record the measurement to use as a reference point when performing the following.

CAUTION
The 15-degree cutter removes material quickly. Work carefully and check the progress often.

8. Reinsert the solid pilot into the valve guide. Be certain the pilot is properly seated. Install the 15-degree cutter onto the solid pilot and lightly cut the seat to remove 1/4 of the existing valve seat.

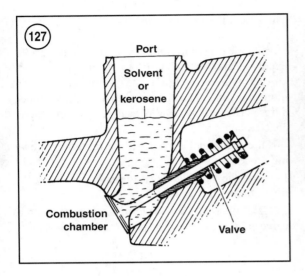

Port

Solvent
or
kerosene

Combustion
chamber

Valve

9. Install the 65-degree cutter onto the solid pilot and lightly cut the seat to remove the lower 1/4 of the existing valve seat.

10. Measure the valve seat with a vernier caliper. Then fit the 45-degree cutter onto the solid pilot and cut the valve seat to the specified seat width in **Table 2**.

11. When the valve seat width is correct, check valve seating as follows.

12. Remove the solid pilot from the cylinder head.

13. Inspect the valve seat-to-valve face impression as described in *Valve Seat Inspection*.

14. The valve seat contact area must be in the center of the valve face area. If the contact area is too high on the valve, or if it is too wide, cut the seat with the 15-degree cutter. This will remove part of the top valve seat area to lower or narrow the contact area.

15. If the contact area is too low on the valve, or if it is too wide, use the 65-degree cutter and remove part of the lower area to raise and widen the contact area.

16. After obtaining the desired valve seat position and angle, use the 45-degree cutter and very lightly clean off any burrs caused by the previous cuts.

17. When the contact area is correct, lap the valve as described in this chapter.

18. Repeat Steps 1-17 for the remaining valve seats.

19. Thoroughly clean the cylinder head and all valve components in solvent, then clean with detergent and hot water and rinse in cold water. Dry with compressed air. Then apply a light coat of engine oil

to all non-aluminum metal surfaces to prevent rust formation.

Valve Lapping

If valve wear or distortion is not excessive, it may be possible to restore the valve seal by lapping the valve to the seat.

1. Smear a light coating of fine-grade valve lapping compound on the seating surface of the valve.

2. Insert the valve into the head.

3. Wet the suction cup of the lapping tool and stick it onto the head of the valve. Lap the valve to the seat by spinning the tool between both hands while lifting and moving the valve around the seat 1/4 turn at a time.

4. Wipe off the valve and seat frequently to check the progress. Lap only enough to achieve a precise seating ring around valve head.

5. Closely examine the valve seat in the cylinder head. The seat must be smooth and even with a polished seating ring.

6. Thoroughly clean the valves and cylinder head in solvent to remove all grinding compound residue.

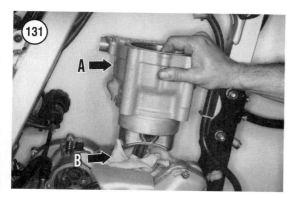

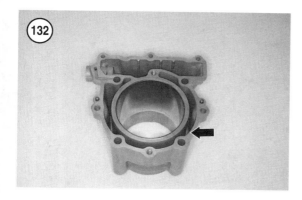

Compound left on the valves or the cylinder head will cause rapid engine wear.

7. After installing the valves into the cylinder head, test each valve for proper seating. Check by pouring solvent into the intake and exhaust ports (**Figure 127**). Solvent must not leak past the valve seats. If leakage occurs, the combustion chamber will appear wet. If solvent leaks past any of the seats, disassemble that valve assembly and repeat the lapping procedure until there is no leakage.

4

CYLINDER

Removal

1. Remove the cylinder head as described in this chapter.
2. Remove all dirt and debris from the cylinder base.
3. If still in place, remove the cylinder head gasket (**Figure 128**) and the two locating dowels (**Figure 129**) from the top of the cylinder.
4. Turn the crankshaft until the piston is at bottom dead center (BDC).
5. On the left side of the cylinder, remove the two Allen bolts (**Figure 130**) securing the cylinder to the crankcase.
6. Pull the cylinder (A, **Figure 131**) straight up and off the piston. If necessary, tap around the perimeter of the cylinder with a rubber or plastic mallet.
7. Place clean shop rags (B, **Figure 131**) into the crankcase opening to prevent objects from falling undetected into the crankcase.
8. Remove the cylinder base gasket. Do not lose the two locating dowels.

Inspection

1. Carefully remove all gasket residue from the top (**Figure 132**) and bottom (**Figure 133**) cylinder gasket surfaces.
2. Thoroughly clean the cylinder with solvent and dry with compressed air. Lightly oil the cylinder block bore to prevent rust.
3. Use low-pressure air to blow out the oil ducts for the camshaft drive chain tensioner (**Figure 134**).
4. Check the cylinder bore (**Figure 135**) for scuff marks, scratches or other damage.
5. Measure the cylinder bore with a bore gauge or inside micrometer (**Figure 136**). Perform the first measurement 55-65 mm (2.17-2.56 in.) below the

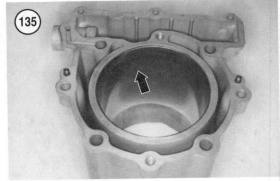

top of the cylinder. Do not measure areas where the rings do not travel.

6. Measure in two axes–aligned with the piston pin and at 90° to the pin. If the measurements exceed the service limits in **Table 2**, replace the cylinder.

> *NOTE*
> *An oversize piston is not available for this engine. If the cylinder is worn past the service limit, it must be replaced.*

Installation

> *NOTE*
> *The following photographs are shown with the piston removed to better illustrate the steps.*

1. Remove all gasket residue and clean the cylinder as described under *Inspection* in this chapter.

2. If removed, install the locating dowels (**Figure 137**) into the crankcase.

3. Install a *new* gasket (**Figure 138**) onto the locating dowels.

4. If removed, install the piston as described in this chapter.

5. Turn the crankshaft until the piston is at top dead center (TDC).

6. Lubricate the cylinder bore, piston and piston rings liberally with clean engine oil.

7. Stagger the piston ring end gaps so they are 90°-180° from the gap of the ring above it.

8. Compress the piston rings with a ring compressor (A, **Figure 139**).

9. Carefully align the cylinder (B, **Figure 139**) with the piston and slide it down. Then continue sliding the cylinder down and past the rings. Remove the

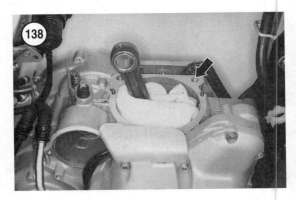

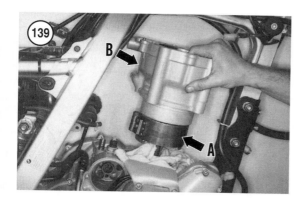

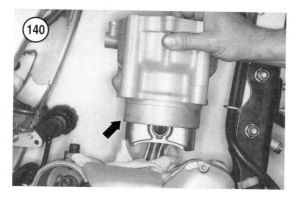

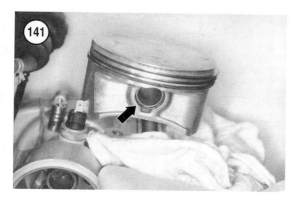

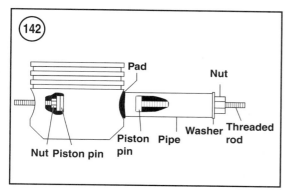

Pad Nut

Piston Pipe Washer Threaded
pin rod

Nut Piston pin

ring compressor once the piston rings enter the cylinder bore (**Figure 140**). Remove the shop rag from the crankcase opening.

10. Run the camshaft drive chain up through the chain cavity. Secure the chain to the frame.

11. Continue to slide the cylinder down onto the crankcase.

12. On the left side of the cylinder, install the two Allen bolts (**Figure 130**) that secure the cylinder to the crankcase. Tighten the bolts securely.

13. Install the cylinder head as described in this chapter.

14. Bleed the oil circuit as described under *Engine Oil Circuit Bleeding* in Chapter Five.

PISTONS AND PISTON RINGS

Piston Removal

1. Remove the cylinder head and cylinder as described in this chapter.

2. Cover the crankcase with a clean shop rag.

> *WARNING*
> *The piston pin retaining rings may spring out of the piston during removal. Wear safety glasses when removing them in Step 3.*

3. Using an awl, pry the piston pin circlip (**Figure 141**) out of one side of the piston. Place your thumb over the hole to help prevent the circlip from flying out during removal.

4. Support the piston and push out the piston pin. If the piston is difficult to remove, use a piston pin removal tool (**Figure 142**).

5. Remove the piston from the connecting rod.

6. Inspect the piston, piston pin and piston rings as described in this chapter.

Piston Rings Inspection and Removal

A three-ring type piston and ring assembly is used. The top and second rings are compression rings. The lower ring is an oil control ring assembly (consisting of two ring rails and an expander spacer).

When measuring the piston rings and piston in this section, compare the actual measurements to the new and service limit specifications in **Table 2**.

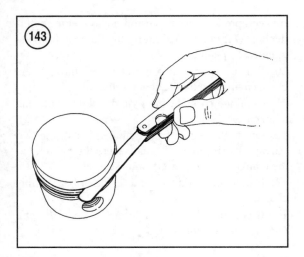

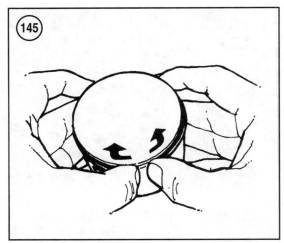

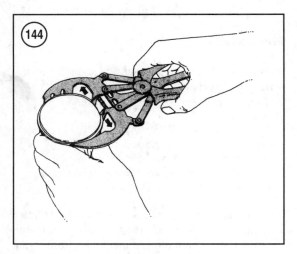

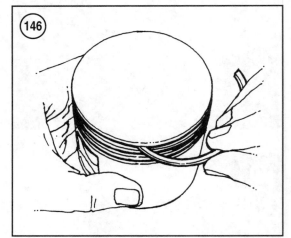

Replace parts that are out of specification or show damage as described in this section.

1. Measure the side clearance of each compression ring in its groove with a flat feeler gauge (**Figure 143**). If the clearance is greater than specified, the rings must be replaced. If the clearance is still excessive with the new rings, the piston must be replaced.

> *WARNING*
> *Piston ring edges are very sharp. Be careful when handling them to avoid cutting your fingers.*

> *NOTE*
> *Store the old rings in the order in which they are removed.*

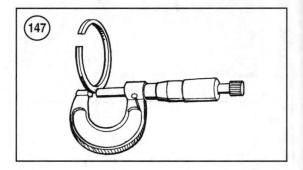

2. Remove the piston rings using a ring expander tool (**Figure 144**) or spread them by hand (**Figure 145**) and remove them.

3. Remove the oil ring assembly by first removing the upper and then the lower ring rails. Then remove the expander spacer.

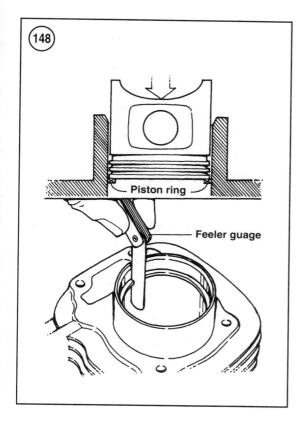

Piston ring

Feeler guage

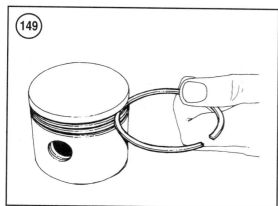

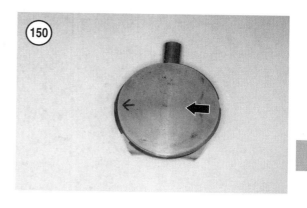

6. Inspect grooves carefully for burrs, nicks or broken or cracked lands. Replace the piston if necessary.

7. Measure the thickness of each compression ring with a micrometer (**Figure 147**). If the thickness is less than specified, replace the ring(s).

8. Insert one piston ring into the top of the cylinder and use the piston to push it squarely into the bore approximately 60 mm (2.36 in.). Measure the ring end gap (**Figure 148**) with a feeler gauge and compare with the specification in **Table 2**. Replace the piston rings as a set if any one ring end gap measurement is excessive. Repeat for each ring.

9. Roll each compression ring around its piston groove as shown in **Figure 149**. The ring must move smoothly with no binding. If a ring binds in its groove, check the groove for damage. Replace the piston if necessary.

Piston Inspection

1. If necessary, remove the piston rings as described in this chapter.

2. Carefully clean the carbon from the piston crown (**Figure 150**) with a soft scraper. Large carbon accumulations reduce piston cooling and result in detonation and piston damage.

CAUTION
Be very careful not to gouge or otherwise damage the piston when removing carbon. Never use a wire brush to clean the piston ring grooves. Do not attempt to remove carbon from the sides of the piston above the top ring or from the cylinder bore near the top. Removing carbon from these two ar-

4. Using a broken piston ring, carefully remove carbon and oil residue from the piston ring grooves (**Figure 146**). Do not remove aluminum material from the ring grooves, as this will increase ring side clearance.

5. Measure each compression ring groove width with a vernier caliper. Measure each groove at several points around the piston. Replace the piston if any groove is worn to the service limit.

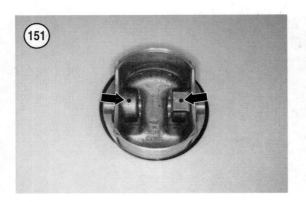

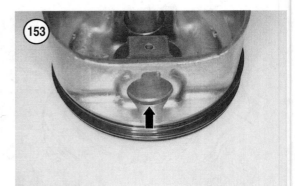

eas may cause increased oil consumption.

3. After cleaning the piston, examine the crown. The crown should show no signs of wear or damage. If the crown appears pecked or spongy-looking, also check the spark plugs, valves and combustion chamber for aluminum deposits. If these deposits are found, the engine is overheating.

4. Examine each ring groove for burrs, dented edges or other damage. Pay particular attention to the top compression ring groove as it usually wears more than the others. The oil rings and grooves generally wear less than compression rings and their grooves. If there is evidence of oil ring groove wear or if the oil ring assembly is tight and difficult to remove, the piston skirt may have collapsed due to excessive heat and is permanently deformed. Replace the piston.

5. Check the oil control holes in the underside of the piston for carbon or oil sludge buildup. Refer to **Figure 151** and **Figure 152**. Clean the holes with wire and blow out with compressed air.

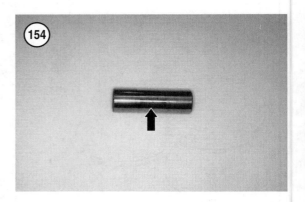

6. Check the piston skirt for cracks or other damage. If a piston shows signs of partial seizure (bits of aluminum build-up on the piston skirt), replace the piston to reduce the possibility of engine noise and further piston seizure.

NOTE
If the piston skirt is worn or scuffed unevenly from side-to-side, the connecting rod may be bent or twisted.

7. Check the circlip groove (**Figure 153**) on each side for wear, cracks or other damage. If the grooves are questionable, check the circlip fit by installing a new circlip into each groove and then attempt to move the circlip from side to side. If the circlip has

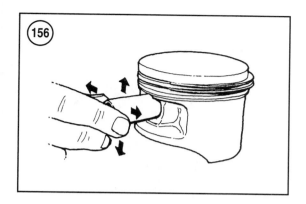

any side play, the groove is worn and the piston must be replaced.

8. Measure piston-to-cylinder clearance as described under *Piston Clearance* in this chapter.

9. If damage or wear indicates piston replacement, select a new piston as described under *Piston Clearance* in this chapter. If the piston, rings and cylinder are not damaged and are dimensionally correct, they can be reused.

Piston Pin Inspection and Clearance

1. Clean the piston pin with solvent and dry thoroughly.

2. Inspect the piston pin (**Figure 154**) for chrome flaking or cracks. Replace if necessary.

3. Oil the piston pin and install it in the connecting rod (**Figure 155**). Slowly rotate the piston pin and check for radial play.

4. Oil the piston pin and install it in the piston (**Figure 156**). Check the piston pin for excessive play.

5. Measure the piston pin-to-piston clearance as follows:

    a. Measure the piston pin diameter with a micrometer (**Figure 157**).

    b. Measure the diameter of the piston pin bore (**Figure 158**) with a snap gauge. Measure the snap gauge with a micrometer.

    c. Subtract the piston pin diameter from the piston pin bore. Check against the specification in **Table 2**.

    d. If out of specification, replace the piston and/or the piston pin.

6. Replace the piston pin and/or piston or connecting rod if necessary.

Piston Clearance

1. Make sure the piston skirt and cylinder bore is clean and dry.

2. Measure the cylinder bore with a bore gauge (**Figure 159**) as described under *Cylinder* in this chapter.

3. Measure the piston diameter with a micrometer at a right angle to the piston pin bore. Measure up 16 mm (0.63 in.) from the bottom edge of the skirt (**Figure 160**).

4. Subtract the piston diameter from the largest bore diameter; the difference is piston-to-cylinder

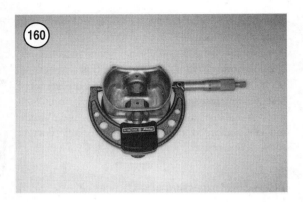

clearance. If the clearance exceeds the specification in **Table 2**, replace the piston or the cylinder.

NOTE
An oversize piston is not available for this engine. If the piston is worn past the service limit, replace it.

Piston Ring Installation

Each piston is equipped with three piston rings: two compression rings and one oil ring assembly as shown in **Figure 161**. The top compression ring is beveled. The lower compression ring is stepped.

1. Wash the piston in hot, soapy water. Then rinse with cold water and dry with compressed air. Make sure the oil control holes in the lower ring groove are clear.

2. Install the oil ring assembly as follows:
   a. The oil ring consists of three rings: a spacer ring and two steel rings.
   b. Install the spacer ring into the lower ring groove. Butt the spacer ring ends together. Do not overlap the ring ends.
   c. Insert one end of the first steel ring into the lower groove so that it is below the spacer ring. Then spiral the other end over the piston crown and into the lower groove. To protect the ring end from scratching the side of the piston, place a piece of shim stock or a thin, flat feeler gauge between the ring and piston.
   d. Repeat substep c to install the other steel ring above the spacer ring.

NOTE
When installing the compression rings, use a ring expander. Do not expand the

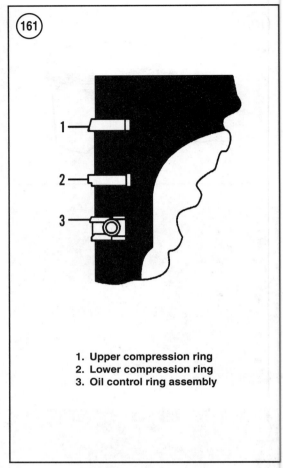

1. **Upper compression ring**
2. **Lower compression ring**
3. **Oil control ring assembly**

rings any more than necessary to install them.

3. Install the lower compression ring with the stepped side facing down.

4. Install the top compression ring with the bevel facing up.

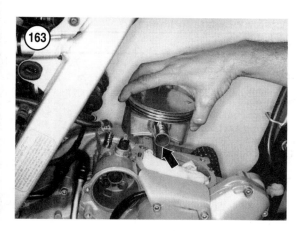

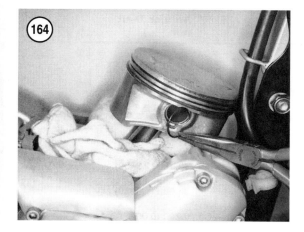

Piston Installation

1. Cover the crankcase openings to avoid dropping a retaining ring into the engine.

2. Install a *new* piston pin retaining ring into one groove in the piston. Make sure the ring seats in the groove completely.

3. Coat the connecting rod bushing and piston pin with assembly oil.

4. Slide the piston pin into the piston until its end is flush with the piston pin boss.

5. Place the piston over the connecting rod with its arrow mark (**Figure 162**) facing toward the front of the engine.

6. Push the piston pin (**Figure 163**) through the connecting rod bushing and into the other side of the piston. Push the piston pin in until it bottoms on the retaining ring.

7. Install the other *new* piston pin retaining ring (**Figure 164**) into the piston groove. Make sure it seats properly in the piston groove (**Figure 165**).

8. Install the cylinder as described in this chapter.

5. Check the ring side clearance with a feeler gauge as shown in **Figure 143**. Check the side clearance in several spots around the piston. If the clearance is larger than the service limit in **Table 2**, replace the piston.

6. Stagger the ring gaps around the piston so they are 90°-180° from the gap of the ring above it.

Table 1 GENERAL ENGINE SPECIFICATIONS

Item	Specifications
Engine type	Liquid cooled single cylinder with balancer shaft and four valve cylinder head operated by double overhead camshafts.
Bore and stroke	100 × 83 mm (3.94 × 3.27 in.)
Displacement	652 cc (39.8 cu. in.)
Compression ratio	9.7:1
Power output	48 hp (35 kW)
Torque (maximum)	57 N•m (42 ft.-lb.) at 5200 rpm
	(continued)

Table 1 GENERAL ENGINE SPECIFICATIONS (continued)

Item	Specifications
Engine speed	
Maximum sustained speed	7000 rpm
Maximum engine speed	7500 rpm
Engine lubrication	Dry sump
Cylinder	Nikasil coated light alloy
Piston	Three ring cast aluminum
Oil filter	Full flow
Oil pumps	Two trochoid pumps driven by the clutch housing
Cooling system	Liquid

Table 2 ENGINE TOP END SERVICE SPECIFICATIONS

Item	New mm (in.)	Service limit mm (in.)
Cylinder head		
Valve guide tilt	–	0.4 (0.016)
Valve guide inner diameter		
Intake and exhaust	6.006-6.018 (0.2365-0.2369)	6.080 (0.2394)
Valve guide projection		
into cylinder head (max.)		
Intake	15.4 (0.61)	–
Exhaust	17.9 (0.70)	–
Valve lifter		
Outside diameter	–	33.400 (1.3150)
Valve lifter bore in head		
Inside diameter	–	33.600 (1.3229)
Clearance in cylinder		
head bore	–	0.200 (0.0079)
Valve seat angle in head		
Intake	45°	–
Exhaust	30°	–
Valve seat width		
Intake	1.2 (0.047)	1.6 (0.063)
Exhaust	1.4 (0.055)	1.8 (0.071)
Valves		
Valve length		
Intake	90.91 (3.579) or 90.76 (3.573)	–
Exhaust	90.65 (3.569) or 90.05 (3.545)	–
Valve head diameter		
Intake	36 (1.41)	–
Exhaust	31 (1.22)	–
Valve stem diameter		
Intake	5.960-5.975 (0.2346-0.2352)	5.950 (0.2342)
Exhaust	5.945-5.969 (0.2341-0.2346)	5.935 (0.2337)
Valve seat width		
Intake	1.05-1.35 (0.041-0.053)	1.60 (0.063)
Exhaust	1.25-1.55 (0.049-0.061)	1.80 (0.071)

(continued)

Table 2 ENGINE TOP END SERVICE SPECIFICATIONS (continued)

Item	New mm (in.)	Service limit mm (in.)
Valves (continued)		
Valve springs		
Free length	45.70 (1.799)	44.50 (1.752)
Camshaft		
Lobe height	–	39.7 (1.56)
Bearing outside diameter	–	21.95 (0.864)
Bearing bore inside diameter		
in camshaft mount	–	22.040 (0.8677)
Oil clearance	–	0.090 (0.0035)
Oil circuit valve		
Coil spring relaxed	13.0 (0.512)	–
Piston outside diameter	99.975-99.985 (3.9361-3.9365)	99.940 (3.9347)
Piston-to-cylinder clearance	–	0.090 (0.004)
Piston pin		
Fit in piston	0.012-0.021 (0.0005-0.0008)	0.050 (0.0020)
Fit in connecting rod	0.015-0.029 (0.0006-0.0011)	0.050 (0.0020)
Piston rings		
Compression ring end gap		
Top and second rings	0.020-0.040 (0.008-0.016)	1.0 (0.04)
Oil control ring	0.020-0.040 (0.008-0.016)	1.0 (0.04)
Compression ring side clearance		
Top and second ring	0.030-0.065 (0.0012-0.0026)	0.150 (0.006)
Oil control ring	0.030-0.065 (0.0012-0.0026)	0.150 (0.006)
Ring thickness		
Top and second rings	1.2 (0.05)	–
Oil control ring	2.45 (0.096)	–
Groove height		
Top and second rings	1.35 (0.053)	–
Oil control ring	2.60 (0.102)	–
Ring side clearance all		
three rings	0.030-0.065 (0.0012-0.0026)	0.150 (0.006)
Cylinder bore	100.000-100.012 (3.9371-3.9376)	100.03 (3.9382)

Table 3 ENGINE TOP END TORQUE SPECIFICATIONS

Item	N•m	in.-lb.	ft.-lb.
Camshaft mount bolts	10	88	–
Camshaft sprocket bolts	50	–	37
Chain			
guide bolt	10	88	–
Chain			
tensioner end plug	40	–	29
Cylinder head cover bolts	10	88	–
	(continued)		

4

Table 3 ENGINE TOP END TORQUE SPECIFICATIONS (continued)

Item	N•m	in.-lb.	ft.-lb.
Cylinder and cylinder head bolts and nuts			
M6	10	88	
M8	28	–	21
M10			
First stage	20	–	15
Final stage	50	–	37

CHAPTER FIVE

ENGINE LOWER END

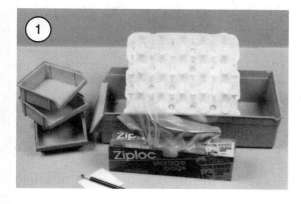

Before removing and disassembling the crankcase, clean the entire engine and frame with a quality commercial degreaser. It is easier to work on a clean engine.

Make certain that all of the necessary hand and special tools are available. Purchase replacement parts before disassembly.

One of the more important aspects of engine overhaul is preparation. Improper preparation before and failing to identify and store parts during removal will make it difficult to reassemble the engine. Before removing the first bolt and to prevent frustration during installation, get a number of boxes, plastic bags and containers (**Figure 1**) and store the parts when removed. Also have on hand a roll of masking tape and a permanent, waterproof marker to label parts as required.

The text makes frequent references to the left and right side of the engine. This refers to the engine as it sits in the frame, not how it may sit on a workbench.

Table 1 and **Table 2** are located at the end of this chapter.

SERVICING ENGINE IN FRAME

Many components can be serviced while the engine is installed in the frame:
1. Cylinder head.
2. Camshafts.
3. Cylinder and piston.

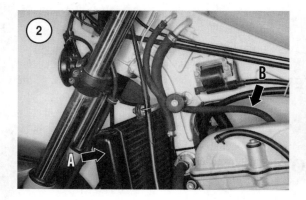

4. Clutch.

5. Starter motor and gears.

6. Alternator stator and rotor.

7. Water pump.

ENGINE

This procedure describes engine removal and installation. To decrease the weight of the engine, remove sub-assemblies from it before removing the engine from the frame. By following this method, the frame can be used as a holding fixture when servicing the engine. Attempting to disassemble the complete engine while placed on a workbench can be more time consuming.

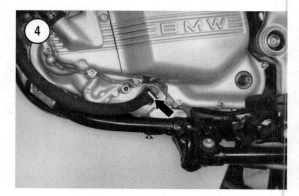

Removal

1. Thoroughly clean the engine of all dirt and debris.

2. Refer to Chapter Fifteen and perform the following:

    a. Remove the seat.

    b. Remove both frame side covers.

    c. Remove both cylinder head side covers.

    d. Remove the fuel tank cover.

    e. Remove the front fairing.

    f. Engine lower guard.

3. Disconnect the negative battery cable as described Chapter Nine.

4. Support the motorcycle on a stand or floor jack. See *Motorcycle Stands* in Chapter Eleven.

5. Remove the fuel tank as described in Chapter Eight.

6. Drain the engine oil as described in Chapter Three.

7. Remove the radiator (A, **Figure 2**) as described in Chapter Ten. Disconnect all coolant hoses from the engine.

8. Remove the thermostat assembly as described in Chapter Ten.

9. Remove both exhaust pipes as described in Chapter Eight. The muffler can remain in place.

10. Disconnect the spark plug leads and tie them up out of the way.

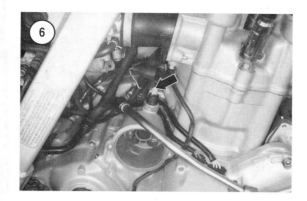

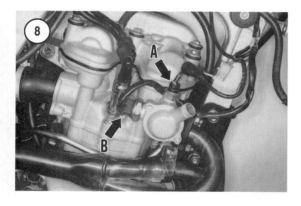

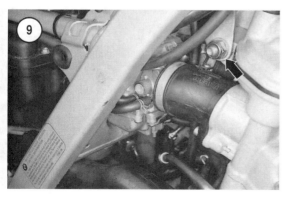

11. Remove the engine drive sprocket and drive chain from the engine as described in Chapter Thirteen.

12. Disconnect the engine breather hose from the cylinder head cover (B, **Figure 2**).

13. Disconnect the oil tank line from the top of the crankcase (**Figure 3**) and from the lower left side of the crankcase (**Figure 4**). Plug the oil lines to prevent dirt from entering the hoses.

14. Disconnect the clutch cable (A, **Figure 5**) from the left crankcase side cover as described under *Clutch Cable Replacement* in Chapter Five.

15. Slide the rubber boot up and disconnect the tachometer drive cable (B, **Figure 5**) from the crankcase.

16. Remove the drive chain driven sprocket as described in Chapter Thirteen.

17. Disconnect the following electrical connectors:
    a. Oil pressure switch (**Figure 6**).
    b. Neutral indicator switch (**Figure 7**).
    c. Engine temperature sensor (A, **Figure 8**).
    d. Cooling fan thermo switch (B, **Figure 8**).

18. Remove the starter motor as described in Chapter Nine.

19. If the engine requires disassembly, remove the following sub-assemblies:
    a. Alternator stator and rotor (Chapter Nine).
    b. Water pump (Chapter Ten).
    c. Clutch (Chapter Six).
    d. Starter motor (Chapter Nine).
    e. Cylinder head and camshafts (Chapter Four).
    f. Cylinder and piston (Chapter Four).

20. Remove the bolts securing the carburetor intake tube to the cylinder head. The carburetors and intake tube can be left in place.

21. If still in place, remove the bolts and washers securing the cylinder head to the frame bracket (**Figure 9**).

22. If necessary, remove the rear wheel as described in Chapter Thirteen.

23. Check the engine to make sure all wiring, hoses and other related components have been disconnected from the engine. Check that nothing will interfere with the removal of the engine from the frame.

24. Remove the following fasteners securing the engine to the sub frame:
    a. Front bolts and nuts (**Figure 10**).
    b. Lower left side (**Figure 11**).
    c. Lower right side.

5

25. Remove the sub-frame and allow the engine to rest on the swing arm pivot bolt (**Figure 12**).

26. Support the engine with a floor jack. Apply enough jack pressure on the crankcase to support it before removing the swing arm pivot bolt.

27. Remove the bearing trim cap on each side covering the swing arm pivot bolt and nut.

28. On the right side, have an assistant hold the swing arm pivot bolt with a socket.

29. On the left side, remove the nut and washers (**Figure 13**) from the swing arm pivot bolt.

30. Place a box under the swing arm to support it securely.

31. On the left side, carefully tap the pivot shaft part way out of the frame.

32. On the right side, slowly withdraw the pivot shaft from the frame and engine crankcase. If necessary, adjust jack pressure under the engine to ease removal of the pivot shaft from the crankcase.

> *WARNING*
> *Due to the weight of a complete engine assembly, have an assistant help to safely remove the engine.*

33. Slowly lower the engine from the frame and remove it.

34. Reinstall the swing arm pivot shaft (**Figure 14**), washer and nut to hold the swing arm in place. Tighten the nut finger-tight.

35. Inspect the sub frame (**Figure 15**) for cracks and damage. Check all welded sections. Repair or replace if necessary.

36. Inspect the sub frame mounting bosses (**Figure 16**) on the frame for damage.

37. Inspect the engine mounting boss (**Figure 17**) at the rear of the frame for damage.

38. Replace leaking or damaged oil hoses.

Installation

Installation is the reverse of removal while noting the following.

1. Check that all wiring, hoses and other related components are out of the way and will not interfere with engine installation.

2. Do not tighten any of the engine mounting bolts and nuts until all are installed. Install *new* self-locking nuts during installation.

3. Install the engine into the frame and install the swing arm pivot bolt through the frame, swing arm

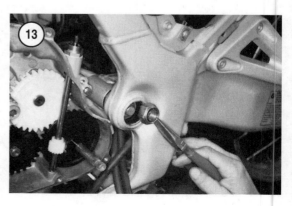

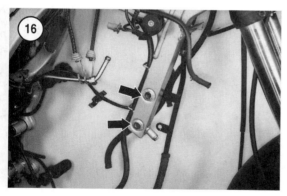

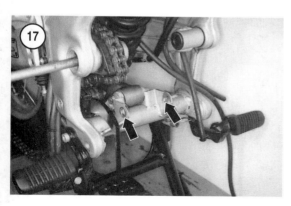

and crankcase. Refer to Chapter Thirteen to install the pivot bolt, washer and nut.

4. Move the engine up into place with a floor jack and install the sub-frame fasteners.

5. Tighten the engine mounting bolts securely. There are no manufacturer's torque specifications. Refer to the general torque specifications in Chapter One.

6. Refill the coolant and engine oil as described in Chapter Three.

7. Bleed the oil circuit as described under *Engine Oil Circuit Bleeding* in this chapter.

8. Start the engine and check or leaks.

CRANKCASE RIGHT SIDE COVER

Removal/Installation

Refer to *Alternator Stator Removal/Installation* in Chapter Nine.

CRANKCASE LEFT SIDE COVER

Removal/Installation

1. Refer to Chapter Fifteen and perform the following:
   a. Remove the seat.
   b. Remove the frame left side cover.
   c. Remove the cylinder head left side cover.
   d. Remove the engine lower cover.

2. Drain the engine oil as described in Chapter Three.

3. Drain the engine coolant as described in Chapter Three.

4. Disconnect the clutch cable (**Figure 18**) from the cover as described in Chapter Six.

5. Remove the water pump cover as described in Chapter Ten.

6. Remove the bolt (**Figure 19**) securing the gearshift lever and slide it off the shaft.

7. Using a crisscross pattern, loosen and remove the Allen bolts securing the crankcase left side cover (**Figure 20**). Note the location of the ground strap (**Figure 21**) at the rear of the cover and the sealing washer (**Figure 22**) on one of the top front bolts.

8. Remove the cover and gasket. Do not lose the locating dowels.

9. Inspect the cover (**Figure 23**) for cracks or damage. Inspect the shift lever oil seal (**Figure 24**) for

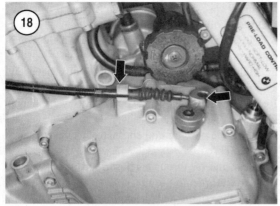

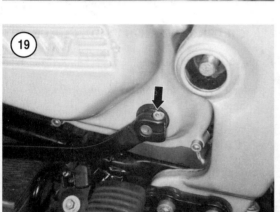

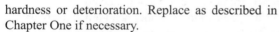

hardness or deterioration. Replace as described in Chapter One if necessary.

10. Install by reversing these removal steps while noting the following:

   a. If removed, install the locating dowels. Refer to **Figure 25** and **Figure 26**.

   b. Install a *new* gasket (**Figure 27**).

   c. Adjust the clutch as described in Chapter Three.

   d. Bleed the oil circuit as described under *Engine Oil Circuit Bleeding* in this chapter.

TACHOMETER DRIVE MECHANISM

Removal/Installation

Refer to **Figure 28**.

1. Slide the rubber boot up and disconnect the tachometer drive cable (**Figure 29**) from the crankcase.

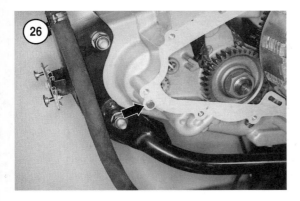

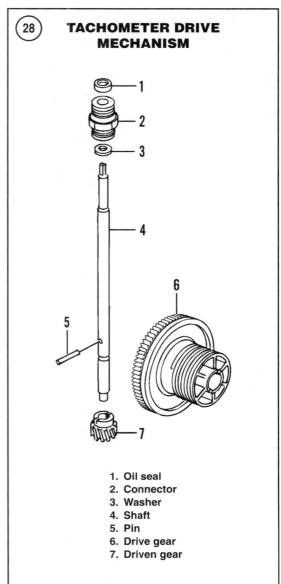

TACHOMETER DRIVE MECHANISM

1. Oil seal
2. Connector
3. Washer
4. Shaft
5. Pin
6. Drive gear
7. Driven gear

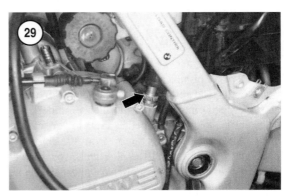

5

2. Remove the clutch assembly as described in Chapter Six.

NOTE
The following photographs are shown with the engine removed and partially disassembled to better illustrate the procedure.

3. Unscrew and remove the connector (**Figure 30**) from the crankcase.

4. Remove the washer (**Figure 31**) from the shaft.

5. Pull the shaft (A, **Figure 32**) up and disengage the lower end from the crankcase receptacle (B).

6. Pull the shaft down and out of the crankcase top opening (**Figure 33**) and remove it.

7. Pull up and remove the drive gear (**Figure 34**) from the shaft.

8. If necessary, remove the pin and slide the driven gear off the shaft.

9. Install by reversing these removal steps. Bleed the oil circuit as described under *Engine Oil Circuit Bleeding* in this chapter.

OIL PUMPS

The two oil pumps are mounted onto the left side of the crankcase under the clutch assembly. There is an upper feed pump, which supplies oil under pressure to the engine components, and a lower scavenger pump, which returns the oil from the engine to the oil tank in the frame. The oil travels from the engine to the oil tank through two interconnecting hoses.

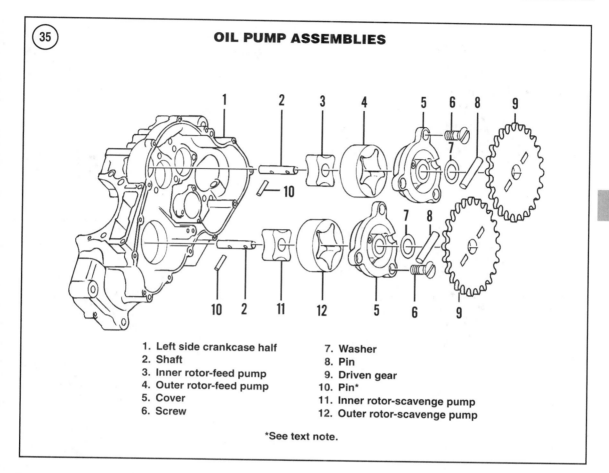

35 **OIL PUMP ASSEMBLIES**

1. Left side crankcase half
2. Shaft
3. Inner rotor-feed pump
4. Outer rotor-feed pump
5. Cover
6. Screw
7. Washer
8. Pin
9. Driven gear
10. Pin*
11. Inner rotor-scavenge pump
12. Outer rotor-scavenge pump

*See text note.

36

Removal/Disassembly

The oil pumps (**Figure 35**) can be removed with the engine in the frame. This procedure is shown with the engine removed and partially disassembled to better illustrate the steps.

NOTE
There are two methods to secure the oil pump driven gears to their shafts. Engines starting with No. 398 298 use a snap ring to secure the driven gear to the shaft. Engines prior to and including No. 398 297 do not use a snap ring.

1. Drain the engine oil as described in Chapter Three.

2. Remove the clutch assembly as described in Chapter Six.

3. Remove the tachometer drive mechanism as described in this chapter.

4. Remove the white idle gear (**Figure 36**).

NOTE
Do not intermix the components from the two different oil pump assemblies. They have developed a wear pattern and must remain as a set.

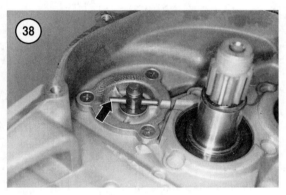

5. On the feed pump, perform the following:

   a. On models so equipped, remove the snap ring (**Figure 37**) securing the driven gear.

   b. Remove the driven gear.

   c. Remove the pin (**Figure 38**) from the shaft.

   d. Remove the washer (**Figure 39**) from the shaft.

6. On the scavenge pump, perform the following:

   a. On models so equipped, remove the snap ring securing the driven gear.

   b. Remove the driven gear (**Figure 40**).

   c. Remove the pin (**Figure 41**) from the shaft.

   d. Remove the washer (**Figure 42**) from the shaft.

> *CAUTION*
> *The cover screws are secured to the crankcase with a medium-strength threadlocking compound. Use an impact driver and appropriate size Phillips bit to loosen the screws. The screw head may be damaged if a normal Phillips screwdriver is used.*

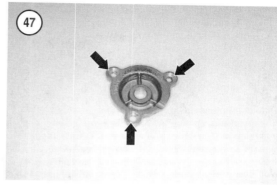

5

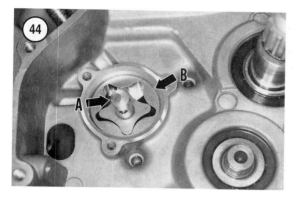

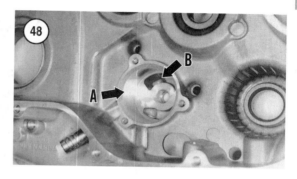

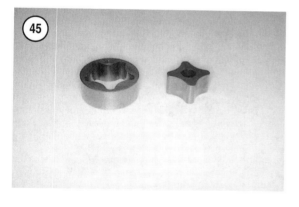

NOTE
The following steps relate to both feed
and scavenge oil pump assemblies.

7. Remove the Phillips screws securing the cover and remove the cover (**Figure 43**).

8. Remove the inner rotor and shaft (A, **Figure 44**) and the outer rotor (B) from the crankcase housing.

9. Repeat Steps 7 and 8 for the other oil pump assembly.

Inspection

Replace any part that is damaged or is worn to the service limit in **Table 1**.

1. Clean all parts thoroughly in solvent and place them on a clean, lint-free cloth.

2. Inspect both sets of rotors (**Figure 45**) for scratches and abrasion.

3. Inspect the cover inner surface (**Figure 46**) for scratches or abrasion.

4. Inspect the cover and the mounting screw holes (**Figure 47**) for damage.

5. Inspect the wall of the oil pump housing (A, **Figure 48**) in the crankcase for scratches caused by the rotors.

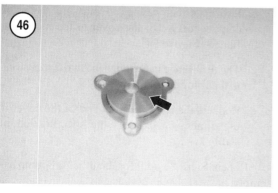

6. Inspect the interior passageways (B, **Figure 48**) of the oil pump housing. Make sure all oil sludge and debris is removed. Apply low-pressure compressed air through all oil pump housing passages.

7. Inspect the driven gears (**Figure 49**) and the white idle gear (**Figure 50**) for chipped or missing teeth. These gears are plastic and are prone to wear and/or damage. Replace as necessary.

8. Check the rotor side clearance as follows:
   a. Install the outer rotor and check the clearance between the outer rotor and the crankcase housing with a flat feeler gauge (**Figure 51**).
   b. Install the shaft and inner rotor into the housing and outer rotor. Check the clearance between the inner tip and outer rotor (**Figure 52**) with a flat feeler gauge.
   c. Replace the rotors as a set if either exceeds the dimension in **Table 2**.

9. Check the rotor endplay clearance as follows:
   a. Install both rotors into the crankcase housing. Use a vernier caliper and measure the distance from the top surface of the rotors to the top surface of the oil pump cover mating surface on the crankcase (**Figure 53**).
   b. Use a vernier caliper to measure the rotor contact surface of the cover to the mounting flange (**Figure 54**).
   c. The difference between these two dimensions is the rotor endplay.
   d. Replace the rotors as a set and/or the cover if the dimension exceeds the specification in **Table 2**.

10. Repeat Steps 8 and 9 for the other oil pump assembly.

Reassembly/Installation

1. Apply clean engine oil to all sliding surfaces prior to installation.

2. Position both rotors with their index marks facing up.

3. Install the outer rotor (B, **Figure 44**), then the inner rotor and shaft (A). Push the rotor and shaft down until it bottoms.

4. Install the cover (**Figure 55**).

5. Apply a medium-strength threadlocking compound to the Phillips screw threads on the cover prior to installation. Install the Phillips screws and tighten to the specification in **Table 2**.

6. Repeat Steps 2-5 for the other oil pump.

7. On the feed pump, perform the following:
   a. Install the washer (**Figure 39**) onto the shaft.
   b. Install the pin (**Figure 38**) into the shaft and center it.
   c. Install the driven gear and index it onto the pin. Push the gear down until it bottoms.
   d. On models so equipped, install the snap ring (**Figure 37**) securing the driven gear. Make sure the snap ring is seated correctly in the shaft groove.

8. On the scavenge pump, perform the following:
   a. Install the washer (**Figure 42**) onto the shaft.
   b. Install the pin onto the shaft and center it (**Figure 41**).
   c. Install the driven gear (**Figure 56**).
   d. On models so equipped, install the snap ring (**Figure 57**) securing the driven gear. Make sure the snap ring is seated correctly in the shaft groove.

9. Install the white idle gear (**Figure 36**).

10. Install the tachometer drive mechanism as described in this chapter.

11. Install the clutch assembly as described in Chapter Six.

12. Refill the engine oil as described in Chapter Three.

13. Bleed the oil circuit as described under *Engine Oil Circuit Bleeding* in this chapter.

PRIMARY DRIVE GEAR AND CAMSHAFT DRIVE CHAIN

Removal/Installation

1. Remove the camshafts as described in Chapter Four.

2. Remove the crankcase left side cover as described in this chapter.

3. To keep the primary drive gear from turning in the next step, insert a soft metal washer (**Figure 58**) between the primary drive gear and the clutch housing.

4. Loosen the primary drive gear 30 mm nut (**Figure 59**). Remove the washer.

5. Remove the clutch assembly as described in Chapter Six.

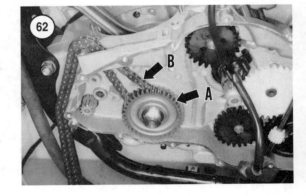

NOTE
The following photographs are shown with the top end removed to better illustrate this procedure. The top end assembly can remain in place for this procedure.

6. Remove the primary drive gear nut (**Figure 60**) and lockwasher (**Figure 61**).

7. Slide the primary drive gear (A, **Figure 62**) off the crankshaft.

8. Guide the camshaft drive chain (B, **Figure 62**) down through the chain cavity and remove the assembly from the crankcase.

9. Do not lose the Woodruff key on the crankshaft.

10. Inspect the primary drive gear as described in this chapter.

11. Inspect the camshaft drive chain as described in Chapter Four.

12. Install by reversing these removal steps while noting the following:

    a. Make sure the Woodruff key is in place on the crankshaft.

    b. Correctly mesh the camshaft drive chain onto the sprocket on the backside of the primary drive gear (**Figure 63**).

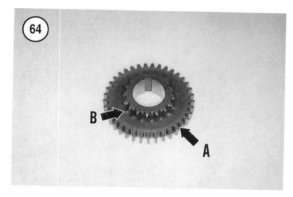

5

c. Install the lockwasher and nut and tighten to the specification in **Table 2**.

d. Bleed the oil circuit as described under *Engine Oil Circuit Bleeding* in this chapter.

Primary Drive Gear Inspection

1. Inspect the primary drive gear for chipped or missing teeth (A, **Figure 64**). If damaged, inspect the clutch housing teeth as they may also be damaged.

2. Inspect the camshaft drive chain sprocket (B, **Figure 64**) for wear or damage. If damaged, inspect the camshaft drive chain and camshaft sprockets for wear (Chapter Four).

3. Check the Woodruff key slot (**Figure 65**) for wear or damage. Replace the gear if necessary.

STARTER CLUTCH AND GEARS

Starter Gears Removal/Installation

NOTE
The photographs shown in this procedure are shown with the engine partially disassembled to better illustrate the steps.

1. Remove the starter motor as described in Chapter Nine.

2. Remove the alternator rotor as described in Chapter Nine.

3. Remove the washer and collar (**Figure 66**) from the idle gear shaft.

4. Remove the starter driven gear (A, **Figure 67**) and thrust washer (B).

5. Remove the idle gear (**Figure 68**).

6. Inspect the gears as described in this chapter.

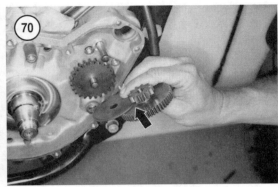

7. Install the idle gear (**Figure 69**) onto the shaft.

8. Position the thrust washer between the two gears of the driven gear (**Figure 70**).

9. Hold the thrust washer in place and install the washer and driven gear onto both shafts (**Figure 71**). Mesh the driven gear onto the idle gear and push the driven gear on until it bottoms.

10. Install the alternator rotor as described in Chapter Nine.

11. Install the collar (**Figure 72**) and washer (**Figure 73**) onto the idle gear shaft.

12. Install the starter motor as described in Chapter Nine.

13. Bleed the oil circuit as described under *Engine Oil Circuit Bleeding* in this chapter.

Starter Clutch
Removal/Inspection/Installation

1. Remove the starter motor as described in Chapter Nine.

2. Remove the alternator rotor as described in Chapter Nine.

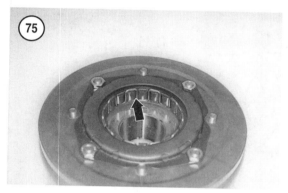

3. Rotate the freewheel gear and remove it from the backside of the alternator rotor (**Figure 74**).

4. Inspect the freewheel rollers (**Figure 75**) for damage or heat distortion. Replace if necessary.

5. Inspect the freewheel gear for chipped or missing teeth (**Figure 76**). If any are damaged, also inspect the gear teeth on the starter idle gear (**Figure 77**).

6. Inspect the freewheel gear bushing (**Figure 78**) for wear or damage.

7. Inspect the freewheel bearing surface (**Figure 79**) where it contacts the rollers for wear or damage.

Disassembly/Assembly

Refer to **Figure 80**.

1. Remove the alternator rotor as described in Chapter Nine.

2. To replace the freewheel perform the following:

CAUTION
The freewheel cover nuts are secured with a high-strength threadlocking compound and may be difficult to loosen.

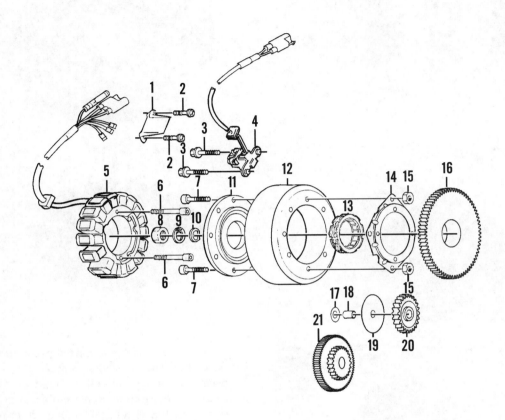

⑧⓪ **ALTERNATOR AND STARTER CLUTCH**

1. Clamp
2. Screw
3. Screw
4. Pickup coil
5. Stator assembly
6. Allen bolt
7. Allen bolt
8. Nut
9. Lockwasher
10. Washer
11. Hub
12. Rotor
13. Freewheel
14. Freewheel cover
15. Nut
16. Freewheel
17. Washer
18. Spacer
19. Thrust washer
20. Starter idle gear
21. Starter driven gear

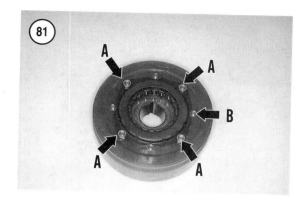

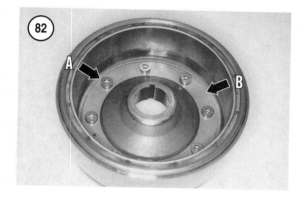

a. Use an impact driver and a suitable size hex nut bit to loosen the freewheel cover nuts (A, **Figure 81**).

b. Remove the nuts and the cover (B, **Figure 81**) and the freewheel from the alternator rotor.

c. Install the freewheel into the alternator rotor with the arrow facing up.

d. Install the cover.

e. Apply a high-strength threadlocking compound to the nut threads prior to installation.

f. Install the nuts and tighten them to the specification in **Table 2**.

3. To replace the hub, perform the following:

CAUTION
The eight Allen bolts have been secured with a high-strength thread-locking compound and may be difficult to loosen.

a. If still in place, remove the freewheel from the alternator as previously described.

b. Use an impact driver and a suitable Allen bolt bit to loosen the eight bolts (A, **Figure 82**) that secure the hub.

c. Remove the bolts and the hub (B, **Figure 82**) from the alternator rotor.

d. Install the hub onto the alternator rotor.

e. Apply a high-strength threadlocking compound to the Allen bolt threads prior to installation.

f. Install the bolts and tighten to the specification in **Table 2**.

CRANKCASE, CRANKSHAFT AND BALANCER SHAFT

Balancer Shaft System

The engine uses a balancer system. This system eliminates the vibration normally associated with a large displacement single cylinder engine. Do *not* disable this feature. If the balancer is eliminated it will result in excessive vibration that may damage the engine and frame.

CAUTION
Any applicable manufacturer's warranty will be voided if the balancer system is modified, disconnected or removed.

Crankcase Disassembly

1. Remove the engine from the frame as described in this chapter.

2. Remove the following components as described in this and various chapters:

a. Cylinder head (Chapter Four).

b. Camshafts (Chapter Four).

c. Cylinder and piston (Chapter Four).

d. Oil pumps (this chapter).

e. Clutch (Chapter Six).

f. Starter motor and gears (Chapter Nine and this chapter).

g. Alternator stator and rotor (Chapter Nine).

h. Water pump (Chapter Ten).

3. Place the crankcase assembly on wooden blocks with the right side facing up.

NOTE
Before removing the crankcase bolts in Step 5, draw an outline of the right side crankcase on cardboard, then punch a hole along the outline to represent the position of each crankcase

5

*bolt. As each bolt is removed, install it
in its correct position.*

4. Loosen the right side crankcase bolts one-quarter turn at a time and in a crisscross pattern.

5. Remove the crankcase bolts and install them in the cardboard holder as follows:

    a. Front and lower seven bolts (**Figure 83**).

    b. Rear four bolts (**Figure 84**).

    c. Two black bolts within the oil filter cavity (A, **Figure 85**) and the single center bolt (B). The two black bolts must be reinstalled in the same location.

> *CAUTION*
> *Crankcase separation requires only slight pressure. Do not gouge the crankcase gasket sealing surfaces by prying the crankcases apart. If damaged, it will result in oil leaks and require crankcase replacement. Make sure all of the crankcase bolts are removed, including the two black bolts (**Figure 86**).*

6. Tap around the perimeter of the crankcase with a plastic mallet to remove the right crankcase half. Use a plastic mallet to tap on the end of the crankshaft and transmission shaft to help release the shafts from the crankcase bearings.

7. Remove the gasket. Set it aside, as it will be used to establish crankshaft end-float. Do not lose the two locating dowels.

8. To remove the gearshift mechanism, refer to **Figure 87** and perform the following:

    a. Remove the washer (**Figure 88**) from the gearshift shaft.

    b. Disengage the shift pawl (A, **Figure 89**) from the shift drum and withdraw the gearshift shaft (B) assembly from the left side crankcase.

    c. Remove the index lever (A, **Figure 90**) and spring (B) from the left side crankcase.

9. To remove the gearshift drum and shift forks, refer to **Figure 91** and perform the following:

    a. Withdraw both shift fork shafts (**Figure 92**).

> *NOTE*
> *Identify the shift forks with a C, R and L as they are removed.*

    b. Remove the center (A, **Figure 93**), right (B) and left (C) shift forks from the shift drum.

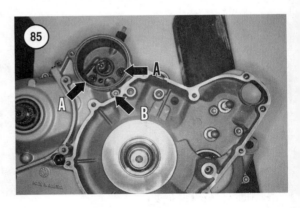

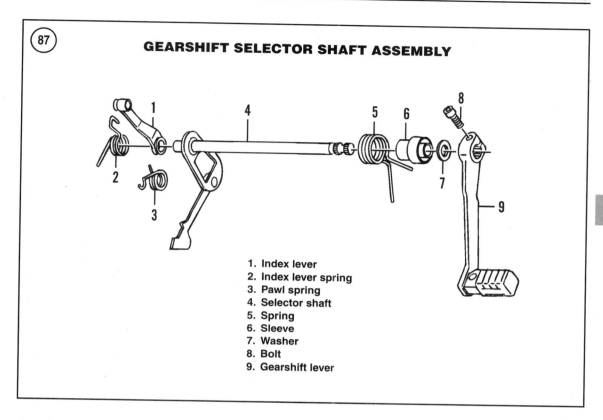

GEARSHIFT SELECTOR SHAFT ASSEMBLY

1. Index lever
2. Index lever spring
3. Pawl spring
4. Selector shaft
5. Spring
6. Sleeve
7. Washer
8. Bolt
9. Gearshift lever

10. Pull straight up and remove the shift drum (**Figure 94**) from the left side crankcase.

11. Pull straight up and remove both transmission shafts from the left side crankcase as an assembly (**Figure 95**).

NOTE
Do not lose the end float shims located on both ends of the crankshaft. The balancer shaft may also be fitted with shims. Remove them and identify them so they will be reinstalled in

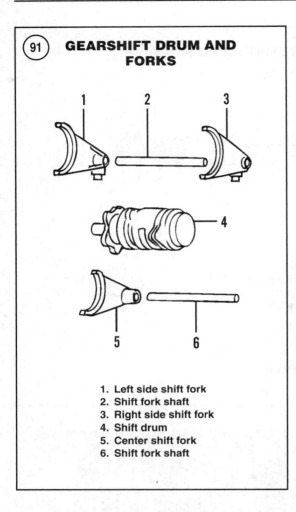

91 **GEARSHIFT DRUM AND FORKS**

1. Left side shift fork
2. Shift fork shaft
3. Right side shift fork
4. Shift drum
5. Center shift fork
6. Shift fork shaft

their original positions and locations during assembly.

12. Pull straight up to remove the crankshaft (A, **Figure 96**), then the balancer shaft (B) from the left side crankcase. There will be a slight click when the crankshaft gear separates from the balancer shaft dual gear. This is normal, as the dual gear is spring loaded.

13. Clean and inspect the crankcase halves, bearings, crankshaft and balancer shaft as described in this chapter.

14. Service the transmission and gearshift mechanism as described in Chapter Seven.

Crankcase Cleaning and Inspection

1. Inspect the crankcase seals for hardness or deterioration. Refer to **Figure 97** and **Figure 98**. Re-

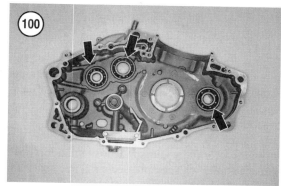

5

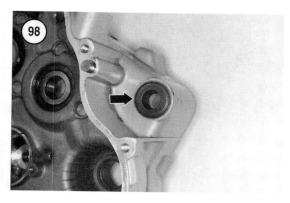

place the seals if necessary, as described in Chapter One.

2. Remove all gasket and sealer residue from all mating surfaces.

3. Clean both crankcase halves and bearings with solvent. Then reclean in hot, soapy water and rinse with clear, cold water.

4. Dry the case halves and bearings with compressed air, if available. When drying the bearings with compressed air, hold the inner bearing races to prevent them from turning. Do not allow the air jet to spin the bearings. After the bearings are dry, lubricate them with transmission oil.

5. Check each crankshaft main bearing (**Figure 99**) in each case half for abrasion and scoring. Replace the bearings as described in this chapter.

6. Turn each ball bearing (**Figure 100**, typical) by hand. The bearings must turn smoothly with no roughness. Replace damaged bearings as described in this chapter.

7. On the left side case half, make sure the oil pump housings (**Figure 101**) are thoroughly clean and free of any oil buildup.

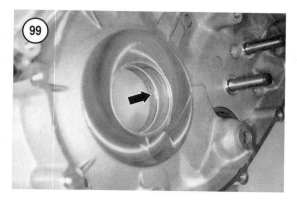

8. Carefully inspect the case halves for cracks and fractures, especially in the lower areas (**Figure 102**) where they are vulnerable to rock damage.

9. Inspect machined surfaces for burrs, cracks or other damage. It may be possible to repair minor damage with a fine-cut file or oilstone. Major damage may require welding and machining work or replacing the crankcase.

10. Check the crankcase stud threaded holes for stripping, cross-threading or deposit buildup. Clean threaded holes with compressed air. If necessary, repair threads with the correct size tap.

11. Check the starter gear shafts (**Figure 103**) for tightness. Tighten if necessary.

12. Remove the screws (A, **Figure 104**) and retaining bar (B), then remove the filter (**Figure 105**). Clean the filter and the receptacle in the crankcase. Reinstall the filter and tighten the screws securely.

13. On the right side crankcase, unscrew the oil relief valve (**Figure 106**). Clean the valve and inspect the spring (A, **Figure 107**) and seal end (B) for wear or damage. Replace if necessary.

Main Bearing Replacement

Two special tools are required to replace the main bearings: the removal drift (BMW part number 11 6 610) and installer drift (BMW part No. 11 6 620).

The bearings are not identical. Note the difference prior to removing them. The right side case bearing is grooved with an oil hole (**Figure 108**) while the left side case bearing is smooth (**Figure 109**).

Note the location of the oil hole (**Figure 108**) and mark its location on the crankcase as a reference point. The new bearing's oil hole must be reinstalled in the exact same location to ensure proper oil flow to the crankshaft.

1. Before heating the crankcases to replace the bearing, place the new bearings in a freezer. Chilling them slightly reduces their overall diameter while the hot crankcase is slightly larger due to heat expansion. This makes installation much easier.

2. Wash the cases thoroughly to remove all traces of oil and other chemical deposits.

3. The bearings are installed with a slight interference fit. Heat the crankcase to a temperature of about 212° F (100° C) in a shop oven or on a hot plate. Heat only one case at a time.

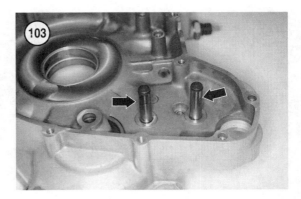

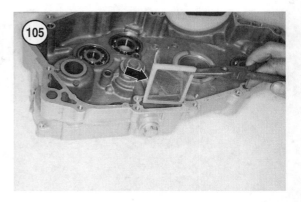

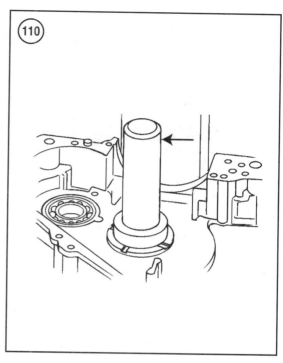

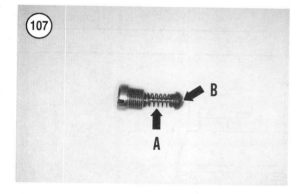

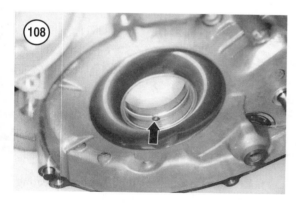

CAUTION
*Do not heat the cases with a torch
(propane or acetylene)—never bring a
flame into contact with the bearing or
case. The direct heat will warp the
case half.*

4. Remove the case from the shop oven or hot plate and hold onto the crankcase with welding gloves—*it is hot!*

5. Place the case on wooden blocks with the inside surface facing up.

6. Place the removal drift over the bearing (**Figure 110**) and carefully drive the bearing out of the crankcase.

7. While the crankcase is still hot, install the new bearing into the crankcase.

8. On the right side, correctly position the bearing's oil hole with the mark on the crankcase. Start the installation by hand with the installer drift. After it has started, lightly tap the bearing into the case with the drift until the drift flange bottoms on the crankcase.

9. On the right side, remove the installer drift and check the bearing's oil hole location in relation to the mark on the crankcase. They must be aligned correctly to ensure oil flow to the crankshaft. If alignment is incorrect, remove the bearing and discard it. Install a new one with the correct alignment.

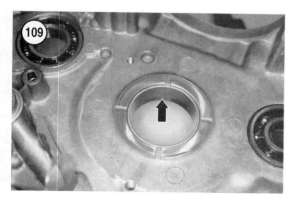

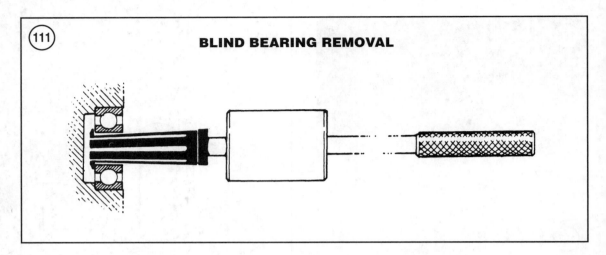

BLIND BEARING REMOVAL

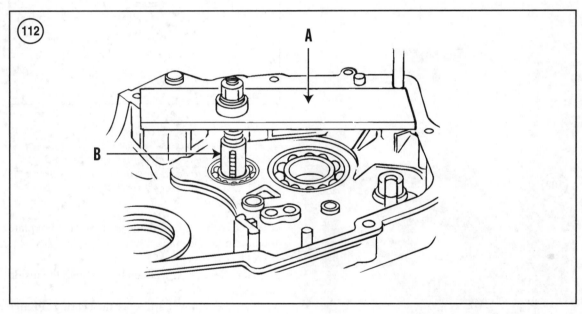

10. Repeat these steps for the other crankcase half.

Ball Bearing Replacement

The ball bearings can be replaced by using an appropriate size socket or blind puller or by using two BMW special tools: the bearing puller plate (BMW part No. 11 6 560) and spreader sleeve (BMW part No. 11 6 563). Both procedures are described.

1. Remove any oil seals as described in Chapter One.

2. Before heating the crankcase to replace the bearings, place the new bearings in a freezer. Chilling them slightly reduces their overall diameter while the hot crankcase expands slightly due to heating. This makes installation much easier.

3. Wash the cases thoroughly to remove all traces of oil and other chemical deposits.

4. The bearings are installed with a slight interference fit. Heat the crankcase to a temperature of about 212° F (100° C) in a shop oven or on a hot plate. Heat only one case at a time.

CAUTION
Do not heat the cases with a torch (propane or acetylene)–never bring a flame into contact with the bearing or case. The direct heat will destroy the

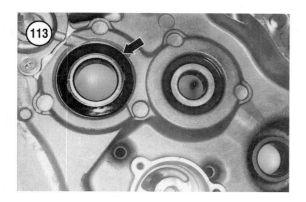

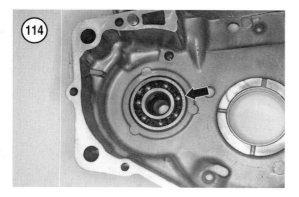

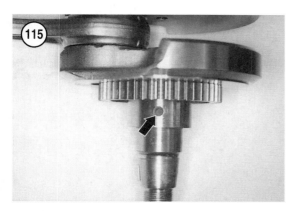

removal tool (**Figure 111**) to remove bearings installed in blind holes.

6B. If using the special tools, perform the following:

a. Install the bearing puller plate over the crankcase half mating surface (A, **Figure 112**).

b. Insert the spreader sleeve (B, **Figure 112**) into the bearing and spread it against the inner race.

c. Tighten the puller plate fastener and withdraw the bearing from the case half.

NOTE
*Install new bearings so the sealed side (**Figure 113**) faces outside.*

7. While the crankcase is still hot, install the new bearing(s) into the crankcase. Install the bearings by hand, if possible. If necessary, lightly tap the bearing(s) into the case with a bearing driver or socket placed on the outer bearing race. Do *not* install the bearings by driving on their inner race. Install the bearing(s) until it seats completely in its mounting bore (**Figure 114**).

Crankshaft and Connecting Rod
Cleaning and Inspection

When measuring the crankshaft in this section, compare the actual measurements to the specifications in **Table 2**. Have the crankshaft serviced if it is out of specification or shows damage.

NOTE
If any portion of the crankshaft and/or connecting rod are worn or damaged, they must be replaced or overhauled as one assembly by a BMW dealership.

1. Clean the crankshaft assembly in solvent and dry it thoroughly with compressed air.

2. Make sure the oil hole (**Figure 115**) is clear. Clean out if necessary and blow out with low pressure compressed air.

3. Inspect the main bearing journal on each end of the crankshaft for wear or abrasion. Refer to **Figure 116** and **Figure 117**.

4. Inspect the connecting rod piston pin bushing for wear or abrasion. Measure the inside diameter (**Figure 118**) with a snap gauge. Measure the snap gauge with a micrometer.

case hardening of the bearing and will warp the case half.

5. Remove the case from the shop oven or hot plate and hold onto the crankcase with welding gloves–*it is hot!*

6A. If special tools are not used, support the crankcase on wooden blocks and drive the bearing out from its opposite side. Use a bearing driver or socket to remove the bearing. Use a blind bearing

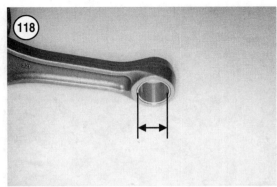

5. Hold the shank portion of the connecting rod (**Figure 119**) where it attaches to the crankshaft. Pull up and down on the connecting rod. Any slight amount of up and down movement indicates excessive lower bearing (**Figure 120**) wear. If there is movement, the crankshaft must be overhauled.

6. Measure connecting rod side-play with a feeler gauge (**Figure 121**) and check it against the service limit in **Table 2**.

7. Inspect the crankshaft balancer drive gear (**Figure 122**) for chipped or missing teeth. If damaged, also inspect the balancer gear teeth for damage.

8. Support the crankshaft on a truing stand or in a lathe and check runout at the clutch end (A, **Figure 123**) and at the alternator end (B) with a dial indicator.

9. To establish main bearing radial play, perform the following:

    a. Measure the crankshaft bearing journal diameter (**Figure 124**) with a micrometer.

    b. Measure the crankcase bearing journal diameter (**Figure 125**) with a bore gauge.

    c. The difference between the two measurements is the radial play.

5

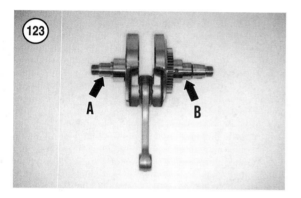

Crankshaft End Float
Inspection and Adjustment

The crankshaft end float must be maintained between the main bearing surfaces on both sides of the
crankcase. The end float is maintained by shims, of
various thicknesses, located on the clutch side of the
crankshaft. A standard thickness shim of 1.0 mm
(0.04 in.) is always installed on the alternator side of
the crankshaft.

1. Disassemble the crankcase as described in this
chapter.

2. Place the left side crankcase on wooden blocks.

3. Install the standard shim (**Figure 126**) on the
clutch side of the crankshaft.

4. Install the crankshaft, with the standard shim in
place, into the left side crankcase (**Figure 127**).

NOTE
Use the same machined straightedge
in Step 5 and Step 8 and place it in the
same position on the components. By
doing this, the thickness of the
straightedge will not have to be com-

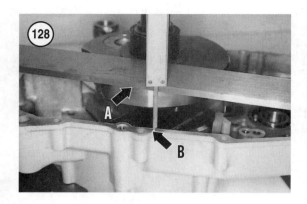

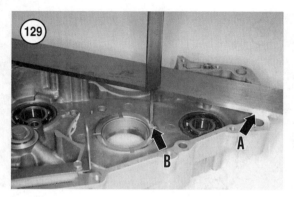

pensated for in establishing the shim thickness.

5. Place a machined straightedge on the crankshaft web (A, **Figure 128**).

6. Use a vernier caliper to measure from the top surface of the straightedge to the crankcase mating surface (B, **Figure 128**). This is *Dimension A*.

7. Remove the crankshaft from the crankcase.

8. Place the same machined straightedge on the crankcase mating surface (A, **Figure 129**) in the same position used in Step 5.

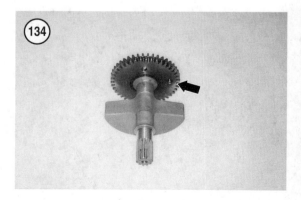

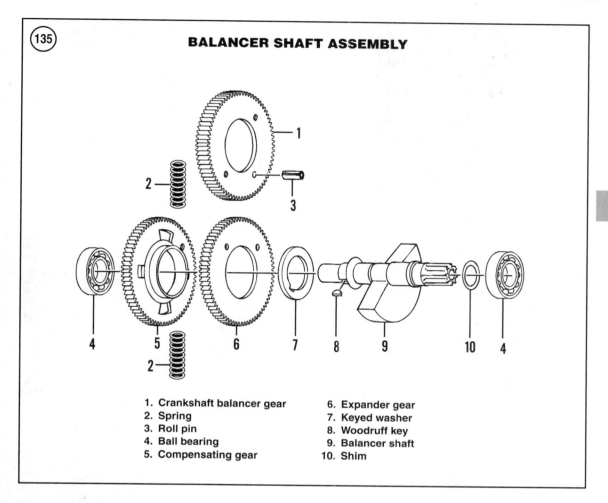

(135)

BALANCER SHAFT ASSEMBLY

1. Crankshaft balancer gear
2. Spring
3. Roll pin
4. Ball bearing
5. Compensating gear
6. Expander gear
7. Keyed washer
8. Woodruff key
9. Balancer shaft
10. Shim

9. Use a vernier caliper to measure from the top surface of the straightedge to the crankcase shim contact surface (B, **Figure 129**). This is *Dimension B*.

10. Measure the thickness of the *old* crankcase mating surface gasket. Do not use a new gasket, as it is thicker.

11. Subtract *Dimension A* from *Dimension B*, then add the thickness of the *old* compressed gasket. This dimension establishes crankshaft end float.

12. If the end float is not within specification, adjust it by installing a shim (**Figure 130**) of a different thickness on the alternator side of the crankshaft.

Balancer Shaft Cleaning and Inspection

1. Clean the balancer shaft in solvent and dry thoroughly with compressed air.

2. Inspect the bearing journal (A, **Figure 131**) on each end of the balancer shaft for wear or abrasion.

3. Inspect the shim mounting surface (**Figure 132**) for wear or damage.

4. Inspect the teeth on the expander and compensating gears (**Figure 133** and **Figure 134**) for chipped or missing teeth. If damaged, also inspect the crankshaft balancer gear teeth for damage.

Balancer Shaft Disassembly/Assembly

Refer to **Figure 135**.

NOTE
Do not disassemble the gears unless one or both gears require replacement.

1. Place the balancer shaft in a vise with soft jaws with the gear side facing up.

2. Insert a pair of flat-blade screwdrivers between the two gears and slowly separate them.

3. Slide the compensating gear off the balancer shaft.

4. Remove the two springs.

5. Slide the expander gear off the balancer shaft.

6. Remove the keyed washer and the Woodruff key from the balancer shaft.

7. Install the Woodruff key and the keyed washer.

8. Assemble the compensating gear, two springs and expander gear. Align the gears so that both gear holes are aligned.

9. Install this assembly onto the balancer shaft. Rotate the gears against the spring so the Woodruff key slots are aligned (**Figure 136**), then slide the assembly onto the shaft. Push it on until it bottoms. If necessary, use a deep socket to tap the gears into place with a mallet until they are seated against the balancer shaft shoulder (B, **Figure 131**).

10. Try to slightly rotate the gears to ensure the springs are operating properly. There must be resistance when trying to rotate the gears.

Crankcase Assembly

1. Clean all parts before assembly.

2. Pack all of the crankcase seals with high-temperature grease.

3. Apply clean engine oil to all sliding and bearing surfaces.

4. Place the right side case half on wooden blocks on the workbench with the inside surface facing up.

NOTE
The compensating gear and expander
gear teeth must be aligned, and held

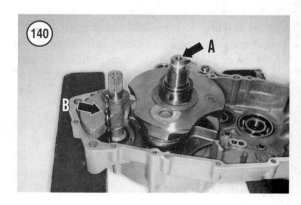

5

6. Install the balancer shaft (**Figure 139**) into the crankcase and align its index mark with the one in the crankcase.

7. With the right side shim in place, install the crankshaft partially into the crankcase (A, **Figure 140**). Rotate the crankshaft until its index mark aligns with the one in the crankcase. Push the crankshaft down and mesh it with the balancer shaft gear.

CAUTION
Incorrect alignment of the balancer shaft with the crankshaft will result in severe engine vibration and lead to internal engine damage. The index marks must be correctly aligned as shown in Step 8.

8. After both shafts are installed, ensure that the index marks on both shafts are aligned with the index marks on the crankcase (**Figure 141**).

9. Remove the drill bit (B, **Figure 140**) from the balancer shaft.

10. Use a plastic mallet to tap on the balance and crankshaft ends (**Figure 142**) to correctly seat them in the crankcase.

11. Make sure the shim (**Figure 143**) is in place on the left side of the balancer shaft and the crankshaft.

12. Mesh the mainshaft and countershaft together by hand, then install them into the crankcase (**Figure 144**). Push both shaft assemblies down until they are correctly seated in the ball bearings. When properly installed, the mainshaft first gear will stick up above the countershaft first gear as shown in **Figure 145**.

13. Rotate both transmission shafts to ensure they rotate freely in the crankcase bearings.

in this alignment, in order to properly mesh with the crankshaft gear teeth in Step 7.

5. Align the holes in the two balancer shaft gears. Insert a 5/16 in. drill bit through the holes to keep the gears aligned (A, **Figure 137**). Push the drill bit in until it is flush with the bottom surface of the compensating gear (**Figure 138**). The two gears are now aligned correctly (B, **Figure 137**).

14. Install the shift drum (**Figure 146**) into the crankcase bushing. Press it into place until it bottoms.

NOTE
Refer to the identification marks made in (bf ital)Disassembly Step 9.

15. Install the center (A, **Figure 147**), right (B) and left (C) shift forks into their respective gears.
16. Move the shift forks over and into mesh with the shift drum grooves (**Figure 148**).

NOTE
Make sure both shift fork shafts bottom out solidly after installing them.

17. Align the shift forks with the shift fork shaft receptacles in the crankcase, then install both shift fork shafts (**Figure 149**). Ensure that the shift fork guide pins are correctly engaged with the shift drum grooves (**Figure 150**).
18. To install the gearshift mechanism, refer to **Figure 151** and perform the following:
  a. Install the index lever (A, **Figure 152**) and spring (B) onto the left side crankcase. Hook

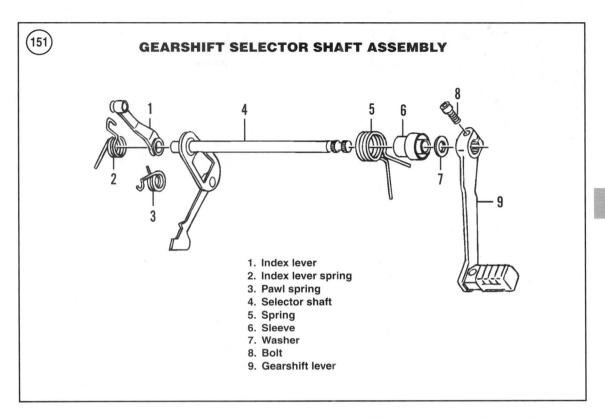

GEARSHIFT SELECTOR SHAFT ASSEMBLY

1. Index lever
2. Index lever spring
3. Pawl spring
4. Selector shaft
5. Spring
6. Sleeve
7. Washer
8. Bolt
9. Gearshift lever

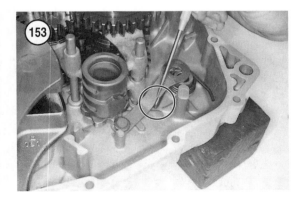

the spring onto the index lever as shown in **Figure 153**.

b. Install the gearshift shaft assembly into the left side crankcase (**Figure 154**).

c. Engage the shift pawl (**Figure 155**) into the shift drum.

d. Push the shift shaft down into the crankcase receptacle until it bottoms.

e. Install the washer (**Figure 156**) onto the gearshift shaft.

19. Lubricate the transmission gears and shift forks with clean engine oil.

20. Install the gearshift lever (**Figure 157**) onto the gearshift shaft and tighten the pinch bolt.

NOTE
Step 21 is best done with the aid of an assistant, as the assemblies are loose and do not spin very easily. Have the assistant spin the transmission shafts while turning the shift drum through all gears.

21. Spin the transmission shafts and shift through all gears using the gearshift lever. Make sure to shift into all five gears. This is the time to find that something may be installed incorrectly–not after the crankcase is completely assembled. Remove the gearshift lever.

22. Thoroughly clean both crankcase mating surfaces with an aerosol parts cleaner to remove all oil residue.

23. Install a *new* crankcase gasket (**Figure 158**). Make sure all holes are aligned with the crankcase.

24. If removed, install the two locating dowels into the left crankcase. Refer to **Figure 159** and **Figure 160**.

25. Carefully install the left side case half onto the right side.

26. Start it over the shafts and push it down until it is against the right side case half. When doing so, stop often to check that both case surfaces remain parallel (**Figure 161**). It may be necessary to tap the left side case near the crankshaft and countershaft to maintain this alignment. Check that all two dowel pins engage the left side case when the halves come together. When the case halves bottom out, check that the gasket surfaces are flush all the way around

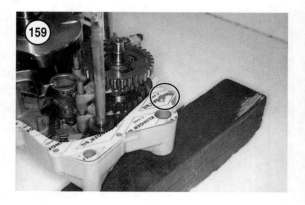

5

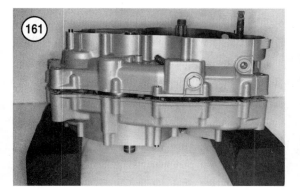

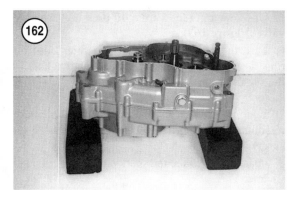

the engine (**Figure 162**). Check also that the mainshaft, countershaft, shift drum and crankshaft rotate freely. There must be no binding with any shaft.

> *CAUTION*
> *The case halves must fit together completely. If not, do not try to pull them together with the fasteners. Separate the case halves and investigate the cause of the interference. If the transmission shafts were disassembled, check to make sure that a gear was not installed backwards. Do not risk damage by trying to force the cases together.*

27. Install all of the crankcase bolts and tighten finger-tight as follows:

    a. Front and lower seven bolts (**Figure 163**).

    b. Rear four bolts (**Figure 164**).

> *CAUTION*
> *Do not forget the two black bolts (**Figure 165**) within the oil filter cavity.*

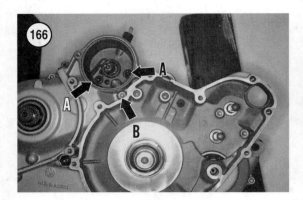

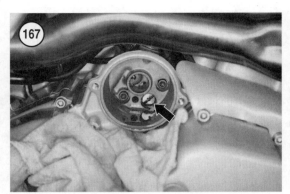

c. Two black bolts within the oil filter cavity (A, **Figure 166**) and the single center bolt (B). The two black bolts must be reinstalled in this location.

28. Using a crisscross pattern, tighten the bolts in two to three stages to the specification in **Table 2**.

29. Install the following components as described in this and other chapters:

    a. Water pump (Chapter Ten).

    b. Alternator stator and rotor (Chapter Nine).

    c. Starter motor and gears (Chapter Nine and this chapter).

    d. Clutch (Chapter Six).

    e. Oil pumps (this chapter).

    f. Cylinder and piston (Chapter Four).

    g. Camshafts (Chapter Four).

    h. Cylinder head (Chapter Four).

30. Install the engine into the frame as described in this chapter.

31. Bleed the oil circuit as described under *Engine Oil Circuit Bleeding* in this chapter.

ENGINE OIL CIRCUIT BLEEDING

Whenever any portion of the engine has been removed and the oil system completely drained, bleed the oil circuit to ensure proper oil circulation.

1. Remove the fuel tank as described in Chapter Eight.

2. Remove the oil filter as described in Chapter Three.

3. Remove one spark plug as described in Chapter Three.

4. Place a shop cloth under the oil filter cavity in the crankcase to catch oil as it runs out in the following steps.

5. Unscrew and remove the oil pressure retaining valve (**Figure 167**).

6. Turn the engine over with the starter until oil runs out of the oil pressure retaining valve hole in the oil filter cavity (**Figure 168**). Stop the starter motor.

7. Wipe up expelled oil and install the oil pressure retaining valve (**Figure 169**). Tighten the valve securely.

8. Install the oil filter and spark plug as described in Chapter Three.

9. Place a shop cloth under the oil return hose (**Figure 170**) to catch oil as it runs out in the following step. Loosen the hose clamp and disconnect the hose from the frame fitting.

10. Turn the engine over with the starter until oil runs out of the oil return hose. Stop the starter motor.

11. Connect the oil return hose to the fitting and tighten the clamp securely.

12. Install the fuel tank as described in Chapter Eight.

13. Install the spark plug as described in Chapter Three.

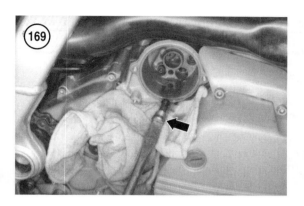

5

14. Check the oil level as described in Chapter Three and top off if necessary.

ENGINE BREAK-IN

Following cylinder service (honing, new rings) and major lower end work, break the engine in as though it were new. The service and performance life of the engine depends on a careful and sensible break-in.

1. For the first 50 mi. (80 km), maintain engine speed below 2500 rpm in any gear. However, do not lug the engine. Do not exceed 50 mph during this period.

2. From 50-500 mi. (80-804 km), vary the engine speed. Avoid prolonged steady running at one engine speed. During this period, increase engine speed to 3000 rpm. Do not exceed 55 mph during this period.

3. After the first 500 mi. (804 km), the engine break-in is complete.

Table 1 ENGINE LOWER END SERVICE SPECIFICATIONS

Item	New mm (in.)	Service limit mm (in.)
Compensating gear and expander gear maximum spread	–	6.2 (0.244)
Crankshaft		
Bearing		
Journal diameter	–	47.975 (1.8888)
Radial play	0.030-0.070 (0.0012-0.0028)	0.10 (0.004)
Runout		
Clutch end	–	0.03 (0.0012)
Alternator end	–	0.05 (0.0019)
Connecting rod side clearance	–	0.80 (0.031)
Connecting rod radial clearance	–	0.80 (0.031)
Small end bore inside diameter	–	22.04 (0.868)
End float	–	0.1-0.3 (0.004-0.012)
Oil pump		
Inner rotor–to–outer rotor clearance	–	0.25 (0.010)
Outer rotor–to–housing clearance	–	0.25 (0.010)
Rotor end play		0.20 (0.008)

Table 2 ENGINE LOWER END TORQUE SPECIFICATIONS

Item	N•m	in.-lb.	ft.-lb.
Alternator			
Hub Allen bolt	10	88	–
Rotor/starter			
freewheel nuts	10	88	–
Crankcase bolts	10	88	–
Engine oil drain plug	40	–	29
Oil filter cover bolt	10	88	–
Oil pressure			
retaining valve	24	–	20
Oil pressure switch	15	–	11
Oil pressure valve	24	–	20
Oil pump cover			
screws	6	53	–
Oil tank drain screw	10	88	–
Primary drive gear nut	180	–	132

CLUTCH

This chapter describes service procedures for the clutch assembly.

Specifications are in **Table 1** and **Table 2** at the end of this chapter.

CLUTCH RELEASE LEVER AND BEARINGS

The clutch release mechanism (**Figure 1**) is mounted in the crankcase left side cover and can be removed with the engine installed in the frame.

Removal/Installation

1. Disconnect the negative battery cable as described in Chapter Eight.

2. At the clutch lever, slide the rubber boot (A, **Figure 2**) off the cable adjuster.

3. Loosen the adjuster locknut (B, **Figure 2**) and turn the adjuster (C) to obtain maximum cable slack.

4. Disconnect the clutch cable from the release lever (A, **Figure 3**) and from the retainer on the left side crankcase cover (B).

5. Remove the bolt (A, **Figure 4**) securing the release lever and remove the lever (B).

6. Remove the crankcase left side cover as described in Chapter Five.

7. Remove the snap ring (**Figure 5**) securing the release shaft in the side cover.

8. Carefully withdraw the release shaft (**Figure 6**) out of the crankcase left side cover.

9. Inspect the release arm and shaft for cracks, deep scoring or excessive wear. Replace as necessary.

10. Install the release shaft into the crankcase left side cover.

11. If removed, carefully tap the new oil seal into place in the crankcase left side cover.

12. Install a *new* snap ring (**Figure 5**) securing the release shaft in the side cover. Make sure the snap ring is correctly seated in the shaft groove.

13. Install the release lever (B, **Figure 4**) and bolt (A). Tighten the bolt securely.

14. Install the crankcase left side cover as described in Chapter Five.

15. Connect the clutch cable onto the crankcase left side cover boss (B, **Figure 3**) and onto the release lever (A).

16. Adjust the clutch as described in Chapter Three.

Bearing Replacement

> *NOTE*
> *Do not remove the needle bearing unless they are going to be replaced.*

1. Using a puller (BMW part No. 21 4 610), or an equivalent, pull both needle bearings and the oil seal from the crankcase left side cover at the same time.

2. Install new needle bearings using a drift (BMW part No. 21 4 640) or an equivalent. Install the lower bearings first, then the upper needle bearings.

3. Install the *new* oil seal onto the release shaft.

CLUTCH

The clutch is a wet (operates immersed in the engine oil supply) multiplate-type. The clutch hub is splined to the transmission mainshaft and the clutch housing can rotate freely on the mainshaft. The clutch housing is geared to the primary drive gear attached to the crankshaft.

CLUTCH SERVICE

Removal

Refer to **Figure 7**.

1. Disconnect the negative battery cable as described in Chapter Nine.

2. Remove the crankcase left side cover as described in Chapter Five.

3. Loosen the pressure plate bolts (**Figure 8**) in a crisscross pattern, then remove the bolts and springs.

4. Remove the pressure plate (**Figure 9**).

5. Remove the clutch plates and friction discs from the clutch housing. Keep them in the order of removal.

6. Straighten the locking tab (**Figure 10**) on the clutch nut.

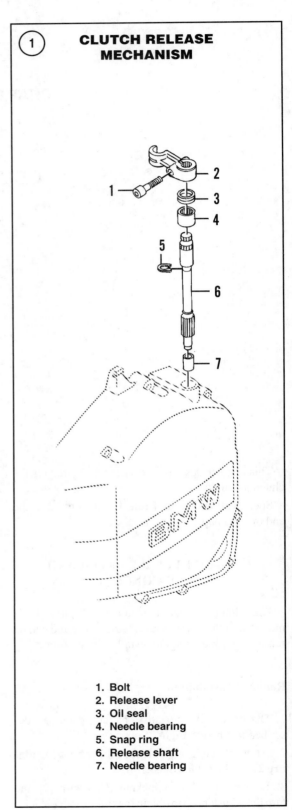

① CLUTCH RELEASE MECHANISM

1. Bolt
2. Release lever
3. Oil seal
4. Needle bearing
5. Snap ring
6. Release shaft
7. Needle bearing

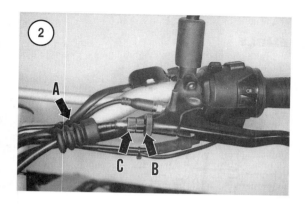

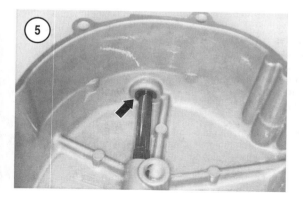

6

CAUTION
*When using the clutch holder in Step
7, make sure to secure it squarely onto
the clutch hub. If the clutch holder
starts to slip, stop loosening the clutch
nut and reposition the clutch holder. If
the clutch holder slips while loosening the clutch nut, it may damage the
clutch hub splines.*

7. Hold the clutch hub with a clutch holder (A, **Figure 11**). Loosen the 27 mm clutch nut (B).

8. Remove the clutch nut (B, **Figure 11**) and splined lockwasher (A, **Figure 12**).

9. Remove the clutch hub (B, **Figure 12**).

10. Remove the splined washer (**Figure 13**).

11. Remove the clutch housing (**Figure 14**) from the transmission shaft.

12. Remove the two needle bearings (**Figure 15**) and washer (A, **Figure 16**) from the transmission shaft.

13. If necessary, remove the O-ring (B, **Figure 16**) from the mainshaft groove.

14. Inspect the clutch assembly as described under *Clutch Inspection* in this chapter.

Installation

1. Coat all clutch parts with engine oil before re-assembly.

2. Apply Optimoly MP3 grease to the transmission shaft splines.

3. Install the washer (A, **Figure 17**) onto the mainshaft.

4. If removed, install the O-ring (A, **Figure 18**).

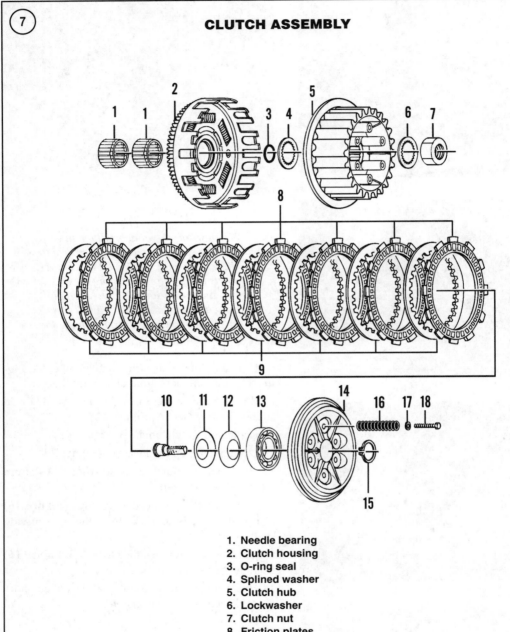

CLUTCH ASSEMBLY

1. Needle bearing
2. Clutch housing
3. O-ring seal
4. Splined washer
5. Clutch hub
6. Lockwasher
7. Clutch nut
8. Friction plates
9. Clutch plates
10. Release head
11. Plate spring-inner
12. Plate spring-outer
13. Ball bearing
14. Pressure plate
15. Snap ring
16. Spring
17. Washer
18. Bolt

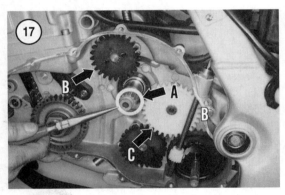

5. Install the smaller needle bearing (B, **Figure 18**) then the larger needle bearing (**Figure 15**) onto the transmission mainshaft.

> *CAUTION*
> *The black oil pump driven gear (B, **Figure 17**) and the white oil pump idler gear (C) are plastic and may be easily damaged during clutch housing installation. The gear (**Figure 19**) on the backside of the clutch hub must mesh properly with these two gears during installation, or they will be damaged.*

6. Partially install the clutch housing (**Figure 14**) onto the mainshaft. Use a scribe to slowly rotate both black oil pump driven gears to ensure proper gear engagement. Refer to **Figure 20** and **Figure 21**. The lower black gear rotates the white oil pump idler gear. Also, the clutch hub must mesh properly with the primary drive gear (**Figure 22**).

7. Once all three gears are meshed correctly, push the clutch housing on until it bottoms.

6

8. Position the splined washer with the chamfered side going on first and install the splined washer (**Figure 13**).

9. Install the clutch hub (B, **Figure 12**) and the splined lockwasher (A).

10. Apply Loctite 243, or an equivalent, to the clutch nut threads.

11. Install the clutch nut (B, **Figure 11**) and tighten it finger-tight.

12. Hold the clutch hub with the same clutch holder tool (A, **Figure 23**) used during disassembly, then tighten the clutch nut (B) to the torque specification in **Table 2**. Remove the clutch holder tool.

13. Install the clutch plates as follows:

   a. If not already done, lubricate the friction plates and clutch plates with engine oil.

   b. First install a clutch plate (**Figure 24**), then a friction plate (**Figure 25**), then a clutch plate. Continue to alternately install the friction plates and clutch plates.

   c. Install the last friction plate (**Figure 26**) into the offset grooves in the clutch hub (**Figure 27**).

14. Install the pressure plate (**Figure 28**) over the clutch hub. Make sure the pressure plate seats flush against the outer friction disc. If not, the pressure plate is not installed correctly. Remove it and reinstall it correctly.

15. Install the clutch springs (**Figure 29**) and bolts and washers (**Figure 30**). Tighten the bolts in a crisscross pattern in two or three steps to the specification in **Table 2**.

16. Rotate the release head so the gear teeth (**Figure 31**) are facing toward the rear to ensure proper engagement with the release shaft gears.

17. Install the crankcase left side cover as described in Chapter Five.

18. Refill the engine with the correct type and quantity of oil as described in Chapter Three.

19. Check and adjust the clutch as described in Chapter Three.

20. Connect the negative battery cable as described in Chapter Nine.

21. Shift the transmission into NEUTRAL and start the engine. After the engine warms up, pull the clutch in and shift the transmission into first gear. Note the following:

   a. If the clutch makes a loud grinding and spinning noise immediately after starting the engine, either the engine is out of oil or the new clutch plates were not previously lubricated with oil.

   b. If the motorcycle jumps forward and stalls or creeps with the transmission in gear and the clutch lever pulled in, recheck the clutch adjustment. If the clutch will not adjust properly, either the clutch cable or friction plates are excessively worn. Replace them.

   c. If the clutch adjustment is correct, operate the clutch lever while watching the clutch release

lever on the crankcase left side cover. The lever should move back and forth out as the clutch lever is operated by hand.

   d. If the clutch adjustment, clutch cable and clutch release lever all seem to be working correctly, the clutch may have been assembled incorrectly or there is a broken part in the clutch. Disassemble the clutch as described in this chapter and inspect the parts.

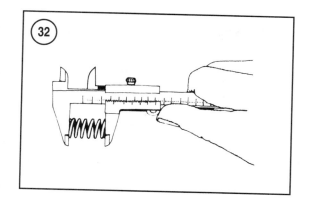

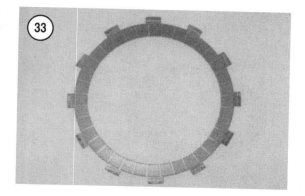

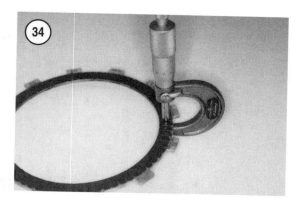

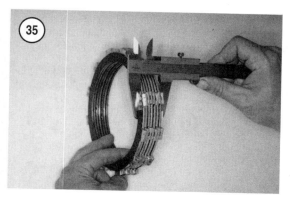

Clutch Inspection

When measuring the clutch components, compare the actual measurements to the specifications in **Table 1**. Replace parts that are out of specification or show damage as described in this section.

1. Clean all parts in solvent and dry.
2. Measure the free length of each clutch spring (**Figure 32**) with a vernier caliper. Replace the springs as a set if any one spring is too short.
3. Inspect the friction plates as follows:

> *NOTE*
> *If any friction plate is damaged or out of specification as described in the following steps, replace all of the friction plates as a set. Never replace individual plates.*

6

  a. The friction material used on the friction plate (**Figure 33**) is bonded to an aluminum plate for warp resistance and durability. Inspect the friction material for excessive or uneven wear, cracks and other damage. Check the disc tangs for surface damage. The sides of the disc tangs where they contact the clutch housing fingers must be smooth; otherwise, the discs cannot engage and disengage correctly.

> *NOTE*
> *If the plate tangs are damaged, inspect the clutch housing fingers carefully as described later in this section.*

  b. Measure the thickness of each friction plate with a vernier caliper, or micrometer (**Figure 34**). Measure at several places around the plate.

  c. Stack the seven friction plates and measure the height (**Figure 35**).

  d. Place each friction plate on a flat surface and measure for warp with a feeler gauge (**Figure 36**).

4. Inspect the clutch plates (**Figure 37**) as follows:

  a. Inspect the clutch plates for cracks, damage or color change. Overheated clutch plates will have a blue discoloration.

  b. Check the clutch plates for oil glaze buildup. Remove by lightly sanding both sides of each plate with 400-grit sandpaper placed on a surface plate or piece of glass.

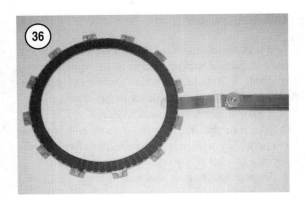

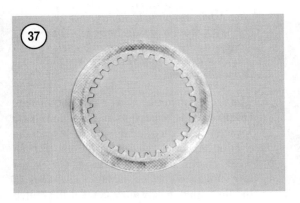

c. Place each clutch plate on a flat surface and check for warp with a feeler gauge (**Figure 38**).

d. The clutch plate inner teeth mesh with the clutch hub splines. Check the clutch plate teeth for any roughness or damage. The teeth contact surfaces must be smooth; otherwise, the plates cannot engage and disengage correctly.

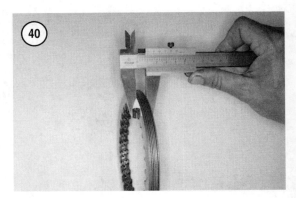

NOTE
If the clutch plate teeth are damaged, inspect the clutch hub splines carefully as described later in this section.

e. Measure the thickness of each clutch plate with a vernier caliper or micrometer (**Figure 39**). Measure at several places around the plate.

f. Stack the seven clutch plates together and measure the height (**Figure 40**).

g. Measure the outer diameter of the clutch plates (**Figure 41**).

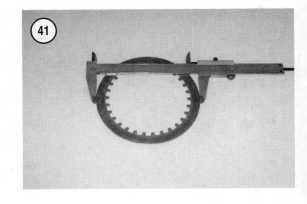

5. Inspect the clutch hub for the following conditions:

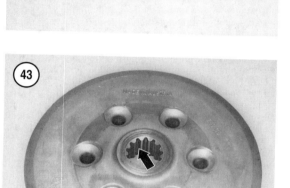

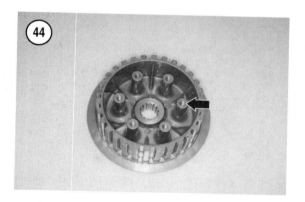

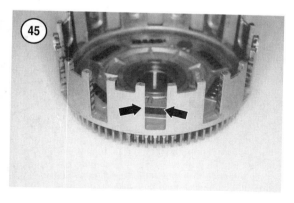

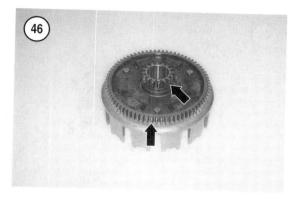

6

a. The clutch plate teeth slide in the clutch hub splines (**Figure 42**). Inspect the splines for rough spots, grooves or other damage. Repair minor damage with a file or oil stone. If the damage is excessive, replace the clutch hub.

b. Inspect the clutch hub splines (**Figure 43**) for rough spots, grooves or other damage. Repair minor damage with a fine cut file or oil stone. If damage is severe, replace the clutch hub. The splines must be in good condition so the clutch plates can slide freely.

c. Inspect the spring towers and threads (**Figure 44**) for thread damage or cracks at the base of the tower. Repair thread damage with the correct size metric tap. If a tower(s) is cracked or damaged, replace the clutch hub.

6. Check the clutch housing for the following conditions:

a. Inspect the clutch housing grooves for cracks or galling (**Figure 45**). Inspect the grooves for cracks or galling. Repair minor damage with a file. If the damage is excessive, replace the clutch housing. The grooves must be in good condition so the friction plates can slide freely.

b. Check the two clutch housing gears (**Figure 46**) for excessive wear, pitting, chipped gear teeth or other damage.

c. Check the clutch housing bore (A, **Figure 47**) where the needle bearings ride for cracks, pitting or other damage.

d. Insert the needle bearings into the housing bore (**Figure 48**) and rotate them. The bearings must rotate smoothly.

e. Inspect the damper springs (B, **Figure 47**) for damage or sagging.

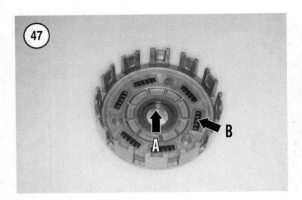

7. Check the needle bearings for excessive wear and damage.

8. Turn the pressure plate bearing (**Figure 49**) inner race by hand. The bearing must turn smoothly.

9. Check the pressure plate (**Figure 50**) for cracks or other damage.

10. If necessary, remove the snap ring (A, **Figure 51**) securing the release head (B). Remove the release head and washers (**Figure 52**) and check for worn or damaged parts. Reinstall (**Figure 53**) and secure with the snap ring.

11. Check each splined washer for nicks, burrs or damage.

12. Inspect the O-ring in the mainshaft groove behind the splines for hardness or deterioration. Replace if necessary.

CLUTCH CABLE REPLACEMENT

1. Disconnect the negative battery cable as described in Chapter Nine.

2. Remove the seat as described in Chapter Fifteen.

3. Remove the fuel tank as described in Chapter Eight.

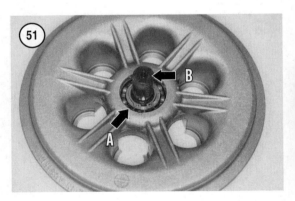

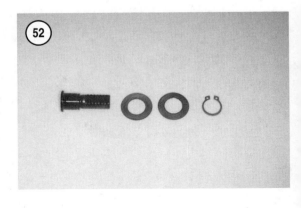

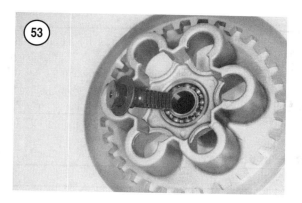

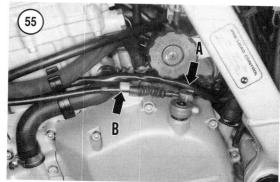

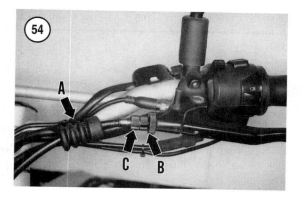

4. At the clutch lever, slide the rubber boot (A, **Figure 54**) off the cable adjuster.

5. Loosen the adjuster locknut (B, **Figure 54**) and turn the adjuster (C) to obtain the maximum cable slack.

6. Disconnect the clutch cable from the hand lever.

7. Disconnect the clutch cable from the release lever (A, **Figure 55**) and from the retainer on the left side crankcase cover (B).

NOTE
Prior to removal, make a drawing of the cable routing through the frame. It is easy to forget the cable's routing path after removing it. Replace the ca-

ble exactly as it was, avoiding any sharp turns.

8. Pull the cable out of any retaining clips on the frame and radiator support (**Figure 56**).

9. Remove the cable and replace it with a new one.

10. Lubricate the clutch before reconnecting it in the following steps. Refer to Chapter Three.

11. Install by reversing these removal steps. Make sure it is correctly routed with no sharp turns. Adjust the clutch cable as described in Chapter Three.

Table 1 CLUTCH SPECIFICATIONS	
Clutch type	Wet multiplate
Clutch lever free play	1.5-2.5 mm (0.06-0.10 in.)
Friction plate thickness	
Individual	3.45-3.55 mm (0.136-0.140 in.)
Service limit stack of all 7	24.0 mm (0.945)
Friction plate distortion limit	0.15 mm (0.006 in.)
	(continued)

Table 1 CLUTCH SPECIFICATIONS (continued)

Steel clutch plate	
Service limit stack of all 7	35.0 mm (1.38 in.)
Distortion limit	0.15 mm (0.006 in.)
Outer diameter (new)	145 mm (5.71 in.)
Clutch springs	
Wear limit	43.0 mm (1.693 in.)

Table 2 CLUTCH TORQUE SPECIFICATIONS

Item	N•m	in.-lb.	ft.-lb.
Pressure plate			
spring bolts	10	88	–
Clutch nut	140	–	103

CHAPTER SEVEN

TRANSMISSION AND GEARSHIFT MECHANISM

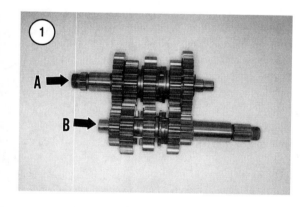

This chapter describes disassembly and assembly of the transmission shafts and internal shift mechanism.

Transmission specifications are in **Table 1** and **Table 2** at the end of the chapter.

TRANSMISSION OPERATION

The transmission has five pairs of constantly meshed gears on the countershaft (A, **Figure 1**) and mainshaft (B). Each pair of meshed gears provides one gear ratio. In each pair, one of the gears is locked to its shaft and always turns with it. The other gear is not locked to its shaft and can spin freely on it. Next to each free-spinning gear is a third gear that is splined to the same shaft, always turning with it. This third gear can slide from side to side along the shaft splines. The side of the sliding gear and the free-spinning gear have mating dogs and slots. When the sliding gear moves up against the free-spinning gear, the two gears are locked together, locking the free spinning gear to its shaft. Since both meshed mainshaft and countershaft gears are now locked to their shafts, power is transmitted at that gear ratio.

Shift Drum and Forks

Each sliding gear has a deep groove machined around its outside (**Figure 2**). The curved shift fork arm rides in this groove, controlling the side-to-side sliding of the gear, and therefore the selection of different gear ratios. Each shift fork (A, **Figure 3**) slides back and forth on a shaft, and has a pin (B) that rides in a groove machined in the shift drum (**Figure 4**). When the shift linkage rotates the shift drum, the zigzag grooves move the shift forks and sliding gears back and forth.

TRANSMISSION

Removal/Installation

Remove and install the transmission and internal shift mechanism as described under *Crankcase Disassembly/Assembly* in Chapter Five.

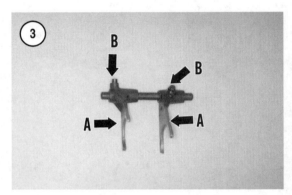

Preliminary Inspection

1. After the transmission shaft assemblies have been removed from the crankcase, clean and inspect the assemblies prior to disassembling them. Place the assembled shaft into a large can or plastic bucket and thoroughly clean it with a petroleum-based solvent, such as kerosene, and a stiff brush. Dry with compressed air or let it sit on rags to drip-dry. Repeat for the other shaft assembly.

2. After they have been cleaned, visually inspect the components of the assemblies for excessive wear. Any burrs, pitting or roughness on the gear teeth will cause wear on the mating gear. Minor roughness can be cleaned up with an oilstone, but there is little point in attempting to remove deep scars.

> *NOTE*
> *Replace defective gears. It is a good idea to replace the mating gear on the other shaft, even though it may not show as much wear or damage.*

3. Carefully check the engagement dogs. If any is chipped, worn, rounded or missing, the affected gear must be replaced.

4. Rotate the transmission bearings (**Figure 5**) by hand. Check for roughness, noise and radial play. Replace any bearing that is suspect.

5. If the transmission shafts are satisfactory and are not going to be disassembled, apply assembly oil or engine oil to all components and reinstall them in the crankcase as described in Chapter Five.

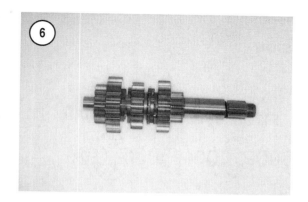

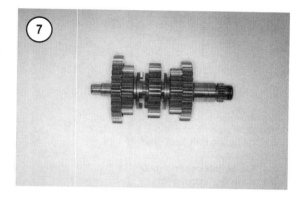

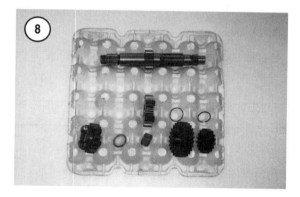

NOTE
If disassembling a used, high-mileage transmission for the first time, pay particular attention to any additional shims that may have been added by a previous owner. These may have been added to take up the tolerance of worn components and must be reinstalled in the same position since the shims have developed a gear wear pattern. If new parts are going to be installed, these shims may be eliminated. This is something that will have to be determined upon reassembly.

Transmission Service Notes

1. As a part is removed from the shaft, set it in the exact order of removal and in the same position from which it was removed. Refer to **Figure 6** for the mainshaft and **Figure 7** for the countershaft. This is an easy way to remember the correct relationship of all parts.

2. Store the transmission gears, washers and snap rings in a divided container, such as a restaurant size egg carton (**Figure 8**) to maintain component alignment and position.

3. The snap rings are a tight fit on the transmission shafts. All snap rings must be replaced during assembly.

4. Snap rings turn and fold over, making removal and installation difficult. To ease replacement, open the snap rings with a pair of snap ring pliers while at the same time holding the back of the snap ring with another pair of pliers. Remove the snap ring (**Figure 9**). Repeat for installation.

TRANSMISSION OVERHAUL

The overhaul procedures refer to the transmission mainshaft and countershaft. The term mainshaft refers to the transmission input shaft. The mainshaft is connected to the clutch outer hub, which is driven by the primary drive gear on the crankshaft. The term countershaft refers to the transmission output shaft. The countershaft drives the engine drive sprocket.

CAUTION
Do not expand the split needle bearings any more than necessary to slide

7

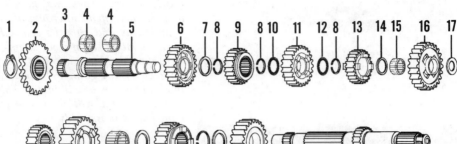

TRANSMISSION

1. Snap ring (models so equipped)
2. Drive sprocket
3. O-ring
4. Split needle bearing
5. Countershaft
6. Countershaft second gear
7. Washer
8. Snap ring
9. Countershaft fifth gear
10. Washer
11. Countershaft third gear
12. Dished splined washer
13. Countershaft fourth gear
14. Washer
15. Split needle bearing
16. Countershaft first gear
17. Washer
18. Mainshaft second gear
19. Mainshaft fifth gear
20. Split needle bearing
21. Washer
22. Mainshaft third gear
23. Washer
24. Mainshaft fourth gear
25. Mainshaft/first gear

them off and onto the shafts. The bearing carriers are plastic and will fracture if expanded too far.

NOTE
BMW uses different terms for the transmission shafts than those referred to in this manual. BMW refers to the mainshaft as the countershaft and also refers to the countershaft as the mainshaft. Keep this in mind when ordering transmission parts. If necessary, refer to the illustrations in this manual when ordering part(s).

Mainshaft Disassembly

Refer to **Figure 10**.

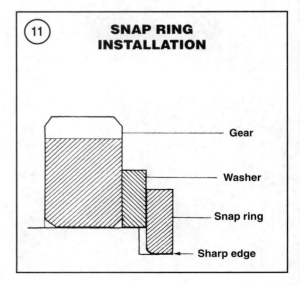

SNAP RING INSTALLATION

- Gear
- Washer
- Snap ring
- Sharp edge

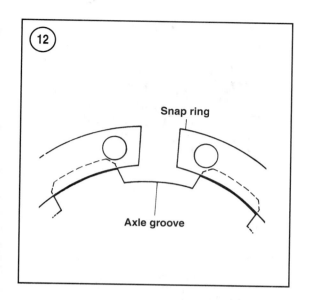

Snap ring

Axle groove

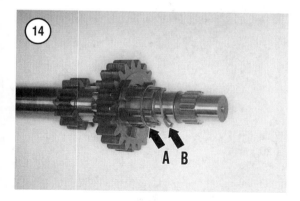

1. If not cleaned in the *Preliminary Inspection* sequence, place the assembled shaft in a large can or plastic bucket and thoroughly clean it with solvent and a stiff brush. Dry with compressed air or let the shaft dry on rags.

2. Slide off the second gear.

3. Slide off the fifth gear and carefully remove the split needle bearing.
4. Slide off the washer.
5. Slide off the third gear.
6. Remove the snap ring and slide off the washer.
7. Slide off the fourth gear.
8. Keep the parts in the exact order of removal and note their installed positions (**Figure 8**).
9. Inspect the mainshaft components as described in this chapter

Mainshaft Assembly

1. Before assembling the mainshaft, note the following:
   a. Always install a *new* snap ring.
   b. Install the snap ring with its chamfered edge facing *away* from the thrust load (**Figure 11**).
   c. Align the snap ring end gaps with the transmission shaft grooves (**Figure 12**).
   d. Lubricate all sliding surfaces with engine oil.
2. Position the fourth gear with the shift dog receptacles going on last and install the fourth gear (**Figure 13**).
3. Slide on the washer (A, **Figure 14**) and install the snap ring (B). Make sure the snap ring is correctly seated in the mainshaft groove (**Figure 15**).
4. Position the third gear with the shift fork groove (A, **Figure 16**) going on first and install the third gear (B).
5. Install the washer (**Figure 17**).
6. Carefully install the split needle bearing (**Figure 18**) and push it up against the third gear.
7. Position the fifth gear with the shift dogs going on first and install the fifth gear (**Figure 19**) onto the split needle bearing.

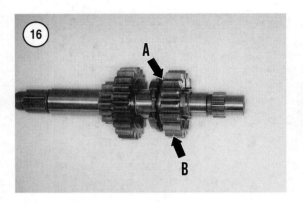

8. Slide on the second gear (**Figure 20**).

9. Refer to **Figure 21** for gear placement. Make sure the snap ring is correctly seated in the mainshaft groove.

10. Make sure each gear engages the adjoining gear properly, where applicable. Spin any non-splined gear on the shaft and check for smooth operation.

Countershaft Disassembly

Refer to **Figure 10**.

1. If not cleaned in the *Preliminary Inspection* sequence, place the assembled shaft into a large can or plastic bucket and thoroughly clean with solvent and a stiff brush. Dry with compressed air or let it sit on rags to dry.

2. Slide off the washer and the first gear.

3. Carefully remove the split needle bearing and washer.

4. Slide off the fourth gear.

> *NOTE*
> *The third gear must slide down the countershaft to access the snap ring securing the third gear.*

5. Release the snap ring located between the third and fifth gear from the snap ring groove. Slide the snap ring (**Figure 22**) toward the fifth gear along with the adjacent washer.

6. Slide the third gear toward the fifth gear to access the snap ring hidden by the splined dished washer (**Figure 23**).

7. Remove the snap ring (A, **Figure 24**) and slide off the splined dished washer (B).

8. Slide off the third gear.

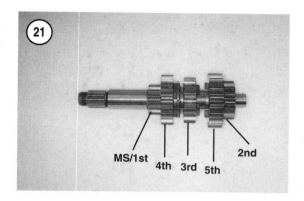

9. Carefully remove the split needle bearing and splined washer.

10. Remove the snap ring and slide off the fifth gear.

11. Remove the snap ring and slide off the washer.

12. Slide off the second gear.

13. Carefully remove the split needle bearing from the transmission shaft groove.

14. Keep the parts in the exact order of removal and note their installed orientations (**Figure 25**).

15. Inspect the countershaft components as described in this chapter

Countershaft Assembly

1. Before assembling the countershaft, note the following:

    a. Always install *new* snap rings.

    b. Install the snap rings with the chamfered edge facing *away* from the thrust load (**Figure 11**).

    c. Align all snap ring end gaps with the transmission shaft grooves (**Figure 12**).

    d. Lubricate all sliding surfaces with engine oil.

2. Carefully install the split needle bearing (**Figure 26**) into the transmission shaft groove.

3. Position the second gear with the shift dog receptacle side going on last and slide on the second gear (**Figure 27**).

4. Slide the washer (A, **Figure 28**) and install the snap ring (B). Make sure the snap ring is correctly seated in the countershaft groove (**Figure 29**).

5. Position the fifth gear with the shift fork groove (**Figure 30**) going on last and install the fifth gear (**Figure 31**).

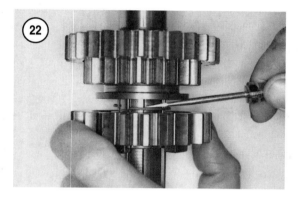

NOTE
The snap ring installed in Step 6 must be positioned down on the shaft so the

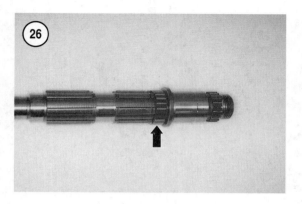

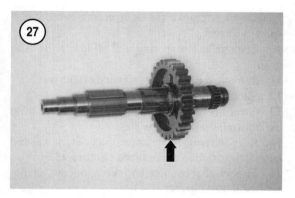

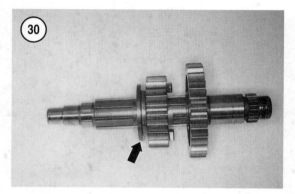

third gear snap ring can be installed in Step 10.

6. Install the snap ring, but do not position it into the correct countershaft groove. Push the snap ring up against the fifth gear (**Figure 32**).

7. Slide on the splined washer and push it against the snap ring (**Figure 33**).

8. Carefully install the split needle bearing (**Figure 34**) into the transmission shaft groove.

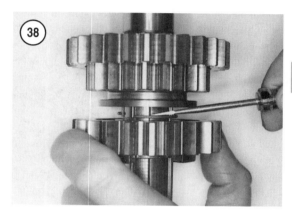

7

9. Position the third gear with the shift dog side going on last and slide on the third gear (**Figure 35**). Push the third gear down against the fifth gear.

10. Position the splined dished washer (A, **Figure 36**) with the recessed, or dished, side going on last. Slide it down against the third gear.

11. Install the snap ring (B, **Figure 36**) into the countershaft groove (**Figure 37**). Make sure it is seated correctly in the countershaft groove.

12. Slide the splined dished washer back onto the snap ring.

13. Move the third gear up against the dished washer and snap ring.

14. Slide the washer, installed in Step 7, against the third gear and install the snap ring into the correct countershaft groove (**Figure 38**). Make sure the snap ring is correctly seated correctly in the countershaft groove.

15. Position the fourth gear with the shift fork groove (**Figure 39**) going on first and install the fourth gear (**Figure 40**).

16. Install the washer (**Figure 41**).

B   A

17. Carefully install the split needle bearing (**Figure 42**) into the transmission shaft.

> *NOTE*
> *The first gear is not symmetrical and must be installed correctly. The side with the deepest recess shown in **Figure 43** must go on first for the transmission to operate correctly.*

18. Position the first gear with the deeper recess side going on first and install the first gear (**Figure 44**).

19. Install the washer (**Figure 45**).

20. Refer to **Figure 46** for correct placement of all gears. Make sure all snap rings are correctly seated in the countershaft grooves.

21. After both transmission shafts have been assembled, mesh the two assemblies together in the correct position (**Figure 47**). Check that each gear engages to the adjoining gear properly, where applicable. This is the last check prior to installing the shaft assemblies into the crankcase; make sure they are correctly assembled.

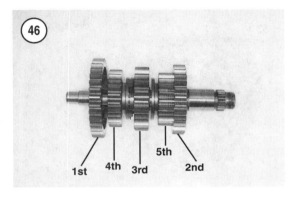

1st 4th 3rd 5th 2nd

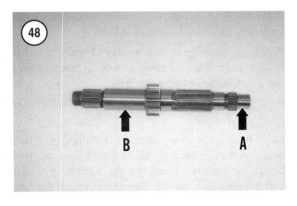

B A

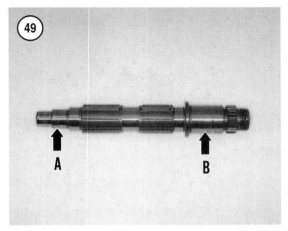

A B

TRANSMISSION INSPECTION

Maintain the alignment of the transmission components when cleaning and inspecting the individual parts in the following section. To prevent intermixing the parts, work on only one shaft at a time.

Refer to **Table 2** and inspect the dimensions of the indicated shafts. Replace parts that show excessive wear or damage as described in this section.

CAUTION
Do not clean the split bearings in solvent. It is difficult to remove all traces of solvent from the plastic bearing retainers. Flush the bearings clean with new transmission oil.

1. Clean and dry the shaft assemblies.
2. Inspect the mainshaft and countershaft:
    a. Worn or damages splines.
    b. On the mainshaft, missing, broken or chipped first gear teeth.
    c. Excessively worn or damaged bearing surfaces.
    d. Cracked or rounded-off snap ring grooves.
3. Measure the outer diameter of each end of both shafts as follows:
    a. On the mainshaft, measure the alternator side (A, **Figure 48**) and the clutch housing side (B).
    b. On the countershaft, measure the alternator side (A, **Figure 49**) and the clutch housing side (B).
4. Check each gear for excessive wear, burrs, pitting, or chipped or missing teeth. Check the inner

splines on sliding gears. Refer to **Figure 50** and **Figure 51**. Check the bore (**Figure 52**) on gears that ride on the shaft, or on the needle bearings, for excessive wear or damage.

5. To check stationary gears for wear, install them on their correct shaft along with the needle bearings (**Figure 53**), and in their original operating position. If necessary, use the old snap rings to secure them in place. Then spin the gear by hand. The gear should turn smoothly. A rough-turning gear indicates heat damage–check for a dark blue color or galling on the operating surfaces. Also check the needle bearing for damage. Rocking indicates excessive wear, either to the gear, the needle bearing or shaft or a combination of all three.

6. To check the sliding gears, install them on their correct shaft in their original operating position. The gear should slide back and forth without any binding or excessive play.

7. Check the dogs (**Figure 54**) on the gears for excessive wear, rounding, cracks or other damage. When wear is noticeable, make sure it is consistent on each gear dog. If one dog is worn more than the others, the others will be overstressed during opera-

tion and will eventually crack and fail. Check engaging gears as described in Step 9.

8. Check each gear dog recess (**Figure 55**) for cracks, rounding and other damage. Check engaging gears as described in Step 9.

9. Check the shift fork groove (**Figure 56**) for wear and other damage.

10. Check engaging gears by installing the two gears on their respective shaft and in their original operating position. Mesh the gears together. Twist one gear against the other and then check the dog

55

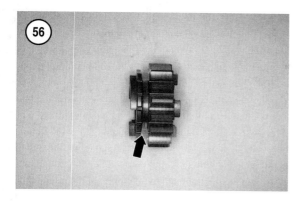

56

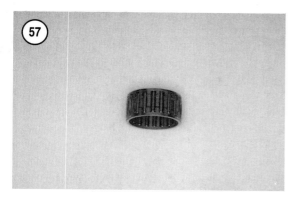

57

58

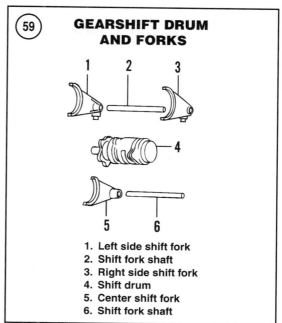

59

GEARSHIFT DRUM AND FORKS

1. Left side shift fork
2. Shift fork shaft
3. Right side shift fork
4. Shift drum
5. Center shift fork
6. Shift fork shaft

engagement. Then reverse the thrust load to check in the other operating position. Make sure the engagement in both directions is positive and without any slippage. Check that there is equal engagement across all of the engagement dogs.

NOTE
*When there is excessive or uneven wear to the gear engagement dogs, check the shift forks carefully for bending and other damage. Refer to **Internal Shift Mechanism** in this chapter.*

NOTE
Replace defective gears along with their mating gears, though they may not show as much wear or damage.

11. Check the split needle bearings (**Figure 57**) for excessive wear or damage.
12. Replace all of the snap rings during assembly. In addition, check the washers (**Figure 58**) for burn marks, scoring or cracks and replace as necessary.

INTERNAL SHIFT MECHANISM

Removal/Installation

Refer to **Figure 59** and **Figure 60**.

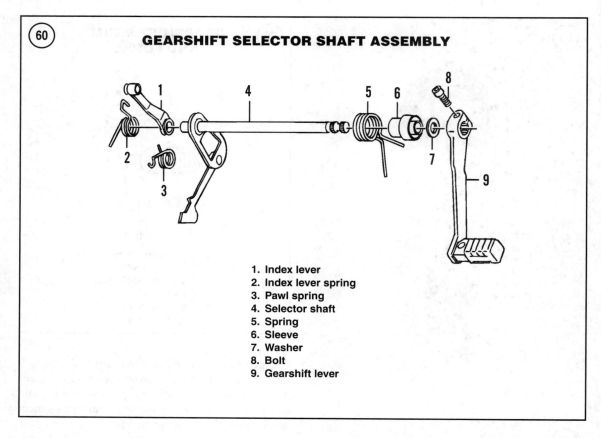

(60)

GEARSHIFT SELECTOR SHAFT ASSEMBLY

1. Index lever
2. Index lever spring
3. Pawl spring
4. Selector shaft
5. Spring
6. Sleeve
7. Washer
8. Bolt
9. Gearshift lever

Remove and install the transmission and internal shift mechanism as described in Chapter Five.

Shift Drum Inspection

1. Thoroughly clean the shift drum assembly in solvent and dry.

2. Check the shift drum (**Figure 61**) for:

   a. Scored or damaged bearing surfaces.

   b. Excessively worn or damaged grooves.

3. Inspect the shift cam (**Figure 62**) for wear or damage.

4. Check the neutral switch pin and insulator disc (**Figure 63**) for wear or damage.

Shift Fork Inspection

When measuring the shift fork components in this section, compare the actual measurements to the specifications listed in **Table 2**. Replace parts that are out of specification or damaged.

(61)

(62)

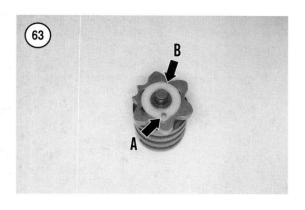

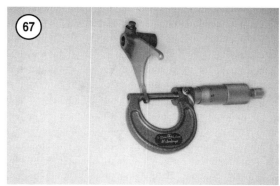

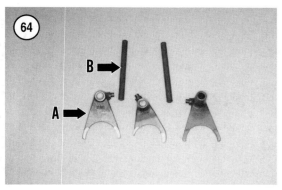

1. Inspect each shift fork (A, **Figure 64**) for signs of wear or damage. Examine the shift forks at the points where they contact the slider gear. These surfaces must be smooth with no signs of excessive wear, bending, cracking, heat discoloration or other damage.

2. Check each shift fork for arc-shaped wear or burn marks (**Figure 65**). These marks indicate a bent shift fork.

3. Check the shift fork shafts (B, **Figure 64**) for bending or other damage. Install each shift fork (**Figure 66**) on its shaft and slide it back and forth. Each shift fork must slide smoothly with no binding or tight spots. If there is any binding, check the shaft closely for bending.

4. Measure the thickness of each shift fork finger (**Figure 67**).

5. Measure the outside diameter of the shift fork guide pin (**Figure 68**).

Selector Shaft Assembly Inspection

1. Clean all parts in solvent and dry with compressed air.

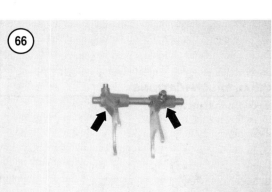

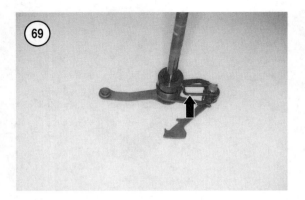

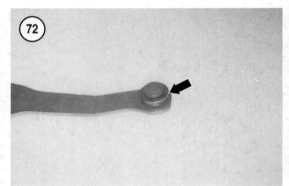

2. Inspect the index lever spring (**Figure 69**) on the selector shaft assembly. If it is broken or weak, it must be replaced.

3. Inspect the selector shaft assembly (**Figure 70**) for bending, wear or other damage; replace, if necessary.

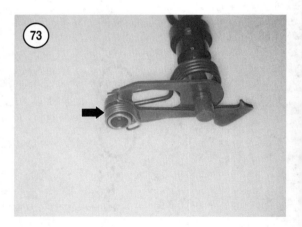

4. Inspect the index lever (**Figure 71**) and related parts for wear or damage. Replace any worn or damaged parts. Make sure the index lever roller (**Figure 72**) operates smoothly.

5. Inspect the pawl spring (**Figure 73**) on the selector shaft assembly. If broken or weak, it must be replaced.

Table 1 TRANSMISSION GENERAL SPECIFICATIONS

Transmission type	5-speed, constant mesh
Gear ratios	
First	2.750
Second	1.750
Third	1.313
Fourth	1.045
Fifth	0.875

Table 2 TRANSMISSION SERVICE SPECIFICATIONS

Item	mm	in.
Countershaft wear limit diameter		
Alternator side	16.98	0.669
Clutch side	24.97	0.983
Mainshaft wear limit diameter		
Alternator side	24.98	0.983
Clutch side	16.98	0.669
Shift forks		
Finger wear limit thickness	3.45	0.136
Guide pin wear limit diameter	5.85	0.230

7

CHAPTER EIGHT

FUEL, EXHAUST AND EMISSION CONTROL SYSTEMS

The fuel system consists of the fuel tank, fuel shutoff valve, dual Mikuni side-draft carburetors and the air filter housing.

The emission control consists of a closed loop crankcase ventilation, a catalytic converter on all models, a secondary air system on U.S. and Switzerland models and the evaporative emission control system on all California models.

This chapter includes service procedures for all parts of the fuel system and the air filter air box. Air filter service is covered in Chapter Three.

Carburetor specifications are in **Table 1** at the end of the chapter.

WARNING
Gasoline is a known carcinogen, as well as an extremely flammable liquid, and must be handled carefully. Wear latex gloves to avoid contact. If gasoline does contact skin, immediately and thoroughly wash the area with soap and warm water.

CARBURETOR OPERATION

An understanding of the function of each of the carburetor components and their relation to one another is a valuable aid for pinpointing a source of carburetor trouble.

The carburetor's purpose is to supply and atomize fuel and mix it in correct proportions with air that is drawn in through the air intake. At the primary throttle opening (idle), a small amount of fuel is siphoned through the pilot jet by the incoming air. As the throttle is opened further, the air stream begins to siphon fuel through the main jet and needle jet. The tapered needle increases the effective flow capacity of the needle jet as it is lifted, in that it occupies progressively less of the area of the jet. At full throttle, the carburetor venturi is fully open and the needle lifts far enough to permit the main jet to flow at full capacity.

The choke circuit is a starting enrichment valve system in which the control lever on the handlebar left side handlebar grip opens an enrichment valve,

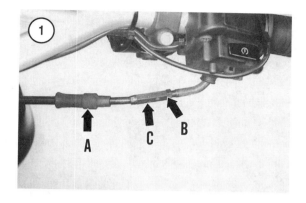

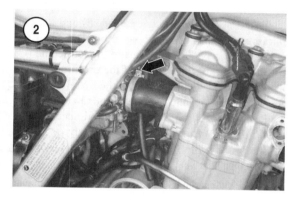

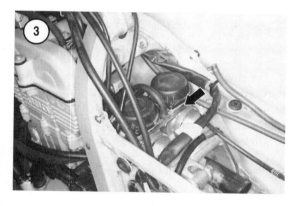

rather than closing a butterfly in the venturi area as on some carburetors. In the open position, the slow jet discharges a stream of fuel into the carburetor venturi to enrich the mixture when the engine is cold.

The accelerator pump circuit reduces engine hesitation by injecting a fine spray of fuel into the carburetor intake passage during sudden acceleration.

CARBURETOR

Removal

1. Remove the seat as described in Chapter Fifteen.
2. Remove the fuel tank as described in this chapter.
3. Remove the battery as described in Chapter Three.
4. Remove the battery box as described in Chapter Nine.
5. Remove the air filter box as described in this chapter.
6. At the handlebar, perform the following:
   a. Slide the rubber boot (A, **Figure 1**) off the cable adjuster.
   b. Loosen the adjuster locknut (B, **Figure 1**) and turn the adjuster (C) to obtain maximum cable slack.
7. Loosen the hose clamp screw (**Figure 2**) on each carburetor at the intake stub pipe on the cylinder head.
8. Carefully pull the carburetor assembly (**Figure 3**) straight back out of the intake stub pipe.
9. Loosen the locknut (A, **Figure 4**) and disconnect the starting enrichment (choke) valve cable from the left side carburetor body. Move the end of the cable out of the way.
10. Disconnect the throttle cable from the carburetor throttle wheel (B, **Figure 4**).
11. Disconnect the fuel supply hose (C, **Figure 4**) from the carburetor fitting.
12. Drain the gasoline from the carburetor assembly.
13. Insert a clean lint-free shop cloth into the intake stub pipe openings.

Installation

1. If removed, install the hose clamps onto the intake stub pipe.

2. Connect the fuel supply hose (C, **Figure 4**) onto the carburetor fitting.

3. Connect the throttle cable onto the carburetor throttle wheel (B, **Figure 4**).

4. Position the starting enrichment valve cable into the carburetor, then tighten the locknut (A, **Figure 4**) securely.

5. Remove the cloths from the intake stub pipe openings.

6. Carefully install the carburetor assembly (**Figure 3**) straight onto the intake stub pipe. Push the assembly in until it bottoms.

> *CAUTION*
> *The carburetor assembly must fit squarely onto the intake stub pipe. If misaligned, it may result in a vacuum leak.*

7. Tighten the hose clamp screws securely (**Figure 2**).

8. Make sure the vent tube is positioned correctly as shown in **Figure 5** to avoid contact with the throttle linkage.

9. Operate the hand throttle a few times, making sure the throttle wheel operates smoothly with no binding. If there is any binding, check the vent tube position as previously described.

10. Install the air filter box as described in this chapter.

11. Install the battery box as described in Chapter Nine.

12. Install the battery as described in Chapter Three.

13. Install the fuel tank as described in this chapter.

14. Install the seat as described in Chapter Fifteen.

15. Adjust the throttle cable as described in Chapter Three.

16. Adjust the idle speed as described in Chapter Three.

Disassembly

To avoid the accidental interchange of parts, disassemble, clean and reassemble one carburetor at a time.

1. Remove the carburetor assembly (**Figure 6**) as described in this chapter.

2. Remove the screws (**Figure 7**) that secure the top cover and remove the cover.

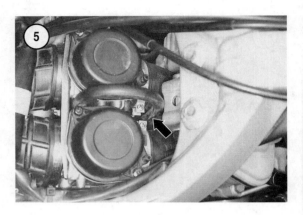

3. Withdraw the spring (A, **Figure 8**) and the diaphragm and throttle slide assembly (B) from the carburetor body. Do not damage the jet needle (C) extending out of the bottom of the throttle slide.

4. Remove the screws securing the float bowl (**Figure 9**) and remove the float bowl and O-ring gasket.

5. Remove the float holder, float and needle valve (A, **Figure 10**) from the carburetor body.

6. Remove the rubber plug (B, **Figure 10**) covering the mixture screw.

> *NOTE*
> *Prior to removing the mixture screw, carefully screw it in until it **lightly** seats. Record the number of turns so it can be installed in the same position.*

7. Unscrew the mixture screw (**Figure 11**). Remove the screw, the spring, shim washer and O-ring.

8. Unscrew and remove the idle jet (**Figure 12**).

9. Unscrew and remove the main jet (A, **Figure 13**).

10. Remove the needle valve seat (B, **Figure 13**).

11. Remove the semi-circular slide (**Figure 14**) and O-ring and main jet nozzle from the carburetor body.

12. Carefully withdraw the jet needle assembly from the throttle slide/diaphragm assembly.

Cleaning and Inspection

Replace worn or damaged parts as described in this section.

> *CAUTION*
> *The carburetor body is equipped with plastic parts that cannot be removed.*

CARBURETOR

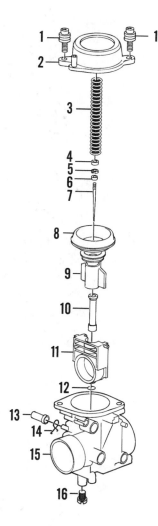

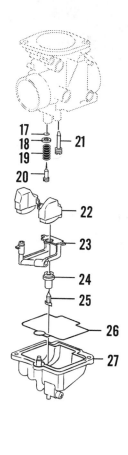

8

1. Screw
2. Top cover
3. Spring
4. Spring support
5. Circlip
6. Plastic ring
7. Jet needle
8. Diaphragm
9. Throttle slide
10. Main jet nozzle
11. Semi-circular slide
12. O-ring
13. Cap
14. Clamp

15. Main body
16. Main jet
17. O-ring
18. Shim washer
19. Spring
20. Mixture screw
21. Idle jet
22. Float
23. Float holder
24. Needle valve seat
25. Needle valve
26. O-ring gasket
27. Float chamber

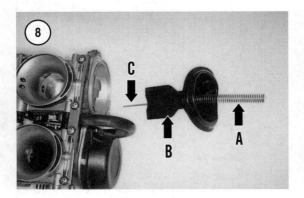

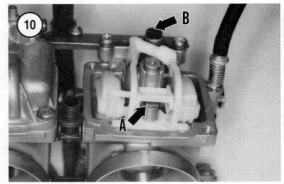

> *Do not dip the carburetor body, O-rings, float assembly, needle valve or diaphragm in a caustic carburetor cleaner that can damage these parts. The use of a caustic carburetor cleaning solvent is not recommended. Instead, clean the carburetor and related parts in a petroleum-based solvent, or Simple Green. Then rinse in clean water.*

1. Initially clean all parts in a mild petroleum based cleaning solution. Then clean in hot soap and water and rinse with cold water. Dry with compressed air.

> *CAUTION*
> *If compressed air is not available, allow the parts to air-dry or use a clean lint-free cloth. Do **not** use a paper towel to dry carburetor parts, as small paper particles may plug openings in the carburetor housing or jets.*

2. Allow the carburetors to dry thoroughly before assembly and dry with compressed air. Blow out the jets and the needle jet holder with compressed air.

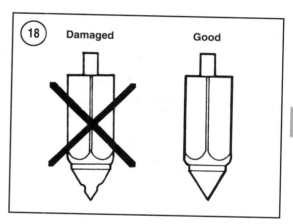

Damaged   Good

8

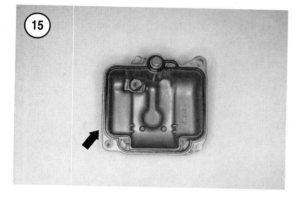

CAUTION
*Do **not** use wire or drill bits to clean jets, as minor gouges in the jet can alter flow rate and the air/fuel mixture.*

3. Inspect the float bowl O-ring gasket (**Figure 15**) for hardness or deterioration.

4. Inspect the throttle slide diaphragm (A, **Figure 16**) for cracks or deterioration. Check the throttle slide sides (B) for excessive wear. Install the throttle slide into the carburetor body and move it up and down in the semi-circular slide. The throttle slide should move smoothly with no binding or excessive play. If there is excessive play, the throttle slide and/or semi-circular slide must be replaced.

5. Inspect the needle valve tapered end (**Figure 17**) for steps, uneven wear or other damage (**Figure 18**).

6. Inspect the needle valve seat for steps, uneven wear or other damage. Insert the needle valve and slowly move it back and forth to check for smooth operation. If either part is worn or damaged, replace both parts as a pair for maximum performance.

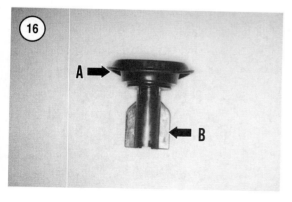

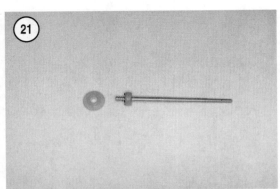

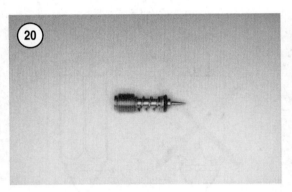

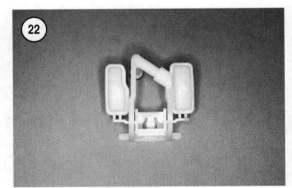

7. Inspect the main jet nozzle, main jet and idle jet (**Figure 19**). Make sure all holes are open and none of the parts are either worn or damaged.

8. Inspect the mixture screw, spring, shim washer and O-ring (**Figure 20**) for deterioration or damage.

9. Inspect the jet needle, plastic ring, circlip and spring support (**Figure 21**) for deterioration or damage.

10. Inspect the jet needle tapered end for steps, uneven wear or other damage.

11. Inspect the float (**Figure 22**) for deterioration or damage. Place it in a container of water and push it down. If the float sinks or if bubbles appear, a leak is indicated. Replace the float.

12. Inspect the semi-circular slide (**Figure 23**) for wear or damage.

13. Make sure the throttle plate (A, **Figure 24**) screws are tight. Tighten if necessary.

14. Move the throttle wheel (B, **Figure 24**) back and forth from stop-to-stop and check for free movement. The throttle lever should move smoothly and return under spring tension.

15. Check the throttle wheel return spring for free movement. Make sure the spring rotates the throttle wheel back to the stop position with no hesitation.

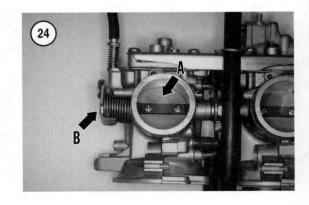

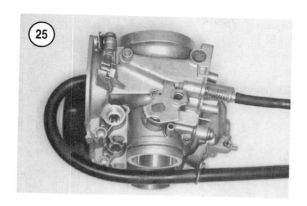

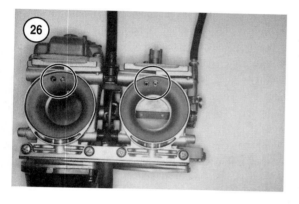

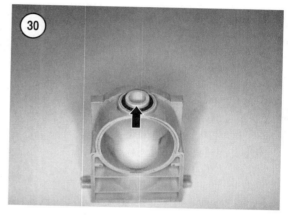

8

16. Make sure all openings in the carburetor housing are clear of all debris. Refer to **Figures 26-28**. Apply compressed air to all openings.

17. Inspect the carburetor body **(Figure 25)** for internal or external damage. If damaged, replace the carburetor assembly, as the body cannot be replaced separately.

18. Check the top cover for cracks or damage.

19. Check the starting enrichment valve and cable for damage.

20. Carefully pull the fuel strainer (**Figure 29**) from the fuel inlet fitting and clean out if necessary.

Assembly

1. If the semi-circular slide was disassembled, install a *new* O-ring (**Figure 30**) and install the main jet nozzle (**Figure 31**).

> *NOTE*
> *The flat on the main jet nozzle (A, **Figure 32**) must align with the small*

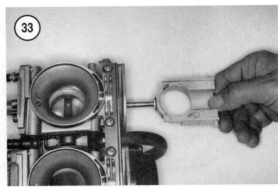

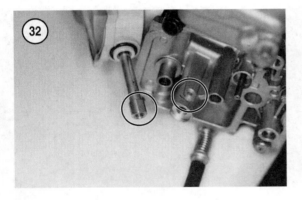

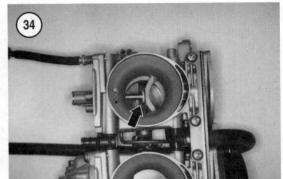

raised pin (B) on the raised tunnel in
the main body.

2. Install the semi-circular slide and main jet nozzle (**Figure 33**) into the carburetor body. Align the
main jet nozzle with the small raised pin, then push
it down until it bottoms (**Figure 34**).

3. Install the main jet (**Figure 35**) and tighten securely.

4. Install a *new* O-ring (**Figure 36**) onto the needle
valve seat and install the needle valve seat (**Figure
37**).

5. Install the idle jet (**Figure 38**) and tighten securely.

6. Install the mixture screw (**Figure 39**), spring,
shim washer and O-ring and lightly seat it. Then
back the screw out the number of turns recorded
during disassembly.

7. Install the rubber plug (**Figure 40**) and press it
down until it is seated.

8. Install the O-ring (**Figure 41**) onto the float
holder.

9. Install the float and float holder (**Figure 42**) onto
the carburetor body. Push the float holder down until it bottoms.

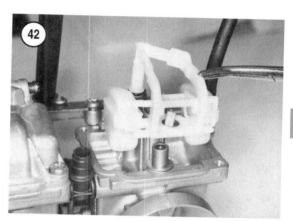

8

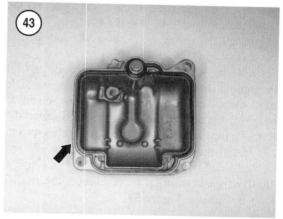

10. Check the float level as described in this chapter.

11. Make sure the float bowl O-ring gasket (**Figure 43**) is in place and install the float bowl (**Figure 44**). Tighten the screws securely.

12. Carefully insert the jet needle assembly (**Figure 45**) into the throttle slide/diaphragm assembly.

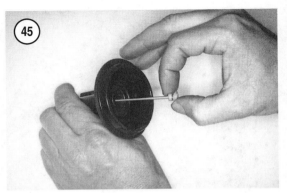

Insert the spring support on top of the jet needle to hold the jet needle in place.

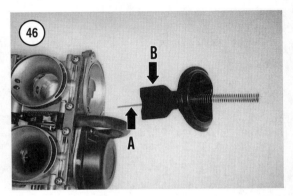

> *CAUTION*
> *During installation, do not damage the jet needle (A, **Figure 46**) extending out of the bottom of the throttle slide.*

13. Align the slides (B, **Figure 46**) on the throttle slide with the grooves in the carburetor and semi-circular slide bore. The slides on the throttle slide are offset, so the throttle slide can only be installed one way. Install the diaphragm and throttle slide assembly into the carburetor body.

14. Seat the outer edge of the diaphragm into the carburetor body groove (**Figure 47**).

15. Install the spring (A, **Figure 48**) and the top cover (B).

16. Hold the carburetor top cover in place and lift the throttle slide with your finger. The throttle slide must move smoothly. If the throttle movement is rough or sluggish, the spring is installed incorrectly. Remove the carburetor top and reinstall the spring.

17. Install the top cover screws (**Figure 49**) and tighten securely.

18. If removed, position the vent tube in the bracket loop as shown in **Figure 50**.

Float Adjustment

The carburetor must be removed and partially disassembled for this adjustment.

1. Remove the carburetor as described in this chapter.

2. Remove the screws securing the float bowl (**Figure 44**) and remove the float bowl and O-ring gasket.

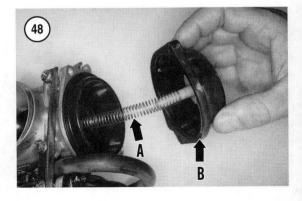

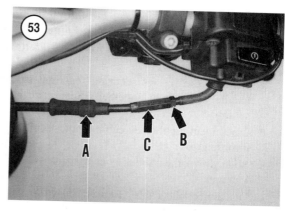

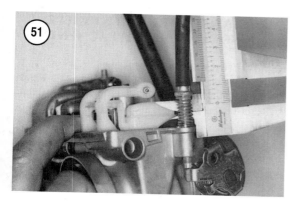

3. Hold the float holder securely in place during this procedure.

4. Tilt the carburetor upward about 30° until the float tang makes contact with the needle valve. The under side of the float must be parallel to the seating surface of the float chamber.

5. At this point the under side of the float should be 14.6 mm (0.57 in.) above the seating surface of the float bowl (**Figure 51**).

6. If the float level is incorrect, carefully bend the float tang (**Figure 52**) to achieve the correct height.

7. Recheck the float level.

8. Repeat these steps until the float level is correct.

9. Install the float bowl and carburetor as described in this chapter.

THROTTLE CABLE

Removal/Installation

1. Remove the seat as described in Chapter Fifteen.

2. Remove the fuel tank as described in this chapter.

3. Record the throttle cable routing from the carburetor through the frame to the right side handlebar.

4. At the handlebar, perform the following:

    a. Slide the rubber boot (A, **Figure 53**) off the cable adjuster.

    b. Loosen the adjuster locknut (B, **Figure 53**) and turn the adjuster (C) to obtain maximum cable slack.

NOTE
In Step 5, the carburetor is shown partially removed to better illustrate the step.

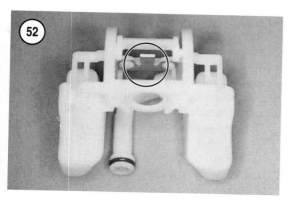

5. On the left side, disconnect the throttle cable from the carburetor throttle wheel (A, **Figure 54**).

6. Disconnect the throttle cable from the throttle grip as follows:

    a. Remove the screws securing the right side handlebar switch together. Separate the switch.

    b. Disconnect the throttle cable nipple from the throttle grip.

    c. Slide down the rubber boot and loosen the locknut.

    d. Disconnect the cable (**Figure 55**) from the lower portion of the handlebar switch assembly.

7. Remove all tie-wraps securing the throttle cable from the frame backbone.

8. Disconnect the cable from the wire loop (**Figure 56**) on the right side of the steering head.

9. Remove the cable from the frame.

10. Remove the bolt and weight and slide the throttle grip off the handlebar.

11. Clean the throttle grip assembly and dry thoroughly. Check the throttle slots for cracks or other damage. Replace the throttle if necessary.

12. Clean the throttle area on the handlebar with solvent.

13. Installation is the reverse of these steps while noting the following:

    a. Apply a light coat of Shell Retinax EP2, or an equivalent, to the handlebar prior to installing the throttle grip.

    b. Adjust the throttle cable as described in Chapter Three.

    c. Install all removed components.

    d. Start the engine and allow it to idle in NEUTRAL. Then turn the handlebar from side to side. Do not operate the throttle. If the engine speed increases when turning the handlebar assembly, the throttle cable is routed incorrectly or damaged. Recheck cable routing and adjustment.

WARNING
Do not ride the motorcycle until the throttle cables are properly adjusted. Improper cable routing and adjustment can cause the throttle to stick open. This could cause loss of control. Recheck the work before riding the motorcycle.

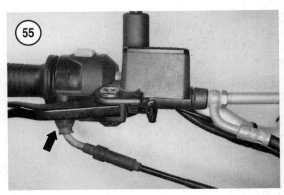

STARTING ENRICHMENT VALVE (CHOKE) CABLE REPLACMENT

Removal/Installation

1. Remove the seat as described in Chapter Fifteen.

2. Remove the fuel tank as described in this chapter.

3. Record the starting enrichment valve cable routing from the carburetor through the frame to the left side handlebar.

NOTE
In Step 4, the carburetor is shown partially removed to better illustrate the step.

4. Loosen the locknut and disconnect the starting enrichment valve cable (B, **Figure 54**).

5. Disconnect the starting enrichment valve cable from the left side handlebar switch as follows:

    a. Remove the screws that secure the left side handlebar switch together. Separate the switch.

    b. Disconnect the cable nipple from the control lever

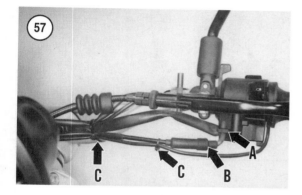

c. Loosen the cable locknut (A, **Figure 57**).

d. Disconnect the cable (B, **Figure 57**) from the lower portion of the handlebar switch assembly.

6. Remove all tie-wraps (C, **Figure 57**) securing the starting enrichment valve cable from the left side switch and handlebar heater cables.

7. Disconnect the cable from the wire loops on the left side of the steering head and frame back bone.

8. Installation is the reverse of these steps while noting the following:

    a. Apply a light coat of Shell Retinax EP2, or an equivalent, to the starting enrichment valve lever and handlebar area. Move the lever back and forth to check for free movement.

    b. Install all components removed.

FUEL TANK

WARNING
Some fuel may spill from the fuel tank hose when performing this procedure. Because gasoline is extremely flammable and explosive, perform this

procedure away from all open flames (including appliance pilot lights) and sparks. Do not smoke or allow anyone to smoke in the work area, as an explosion and fire may occur. Always work in a well-ventilated area. Wipe up any spills immediately.

WARNING
Make sure to route the fuel tank vapor hoses so that they cannot contact any hot engine or exhaust component. These hoses contain flammable vapors. If a hose melts from contacting a hot part, leaking vapors may ignite and cause a fire.

Removal

Refer to **Figure 58**.

1. Disconnect the negative battery cable as described in Chapter Nine.

2. Turn the fuel valve to the OFF position (A, **Figure 59**).

3. Remove the hose clamp and disconnect the fuel hose (B, **Figure 59**) from the valve.

4A. On F650 ST models, remove the fuel filler cap as follows:

    a. Using the ignition key, open the fuel filler cap and remove it.

    b. Remove the screws securing the neck ring and remove the upper neck ring.

4B. On F650 models, remove the fuel filler cap as follows:

    a. Using the ignition key, open the fuel filler cap.

NOTE
*It is not necessary to remove the following screws. Loosen and leave them in place on the flange (**Figure 60**). This will lessen the chance of dropping the screws into the fuel tank.*

    b. Loosen the Torx screws (A, **Figure 61**) securing the fuel filler cap to the fuel tank. Be careful not to drop the single inner Torx screw (B) into the fuel tank.

    c. Pull the filler cap assembly straight up and off the fuel tank and cover.

5. Refer to Chapter Fifteen and perform the following:

    a. Remove the seat.

8

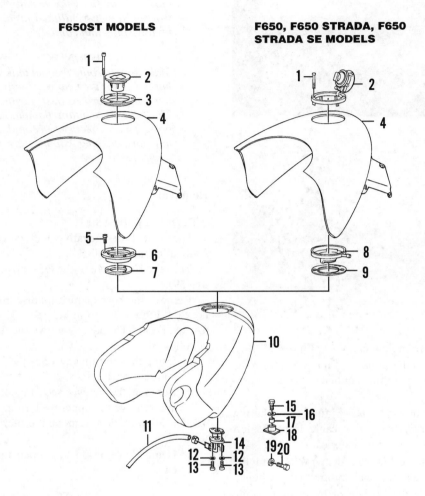

FUEL TANK AND COVER

F650ST MODELS

F650, F650 STRADA, F650 STRADA SE MODELS

1. Bolt
2. Filler cap
3. Neck ring-upper
4. Fuel tank cover
5. Bolt
6. Neck ring
7. Gasket
8. Catch ring
9. Gasket
10. Fuel tank
11. Fuel hose
12. Washer
13. Screw
14. Shutoff valve
15. Screw
16. Washer
17. Collar
18. Post
19. Washer
20. Bolt

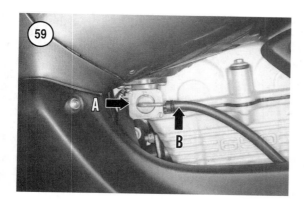

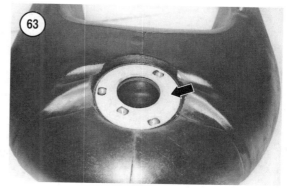

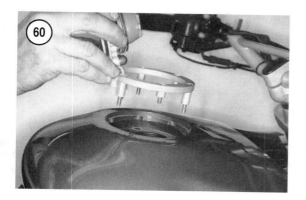

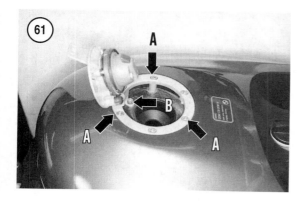

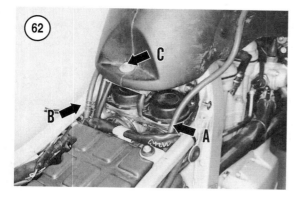

b. Remove the cylinder head cover on both sides.

c. Remove the fuel tank cover.

6. Disconnect the fuel tank evaporation vent hose connector (A, **Figure 62**) at the frame cross member. Leave the remaining vent hose routed through the frame to the charcoal canister.

7. Disconnect the fuel tank overflow connector (B, **Figure 62**) at the frame cross member. Leave the remaining overflow hose routed through frame.

8. At the rear of the fuel tank, remove the bolt, washer and collar (C, **Figure 62**) securing the fuel tank to the frame.

9. Carefully pull the fuel tank toward the rear and up to lift it off the frame.

> *WARNING*
> *Store the fuel tank in a safe place—away from open flames or where it could be damaged.*

10. Drain any remaining fuel left in the tank into a gas can.

11. Inspect the fuel tank and the filler cap as described in this chapter.

Installation

1. On F650 models, make sure the gasket (**Figure 63**) and overflow and vent hose assembly (**Figure 64**) are in place on top of the fuel tank.

2. Install the fuel tank onto the frame and move it into position.

3. At the rear of the fuel tank, install the collar, washer and bolt (C, **Figure 62**) that secure the fuel tank to the frame.

4. Connect the fuel tank overflow connector (B, **Figure 62**) to the remaining overflow hose at the

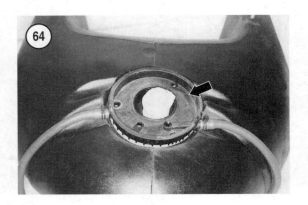

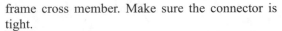

frame cross member. Make sure the connector is tight.

5. Connect the fuel tank evaporation vent hose connector (A, **Figure 62**) to the remaining charcoal canister vent hose at the frame cross member. Make sure the connector is tight.

6. Correctly position the fuel tank evaporation vent hose (**Figure 65**) into the recess on the right side of the fuel tank.

7. Correctly position the fuel tank overflow hose (**Figure 66**) into the recess on the left side of the fuel tank.

8. Make sure to locate all hoses and cables between the fuel tank and the frame cross member as shown in **Figure 67**.

9. Refer to Chapter Fifteen and perform the following:

    a. Install the fuel tank cover.

    b. Install the cylinder head cover on both sides.

    c. Install the seat.

10A. On F650 ST models, remove the fuel filler cap as follows:

    a. Install the upper neck ring and screws. Tighten the screws securely.

    b. Install the fuel filler cap and lock it.

10B. On F650 models, install the fuel filler cap as follows:

    a. With the screws in place, install the filler cap assembly straight down and onto the fuel tank and cover.

    b. Tighten the Torx screws (A and B, **Figure 61**) that secure the fuel filler cap to the fuel tank. Tighten the screws securely, but do not overtighten as the threaded inserts in the fuel tank may pull out.

    c. Close the fuel filler cap.

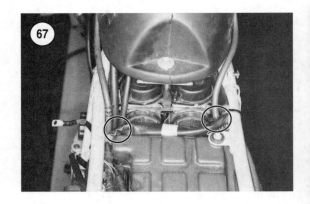

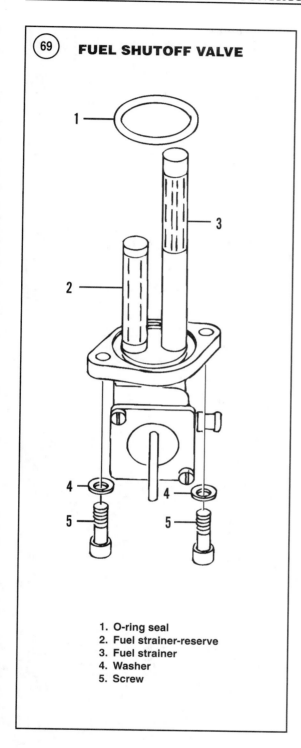

(69) FUEL SHUTOFF VALVE

1. O-ring seal
2. Fuel strainer-reserve
3. Fuel strainer
4. Washer
5. Screw

13. Connect the negative battery cable as described in Chapter Nine.

Inspection

1. Inspect the gasket (**Figure 63**) for hardness or deterioration. Replace if necessary.
2. Inspect the overflow and vent hose assembly (**Figure 64**). Make sure the hoses are clear and not cracked or deteriorated. Replace damaged hoses with the same type and size materials.
3. Check the fuel line for damage. The fuel line must be flexible and strong enough to withstand engine heat and vibration.
4. Check the fuel tank mounting tab for cracking or damage.
5. Inspect the threaded inserts (**Figure 64**) for looseness and thread damage. The individual inserts are not available and if any are damaged, replace the fuel tank.
6. Inspect the tank for contamination. If necessary, clean and flush the tank.
7. Inspect the fuel tank for leaks.
8. Inspect the fuel filler cap (**Figure 68**) for rust. Check the gasket surfaces for deterioration and hardness. If damaged, replace the fuel filler cap.

FUEL SHUTOFF VALVE

Removal/Installation

Refer to **Figure 69**.

> *WARNING*
> *Gasoline is very volatile and presents an extreme fire hazard. Be sure to work in a well-ventilated area away from any open flames (including pilot lights on household appliances). Do not allow anyone to smoke in the area and have a fire extinguisher rated for gasoline fires nearby.*

1. Disconnect the negative battery cable as described in Chapter Nine.
2. Turn the fuel valve to the OFF position (A, **Figure 70**).
3. Remove the hose clamp and disconnect the fuel hose (B, **Figure 70**) from the valve.
4. Attach a fuel hose to the fuel shutoff valve, turn the valve to the RES position and drain the gasoline

11. Reconnect the fuel hose (B, **Figure 59**) to the fuel valve and secure it with a *new* hose clamp.
12. Refill the tank, turn the fuel valve to the ON position and check for leaks.

8

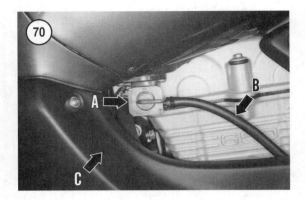

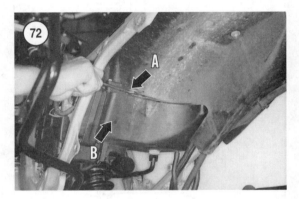

from the fuel tank into a suitable container. Turn the valve to the OFF position.

5. Remove the left side cylinder head cover (C, **Figure 70**) as described in Chapter Fifteen.

NOTE
*The fuel shutoff valve can be removed with the fuel tank in place. **Figure 71** is shown with the fuel tank removed to better illustrate the step.*

6. Remove the screws and washers that secure the fuel shutoff valve (**Figure 71**), then remove the fuel shutoff valve and O-ring from the fuel tank. Place a shop cloth into the opening to prevent debris entering and to stop the flow of any residual gasoline.

7. Installation is the reverse of these steps while noting the following:
   a. Install a *new* O-ring gasket onto the fuel shut-off valve, then install the filter.
   b. Install the valve onto the fuel tank and tighten the screws securely.
   c. Refill the fuel tank and check for leaks.

Cleaning and Inspection

1. Inspect the filter mounted on top of the fuel valve. Remove and clean all contamination from the filter. Replace the filter if damaged.
2. Inspect the fuel valve for leakage or damage.
3. Check the O-ring for hardness or deterioration.

AIR FILTER AIR BOX

Removal/Installation

1. Refer to Chapter Fifteen and perform the following:

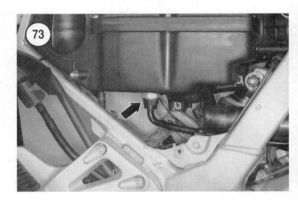

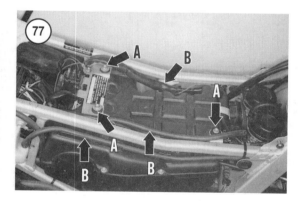

a. Remove the seat.

b. Remove both frame side covers.

c. On models so equipped, remove the saddle-bags.

2. Remove the battery and battery box as described in Chapter Nine.

3. Working under the rear mudguard, remove the bolt and washer (A, **Figure 72**) that secure the rear of the air box (B) to the rear fender.

4. On U.S. and Switzerland models, unscrew the secondary air system pipe fitting (**Figure 73**) from the base of the air filter.

5. Remove the bolt (**Figure 74**) securing the rear caliper remote reservoir to the air box. Move the reservoir out of the way, but keep it upright to avoid letting air into the brake system.

6. Remove the air intake scoop (**Figure 75**).

7. Loosen the clamp screws (**Figure 76**) securing the air box to the carburetor assembly on both sides.

8. Remove the three bolts, washers and lockwashers (A, **Figure 77**) securing the air box and the front mounting strap to the top of the frame. Remove the mounting strap.

9. Note the location of all electrical wires and hoses (B, **Figure 77**) that run along the upper side of the air box and the frame rails. During installation, these wires and hoses must be located correctly to avoid being pinched when the seat is installed.

10. Carefully work the air box (**Figure 78**) free and remove it from the frame.

11. Inspect the air box (**Figure 79**) for cracks or joint seam separation.

12. On U.S. and Switzerland models, check the tightness of the secondary air system EGR valve (**Figure 80**). Tighten securely if necessary.

13. Installation is the reverse of these steps.

EXHAUST SYSTEM

Removal

Refer to **Figure 81**.

NOTE
If the system joints are corroded or rusty, spray all connections with WD-40, or an equivalent, and allow the penetrating oil to soak in sufficiently to free the rusted joints.

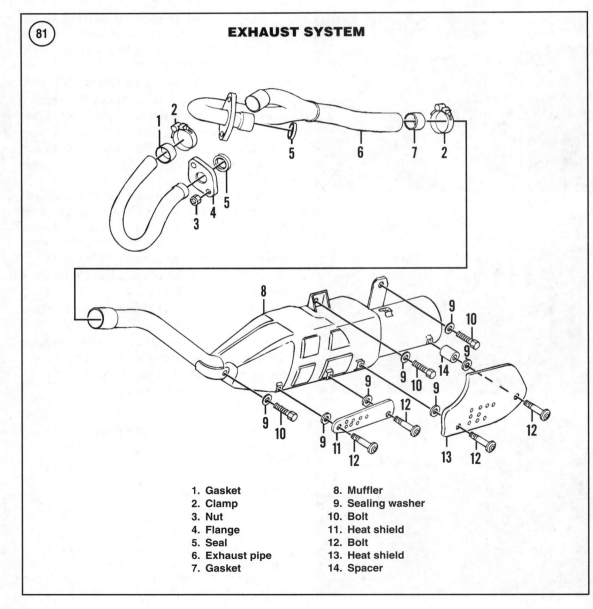

EXHAUST SYSTEM

1. Gasket
2. Clamp
3. Nut
4. Flange
5. Seal
6. Exhaust pipe
7. Gasket
8. Muffler
9. Sealing washer
10. Bolt
11. Heat shield
12. Bolt
13. Heat shield
14. Spacer

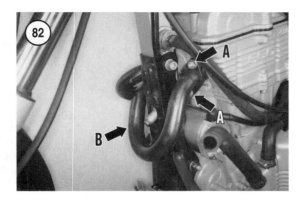

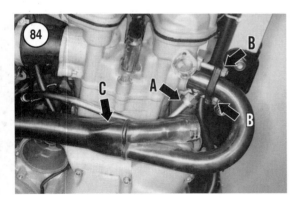

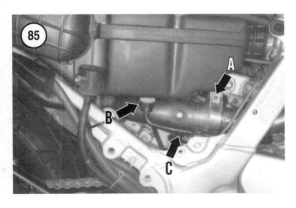

1. Support the motorcycle on a work stand. See *Bike Stands* in Chapter Nine.
2. Remove the left side exhaust pipe, as follows:
    a. Remove the radiator as described in Chapter Ten.
    b. Remove the nuts (A, **Figure 82**) securing the left side exhaust pipe to the cylinder head.
    c. Loosen the clamp (**Figure 83**) securing the left side exhaust pipe to the right side exhaust pipe.
    d. Work the left side exhaust pipe free from the right side exhaust pipe and remove the left side exhaust pipe (B, **Figure 82**).
3. To remove the right side exhaust pipe, perform the following:
    a. If still in place, remove the radiator as described in Chapter Ten.
    b. If still in place, remove the left side exhaust pipe as described in this chapter.
    c. On U.S. and Switzerland models, unscrew the secondary air system pipe fitting (A, **Figure 84**) from the right side exhaust pipe.
    d. Remove the nuts (B, **Figure 84**) securing the right side exhaust pipe to the cylinder head.
    e. Loosen the clamp (A, **Figure 85**) securing the right side exhaust pipe to the muffler.
    f. Work the right side exhaust pipe free from the muffler, pull the exhaust pipe forward and remove the right side exhaust pipe (C, **Figure 84**).
4. To remove the muffler, perform the following:
    a. On models so equipped, remove both saddlebags as described in Chapter Fifteen.
    b. Remove the rear wheel as described in Chapter Eleven.
    c. Loosen the clamp (A, **Figure 85**) that secures the right side exhaust pipe to the muffler.
    d. On U.S. and Switzerland models, unscrew the secondary air system pipe fitting (B, **Figure 85**) from the base of the air filter. Lower the pipe (C, **Figure 85**) away from the air filter air box and the exhaust pipe.
    e. Remove the bolts (**Figure 86**) securing the muffler to the frame. Do not lose the frame cover bumper strap (**Figure 87**) on the front bolt.
    f. Slowly work the muffler free from the right side exhaust pipe and frame area and remove the muffler out through the rear of the frame.

8

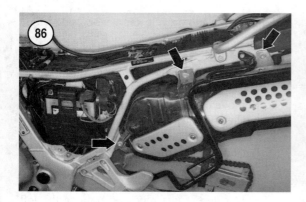

Do not lose the shim located at the right side exhaust pipe clamp.

5. Inspect the exhaust system as described in this chapter.

6. Store the exhaust system components in a safe place until they are reinstalled.

7. Installation is the reverse of these steps while noting the following:

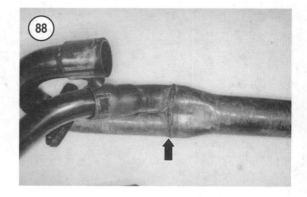

> *NOTE*
> *To eliminate exhaust leaks, do not tighten any of the mounting bolts and nuts or the clamps until all of the exhaust components are in place.*

a. Scrape the exhaust port surfaces of carbon residue. Then wipe the port with a rag to ensure good gasket fit.

b. Install a *new* exhaust port gasket into each exhaust port.

c. Install the frame cover bumper strap (**Figure 87**) on the muffler front mounting bolt.

d. Tighten the exhaust pipes-to-cylinder head nuts to the torque specification in **Table 2**.

e. Tighten the remaining bolts and clamp screws securely.

f. Start the engine and check for leaks.

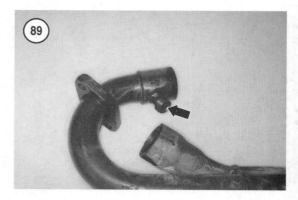

Inspection

Refer to **Figure 81**.

1. Replace rusted or damaged exhaust system components.

2. Remove all rust from exhaust pipes and muffler mating surfaces.

3. Inspect all welded sections of the pipes (**Figure 88**).

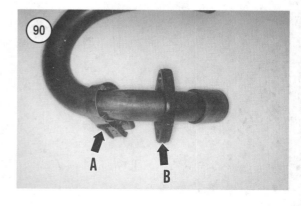

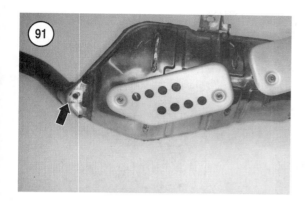

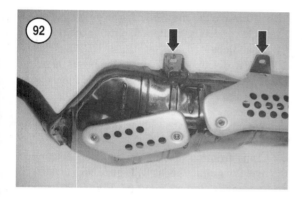

4. On U.S. and Switzerland models, check the threads on the secondary air system fitting (**Figure 89**) for damage.

5. Check the clamps (A, **Figure 90**) and flange (B) for damage.

6. Inspect the muffler threaded hole for the front mount (**Figure 91**) for thread damage. Clean out if necessary.

7. Inspect the muffler two upper mounting tabs (**Figure 92**) for cracking or damage.

8. Replace all worn or damaged heat shields (**Figure 93**) as required.

CRANKCASE BREATHER SYSTEM

Check the breather hose from the top of the camshaft cover (**Figure 94**) to the fitting on the oil tank section of the frame (**Figure 95**). Remove the hose and clean out if necessary.

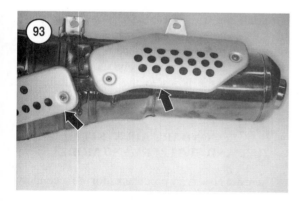

EVAPORATIVE EMISSION CONTROL SYSTEM (CALIFORNIA MODELS)

An evaporative emission control system prevents gasoline vapor from escaping into the atmosphere.

When the engine is not running, the system directs fuel vapors from the fuel system into the charcoal canister. This prevents hydrocarbons escaping into the atmosphere.

When the engine is running, these vapors are drawn into the carburetor, where they are burned.

The vapor valve also prevents gasoline vapor from escaping from the carbon canister if the motorcycle falls onto its side.

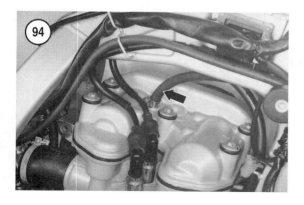

Inspection/Replacement

Before removing the hoses from any of the parts, label the hose and the fitting with a piece of masking tape.

1. Check all emission control lines and hoses to make sure they are correctly routed and connected.

> *WARNING*
> *Make sure the fuel tank vapor hoses are routed so they cannot contact any hot engine or exhaust component. These hoses contain flammable vapor. If a hose melts from contacting a hot part, leaking vapor may ignite and cause severe motorcycle damage and rider injury.*

2. Make sure there are no kinks in the lines or hoses. Also inspect the hose and lines for excessive wear or burning on lines that are routed near engine hot spots.

3. Check the physical condition of all lines and hoses in the system. Check for cuts, tears or loose connections. These lines and hoses are subjected to various temperature and operating conditions and eventually become brittle and crack. Replace damaged lines and hoses.

4. Check all components in the emission control system for damage, such as broken fittings or broken nipples on the component.

EVAPORATIVE EMISSION CONTROL SYSTEM SERVICE

Carbon Canister Replacement

1. Refer to Chapter Fifteen and perform the following:
   a. Remove the seat.

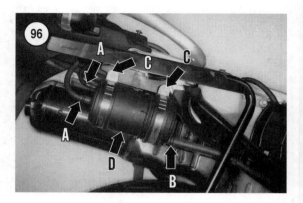

b. Remove the right side frame cover.
   c. On models so equipped, remove the right side saddlebag.

2. Prior to disconnecting any of the hoses, label the hoses and the canister fittings. Plug the open end of each hose to prevent contamination.

3. At the back surface of the canister, disconnect the fuel tank inlet hose and the outlet hose (A, **Figure 96**).

4. At the front surface of the canister, disconnect the overflow outlet hose (B, **Figure 96**).

5. Loosen the clamp screws (C, **Figure 96**) and remove the canister (D) from the frame.

6. Install the carbon canister by reversing these steps while noting the following:
   a. Slide the canister onto the frame and tighten the clamp screws securely.
   b. Attach the hoses to the correct fittings as noted during removal.

SECONDARY AIR SYSTEM (U.S. AND SWITZERLAND MODELS)

There are no service procedures for the secondary air system other than to check the pipe and fittings for tightness and/or damage.

Table 1 CARBURETOR SPECIFICATIONS

Item	Specification
Carburetor	Mikuni
Carburetor type	BST 33-B-316
Main jet	140
Main air jet	0.6
Jet needle	5E 94-4
Jet needle clip position	fourth groove from top
	(continued)

Table 1 CARBURETOR SPECIFICATIONS (continued)

Item	Specification
Needle jet	0-2
Throttle butterfly	105
Idle jet	41.4
Idle air jet	1.5
Float level	14.6 mm (0.57 in.)
Idle speed	1300-1400 rpm
Idle mixture screw	3 1/2 turns out

Table 2 EXHAUST SYSTEM TORQUE SPECIFICATIONS

Item	N•m	in.-lb.	ft-lb.
CO measurement screw plug	10	88	–
Exhaust pipe–to–cylinder head nuts	10	88	–
Frame mounting bolts	25	–	18
Muffler cover screws	12	106	–

8

CHAPTER NINE

ELECTRICAL SYSTEM

This chapter contains service and test procedures for all electrical and ignition system components. Spark plug service information is covered in Chapter Three. Specifications are in **Tables 1-3** at the end of the chapter. The wiring diagram is at the end of the manual.

The electrical system includes the following systems:
1. Charging system.
2. Ignition system.
3. Starting system.
4. Lighting system.
5. Switches and other electrical components.

PRELIMINARY INSPECTIONS

Wiring and Connectors

Many electrical troubles are the result of damaged wiring, or contaminated or loose connectors.

The location of the connectors varies by model year. The photographs in this chapter may not represent the model year being serviced. Also, if the motorcycle has been serviced previously, the connector may be in a different location.

Always compare the wire colors with the wiring diagram to verify that the correct component has been identified. Also, follow the wire from the specific component to where it connects to the wiring harness or to another electrical component.

Perform the following steps first if an electrical system fault is encountered.
1. Inspect all wiring for fraying, burning and any other visual damage.
2. Check the condition of the 20-amp main fuse. Replace it if necessary.
3. Check the condition of the individual fuse(s) for each circuit. Replace it if necessary.
4. Inspect the battery as described in Chapter Three. Make sure it is fully charged and that the battery cables are clean and securely attached to the battery terminals.
5. Clean connectors with an aerosol electrical contact cleaner. After a thorough cleaning, pack multi-pin electrical connectors with dielectric grease to seal out moisture.

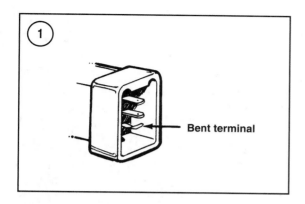

Bent terminal

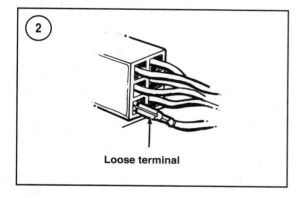

Loose terminal

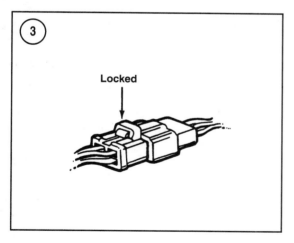

Locked

6. Disconnect electrical connectors in the suspect circuits and check for bent male terminals (**Figure 1**). A bent terminal will not connect to the female terminal, causing an open circuit. Check each female terminal.

7. Make sure that the metal terminals on the end of each wire are pushed all the way into the plastic connector (**Figure 2**). If not, carefully push them in with a narrow-blade screwdriver.

8. After everything is checked, push the connectors together and make sure they are fully engaged and locked together (**Figure 3**).

9. Never pull on the electrical wires when disconnecting an electrical connector–pull only on the connector plastic housing.

10. Check wiring continuity as follows:

    a. Disconnect the negative battery cable as described in this chapter.

NOTE
When making a continuity test, it is best not to disconnect the electrical connector. Instead, insert the test leads into the back of the connectors and check both sides. Because corrosion between the connector contacts may be causing an open circuit, the trouble may be in the connector instead of with the wiring.

    b. If using an analog ohmmeter, always touch the test leads, then zero adjust the needle according to manufacturer's instructions to assure correct readings.

    c. Attach the test leads to the circuit to be tested.

    d. There should be continuity. If there is no continuity (infinite resistance), there is an open in the circuit.

Electrical Component Resistance Testing

Because the resistance of a component varies with temperature, perform the resistance tests with the component at room temperature (68° F [20° C]). The specifications provided in this manual are based on tests performed at this temperature.

NOTE
When using an analog ohmmeter, always touch the test leads, then zero adjust the needle to ensure correct readings.

Electrical Component Replacement

Most motorcycle dealerships and parts suppliers do not accept returns of electrical parts. Avoid purchasing parts unless the cause of the malfunction has been determined. If a thorough diagnosis has not located the exact cause of the electrical system

9

malfunction, have a BMW dealership determine the possible cause.

Negative Cable

Some of the component replacement procedures and some of the test procedures in this chapter require disconnecting the negative battery cable as a safety precaution.

1. Remove the seat as described in Chapter Fifteen.
2. Remove the frame left side cover as described in Chapter Fifteen.
3. Remove the bolt and nut (**Figure 4**) securing the negative cable to the battery. Move the cable away from the battery to avoid making accidental contact with the battery post.
4. Install the negative cable by reversing these steps and note the following:
   a. If necessary, clean the battery terminals and cables.
   b. Coat the terminals with dielectric grease.

BATTERY BOX

Removal/Installation

1. Remove the battery from the battery box as described in Chapter Three.
2. Remove the bolts (**Figure 5**) securing the battery box to the frame and air filter air box.
3. Remove the battery box.
4. Thoroughly clean the battery box with a soft brush and a baking soda solution. Rinse it thoroughly with clean water and wipe dry with a clean cloth.
5. Check the battery box for cracks or damage and replace if necessary.
6. Install by reversing these removal steps.

CHARGING SYSTEM

The charging system consists of the battery, alternator and a voltage regulator/rectifier. Alternating current generated by the alternator is rectified to direct current. The voltage regulator maintains the voltage to the battery and additional electrical loads, like the lights and ignition system, at a constant voltage regardless of variations in engine speed and load.

A malfunction in the charging system generally causes the battery to remain undercharged. To pre-

vent damage to the alternator and the regulator/rectifier when testing and repairing the charging system, note the following precautions:

1. Always disconnect the negative battery cable, as described in this chapter, before removing a component from the charging system.
2. When it is necessary to charge the battery, remove the battery from the motorcycle and recharge it as described in Chapter Three.
3. Inspect the battery case. Look for bulges or cracks in the case, leaking electrolyte or corrosion build-up.
4. Check the charging system wiring for signs of chafing, deterioration or other damage.
5. Check the wiring for corroded or loose connections. Clean, tighten or reconnect as required.

Current Draw

Perform this test prior to performing the output test.

1. Turn the ignition switch OFF.

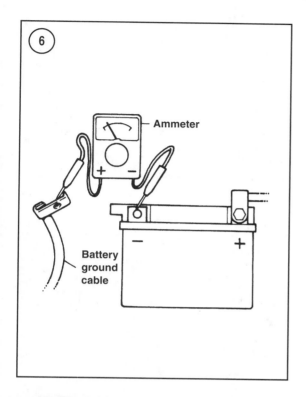

Ammeter

Battery
ground
cable

$-$ $+$

A   B

2. Refer to Chapter Fifteen and perform the following:

  a. Remove the seat.

  b. Remove the frame left side cover.

3. Disconnect the negative battery cable as described in this chapter.

4. Switch the ammeter from its highest to lowest amperage scale while reading the meter scale.

CAUTION
Before connecting the ammeter into the circuit in Step 4, set the meter to its highest amperage scale. This will prevent a possible large current flow from damaging the meter or blowing the meter's fuse, if so equipped.

5. Connect the ammeter between the negative battery cable and the negative terminal of the battery (**Figure 6**). If the needle swings even the slightest amount when the meter is connected, there is a current draw in the system that will discharge the battery.

6. If there is a current draw, the probable causes are:

  a. Damaged battery.

  b. Short circuit in the system.

  c. Loose, dirty or faulty electrical system connectors in the charging system wiring harness system.

7. To determine which circuit is at fault, disconnect individual circuits from the system. If the current draw stops when a particular circuit is disconnected, a fault is indicated in that circuit.

8. Disconnect the ammeter test leads and reconnect the negative battery cable.

Testing

A malfunction in the charging system generally causes the battery to remain undercharged. Perform the following visual inspection to determine the cause of the problem. If the visual inspection proves satisfactory, test the charging system as described under *Charging System* in Chapter Two.

1. Make sure the battery negative (A, **Figure 7**) and positive (B) cables are connected properly. If polarity is reversed, check for a damaged voltage regulator/rectifier.

2. Inspect the terminals for loose or corroded connections. Tighten or clean as required.

3. Inspect the battery case. Look for bulges or cracks in the case, leaking electrolyte or corrosion build-up.

4. Carefully check all connections at the alternator to make sure they are clean and tight.

5. Check the circuit wiring for corroded or loose connections. Clean, tighten or connect as required.

9

ALTERNATOR

Stator Removal/Installation

The alternator stator assembly is attached to the backside of the alternator cover.

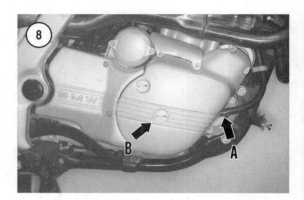

> *NOTE*
> *Some of the photographs in this proce-dure are shown with the engine par-tially disassembled to better illustrate the steps.*

1. Disconnect the negative battery cable as de-scribed in this chapter.
2. Refer to Chapter Fifteen and perform the follow-ing:
   a. Remove the seat.
   b. Remove both frame side covers.
   c. Remove the right side cylinder head cover.
3. Drain the engine oil as described in Chapter Three.
4. Disconnect the breather hose (A, **Figure 8**) from the front of the alternator cover.
5. Unscrew and remove the center plug (B, **Figure 8**) from the alternator cover.

6. Follow the stator assembly wiring harness from the top of the alternator cover to the left side of the motorcycle. Disconnect the electrical connector (**Figure 9**) containing the three yellow wires located above the battery.

> *NOTE*
> *Before removing the wiring harness, make a drawing of the harness routing from the alternator through the frame to the electrical connector above the battery.*

7. Carefully pull the electrical harness out through the frame.
8. Remove the screws securing the alternator cover (**Figure 10**).
9. Screw the handle (BMW part No. 12 5 500) into the cover (**Figure 11**).

> *NOTE*
> *In some cases the handle may not be necessary to remove the cover. The ro-tor magnets are very strong and the handle assists in the removal of the cover. Do not pry the cover loose, as this will result in an oil leak.*

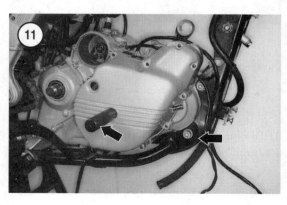

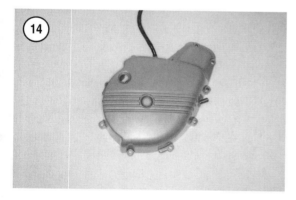

10. Pull straight out on the handle and remove the alternator cover and stator assembly from the crankcase and the rotor. Remove the gasket. Carefully pull the wiring harness out of the frame.

11. Do not lose the locating dowel.

12. Place several shop cloths on the workbench and turn the alternator cover upside down on these cloths.

NOTE
The screws were secured with a threadlocking agent and may be difficult to loosen. Use an impact driver and correct size Allen bit to loosen the bolts.

13. Loosen the Allen bolts securing the alternator stator (**Figure 12**) to the cover.

14. Remove the screws (A, **Figure 13**) securing the harness clamp to the cover.

15. Carefully pull the rubber grommet (B, **Figure 13**) from the cover.

16. Remove the Allen bolts and remove the stator assembly from the cover.

17. Inspect the alternator cover (**Figure 14**) for damage.

18. Install the alternator stator by reversing these removal steps while noting the following:

   a. Apply a non-permanent locking agent to the stator assembly mounting Allen bolts threads prior to installation. Tighten the bolts securely.

   b. The metal clamp (A, **Figure 13**) and screws (B) must be installed in the correct location. The clamp secures the wiring harness to the cover and away from the spinning rotor. If these wires contact the rotor, they will be damaged.

   c. If removed, install the locating dowel (**Figure 15**).

   d. Apply several small dabs of silicone sealer to the backside of the gasket to hold it in place on the crankcase, then install a *new* gasket (**Figure 16**).

   e. Make sure the electrical connector is free of corrosion and is tight.

Rotor Removal/Installation

CAUTION
*Do **not** try to remove the rotor without the BMW rotor removal tool. Any attempt to do so will lead to some form*

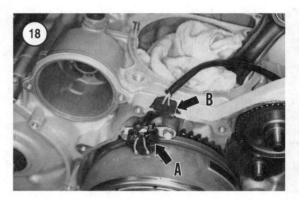

of damage to the engine and/or the rotor. If the rotor removal tool is not available, have the rotor removed by a BMW dealership.

NOTE
On some engines, a strong locking agent was applied to the crankshaft taper where it contacts the inner taper of the rotor to help secure it in place. If this situation exists, rotor removal will be very difficult.

1. Modify the removal tool (BMW part No. 12 5 510) to accept a large adjustable wrench. Grind a flat on each side of the tool as shown in **Figure 17**. Grind the flats down far enough to provide a large surface for the jaws of the wrench.

2. Remove the alternator stator assembly as described in this chapter.

3. Remove the bolts that secure the ignition pickup coil assembly (A, **Figure 18**) to the crankcase.

4. Carefully pull the rubber grommet (B, **Figure 18**) from the crankcase. Move the pickup coil out of the way.

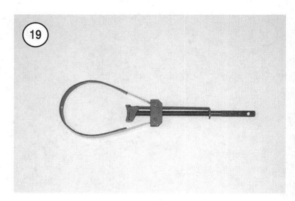

5A. Install a rotor holding tool (**Figure 19**) onto the rotor to prevent the crankshaft from rotating.

5B. If the holding tool is not available, shift the transmission into gear. Have an assistant apply the rear brake to keep the crankshaft from rotating.

6. Loosen and remove the rotor nut (**Figure 20**) and lock washer (**Figure 21**) from the crankshaft.

7. Remove the washer (**Figure 22**) and spacer (**Figure 23**) from the post.

8. Apply a dab of grease to the end of the special tool's center bolt, also apply oil to the center bolt threads. Screw the bolt in and out of the tool several times to make sure it rotates smoothly.

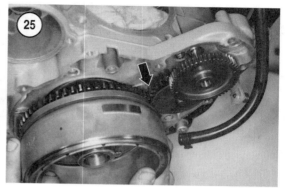

9. Install the rotor removal tool onto the threads of the rotor and tighten securely.

10. Secure the outer portion of the tool with a crescent wrench and turn the tool's center bolt with a wrench. Turn the center bolt until it is very tight against the end of the crankshaft. Tap the end of the center bolt (not the rotor as it will be damaged) firmly with a hammer. Repeatedly tighten the center bolt and tap the bolt with the hammer until the rotor disengages from the crankshaft taper.

CAUTION
If normal rotor removal attempts fail, do not force the puller, as the threads may be stripped from the rotor and cause damage. Take the motorcycle to a BMW dealership and have the rotor removed.

11. Unscrew and remove the rotor removal tool from the rotor.

12. Slowly withdraw the rotor from the crankshaft (**Figure 24**) while disengaging the freewheel gear on the backside of the rotor from the starter idle gear and disc (**Figure 25**).

13. Do not lose the Woodruff key (**Figure 26**) on the crankshaft taper.

14. Inspect the inside of the rotor (**Figure 27**) for metal debris that may be attached to the magnets. Any metal debris will cause severe damage to the alternator stator assembly.

15. Install by reversing these removal steps while noting the following:

   a. Use an aerosol parts cleaner to clean all threadlocking compound residue from the crankshaft and rotor tapers (**Figure 28**). Do *not* use any threadlocking compound on the taper when installing the rotor.

    b. Apply a light coat of medium-strength threadlocking compound to the rotor nut threads prior to installation.

    c. Use the same tool setup (**Figure 29**) used during removal to tighten the rotor nut to the specification in **Table 3**.

VOLTAGE REGULATOR

Testing

There are no test procedures for the voltage regulator/rectifier. If the voltage regulator is suspect, have a BMW dealership check it by installing a test regulator to ensure the suspect unit is faulty. Make sure that nothing has been overlooked before purchasing a new voltage regulator. Most parts suppliers do not accept returns on electrical components.

Removal/Installation

1. Disconnect the negative battery cable as described in this chapter.

2. Refer to Chapter Fifteen and perform the following:

    a. Remove the seat.

    b. Remove both frame side covers.

    c. Remove the left side cylinder head cover.

3. Follow the voltage regulator/rectifier wiring harness (A, **Figure 30**) from the regulator to the top of the battery area. Disconnect the electrical connector (**Figure 31**) containing the three yellow wires located above the battery.

4. Disconnect the two wire harnesses (B, **Figure 30**) containing two wires (one green and one red/white) and disconnect the two-pin electrical connector.

5. Remove the two mounting bolts securing the voltage regulator/rectifier (**Figure 32**) to the top of the rear fender.

6. Carefully remove the regulator and related wiring harnesses from the frame.

7. Install by reversing these removal steps. Apply a light coat of dielectric compound to the electrical connectors prior to installing them.

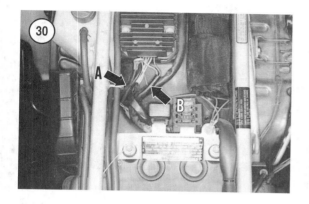

of the high-voltage ignition coil where it is increased, or stepped up, to a high enough voltage to jump the gap between the spark plug electrodes.

The ignition system consists of two ignition coils, two spark plugs and the ignition module.

CDI Cautions

When servicing the CDI system, note the following:

1. Keep all connections between the various units clean and tight. Make sure the wiring connectors are locked together firmly.

2. Never disconnect any of the electrical connections while the engine is running. Otherwise, excessive voltage may damage the coils or igniter unit.

3. When turning the engine over with one spark plug removed, make sure the spark plug is installed in the plug cap and grounded against the cylinder head (**Figure 33**). If not, excessive resistance may damage the igniter unit.

4. The ignition control unit (ICU) unit is mounted in a rubber vibration isolator. Make sure that the ICU unit is mounted correctly. Handle the ICU unit carefully when removing and installing from the top of the rear fender. The ICU unit is a sealed unit. Do not attempt to open it, as this will cause permanent damage.

When servicing the ignition system, refer to the wiring diagram, located at the back of the manual.

CAPACITOR DISCHARGE IGNITION

All models are equipped with a capacitor discharge ignition (CDI) system. This solid state system uses no moving parts.

Alternating current from the alternator is rectified and used to charge the capacitor. As the piston approaches the firing position, a pulse from the pulse coil is rectified, shaped, and then used to trigger the silicone-controlled rectifier. This in turn allows the capacitor to discharge quickly into the primary side

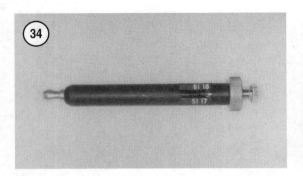

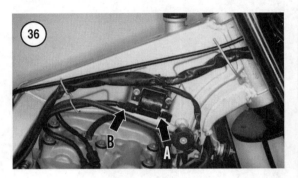

Ignition Coil

Performance test

1. Disconnect the plug wire and remove one of the spark plugs as described in Chapter Three.

> *NOTE*
> *A spark tester is a useful tool for testing the ignition system's spark output.* **Figure 34** *shows the Motion Pro Ignition System Tester (part No. 08-0122). This tool is inserted in the spark plug cap and its base is grounded against the cylinder head. The tool's air gap is adjustable, and it allows the visual inspection of the spark while testing the intensity of the spark.*

2. Insert a clean shop cloth into the spark plug hole in the cylinder head to lessen the chance of gasoline vapors being emitted from the hole.

3. Insert the spark plug (**Figure 33**), or spark tester into its cap and touch the spark plug base against the cylinder head to ground it (**Figure 35**). Position the spark plug so the electrode is visible.

> *WARNING*
> *Mount the spark plug, or tester, away from the spark plug hole in the cylinder so that the spark or tester cannot ignite the gasoline vapors in the cylinder. If the engine is flooded, do not perform this test. The firing of the spark plug can ignite fuel that is ejected through the spark plug hole.*

> *NOTE*
> *If not using a spark tester, always use a new spark plug for this test procedure.*

4. Turn the engine over with the electric starter. A fat blue spark should be evident across the spark plug electrode, or spark tester. If there is strong sunlight on the plug, or tester, shade it so the spark is more visible. Repeat for the other spark plug.

> *WARNING*
> *If necessary, hold onto the spark plug wire with a pair of insulated pliers. Do **not** hold the spark plug, wire or connector, or a serious electrical shock may result.*

5. If a fat blue spark occurs, the ignition coil is good. If not, perform the following resistance test.

Resistance test

1. Refer to *Preliminary Inspections* at the beginning of this chapter.

2. Disconnect the negative battery cable as described in this chapter.

3. Remove the fuel tank as described in Chapter Eight.

4. Disconnect the primary connector (A, **Figure 36**) and the secondary wire (B) from the ignition coil.

5. Use an ohmmeter set at R × 1 to measure the primary coil resistance between the primary terminal

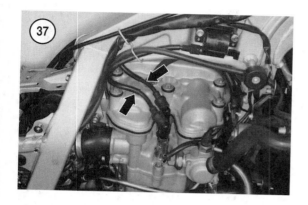

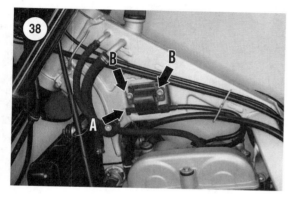

(A, **Figure 36**) and the coil core. Compare the resistance value with the specification in **Table 1**.

6. Use an ohmmeter set at R × 1000 to measure the secondary coil resistance between the secondary coil terminal (B, **Figure 36**) and the coil core. Compare the resistance value with the specification in **Table 1**.

7. If the resistance values are less than specified, there is most likely a short in the coil windings. Replace the coil.

8. If the resistance values are more than specified, this may indicate corrosion or oxidation of the coil's terminals. Thoroughly clean the terminals, then spray with an aerosol electrical contact cleaner. Repeat Step 5 and Step 6 and if the resistance value is still high, replace the coil.

9. If the coil resistance does not meet (or come close to) either of these specifications, the coil must be replaced. If the coil exhibits visible damage, replace it as described in this chapter.

10. Repeat this procedure for the other ignition coil.

Removal/installation

1. Disconnect the negative battery cable as described in this chapter.

2. Remove the fuel tank as described in Chapter Eight.

NOTE
Label all wiring connectors prior to disconnecting them in the following steps.

3. Disconnect the secondary lead (**Figure 37**) from each spark plug.

4. Disconnect the primary connector (A, **Figure 38**) from the ignition coil.

5. Remove the bolts and lockwashers (B, **Figure 38**) that secure the ignition coil to the frame.

6. Remove the ignition coil.

7. Install the ignition coil by reversing these steps.

8. Repeat this procedure for the other ignition coil if necessary.

Ignition Control Unit (ICU)
Testing and Replacement

There are no test procedures for the ICU. If the ICU is suspect, have a BMW dealership check it by installing a test unit to ensure the suspect unit is faulty. Make sure that nothing has been overlooked before purchasing a new ICU. Most parts suppliers will not accept returns on electrical components.

Ignition Control Unit (ICU)
Removal/Installation

The ICU is located behind the seat and under the rear trim panel.

1. Disconnect the negative battery cable as described in this chapter.

2. Remove the seat as described in Chapter Fifteen.

3. Working under the rear trim panel, remove the screws (**Figure 39**) securing the ICU.

4. Disconnect the six-pin electrical connector (A, **Figure 40**) containing five wires.

5. Work the electrical wires and connector under the frame cross member (B, **Figure 40**) and carefully remove the ICU from the frame.

6. Install the ICU by reversing these steps while noting the following:

9

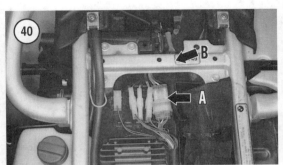

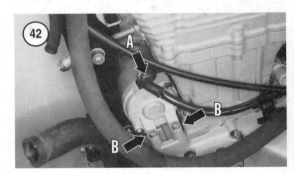

a. Apply a light coat of dielectric compound to the electrical connectors prior to installing them.

b. Make sure the electrical connectors are pushed tightly onto the ICU.

STARTING SYSTEM

When servicing the starting system, refer to the wiring diagram at the back of the manual.

CAUTION
Do not operate the starter for more than five seconds at a time. Let it cool approximately 10 seconds before operating it again.

Troubleshooting

Refer to Chapter Two.

Starter Removal/Installation

NOTE
Some of the photographs in this procedure are shown with the radiator removed to better illustrate the steps.

1. Disconnect the negative battery cable as described in this chapter.

2. Refer to Chapter Fifteen and perform the following:
   a. Remove the seat.
   b. Remove the left side cylinder head cover.
   c. Remove the engine lower cover.

3. Drain the cooling system as described in Chapter Three.

4. Remove the radiator lower hose (**Figure 41**) from the water pump.

5. Slide back the rubber boot (A, **Figure 42**) from the starter motor electrical terminal.

6. Remove the acorn nut (**Figure 43**) securing the positive cable to the starter motor terminal. Move the cable out of the way.

7. Remove the bolts (B, **Figure 42**) securing the starter motor to the crankcase.

8. Carefully pull the starter motor straight out of the crankcase and remove it.

9. If necessary, service the starter motor as described in this chapter.

10. Install the starter motor by reversing these removal steps, while noting the following:

11. Thoroughly clean the starter motor mounting pads on the crankcase and the starter motor mounts.

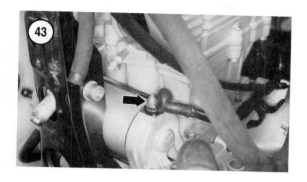

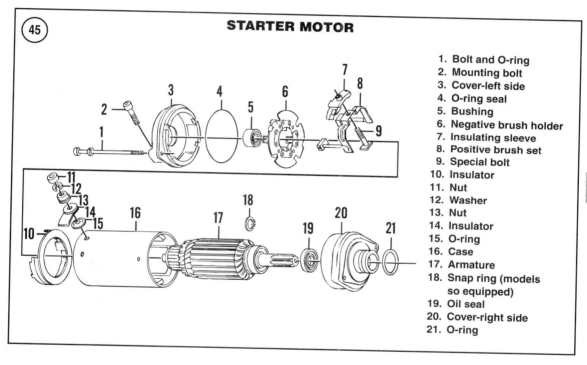

STARTER MOTOR

1. Bolt and O-ring
2. Mounting bolt
3. Cover-left side
4. O-ring seal
5. Bushing
6. Negative brush holder
7. Insulating sleeve
8. Positive brush set
9. Special bolt
10. Insulator
11. Nut
12. Washer
13. Nut
14. Insulator
15. O-ring
16. Case
17. Armature
18. Snap ring (models so equipped)
19. Oil seal
20. Cover-right side
21. O-ring

12. Inspect the starter motor O-ring seal (**Figure 44**) for hardness or deterioration. Replace the O-ring if necessary. Apply clean engine oil to the O-ring prior to installing the starter motor

13. Push the starter motor into the crankcase while guiding the starter motor sprocket onto the starter reduction gear.

14. Install the starter motor mounting bolts (B, **Figure 42**) and tighten securely.

15. Tighten the electrical connector acorn nut (**Figure 43**) securely and pull the rubber boot back into position.

16. Install the radiator lower hose (**Figure 41**) onto the water pump and tighten the clamp securely.

17. Refill the cooling system as described in Chapter Three.

18. Refer to Chapter Fifteen and perform the following:

   a. Install the engine lower cover.

   b. Install the left side cylinder head cover.

   c. Install the seat.

19. Connect the negative battery cable as described in this chapter.

Disassembly

Refer to **Figure 45**.

NOTE
Prior to starter disassembly, check for parts availability for the starter motor

being worked on. Some parts may not be available.

NOTE
As the starter motor is disassembled, lay the parts out in the order of removal.

1. Prior to disassembly, make permanent pen alignment marks on both end covers and the case (**Figure 46**). This will ensure correct alignment during assembly.
2. Remove the case bolts (A, **Figure 47**) and O-ring seals.
3. Remove the right side cover (B, **Figure 47**) from the case.
4. Remove the left side cover and brush holder plate (A, **Figure 48**) from the case. Remove the washers from the shaft.
5. Slide the armature coil out of the case (B, **Figure 48**).

NOTE
Before removing the nuts and washers, record their description and order. They must be reinstalled in the same order to insulate the positive (+) brush plate assembly from the case.

6. Carefully pull the brush holder assembly (A, **Figure 49**) out of the left-hand cover.
7. Remove the nuts, washers, insulator and O-ring (B, **Figure 49**) that secure the brush holder assembly to the left side cover.

CAUTION
*Do not immerse the case or the armature coil (**Figure 50**) in solvent, as the wiring insulation may be damaged. Wipe the windings with a cloth lightly moistened with solvent and thoroughly dry.*

8. Clean all grease, dirt and carbon from all components.
9. Inspect all starter components as described in this chapter.

Assembly

NOTE
In the next step, reinstall all parts in the same order as noted during re-

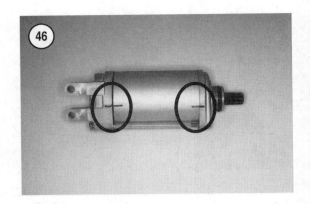

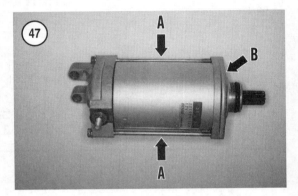

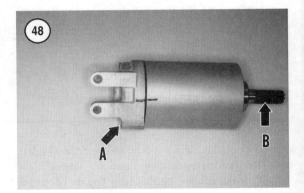

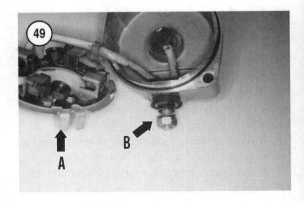

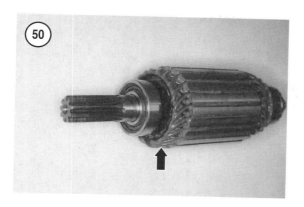

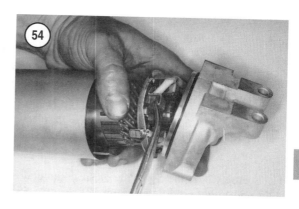

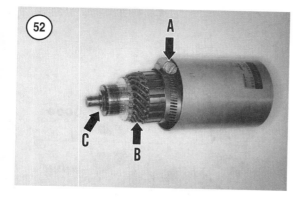

4. To release spring pressure on the brushes, move the spring off of the brush and rest it on the backside of the brush holder (**Figure 51**). Push the brushes back into the holder to allow them to pass by the commutator during the next steps.

NOTE
The armature and left side cover cannot be installed into the case as an assembly. The case magnets are very strong and they will pull the armature directly into the case and out of the left side cover.

5. Install a large hose clamp (A, **Figure 52**) onto the commutator end of the armature.
6. Install the armature into the case (B, **Figure 52**) until the hose clamp stops against the case.
7. Install the washers (C, **Figure 52**) onto the armature shaft.
8. Install the brush holder plate assembly into place onto the commutator (**Figure 53**).
9. Release the brush spring from the brush holder and onto the brush (**Figure 54**). Make sure the brush makes contact with the commutator. Repeat for all four brushes.

moval. This is essential in order to insulate the brush assembly from the case.

1. Install the nut, washers, insulator and O-ring (B, **Figure 49**) securing the brush holder assembly to the left side cover.
2. If removed, install the O-ring onto each end cover.
3. Install the brush holder assembly (A, **Figure 49**) into the left side cover. Align the index tab with the case tab.

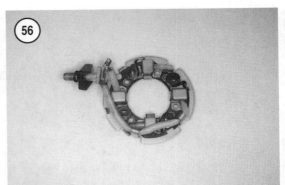

10. Move the left side cover onto the brush holder and align the locating tab (A, **Figure 55**).

> *NOTE*
> *In Step 11, be sure to hold onto the end of the commutator shaft. If released, the commutator will be pulled out of the brush holder and disengage the brushes. This step is best performed with the aid of an assistant.*

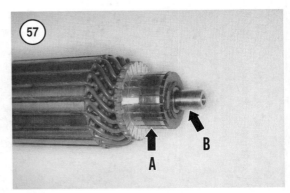

11. Securely hold the right side of the commutator shaft and remove the hose clamp (B, **Figure 55**) from the commutator. Slowly allow the armature, brush holder and left side cover (C) to be pulled into the case by the cover magnets.

12. Push the assembly the rest of the way into the case.

13. Install the right side cover (B, **Figure 47**).

14. Refer to the alignment marks and align both covers with the case (**Figure 46**).

15. Keep the assembly in this position and slowly rotate the armature coil assembly to make sure it rotates freely with the brushes in place.

16. Install the case bolts (A, **Figure 47**) and tighten securely. After the screws are tightened, check the seams to ensure the end covers are pulled tight against the case.

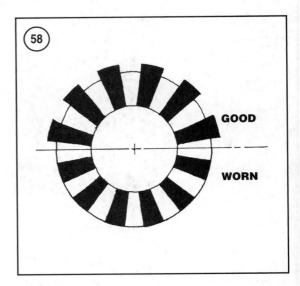

Inspection

1. Inspect each brush in the assembly (**Figure 56**) for abnormal wear. There are no service limit dimensions provided by BMW. Replace as necessary.

2. Inspect the commutator (A, **Figure 57**). The mica in a good commentator is below the surface of the copper bars. On a worn commutator the mica and copper bars may be worn to the same level (**Fig-**

ure 58). If necessary, have the commutator serviced by a dealership or electrical repair shop.

3. Check the entire length of the armature coil assembly for straightness or heat damage. Rotate the right side ball bearing (**Figure 59**) and check for roughness or binding.

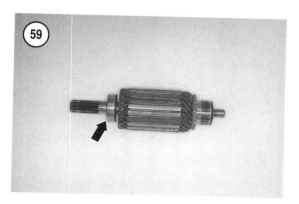

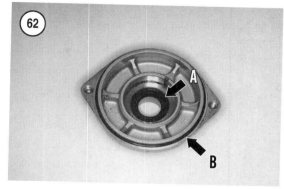

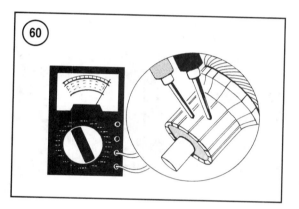

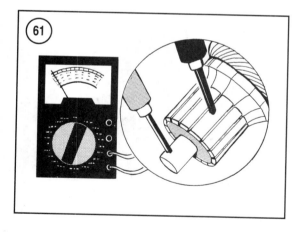

a. Check for continuity between the commutator bars (**Figure 60**); there should be continuity (indicated resistance) between pairs of bars.

b. Check for continuity between the commutator bars and the shaft (**Figure 61**); there should be *no* continuity (infinite resistance).

c. If the unit fails either of these tests, the starter assembly must be replaced. The armature cannot be replaced individually.

7. Inspect the oil seal (A, **Figure 62**) and O-ring seal (B) in the right cover for wear, hardness or damage.

8. Inspect the bushing (**Figure 63**) in the right case for wear. The bushing cannot be replaced, if damaged, the starter must be replaced as this is not a separate part.

9. Inspect the magnets (**Figure 64**) within the case assembly. Make sure they have not picked up any small metal particles. If so, remove them prior to re-assembly. Then inspect for loose, chipped or damaged magnets.

10. Inspect the brush holder and springs for wear or damage. Replace if necessary.

4. Inspect the armature shaft where it rides on the bushing (B, **Figure 57**). Check for wear, burrs or damage. If worn or damaged, replace the starter assembly.

5. Inspect the commutator copper bars (A, **Figure 57**) for discoloration. If a pair of bars are discolored, the armature coils are grounded.

6. Use an ohmmeter to perform the following:

11. Inspect both end covers (**Figure 65**) for wear or damage. If either cover is damaged, the starter must be replaced.

12. Check the long case bolts for thread damage, clean up with the appropriate size metric die. Inspect the O-ring seals for hardness, deterioration or damage. Replace as necessary.

STARTER RELAY REPLACEMENT

1. Disconnect the negative battery cable as described in this chapter.

2. Refer to Chapter Fifteen and perform the following:

   a. Remove the seat.

   b. Remove the frame left side cover.

3. Disconnect the starter relay primary electrical connector (A, **Figure 66**).

4. Remove the nuts and disconnect the starter motor-to-starter relay red and black cables at the starter relay (B, **Figure 66**).

5. Pull the starter relay (C, **Figure 66**) from the rubber mount on the air filter door.

6. Install by reversing these removal steps while noting the following:

   a. Install both electrical red and black cables to the relay and tighten the nuts securely.

   b. Make sure the electrical connectors are on tight and that the rubber boot is properly installed to keep out moisture.

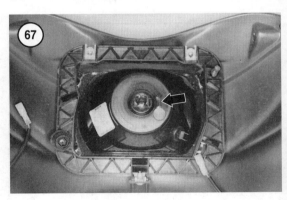

LIGHTING SYSTEM

The lighting system consists of a headlight, taillight/brake light combination and turn signals.

Always use the correct wattage bulb. Using a larger wattage bulb will give a dim light and a smaller wattage bulb will burn out prematurely. Refer to **Table 2** for bulb specifications.

Headlight Bulb Replacement

> *WARNING*
> *If the headlight has just burned out or just turned off, it will be hot. Allow the bulb to cool prior to removal.*

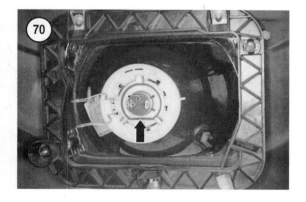

CAUTION
All models are equipped with a quartz-halogen bulb. Do not touch the bulb glass. Traces of oil on the bulb drastically reduce the life of the bulb. Clean all traces of oil from the bulb glass with a cloth moistened in alcohol or lacquer thinner.

NOTE
The following photographs are shown with the front fairing removed to better illustrate the steps.

1. Turn the handlebar all the way to the left.

2. Reach under the front fairing to disconnect the electrical connector from the back of the lens unit and bulb.

3. Remove the rubber cover (**Figure 67**) from the back of the lens assembly. Check the rubber boot for tears or deterioration; replace if necessary.

4. Unhook the bulb retaining hook (**Figure 68**) and pivot it out of the way.

5. Remove and discard the blown bulb (**Figure 69**).

6. Position the new bulb with the flat portion at the bottom (**Figure 70**) and install the bulb.

7. Hook the spring retainer hook over the bulb to hold it in place.

8. Install the rubber boot and makes sure it is correctly seated against the bulb and the retainer.

9. Check headlight operation.

10. Check headlight adjustment as described in this chapter.

Headlight Adjustment

Adjust the headlight horizontally and vertically according to local Department of Motor Vehicle regulations.

1. To adjust the headlight horizontally, perform the following:

   a. Remove the screws securing the windshield and under cover (**Figure 71**).

   b. Use a Phillips screwdriver to turn the upper right side adjust screw (**Figure 72**) until the aim is correct.

   c. Install the under cover and windshield.

2. To adjust the headlight vertically, turn the large knurled knob (**Figure 73**) until the aim is correct.

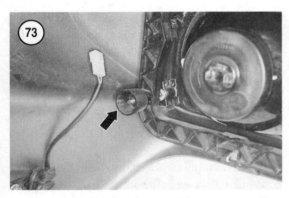

Position Bulb Replacement

NOTE
The following photographs are shown
with the front fairing removed to better
illustrate the steps.

1. Turn the handlebar all the way to the left.
2. Reach under the front fairing and disconnect the electrical connector from the back of the position bulb.
3. Carefully pull the bulb and socket (**Figure 74**) from the front fairing grommet.
4. Discard the blown bulb (**Figure 75**).
5. Install the new bulb and push it into the grommet until it bottoms.
6. Connect the electrical connector onto the back of the position bulb.

Turn Signal Bulb Replacement (Front and Rear)

1. Remove the screws securing the lens, then remove the lens. Refer to **Figure 76** for the front and **Figure 77** for the rear.

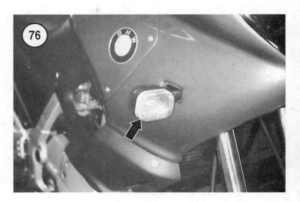

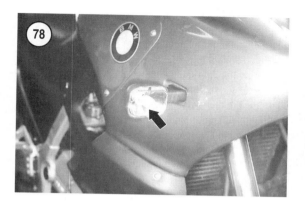

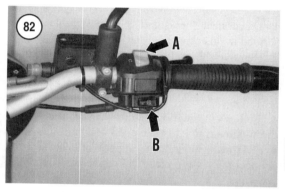

9

2. Push in on the bulb and rotate it to remove the blown bulb. Refer to **Figure 78** for the front and **Figure 79** for the rear.

3. Install a new bulb and lens.

4. Install the screws and tighten securely. Do not overtighten the screws, as the lens may crack.

Taillight/Brake Light Replacement

1. Remove the screws that secure the lens (**Figure 80**).

2. Push in on the bulb and rotate it to remove the blown bulb (**Figure 81**).

3. Install a new bulb, then install the socket assembly into the lens.

SWITCHES

Testing

If a switch is suspect, refer to the wiring diagram at the back of the manual. Test the switch circuit wires with an ohmmeter or test light while operating the switch. Make sure that nothing has been overlooked before purchasing a new switch. Most parts suppliers do not accept returns on electrical components. Consider having a BMW dealership check it by installing a test switch.

Right Side Handlebar Switch Housing Replacement

The right side handlebar switch housing contains the engine stop switch (A, **Figure 82**), start button (B), front brake light switch (electrical connectors only–the switch is separate), and headlight switch (non-U.S. & Canada models).

NOTE
The two (or three) switches located within the right side handlebar switch housing are not available separately. If one switch is damaged, the entire right-hand switch housing assembly must be replaced. The front brake light switch is a separate unit and can be replaced separately, only the wiring harness is combined with the other switch assembly.

1. Disconnect the negative battery cable as described in this chapter.
2. Remove the fuel tank as described in Chapter Eight.
3. Remove the upper fairing as described in Chapter Fifteen.
4. Follow the wiring harness from the switch through the frame to the electrical connectors (**Figure 83**) on the inner fairing support . Locate and disconnect the six-pin electrical connector containing six wires.
5. Disconnect the two-pin electrical connector for the front brake light switch.
6. At the throttle grip, perform the following:
    a. Slide the rubber boot (A, **Figure 84**) off the cable adjuster.
    b. Loosen the adjuster locknut (B, **Figure 84**) and turn the adjuster (C) to obtain the maximum amount of cable slack.
7. Remove the screws that secure the right side switch assembly (A, **Figure 85**) together and separate the switch assembly.
8. Remove any plastic clamps (B, **Figure 85**) that secure the switch wiring harness to the handlebar and frame. Carefully pull the wires out through the opening under the inner panel.
9. Disconnect the throttle cable from the throttle grip.
10. Remove the switch assembly from the handlebar and frame.
11. Install by reversing these removal steps while noting the following:
    a. Connect the throttle cable onto the throttle grip and switch housing.
    b. Align the locating pin with the hole in the handlebar and install the switch onto the handlebar.

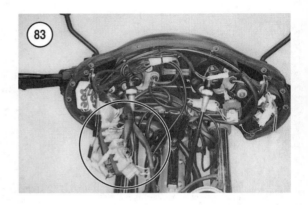

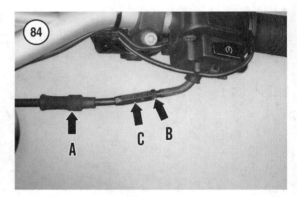

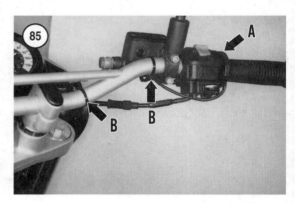

c. Install the screws and tighten securely.

d. Make sure the electrical connector is free of corrosion and is tight.

e. Check the operation of each switch mounted in the right side switch housing.

f. Operate the throttle lever and make sure the throttle linkage is operating correctly and with no binding. If operation is incorrect or there is binding, carefully check that the cable is attached correctly and there are no tight bends in the cable.

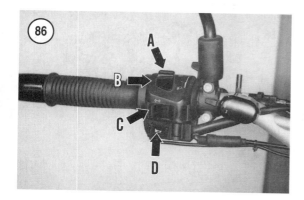

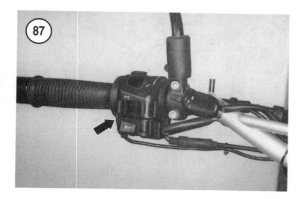

g. Adjust the throttle cable as described in Chapter Three.

Left Side Handlebar Switch Housing Replacement

The left side handlebar switch housing contains the headlight flasher button (A, **Figure 86**), headlight dimmer switch (B), turn signal switch (C), and horn button (D).

> *NOTE*
> *The four switches located within the left side handlebar switch housing are not available separately. If one switch is damaged, the entire right side switch housing assembly must be replaced.*

1. Disconnect the negative battery cable as described in this chapter.
2. Remove the fuel tank as described in Chapter Eight.
3. Remove the upper fairing as described in Chapter Fifteen.

4. Follow the wiring harness from the switch through the frame to the electrical connectors (**Figure 83**) on the inner fairing support. Locate and disconnect the ten-pin electrical connector containing nine wires.
5. Remove the screws securing the left side switch assembly (**Figure 87**) together and separate the switch assembly.
6. Remove any plastic clamps securing the switch wiring harness to the handlebar and frame. Carefully pull the wires out through the opening under the inner panel.
7. Disconnect the throttle cable from the throttle grip.
8. Remove the switch assembly from the handlebar and frame.
9. Install by reversing these removal steps while noting the following:
    a. Align the locating pin with the hole in the handlebar and install the switch onto the handlebar.
    b. Install the screws and tighten them securely.
    c. Make sure the electrical connector is free of corrosion and is tight.
    d. Check the operation of each switch mounted in the left side switch housing.
    e. Operate the choke lever and make sure the linkage is operating correctly and with no binding. If operation is incorrect or there is binding, carefully check that the cable is attached correctly and there are no tight bends in the cable.

Front Brake Light Switch Replacement

1. Disconnect the negative battery cable as described in this chapter.
2. Remove the fuel tank as described in Chapter Eight.
3. Remove the upper fairing as described in Chapter Fifteen.
4. Remove the small screws securing the brake light switch (**Figure 88**) to the master cylinder. Reinstall the screws onto the switch to prevent misplacing them.
5. Follow the wiring harness from the switch through the frame to the electrical connectors (**Figure 83**) on the inner fairing support. Locate and disconnect the two-pin electrical connector containing two wires.

9

6. Remove any plastic clamps securing the switch wiring harness to the handlebar and frame. Carefully pull the wires out through the opening under the inner panel.

7. Install by reversing these removal steps while noting the following:

   a. Install the small screws and tighten securely.
   b. Make sure the electrical connector is free of corrosion and is tight.
   c. Check the operation of the switch.

Rear Brake Light Switch Replacement

1. Refer to Chapter Fifteen and perform the following:

   a. Remove the seat.
   b. Remove the frame right side cover.

2. Remove the rear wheel as described in Chapter Eleven.

> *NOTE*
> *The following photographs show the rear swing arm removed to better illustrate the steps.*

3. Remove the Allen bolt securing the rear brake light switch (**Figure 89**) to the frame. Move the switch away from the frame and brake pedal. Do not damage the thin metal finger that touches the brake pedal.

4. Follow the wiring harness (**Figure 90**) from the switch through the frame to the electrical connector located adjacent to the voltage regulator/rectifier.

5. Remove any plastic clamps securing the switch wiring harness to the frame and adjacent hoses. Carefully pull the wires out through the frame.

6. Install by reversing these removal steps while noting the following:

   a. Install the small Allen bolt and tighten securely.
   b. Make sure the electrical connector is free of corrosion and is tight.
   c. Check the operation of the switch.

**Ignition Switch/Steering Lock
Removal/Installation**

1. Remove the upper fairing as described in Chapter Fifteen.

2. Remove the upper fork bridge (A, **Figure 91**) as described in Chapter Twelve.

3. Disconnect the ignition switch four-pin and three-pin electrical connectors (B, **Figure 91**).

4. Remove the screws that secure the ignition switch to the steering lock assembly on the bottom surface of the upper fork bridge.

5. Remove the ignition switch.

6. To remove the steering lock, perform the following:

   a. Remove the ignition switch as previously described.
   b. Insert the drill bushing (BMW part No. 51 0 520) into the hole of the shear bolt.
   c. Use a 5 mm (0.20 in.) drill bit to drill out the shear bolt to a minimum depth of 6 mm (0.24 in.). Remove the drill bit.
   d. Use an 8 mm (0.31 in.) drill bit to drill out the shear bolt to a minimum depth of 5 mm (0.20 in.). Remove the drill bit and the drill bushing.
   e. Repeat for the remaining shear bolt.
   f. Remove the steering lock assembly from the upper fork bridge.
   g. Install new shear bolts and tighten until they break off.

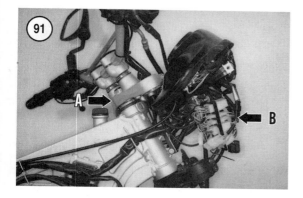

7. Install by reversing these removal steps while noting the following:

   a. Tighten the mounting bolts securely.

   b. Make sure the electrical connectors are free of corrosion and are tight.

   c. Check the operation of the switch.

Oil Pressure Switch Testing and Replacement

The oil pressure switch is located on the right side of the crankcase above the oil filter cavity.

1. Remove the exhaust pipe as described in Chapter Eight.

2. Remove the rubber boot and disconnect the electrical connector from the switch.

3. Turn the ignition switch ON.

4. Ground the switch wire to bare metal on the engine.

5. The oil pressure indicator lamp on the instrument panel must light.

6. If the indicator lamp does not light, check for a defective indicator lamp and inspect all wiring between the switch and the indicator lamp.

7A. If the oil pressure warning light operates properly, attach the electrical connector to the pressure switch. Make sure the connection is tight and oil-free. Slide the rubber boot back into position.

7B. If the warning light remains ON when the engine is running, shut the engine off. Check the engine lubrication system as described in Chapter Two.

NOTE
The following photograph shows the engine partially disassembled to better illustrate this step.

8. To replace the switch, perform the following:

   a. Unscrew the switch (**Figure 92**) from the engine.

   b. Apply a light coat of sealant to the switch threads prior to installation.

   c. Install the switch and tighten securely.

   d. Test the new switch as described in Steps 3-6.

9. Install the exhaust pipe as described in Chapter Eight.

Neutral Indicator Switch Testing and Replacement

The neutral indicator switch is located on the right side of the crankcase behind the alternator housing.

1. Remove the drive sprocket cover as described in Chapter Eleven.

2. Shift the transmission into neutral.

3. Disconnect the electrical connector (**Figure 93**) from the neutral indicator switch.

4. Turn the ignition switch ON.

5. Ground the switch wire to bare metal on the engine.

6. If the neutral indicator lamp lights, the neutral switch is defective. Replace the neutral indicator switch and retest.

9

7. If the neutral indicator lamp does not light, check for a defective indicator lamp, faulty wiring or a loose or corroded connection.

8A. If the neutral switch operates correctly, attach the electrical connector to the neutral switch. Make sure the connection is tight and free from oil.

8B. If the neutral switch is defective, replace the neutral indicator switch.

NOTE
The following photograph shows the engine disassembled to better illustrate this step.

9. To replace the old switch, perform the following:
   a. Shift the transmission into NEUTRAL.
   b. Unscrew and remove the neutral switch (**Figure 94**) from the crankcase.
   c. Apply a light coat of sealant to the switch threads prior to installation.
   d. Install the switch and tighten securely.
   e. Test the new switch as described in Steps 2-4.

HORN

The horn (**Figure 95**) is mounted on the lower fork bridge under the front fairing.

Testing

The following photograph shows the front fairing removed to better illustrate the steps.

1. Working under the front fairing, disconnect the electrical connector (A, **Figure 96**) from the horn terminal.
2. Connect a voltmeter as follows:
   a. Positive test lead to the brown/violet wire terminal in the electrical connector.
   b. Negative test lead to ground.
3. Turn the ignition switch to the ON position.
4. Depress the horn button. If battery voltage is present the horn is faulty or is not grounded properly. If there is no battery voltage, either the horn switch or the horn wiring is faulty.
5. Replace the horn or horn switch as necessary.

Replacement

The following photograph shows the front fairing removed to better illustrate the steps.

1. Disconnect the negative battery cable as described in this chapter.

2. Working under the front fairing, disconnect the electrical connector (A, **Figure 96**) from the horn terminal.

3. Remove the nut (B, **Figure 96**) that secures the horn assembly to the lower fork bridge.

4. Install the horn by reversing these removal steps. Note the following.

   a. Make sure the electrical connectors and horn spade terminals are free of corrosion.

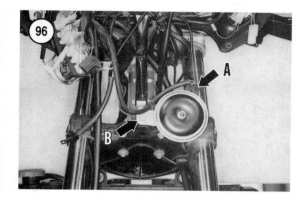

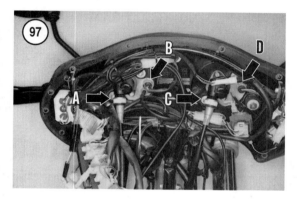

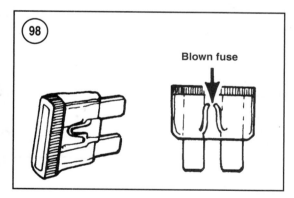

Blown fuse

b. Connect the wires to the horn's terminal.

c. Check that the horn operates correctly.

INSTRUMENTS

Removal/Installation

1. Disconnect the negative battery cable as described in this chapter.

2. Remove the front fairing as described in Chapter Fifteen.

3. To remove the speedometer, perform the following:

a. Unscrew and remove the speedometer cable (A, **Figure 97**) from the back of the instrument.

b. Withdraw the illumination light bulb and socket assembly (B, **Figure 97**) from the back of the speedometer.

c. Remove the screws and/nuts securing the speedometer to the mounting bracket.

d. Carefully remove the speedometer from the front of the inner front fairing.

4. To remove the tachometer, perform the following:

a. Unscrew and remove the tachometer cable (C, **Figure 97**) from the back of the instrument.

b. Withdraw the illumination light bulb and socket assembly (D, **Figure 97**) from the back of the tachometer.

c. Remove the screws and/nuts securing the tachometer to the mounting bracket.

d. Carefully remove the tachometer from the front of the inner front fairing.

5. Store the meters in a safe place.

6. Install by reversing these steps, while noting the following:

a. Install the instruments into the mounting brackets. Press firmly until the instrument is correctly seated and secured by the screws or nuts.

b. Connect the negative battery cable as described in this chapter.

FUSES

All models are equipped with three fuses to protect the electrical system. The fuses located under the seat. Refer to **Table 1** for fuse ratings.

If there is an electrical failure, first check for a blown fuse. The link in the element will be broken (**Figure 98**).

Whenever the fuse blows, find out the reason for the failure before replacing the fuse. Usually, the trouble is a short circuit in the wiring. This may be caused by worn-through insulation or a disconnected wire shorted to ground. Check the circuit that the fuse protects.

9

Fuse Replacement

1. Remove the seat as described in Chapter Fifteen.

2. Disconnect the negative battery cable as described in this chapter.

3. The fuse location is as follows:

   a. Ignition fuse (A, **Figure 99**).

   b. Lights, horn and starter fuse (B).

   c. Main fuse (C).

4. Locate the blown fuse and install a new one of the *same* amperage.

> *NOTE*
> *There are spaces for three additional spare fuses of each rating within the fuse block. Always carry spare fuses.*

WIRING DIAGRAM

The wiring diagram is located at the back of the manual.

Table 1 ELECTRICAL SPECIFICATIONS

Item	Specification
Battery capacity	12 volts, 12 amp hour
Alternator	
Output	14 volts, 280 watts
Coil output	0.20–0.50 ohm
Inductive sensor	190-300 ohms
Ignition coil	
Primary resistance	0.2-0.5 ohm
Secondary resistance	6000-13,000 ohms
Fuses	
Main	20 amp
Lights, horn, starter	15 amp
Ignition	7.5 amp

Table 2 REPLACEMENT BULBS

Item	Size	Type
Headlamp	12V 60/55	H4 halogen
Parking lamp	12V 4W	T8/4
Brake/tail lamp	12 V 21/5 W	P25-2
Turn signal lamp	12V 10W	P25-1

Table 3 ELECTRICAL SYSTEM TORQUE SPECIFICATIONS

Item	N•m	in.-lb.	ft-lb.
Alternator rotor nut	180	–	133

CHAPTER TEN

COOLING SYSTEM

The cooling system consists of a single radiator, reserve tank, a radiator cap, water pump and hoses. During operation, the coolant heats and expands, thus pressurizing the system. The radiator cap seals the system. Water and anti-freeze that was cooled in the radiator is pumped down through the radiator and into the cylinder and cylinder head. Next, the coolant passes through the water jackets and back into the radiator. Finally, the coolant flows down through the radiator where it is cooled once again.

The water pump requires no routine maintenance and can be serviced after first removing the left side crankcase cover. The thermostat and cooling fan can be serviced with the engine mounted in the frame.

This chapter describes repair and replacement of cooling system components. To protect the engine and cooling system, drain and flush the cooling system at least once a year. Refer to *Coolant Change* in Chapter Three.

Cooling system specifications are in **Table 1**.

SAFETY PRECAUTIONS

Keep safety precautions in mind to prevent injury. *Never* remove the radiator cap (**Figure 1**) when the engine is hot. Instead, wait until the system cools down. When removing the radiator cap, first place a rag over the cap and stand off to one side of the radiator. Then slowly turn the radiator cap to its safety stop to allow system pressure to escape, then push the cap down and turn it to release it from the groove in the top of the radiator. Always check the coolant level in the coolant reservoir tank (**Figure 2**) *before* the first ride of the day.

Anti-freeze is an environmental toxin and cannot legally be disposed of by flushing it down a drain or pouring it onto the ground. Place the old antifreeze into a suitable container and dispose of it according to local EPA regulations. Do not store coolant where it is accessible to children or pets.

HOSES AND HOSE CLAMPS

Hoses deteriorate with age and should be replaced whenever they show signs of cracking or leakage. The spray of hot coolant from a cracked hose can injure the rider. Loss of coolant can also cause the engine to overheat.

Whenever any component of the cooling system is removed, inspect the adjoining hose(s) to determine if replacement is necessary.

The small diameter coolant hoses are very stiff and are sometimes difficult to install. Prior to installing the hoses, soak the ends in hot water to make them pliable and they will slide on much easier. Do not apply any type of lubricant to the inner surfaces of the hoses, as the hose may slip off when the engine is running, even with the hose clamp securely in place.

1. Make sure the cooling system is cool before removing any coolant hose.

2. Make sure to replace the hoses with BMW replacement hoses, since they are formed to a specific shape and are of the correct length and inner diameter.

3. Loosen the hose clamps on the hose that is to be replaced. Slide the clamps back off of the component fittings.

> *CAUTION*
> *Do not pry or twist too hard while attempting to remove a stubborn hose from the radiator. The aluminum radiator inlets and outlets are fragile and easily damaged.*

4. Twist the hose to release it from the fitting. If the hose has been installed for some time, it will probably be difficult to break loose. If so, carefully insert a small pick tool or screwdriver between the hose and fitting. Work the tool around the fitting to break the seal and carefully pry the hose from the fitting.

5. Examine the fittings for cracks or other damage. Repair or replace as necessary. If the fitting is good, use a wirebrush to clean off any hose residue that may have transferred to the fitting. Wipe clean with a cloth.

6. Inspect the hose clamps for rust and corrosion, and replace if necessary. The hose clamps are as important as the hoses. If they do not hold the hose in place tightly, there will be a coolant leak. For best results, always use the screw adjusting-type hose clamps.

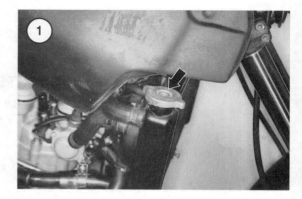

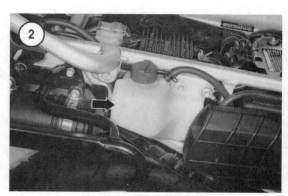

7. With the hose installed correctly on the fitting, position the hose clamp back away from the end of the hose approximately 1/2-inch (12.78 mm). Make sure the hose clamp is still positioned over the fitting and tighten the clamps securely.

COOLING SYSTEM INSPECTION

1. Check the radiator for clogged or damaged fins.

2. To clean a clogged radiator, gently blow compressed air from the rear (engine side). Do not place

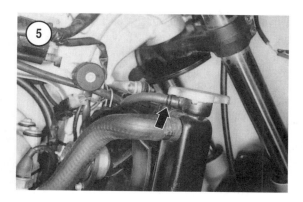

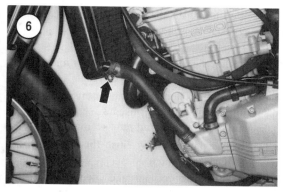

the air nozzle directly against the radiator. Blow air directly perpendicular to the radiator fins; never blow air at an angle against the fins.

3. Check the radiator for loose or missing mounting bolts.

4. Check all coolant hoses for cracks or damage. Replace any questionable parts. Make sure the hose clamps are tight, but not so tight that they cut the hoses.

5. Make sure the overflow hose (**Figure 3**) is connected to the radiator fitting next to the cap and is not clogged or damaged.

6. Pressure test the cooling system as described in Chapter Three.

7. If there is coolant loss, the system is leaking. Check the cooling system hoses, water pump and water jackets (cylinder and cylinder head) carefully.

RADIATOR AND COOLING FAN

Removal/Installation

1. Support the motorcycle with the front wheel off the ground. See *Bike Stands* in Chapter Eleven.

2. Refer to Chapter Fifteen and perform the following:
   a. Front faring.
   b. Remove the engine lower shroud.
   c. Radiator shroud.

3. Remove the fuel tank as described in Chapter Eight.

4. Drain the cooling system as described in Chapter Three.

> *WARNING*
> *Coolant is very slippery if spilled on a concrete floor or a similar surface. Do not walk on spilled coolant–wipe it off immediately. Wipe off any coolant that may get onto your shoes.*

> *NOTE*
> *Even though the cooling system has been drained, there will be some residual coolant remaining in the radiator and hoses. Place a drain pan under each hose as it is removed. Also have shop rags handy to wipe up any spilled coolant.*

5. Disconnect the cooling fan electrical connector (**Figure 4**).

6. Disconnect the overflow hose from the radiator fitting (**Figure 5**).

7. Disconnect the radiator hose (**Figure 6**) from the bottom of the radiator.

8. Disconnect the radiator top hose from the top of the radiator or the thermostat housing (**Figure 7**).

9. Remove the bolts, nuts and washers (**Figure 8**) securing the radiator to the frame mounting bracket.

10. Carefully move the radiator up and off the lower mounting bracket (**Figure 9**) and remove it from the frame.

10

11. Install the radiators by reversing these removal steps while noting the following:

    a. If removed, be sure to reinstall the collars within the rubber mounting bushings (**Figure 10**).

    b. Do not tighten the radiator mounting bolts and nuts until all hoses are in place. Then tighten the bolts and nuts securely.

    c. Route the overflow hose through the hose guide on the radiator.

    d. Add engine coolant and bleed the cooling system as described in Chapter Three.

Inspection

1. Flush off the exterior of the radiator with a low-pressure stream of water from a garden hose. Spray the front and back of the radiator to remove all dirt and debris. *Carefully* use a whisk broom or stiff paintbrush to remove any stubborn dirt.

> *CAUTION*
> *Do not damage the cooling fins and tubes.*

2. Examine the radiator cooling surface for damage (A, **Figure 11**). If the radiator is slightly damaged and is repairable, refer service to a radiator repair shop.

3. Carefully straighten out any bent cooling fins with a wide-blade screwdriver. Replace the radiator if it is damaged across 20% or more of its frontal area.

4. Check for cracks or leakage (usually a moss-green colored residue) at the filler neck, the inlet and outlet hose fittings and the upper and lower tank seams (B, **Figure 11**).

5. Check for missing or damaged radiator mounting bushings and collars (**Figure 12**). Replace, if necessary.

6. Inspect the radiator cap (**Figure 13**) and seal for damage. Check for a bent or distorted cap. Raise the vacuum valve and rubber seal and rinse the cap with water to flush away any loose rust or dirt particles. If the condition of the radiator cap is in doubt, pressure check it as described in Chapter Three.

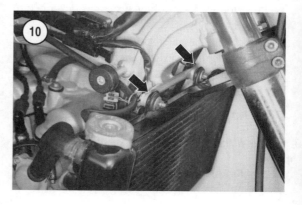

7. Check all coolant hoses for cracks, bulges or other damage, and replace if necessary.

8. Replace damaged or corroded hose clamps.

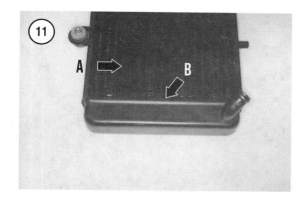

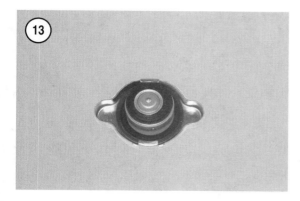

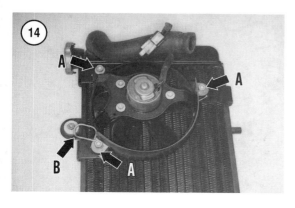

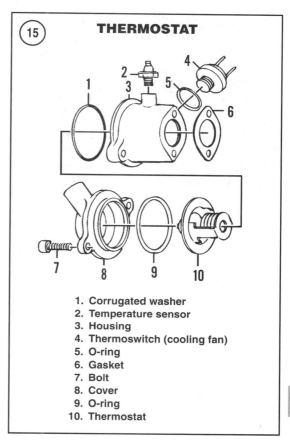

THERMOSTAT

1. Corrugated washer
2. Temperature sensor
3. Housing
4. Thermoswitch (cooling fan)
5. O-ring
6. Gasket
7. Bolt
8. Cover
9. O-ring
10. Thermostat

10

COOLING FAN

Removal/Installation

Replacement parts for the fan assembly are not available. If the fan motor is defective the entire fan assembly must be replaced.

1. Remove the radiator as described in this chapter.
2. Place a blanket or large towels on the workbench to protect the radiator.
3. Remove the fasteners (A, **Figure 14**) that secure the fan shroud and carefully detach the fan assembly from the radiator.
4. Install by reversing these removal steps. Be sure to attach the overflow hose guide (B, **Figure 14**) to the upper left side screw location.

THERMOSTAT

Removal/Installation

Refer to **Figure 15**.

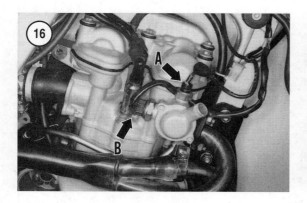

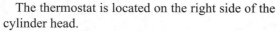

The thermostat is located on the right side of the cylinder head.

1. Refer to Chapter Fifteen and perform the following:

    a. Remove the seat.

    b. Remove the fairing.

2. Remove the fuel tank as described in Chapter Eight.

3. Drain the cooling system as described under *Coolant Change* in Chapter Three.

4. Disconnect the radiator top hose from the top of the radiator or thermostat housing (**Figure 7**).

> *NOTE*
> *The following photographs show the radiator assembly removed to better illustrate the steps.*

5. Disconnect the electrical connector from the engine coolant temperature sensor (A, **Figure 16**) and the coolant thermoswitch (B) for the cooling fan.

6. Remove the bolts (A, **Figure 17**) securing the thermostat cover (B), then remove the cover and O-ring gasket.

7. Remove the thermostat (**Figure 18**) and corrugated washer from the thermostat housing.

8. If necessary, remove the stainless steel bolts (A, **Figure 19**) securing the thermostat housing (B) to the cylinder head and remove the housing and gasket.

9. If necessary, test the thermostat as described in this chapter.

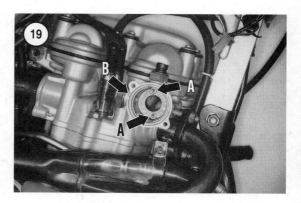

10. Install by reversing these removal steps while noting the following:

    a. If removed, install a *new* gasket on the housing (B, **Figure 19**) and make sure to use the stainless steel bolts (A) to secure the cover. Any other type of screw will rust.

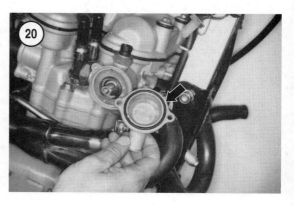

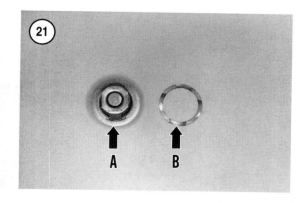

A   B

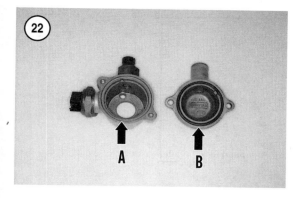

A   B

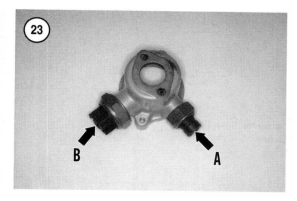

B   A

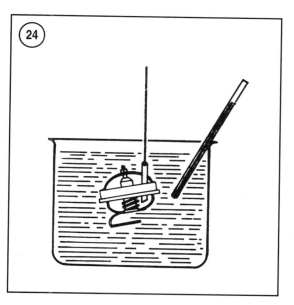

Inspection

1. Inspect the thermostat (A, **Figure 21**) for damage and make sure the spring has not sagged or broken.

2. Check the corrugated washer (B, **Figure 21**) for damage.

3. Clean the inside of the thermostat housing (A, **Figure 22**) of any debris or old coolant residue. Make sure the opening leading to the hose is clear.

4. Inspect the cover for corrosion or damage. Replace the O-ring gasket (B, **Figure 22**) if it is hard or deteriorated.

5. Check the engine coolant temperature sensor (A, **Figure 23**) and the coolant thermoswitch (B) for signs of coolant leakage where they attach to the housing. Tighten if necessary.

Testing

Test the thermostat to ensure proper operation. Replace the thermostat if it remains open at normal room temperature or stays closed after the specified temperature has been reached during the test procedure.

Suspend the thermostat in a pan of water (**Figure 24**). Place a thermometer in the pan of water (use a cooking or candy thermometer that is rated higher than the test temperature). Gradually heat the water and continue to gently stir the water until it reaches

NOTE
The thermostat is not equipped with an air-bleed hole and can be installed into the housing in any orientation.

b. Install the cover O-ring gasket (**Figure 20**).

c. Tighten the bolts securely.

d. Refill the cooling system with the recommended type and quantity of coolant as described in Chapter Three.

10

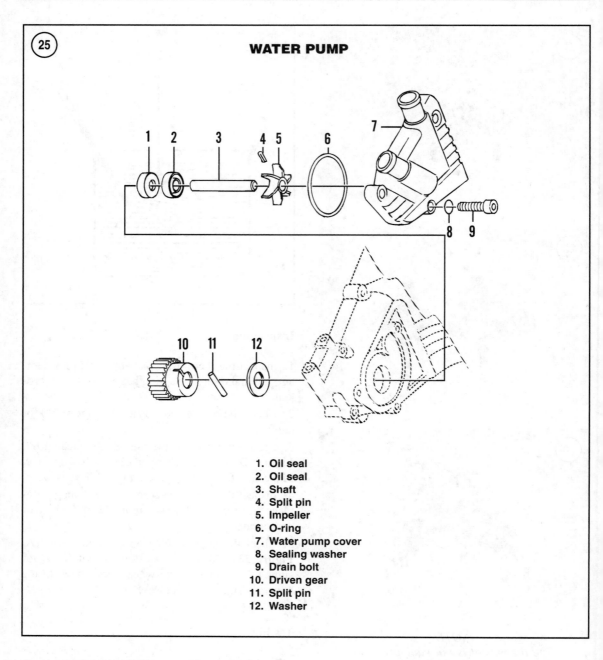

WATER PUMP

1. Oil seal
2. Oil seal
3. Shaft
4. Split pin
5. Impeller
6. O-ring
7. Water pump cover
8. Sealing washer
9. Drain bolt
10. Driven gear
11. Split pin
12. Washer

the temperature in **Table 1**. At this temperature the thermostat valve should open.

NOTE
Valve operation is sometimes slow; it may take 3-5 minutes for the valve to open completely. If the valve fails to open, replace the thermostat. Make sure to replace it with one of the same temperature rating.

WATER PUMP

The water pump (**Figure 25**) is mounted inside the right crankcase cover.

Water Pump Cover Removal/Installation

1. Drain the cooling system as described under *Coolant Change* in Chapter Three.

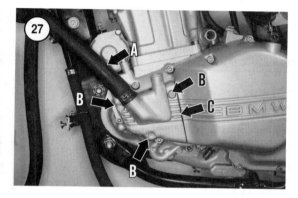

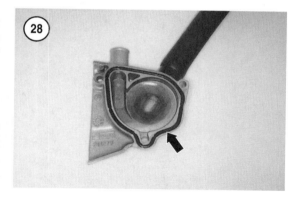

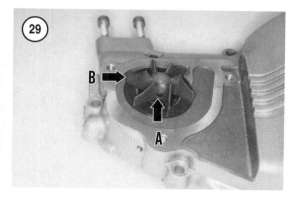

2. Refer to Chapter Fifteen and perform the following:
   a. Remove the seat.
   b. Remove the left side cylinder head cover.
3. Disconnect the rear coolant hose (**Figure 26**) and the front coolant hose (A, **Figure 27**) from the cover.
4. Loosen the water pump cover mounting bolts (B, **Figure 27**) in a crisscross pattern. Remove the bolts.
5. Remove the water pump cover (C, **Figure 27**) and O-ring gasket.
6. Remove the crankcase left side cover as described in Chapter Five.
7. Clean the cover in solvent and thoroughly dry. Inspect the cover for wear or damage and replace if necessary.
8. Inspect the O-ring seal (**Figure 28**) for hardness or deterioration. Replace if necessary.
9. Install by reversing these removal steps while noting the following:
   a. Securely tighten the bolts in a crisscross pattern.
   b. Connect the coolant hoses onto the cover. Fit the hose clamp into position and tighten the clamp securely
   c. Refill the cooling system as described under *Coolant Change* in Chapter Three.

Disassembly/Assembly

1. Remove the crankcase left side cover as described in Chapter Five.
2. Place the crankcase left side cover right side up on the workbench.
3. Carefully drive out the split pin (A, **Figure 29**) and remove the impeller (B) from the shaft.
4. Turn the crankcase left side cover upside down on the workbench.
5. Carefully drive out the split pin and remove the impeller driven gear (**Figure 30**) and washer from the shaft.
6. Withdraw the shaft from the crankcase left side cover.
7. Assemble by reversing these disassembly steps.

Inspection

1. Clean all parts in solvent and thoroughly dry.

10

2. Inspect the impeller driven gear for broken or missing teeth.

3. Inspect the impeller shaft for burrs, excessive wear or damage. Pay close attention to the point on the shaft where the oil seals ride. Replace the impeller shaft if there is any wear or scoring.

4. Inspect the impeller blades for corrosion and damage.

5. Inspect the oil seals for damage. If necessary, replace the oil seals as described in Chapter One.

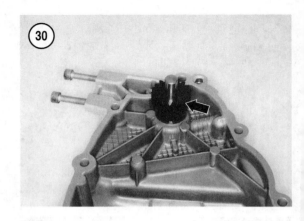

Table 1 COOLING SYSTEM SPECIFICATIONS

Capacity	
Cooling system	1.2 L (1.27 U.S. qt./2.11 lmp. pts.)
	BMW antifreeze
Recovery tank	200 cc (6.7 U.S. oz./5.6 lmp. oz.)
Antifreeze/distilled water ratio	50% antifreeze/50% distilled water
	Protection down to -25° C (-13° F)
Thermostat	
Opens at	72-75° C (162-167° F)
Opening	7.5 mm (0.30 in.) at 87° C (189° F)
Pressure test	98 kPa (14.23 psi)

CHAPTER ELEVEN

WHEELS, HUBS, TIRES
AND DRIVE CHAIN

This chapter describes disassembly and repair of the front and rear wheels, hubs, tires and drive chain service. For routine maintenance, see Chapter Three.

Tables 1-3 are at the end of the chapter.

BIKE STANDS

Many procedures in this chapter require that the front or rear wheel be lifted off the ground. To do this, a quality motorcycle front end stand (**Figure 1**), or swing arm stand, or suitable size jack is required. Before purchasing or using a stand, check the manufacturer's instructions to make sure it is designed for these models. If any adjustments or accessories are required to the motorcycle and/or stand, perform the necessary adjustments or install the correct parts before lifting the motorcycle. When using the stand, have an assistant standing by to help. Some means to tie down the motorcycle may also be required. After lifting the motorcycle

on a stand, make sure it is properly supported before walking away from it.

FRONT WHEEL

Removal

1. Support the motorcycle with the front wheel off the ground. See *Bike Stands* in this chapter.
2. Remove the front fender as described in Chapter Fifteen.
3. Remove the front brake caliper as described in Chapter Fourteen.
4. Remove the plug (**Figure 2**) from end of the front axle.
5. Loosen the front axle holder nuts (A, **Figure 3**).
6. Loosen the front axle shaft (B, **Figure 3**).
7. Remove the front axle holder nuts and holder.
8. Prior to removing the front axle, note the location of the speedometer drive and the left side spacer. These parts must be reinstalled on the correct side during installation.

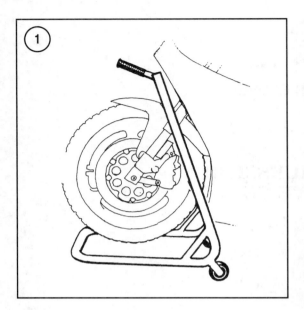

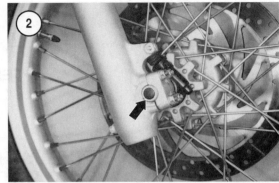

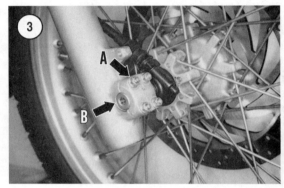

9. Hold onto the front wheel and withdraw the front axle (A, **Figure 4**) from the right side. Do not lose the left side spacer (**Figure 5**).

10. Move the speedometer drive and cable (B, **Figure 4**) out of the way.

> *NOTE*
> *Place a plastic or wooden spacer between the brake pads in place of the disc. Then, if the brake lever is inadvertently applied, the pistons will not be forced out of the caliper. If this occurs, disassemble the caliper to reseat the pistons.*

11. Pull the wheel away from the fork sliders to remove it.

12. Remove the speedometer drive unit and felt seal from the right side and remove the spacer from the left side.

> *CAUTION*
> *Do not set the wheel down on the brake disc surface, as it may be damaged.*

13. Inspect the front wheel assembly as described in this chapter.

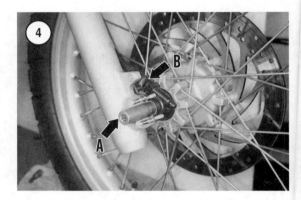

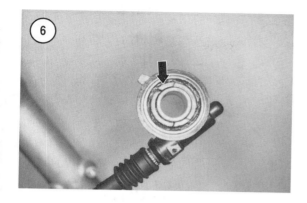

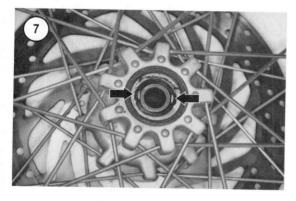

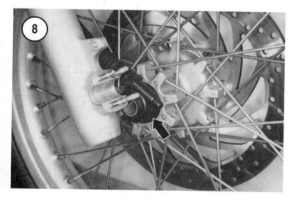

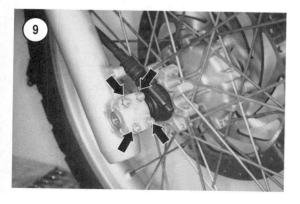

Installation

1. Clean the axle in solvent and dry thoroughly. Make sure the axle bearing surfaces on both fork sliders and the axle are free of burrs and nicks.

2. Apply Shell Retinax EP2 grease, or an equivalent, to the axle prior to installation. Also apply to the speedometer drive unit.

3. Install the wheel into position between the fork sliders.

4. Align the speedometer drive unit dog receptacles (**Figure 6**) with the speedometer drive dogs in the wheel (**Figure 7**) and install it onto the wheel hub (**Figure 8**).

5. Install the spacer (**Figure 5**) onto the left side wheel hub.

6. Lift the wheel into position and install the axle from the right side (A, **Figure 4**). Push the front axle through the right side fork slider, the speedometer drive unit and hub.

7. Position the front axle holder with the UP arrow facing up and install it (A, **Figure 3**). Tighten the nuts only finger-tight at this time.

8. Screw the axle into place in the left side slider and tighten to the specification in **Table 2**.

9. Install the front brake caliper as described in Chapter Fourteen.

10. Remove the stand and lower the front wheel onto the ground.

11. Sit on the motorcycle, apply the front brake and compress the front fork several times to seat the front axle within the fork sliders. Place the motorcycle on the side stand.

12. On the right side fork slider, tighten the nuts on the front axle holder (**Figure 9**). Tighten the upper nuts first then the lower nuts to the specification in **Table 2**. This will leave a gap at the bottom of the front axle holder (**Figure 10**).

13. Install the plug (**Figure 2**) into the front axle.

14. Install the front fender as described in Chapter Fifteen.

Inspection

Replace any worn or damaged parts as described in this section.

1. Turn each bearing inner race (**Figure 11**) by hand. The bearing must turn smoothly. Some axial play (end play) is normal, but radial play (side play) must be negligible. See **Figure 12**. If the bearing is

11

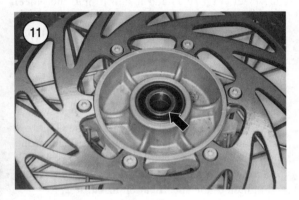

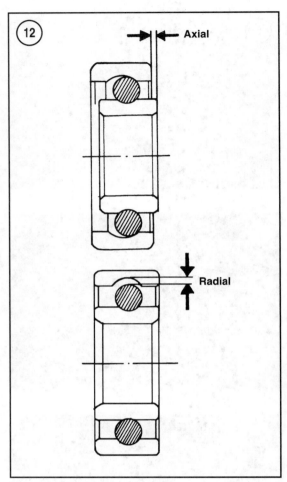

damaged, replace both bearings as a set. Refer to *Front and Rear Hubs* in this chapter.

2. Clean the axle and axle spacers in solvent to remove all grease and dirt. Make sure the axle contact surfaces are clean and free of dirt and old grease.

3. Check the axle runout with a set of V-blocks and dial indicator (**Figure 13**).

4. Check the spacers for wear, burrs and damage. Replace as necessary.

5. Check the brake disc bolts (**Figure 14**) for tightness. To service the brake disc, refer to Chapter Fourteen.

6. Check wheel runout and spoke tension as described in this chapter.

REAR WHEEL

Removal

1. Support the motorcycle with the rear wheel off the ground. See *Bike Stands* in this chapter.

2. Loosen the axle nut (A, **Figure 15**).

3. Loosen the drive chain tensioner screw (B, **Figure 15**) on each side to allow drive chain slack.

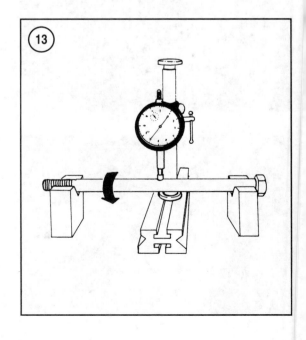

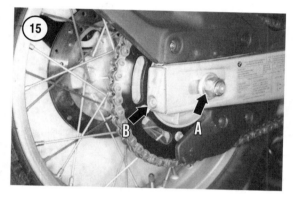

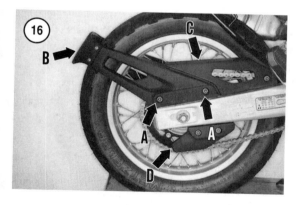

4. Remove the bolts (A, **Figure 16**) on each side that secure the mudguard (B) and remove the mudguard assembly from the swing arm.

5. Remove the screws securing the drive chain guard (C, **Figure 16**) and remove the guard.

6. Remove the screws securing the driven sprocket guard (D, **Figure 16**) and remove the guard.

7. Push the rear wheel forward and remove the drive chain from the driven sprocket.

8. Remove the rear axle nut and washer.

9. Withdraw the rear axle (A, **Figure 17**) and washer (B) while holding onto the rear wheel. Lower the rear wheel to the ground, roll it to the rear and remove it.

10. Remove the rear brake caliper (**Figure 18**) from the swing arm and support it so the hose is not stressed.

11. Remove the right side (A, **Figure 19**) and left side (A, **Figure 20**) spacers from the wheel hub.

CAUTION
Do not set the wheel down on the brake disc surface, as it may be damaged.

NOTE
Place a plastic or wooden spacer between the brake pads in place of the disc. Then, if the brake pedal is inad-

11

vertently depressed, the pistons will not be forced out of the caliper. If this occurs, disassemble the caliper to re-seat the pistons.

12. Inspect the rear wheel as described in this chapter.

Installation

1. Clean the axle in solvent and dry thoroughly. Make sure the bearing surfaces on the axle are free from burrs and nicks.
2. Apply Retinax EP2 grease, or an equivalent, to the axle shaft prior to installation.
3. Position the rear wheel between the swing arm sides and place the drive belt on the sprocket.
4. Install the right side (A, **Figure 19**) and left side (A, **Figure 20**) spacers into the rear wheel oil seals or bearings.
5. Remove the spacer block from between the brake pads.

CAUTION
When installing the rear wheel in the following steps, carefully insert the brake disc between the brake pads in the caliper assembly. Do not force the brake disc, as it can damage the leading edge of both brake pads.

6. Move the rear brake caliper (**Figure 18**) into position on the swing arm.
7. Install the washer (B, **Figure 17**) onto the rear axle.
8. Lift the rear wheel and install the rear axle from the left side (A, **Figure 17**). Install the axle through the swing arm, the rear brake caliper carrier and the other side of the swing arm.
9. After the rear axle is installed, check to make sure both axle spacers are still in place.
10. Install the washer and axle nut (A, **Figure 21**). Do not tighten at this time.
11. Push the rear wheel forward and install the drive chain (B, **Figure 21**) onto the driven sprocket.
12. Adjust the drive chain tension as described in Chapter Three. Tighten the axle nut to the specification in **Table 2**.
13. Rotate the wheel several times to make sure it rotates freely. Then apply the rear brake pedal several times to seat the pads against the disc.

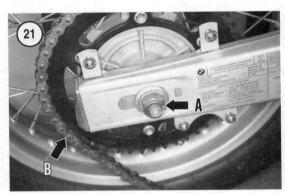

14. Install the driven sprocket guard (D, **Figure 16**), the drive chain guard (C) and the mudguard (B). Tighten all bolts securely.

Inspection

Replace any worn or damaged parts as described in this section.

1. On the rear wheel, inspect the oil seals for excessive wear, hardness, cracks or other damage. Refer to the right side (**Figure 22**) and left side (A, **Figure**

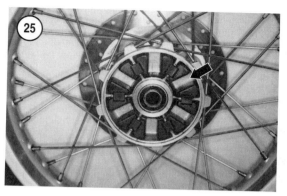

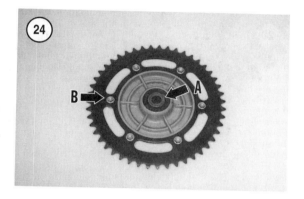

23) in the driven flange. If necessary, replace the seals as described under *Front and Rear Hubs* in this chapter.

2. Turn each bearing inner race (B, **Figure 22**) by hand. The bearing must turn smoothly. Some axial play (end play) is normal, but radial play (side play) must be negligible. See **Figure 12**. If one bearing is damaged, replace both bearings as a set. Refer to *Front and Rear Hubs* in this chapter.

3. Clean the axle and axle spacers in solvent to remove all grease and dirt. Make sure the axle contact surfaces are free of dirt and old grease.

4. Check the axle runout with a set of V-blocks and a dial indicator (**Figure 13**).

5. Check the spacers for wear, burrs and damage. Replace as necessary.

6. Check the brake disc bolts (B, **Figure 20**) for tightness. To service the brake disc, refer to Chapter Twelve.

7. Check the final driven flange sprocket bolts (B, **Figure 19**) for tightness. Service the final driven flange sprocket as described in this chapter.

8. Check wheel runout and spoke tension as described in this chapter.

DRIVEN SPROCKET AND DRIVEN FLANGE

Removal/Disassembly/Assembly/Installation

1. Remove the rear wheel as described in this chapter.

2. If the driven sprocket is going to be removed, loosen the mounting bolts and nuts (B, **Figure 19**) securing the driven sprocket to the driven flange at this time.

NOTE
If the driven flange assembly is difficult to remove from the hub, tap on the back of the sprocket (from the opposite side of the wheel through the wheel spokes) with the wooden handle of a hammer. Tap evenly around the perimeter of the sprocket until the coupling assembly is free of the hub and the rubber dampers.

3. Pull straight up to remove the driven flange assembly (C, **Figure 19**) from the rear hub.

4. If still in place, remove the right side axle spacer (A, **Figure 24**).

5. If necessary, remove the driven sprocket bolts, washer and nuts (B, **Figure 24**) and separate the driven sprocket from the driven flange.

6. Install by reversing these removal steps while noting the following:

   a. Align the rear hub rubber damper receptacles (**Figure 25**) with the driven flange raised webs (**Figure 26**) and install the driven flange. Tap it in until it bottoms.

   b. If removed, tighten the driven sprocket bolts (B, **Figure 24**) and nuts securely after the assembly has been reinstalled in the rear wheel.

11

c. Install the right side axle spacer (A, **Figure 24**).

Inspection

1. Inspect the rubber dampers (**Figure 27**) for signs of damage or deterioration. If damaged, replace as a complete set.

2. Inspect the raised webs where the rubber dampers fit. Check for cracks or wear. If any damage is visible, replace the rear wheel.

3. Inspect the driven flange assembly for cracks or damage, replace if necessary.

4. Inspect the driven sprocket teeth (**Figure 28**). If the teeth are worn (**Figure 29**), replace the driven sprocket as described in this chapter.

> *CAUTION*
> *If the driven sprocket (A, **Figure 30**) requires replacement, also replace the engine drive sprocket (B) and the drive chain. Never install a new drive chain over worn sprockets or a worn drive chain over new sprockets. The old part will wear out the new part prematurely.*

5. If the driven sprocket requires replacement, also inspect the drive chain (Chapter Three) and engine drive sprocket as described in this chapter. They also may be worn and need replacing.

6. Inspect the bearing for excessive axial play (end play) and radial (side play) (**Figure 31**). Replace the bearing if it has an excess amount of free play.

7. On a non-sealed bearing, check the balls for evidence of wear, pitting or excessive heat (bluish tint). Turn the inner race by hand. The bearing must turn smoothly. Replace a questionable bearing. When

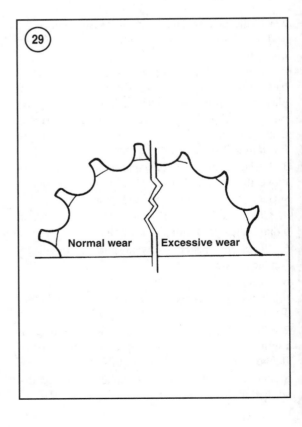

Normal wear   Excessive wear

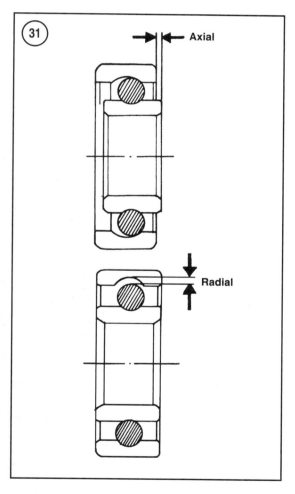

Fully sealed bearings provide better protection from dirt and moisture that passes through worn or damaged oil seals.

Sprocket Runout Inspection

1. Shift the transmission into neutral.

2. Support the motorcycle with the rear wheel off the ground. See *Bike Stands* in this chapter.

3. Place a dial gauge against the rear sprocket near the teeth and drive chain.

4. Slowly rotate the rear wheel and note the readings on the dial indicator. The difference between the lowest and highest dial gauge readings is the amount of runout. The standard runout is 0.4 mm (0.016 in.) with the service limit of 0.5 mm (0.0196 in.). Replace the rear sprocket if the runout is to the service limit.

5. Remove the jack or wooden blocks. Remove the blocks from the front wheel.

FRONT AND REAR HUBS

Sealed ball bearings are installed on each side of the hub. Do not remove the bearing assemblies unless they require replacement.

Preliminary Inspection

Inspect each wheel bearing prior to removing it from the wheel hub.

CAUTION
Do not remove the wheel bearings for inspection purposes, as they will be damaged during the removal process. Remove wheel bearings only if they are to be replaced.

1. Perform Steps 1-3 of *Driven Sprocket and Driven Flange Disassembly.*

2. Turn each bearing by hand. The bearings must turn smoothly.

3. Inspect the play of the inner race of each wheel bearing. Check for excessive axial play and radial play (**Figure 31**). Replace the bearing if it has an excess amount of free play.

replacing the bearing, make sure to take the old bearing along to ensure a perfect match-up.

NOTE
Fully sealed bearings are available from many bearing specialty shops.

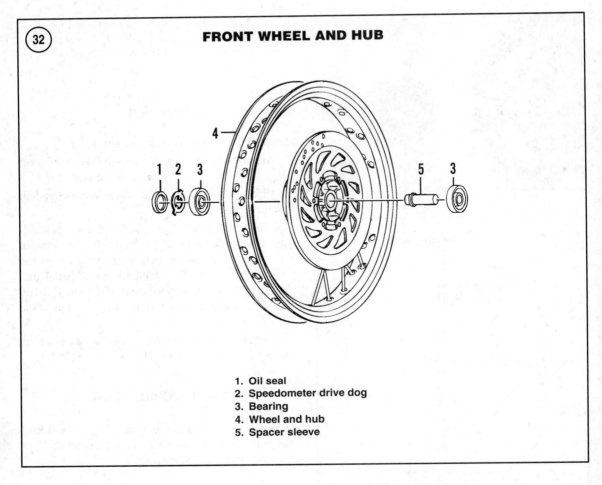

(32)

FRONT WHEEL AND HUB

4

1 2 3

5 3

1. **Oil seal**
2. **Speedometer drive dog**
3. **Bearing**
4. **Wheel and hub**
5. **Spacer sleeve**

Disassembly

This procedure applies to both the front and rear wheel and hub assemblies. Where differences occur between the different hubs, they are identified. Refer to **Figure 32** and **Figure 33**.

1A. Remove the front wheel as described in this chapter.

1B. Remove the rear wheel as described in this chapter.

2. If still in place, remove the axle spacer(s) from each side of the hub.

3A. On the front wheel, pry the right side seal out with a wide-blade screwdriver (A, **Figure 34**). Cushion the screwdriver with a rag (B, **Figure 34**) to avoid damaging the hub or brake disc. Remove the speedometer drive dog.

3B. On the rear wheel, pry the oil seals out with a wide-blade screwdriver (A, **Figure 35**). Refer to the right side (A, **Figure 22**) and left side (**Figure 23**) in

the driven flange. Cushion the screwdriver with a rag (B, **Figure 35**) to avoid damaging the hub or brake disc.

4. If necessary, remove the bolts securing the brake disc and remove the disc.

5. Before proceeding further, inspect the wheel bearings as described in this chapter. If they must be replaced, proceed as follows.

6A. If the special tools are not used, perform the following:

  a. To remove the right- and left-hand bearings and spacer sleeve, insert a soft aluminum or brass drift into one side of the hub.

  b. Push the spacer sleeve over to one side and place the drift on the inner race of the lower bearing.

  c. Tap the bearing out of the hub with a hammer, working around the perimeter of the inner race (**Figure 36**). Remove the bearing and spacer collar.

33

REAR WHEEL AND HUB

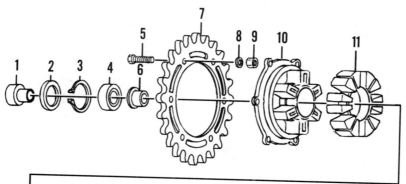

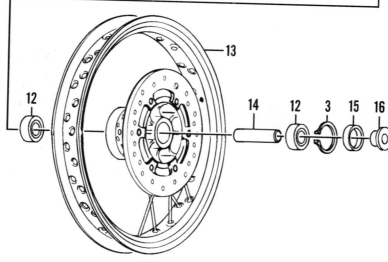

1. Spacer-right side
2. Oil seal
3. Snap ring
4. Bearing (driven flange)
5. Bolt
6. Spacer
7. Driven sprocket
8. Washer
9. Nut
10. Driven flange
11. Rubber dampers
12. Bearing
13. Wheel and hub
14. Spacer sleeve
15. Oil seal
16. Spacer-left side

11

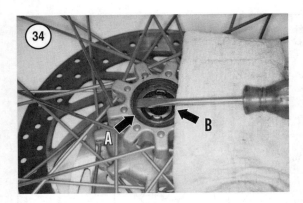

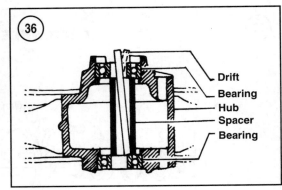

d. Repeat for the bearing on the other side.

NOTE
The Kowa Seiki Wheel Bearing Re-
*mover set (**Figure 37**) can be ordered*
through a K & L Supply Co. dealer.

6B. To remove the bearings with the Kowa Seiki Wheel Bearing Remover set, perform the following:

  a. Select the correct size remover head tool and insert it into the bearing.

  b. Turn the wheel over and insert the remover shaft into the backside of the adapter. Tap the wedge and force it into the slit in the adapter (**Figure 38**). This will force the adapter against the bearing inner race.

  c. Tap on the end of the wedge bar with a hammer to drive the bearing out of the hub. Remove the bearing and the distance collar.

  d. Repeat for the bearing on the other side.

7. Clean the inside and the outside of the hub with solvent. Dry with compressed air.

Assembly

CAUTION
*The removal process will generally damage the bearings. Replace the wheel bearings in pairs along with the one located within the driven sprocket drum. **Never** reinstall them after they are removed; always install **new** bearings.*

1. Blow any debris out of the hub prior to installing the new bearings.

2. Apply a light coat of Shell Retinax EP2, or an equivalent wheel bearing grease, to the bearing seating areas of the hub. This will make bearing installation easier.

CAUTION
Install non-sealed bearings with the single sealed side facing outward. Tap the bearings squarely into place and tap on the outer race only. Do not tap

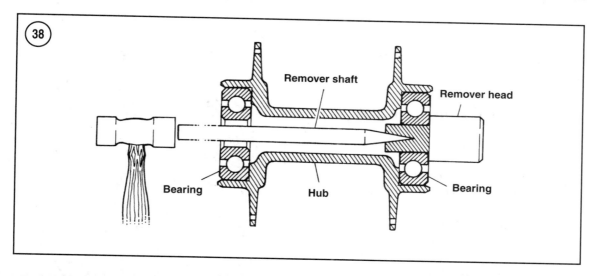

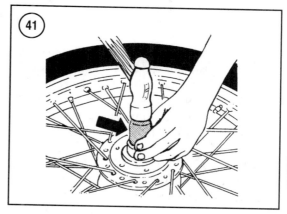

11

on the inner race, or the bearing might be damaged. Be sure that the bearings are completely seated.

3. Select a driver or socket with an outside diameter slightly smaller than the bearing's outside diameter. Refer to **Figure 39** for the front wheel or **Figure 40** for the rear wheel.

4. Tap the right side bearing squarely into place and tap on the outer race only (**Figure 41**). Tap the bearing into the hub bore until it bottoms. Make sure that the bearing is completely seated.

5. Turn the wheel over on the workbench and install the spacer sleeve.

6. Use the same tool setup to drive in the left side bearing.

7A. On the front wheel, install the speedometer drive dog. Install the seal and select a driver with an outside diameter slightly smaller than the seal's outside diameter. Then drive the seal in the bore until it is flush with the outside of the bearing bore.

7B. On the rear wheel, place the seal squarely over the bore opening with the closed side facing out. Then drive the seal in the bore until it is flush with the outside of the bearing bore.

8. If the brake disc was removed, install it as described in Chapter Twelve.

9A. Install the front wheel as described in this chapter.

9B. Install the rear wheel as described in this chapter.

WHEEL RUNOUT

1. Remove the front or rear wheel as described in this chapter.

2. Install the wheel in a wheel truing stand (**Figure 42**) and check the wheel for excessive wobble or runout.

3. If the wheel is not running true, remove the tire from the rim as described in this chapter. Then remount the wheel into the truing stand and measure axial and lateral runout (**Figure 43**) with a pointer or dial indicator. Compare actual runout readings with the service limit specification in **Table 1**. Note the following:

    a. If the wheel bearings, spokes, hub and rim assembly are not damaged, the runout can be corrected by truing the wheel. Refer to *Wheel Service* in this chapter.

    b. If the rim is dented or damaged in any way, the rim must be replaced and the wheel rebuilt.

4. While the wheel is off, perform the following:

    a. Check the brake disc mounting bolts for tightness as described in Chapter Fourteen.

    b. On the rear wheel, check the driven flange sprocket bolts for tightness as described in this chapter.

WHEEL SERVICE

The laced wheel assembly consists of a rim, spokes, nipples and hub containing the bearings, spacer collar and seals.

Component Condition

Riding subjects the wheels to a significant amount of punishment. Therefore, it is important to inspect the wheel regularly for lateral (side-to-side) and radial (up-and-down) runout, even spoke tension and visible rim damage. When a wheel has a noticeable wobble, it is out of true. This is usually caused by loose spokes, but it can be caused by an impact-damaged rim.

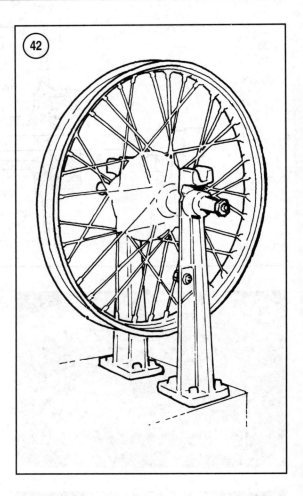

Truing a wheel corrects the lateral and radial runout to bring the wheel back into specification.

The condition of the individual wheel components will effect the ability to successfully true the wheel. Note the following:

1. Spoke condition—Do not attempt to true a wheel with bent or damaged spokes. Doing so places an excessive amount of tension on the spoke and rim. The spoke may break and/or pull through the spoke nipple hole in the rim. Inspect the spokes carefully and replace any that are damaged.

2. Nipple condition—When truing the wheels, the nipples must turn freely on the spoke. However, it is quite common for the spoke threads to become corroded and make it difficult to turn the nipple. Spray a penetrating liquid onto the nipple and allow sufficient time for it to penetrate before trying to force the nipple loose. Work the spoke wrench in both directions and continue to apply penetrating liquid. If the spoke wrench rounds off the nipple, it will be

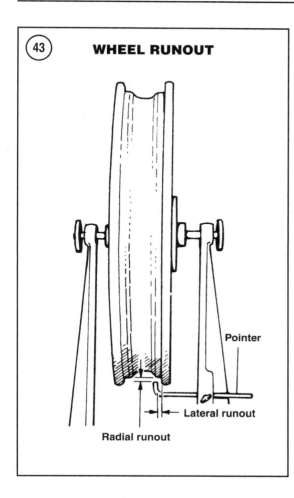

WHEEL RUNOUT

Pointer

Lateral runout

Radial runout

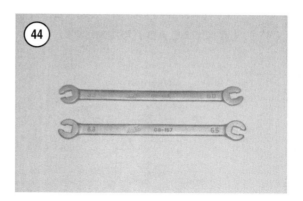

eral (side-to-side) and radial (up-and-down) runout limit specifications.

3. The runout can be checked on the motorcycle by mounting a pointer against the fork or swing arm and slowly rotating the wheel.

4. Perform major wheel truing with the tire removed and the wheel mounted in a truing stand (**Figure 42**). If a stand is not available, mount the wheel on the motorcycle with spacers on each side of the wheel to prevent it from sliding on the axle.

5. Use a spoke nipple wrench of the correct size (**Figure 44**). Using the wrong type of tool or one that is the incorrect size will round off the spoke nipples, making adjustment difficult. Quality spoke wrenches have openings that grip the nipple on four corners to prevent nipple damage. Tighten the spoke nipples securely.

11

necessary to remove the tire from the rim and cut the spoke(s) out of the wheel.

3. Rim condition—Minor rim damage can be corrected by truing the wheel. However, trying to correct excessive runout caused by impact damage will cause hub and rim damage due to spoke overtightening. Inspect the rims for cracks, flat spots or dents. Check the spoke holes for cracks or enlargement. Replace rims with excessive damage.

Wheel Truing Preliminaries

Before checking the runout and truing the wheel, note the following:

1. Make sure the wheel bearings are in good condition. Refer to *Front and Rear Hubs* in this chapter.

2. A small amount of wheel runout is acceptable; do not try to true the wheel to a perfect zero reading. Doing so will result in excessive spoke tension and possible rim and hub damage. **Table 1** lists the lat-

Wheel Truing Procedure

1. Position a pointer facing toward the rim (**Figure 43**). Then spin the wheel slowly and check the lateral and radial runout. If the rim is out of adjustment, continue with Step 2.

NOTE
If there is a large number of loose spokes, check the hub to make sure it is centered in the rim. This must be done visually, as there are no hub and rim centering specifications for these models.

NOTE
The number of spokes to loosen and tighten in Steps 2 and 3 will depend on how far the runout is out of adjustment. As a minimum, always loosen two or three spokes, then tighten the

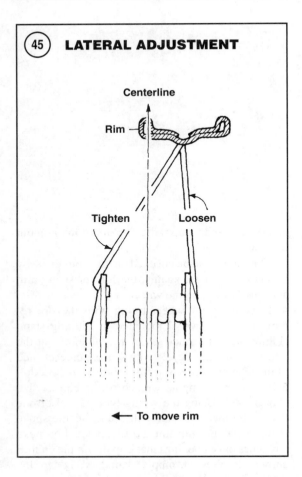

45 **LATERAL ADJUSTMENT**

Centerline

Rim

Tighten   Loosen

◄— To move rim

46

Tighten
(high point)

Hub

Centerline ◄—————————————

Loosen
(low point)

*opposite two or three spokes. If the
runout is excessive and affects a
greater area along the rim, a greater
number of spokes will require adjustment.*

2. If the lateral (side-to-side) runout is out of specification, adjust the wheel by using **Figure 45** as an
example. Always loosen and tighten the spokes an
equal number of turns.

3. If the radial (up and down) runout is out of specification, the hub is not centered in the rim. Draw the
high point of the rim toward the centerline of the
wheel by loosening the spokes in the area of the low
point and tightening the spokes on the side of the
high point (**Figure 46**). Tighten spokes in equal
amounts to prevent distortion.

4. After truing the wheel, seat each spoke in the
hub by tapping it with a flatnose punch and hammer.
Then recheck the spoke tension and wheel runout.
Readjust if necessary.

5. Check the ends of the spokes where they are
threaded in the nipples. Grind off any ends that protrude through the nipples to prevent them from
puncturing the tube.

WHEEL BALANCE

An unbalanced wheel is unsafe. Depending on
the degree of unbalance and the speed of the motorcycle, the rider may experience anything from a
mild vibration to a violent shimmy that may result
in loss of control.

Before attempting to balance the wheel, make
sure the wheel bearings are in good condition and
properly lubricated. The wheel must rotate freely.

1A. Remove the front wheel as described in this
chapter.

1B. Remove the rear wheel as described in this
chapter.

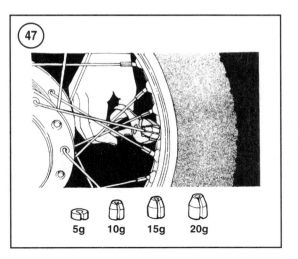

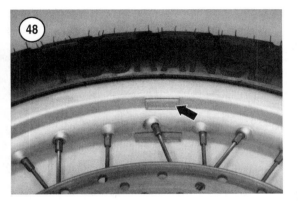

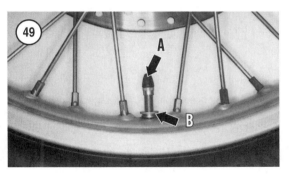

2. Mount the wheel on a fixture so it can rotate freely.

3. Spin the wheel and let it coast to a stop. Mark the tire at the lowest point.

4. Spin the wheel several more times. If the wheel keeps coming to rest at the same point, it is out of balance.

5. Attach a weight to the upper or light side of the wheel on the spoke (**Figure 47**) or stick an adhesive weight onto the rim (**Figure 48**).

6. Experiment with different weights until the wheel comes to a stop at a different position each time it is spun.

7. When fitting weights on laced wheels for the final time, crimp the weights onto the spoke with slip-joint pliers.

TIRES

Tire Safety

After installing new tires on the motorcycle, break them in correctly. Remember that a new tire has relatively poor adhesion to the road surface until it is broken in properly. Do not subject a new tire to any high-speed riding for at least the first 60 miles (100 km).

Even after the tires are broken in properly, avoid aggressive riding until they are warmed up, especially in cold weather. This will lessen the possibility of loss of control of the motorcycle. If using a tire brand other than those originally installed by BMW, refer to the tire manufacturer's recommended pressure. Refer to **Table 3** for original equipment tires.

TIRE CHANGING

Tire and Tube Removal

> *CAUTION*
> *To avoid damage when removing the tire, support the wheel on two wooden blocks, so the brake disc or the driven sprocket does not contact the floor.*

1A. Remove the front wheel as described in this chapter.
1B. Remove the rear wheel as described in this chapter.
2. If not already marked by the tire manufacturer, mark the valve stem location on the tire, so the tire can be installed in the same location for easier balancing.
3. Remove the valve stem cap (A, **Figure 49**) and core from the valve stem and deflate the tire. Remove the valve stem nut (B, **Figure 49**).

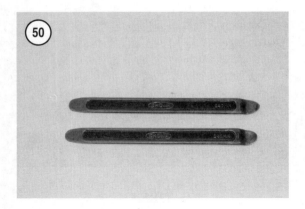

4. Lubricate both beads with soapy water.

CAUTION
*Use only quality tire irons without sharp edges (**Figure 50**). If necessary, file the ends of the tire irons to remove rough edges.*

5. Insert a tire iron under the top bead next to the valve stem (**Figure 51**). Force the bead on the opposite side of the tire into the center of the rim and pry the bead over the rim with the tire iron.

6. Reach inside the tire and remove the valve from the hole in the rim, then remove the tube from the tire.

NOTE
Steps 7 and 8 are required only if it is necessary to completely remove the tire from the rim.

7. Remove the nut and washer and remove the rim lock(s) from inside the tire.

8. Stand the wheel upright. Insert a tire iron between the back bead and the side of the rim that the top bead was pried over (**Figure 52**). Force the bead on the opposite side from the tire iron into the center of the rim. Pry the back bead off the rim working around as with the first.

9. Carefully inspect the tire and wheel rim for any damage as described in the following.

Tire and Wheel Rim Inspection

1. Wipe off the inner surfaces of the wheel rim. Clean off any rubber residue or any oxidation.

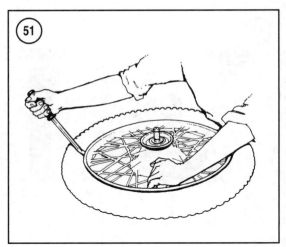

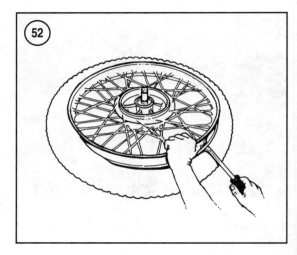

WARNING
Carefully consider whether a tire should be replaced. If there is any doubt about the quality of the existing tire, replace it. Do not take a chance on a tire failure at any speed.

2. If any of the following problems are observed, replace the tire:

   a. A scratch or split on the side wall.

   b. Any type of ply separation.

   c. Tread separation or excessive abnormal wear pattern.

   d. Tread depth worn to the minimum tread depth specification located on the tire sidewall.

   e. The cord is cut in any place.

   f. Flat spots in the tread from skidding.

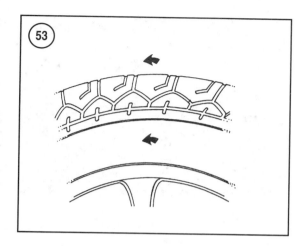

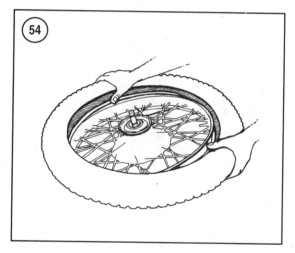

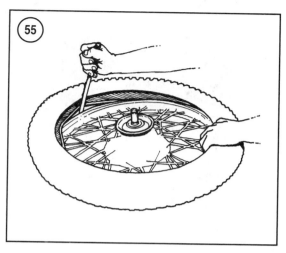

3. Check that the spoke ends do not protrude through the nipples into the center of the rim. That could puncture the tube. Grind or file off any protruding spoke ends.

NOTE
If water and dirt are entering the rim, discard the rubber rim band. Then wrap the rim center with two separate revolutions of duct tape. Punch holes through the tape for the valve stem.

Tire and Tube Installation

NOTE
To make tire installation easier, warming the tire will make it softer and more pliable. Place the tire in a hot place (in the sun or in a hot closed

vehicle). The heat will soften the rubber and ease installation.

1. If a rubber band is used, make sure the band is in place with the rough side facing toward the rim. Align the holes in the band with the holes in the rim.

2. When installing the tire on the rim, make sure the correct tire (either front or rear) is installed on the correct wheel and also that the direction arrow faces the direction of wheel rotation (**Figure 53**).

3. Liberally sprinkle the inside of the rim with talcum powder to reduce chafing between the tire and the tube and to minimize tube damage.

4. If the tire was removed, lubricate one bead with soapy water. Align the tire with the rim and push the tire onto the rim (**Figure 54**). Work around tire in both directions (**Figure 55**).

5. Install the core into the tube valve stem. Put the tire in the tire, making sure not to twist it, then insert the valve stem through the hole in the rim. Inflate the tube just enough to round it out. Too much air will make installation difficult, and too little air increases the chances of pinching the tube with the tire irons.

6. Lubricate the upper tire bead and rim with soapy water.

7. Press the upper bead into the rim opposite the valve stem. Pry the bead into the rim on both sides of the initial point with both hands and work around the rim to the valve stem. If the tire wants to pull up on one side, either use a tire iron or one knee to hold the tire in place. The last few inches are usually the toughest to install, and it is also where most pinched tubes occur. If possible, continue to push the tire

11

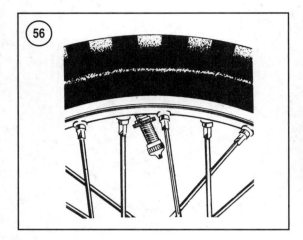

into the rim by hand. Relubricate the bead if necessary. If the tire bead wants to pull out from under the
rim, use both knees to hold the tire in place. If necessary, use a tire iron for the last few inches.

8. Reach inside the tire and wiggle the valve stem
to make sure the tube is not trapped under the bead.
Set the valve squarely in its hole before screwing on
the valve stem nut.

> *NOTE*
> *Make sure the valve stem is not turned
> sideways in the rim as shown in **Fig-
> ure 56**.*

9. Make sure the bead on both sides of the tire fits
evenly around the rim, then relubricate both sides of
the tire. Inflate the tire to approximately 25-30 psi to
ensure the tire is seated properly on the rim. If the
tire is hard to seat, release the air from the tube and
then reinflate.

> *WARNING*
> *Do not overinflate the tire when trying
> to seat the tire onto the rim. The tube
> and tire could burst, causing severe
> injury. Never stand directly over a tire
> while inflating it.*

10. Bounce the wheel several times, rotating it each
time. This will force the tire bead against the rim
flanges.

11. After the tire is properly seated, inflate the tire
pressure to the specification in **Table 3**. Screw on
the valve stem nut but do not tighten it against the
rim. Instead, tighten it against the valve stem cap.
Doing this will prevent the valve stem from pulling
away from the tube if the tire slips on the rim.

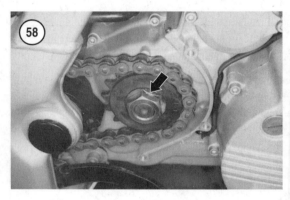

12. Balance the wheel as described in this chapter.

13A. Install the front wheel as described in this
chapter.

13B. Install the rear wheel as described in this chapter.

DRIVE SPROCKET AND CHAIN

The original equipment drive chain is an endless
type *without* a master link. The drive chain can be
removed two different ways and both are included
in this procedure.

To remove and reinstall the original equipment
endless chain, the rear wheel and swing arm must be
removed. The alternate way is to cut the drive chain
and install a new after-market chain equipped with a
master link.

> *NOTE*
> *Replace the driven sprocket when the
> drive chain is replaced. Always re-
> place both sprockets when replacing
> the drive chain; never install a new
> drive chain over worn sprockets.*

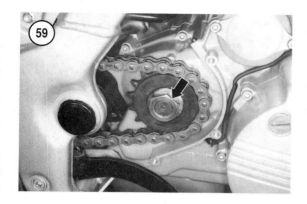

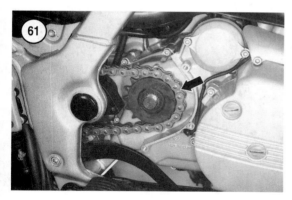

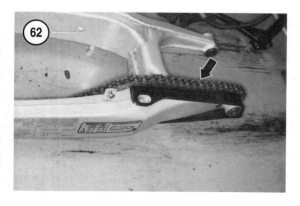

Removal/Installation (Endless Chain Type)

1. Support the motorcycle with the rear wheel off the ground. See *Bike Stands* in this chapter.

2. Remove the screws securing the drive sprocket cover (**Figure 57**) and remove the cover. Depress the rear brake pedal to gain access to the lower screw.

3A. On models equipped with a snap ring, remove the snap ring from the transmission countershaft and discard it.

3B. On models equipped with a nut, perform the following:

    a. Straighten the tab on the lockwasher (**Figure 58**).

    b. Have an assistant hold the rear brake on and loosen the drive sprocket nut (**Figure 59**).

    c. Remove the drive sprocket nut and lockwasher (**Figure 60**).

4. Remove the drive sprocket and drive chain from the transmission countershaft (**Figure 61**). Remove the O-ring from the countershaft and discard it.

5. Remove the rear wheel as described in this chapter.

6. Remove the swing arm as described in Chapter Thirteen.

7. Install the new drive chain over the swing arm (**Figure 62**) and install the swing arm.

8. Install the rear wheel as described in this chapter.

9. Apply engine oil to the *new* O-ring and install it onto the countershaft. Push it on until it bottoms.

10. Position the drive sprocket with the EXT mark facing out.

11. Install the drive sprocket and drive chain (**Figure 61**) onto the transmission countershaft.

12A. On models equipped with a snap ring, install a *new* snap ring onto the transmission shaft and make sure it is properly seated.

12B. On models equipped with a nut, perform the following:

    a. Install a *new* lockwasher and the drive sprocket nut (**Figure 60**).

    b. Have an assistant hold the rear brake on and tighten the drive sprocket nut (**Figure 59**).

    c. Bend down the lockwasher onto one side of the sprocket nut (**Figure 58**).

13. Install the drive sprocket cover (**Figure 57**).

14. Lubricate and adjust the drive chain as described in Chapter Three.

11

Removal/Installation (Master Link Type)

This procedure requires using two special tools that are available from most motorcycle dealerships and parts suppliers. One is the drive chain breaker (**Figure 63**) and the other is the chain riveting tool (**Figure 64**). Make sure to purchase tools that will work on the 520 size chain installed on the motorcycle. Follow the manufacturer's instruction with each special tool.

The original equipment drive chain is an endless type with no master link and must be cut for removal. The drive chain is looped through the swing arm.

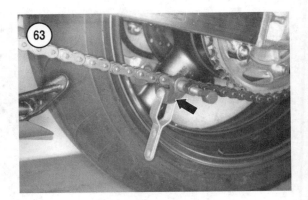

NOTE
If an aftermarket drive chain has been installed, it may be equipped with a master link. If so, follow the drive chain manufacturer's instructions for removal and installation.

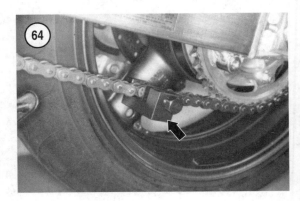

1. Support the motorcycle with the rear wheel off the ground. See *Bike Stands* in this chapter.
2. Loosen the axle nut (A, **Figure 65**).
3. Loosen the drive chain tensioner screw (B, **Figure 65**) on each side to allow drive chain slack.
4. Remove the bolts (A, **Figure 66**) on each side securing the mudguard (B) and remove the mudguard assembly from the swing arm.
5. Remove the screws securing the drive sprocket cover (**Figure 57**) and remove the cover. Depress the rear brake pedal to access the lower screw.

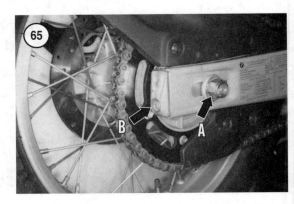

NOTE
When using the chain breaker special tool, apply a small amount of grease to the threaded parts to make removal easier.

6. Install the drive chain breaker tool to the drive chain following the manufacturer's instructions.
7. Tighten the tool pressure bolt (A, **Figure 67**) with the handle (B) or bolt head and force out the drive chain joint pin.
8. Remove the special tool, the joint plate, joint pin and O-rings. Discard all of these parts–they *cannot* be reused.
9. Shift the transmission into neutral.
10. Remove the old drive chain from the driven sprocket, then pull the drive chain out and off the drive sprocket on the engine.

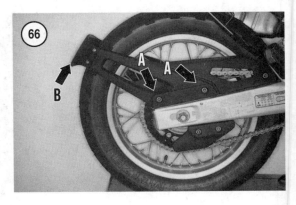

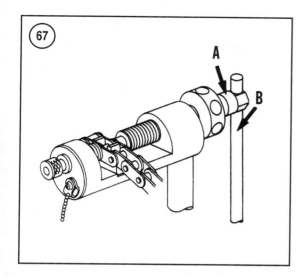

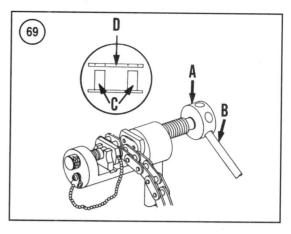

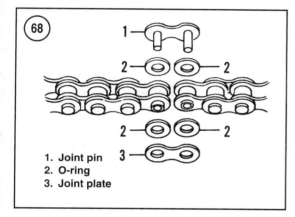

1. Joint pin
2. O-ring
3. Joint plate

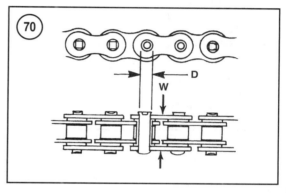

11. Lay the new drive chain along the old drive chain and, if necessary, remove any extra links. The new drive chain must have the *same number* of links as the drive chain that was removed.

12. Install the new drive chain onto the drive sprocket and then onto the driven sprocket on the rear wheel.

13. Refer to **Figure 68** and install the new O-ring seals onto the joint pin.

14. Pull the ends of the drive chain together and insert the joint pin into the chain links from the backside. Push the joint pin all the way in until it bottoms.

15. Install the new O-ring seals onto the joint pin, then install the joint plate.

NOTE
When using the chain riveting special tool, apply a small amount of grease

to the threaded parts to make installation easier.

16. Hold the joint plate in place and install the chain riveting tool to the drive chain following the manufacturer's instructions.

17. Tighten the tool pressure bolt (A, **Figure 69**) with the handle (B) or bolt head and properly align the two joint pins (C) with the respective holes in the joint plate (D). Make sure all four O-rings are still in place.

CAUTION
In the next step, if the joint plate is pressed on farther than specified, the joint pin and joint plate must be removed and discarded. New parts must be installed and Steps 12-18 must be repeated.

18. Press the joint plate over the joint pins until the distance between the joint pin and plate (W, **Figure 70**) is within the specifications listed in the manufacturer's instructions.

19. Remove the special tool.

20. Use the joint pin staking portion of the special tool to stake the pins until the staked pin diameter (D, **Figure 70**) reaches within the specifications listed in the manufacturer's instructions. Use a vernier caliper to measure the staked pins.

21. Remove the special tool.

22. Move the drive chain up and down and check for smooth operation between the new joint assembly and the remainder of the drive chain on each side. If the chain is stiff at this portion of the drive chain, the joint assembly must be removed and a new one installed.

23. Adjust the drive chain as described in Chapter Three.

Table 1 WHEEL SPECIFICATIONS

Tire size	
Front tire	
F650 ST, F650 Strada, SE	100/90 × 18 S tube type
F650	100/90 × 9 57 S tube type
Rear tire	130/80 × 17 65 tube type
Wheel rim size	
Front wheel	2.15 × 19 MT
F650 ST, F650 Strada, SE	2.15 × 18 MT
F650	2.15 × 19 MT
Rear wheel	3.00 × 17 MT
Wheel runout (maximum)	
Lateral and radial	0.25 mm (0.010 in.)

Table 2 WHEEL TORQUE SPECIFICATIONS

Item	N•m	in.-lb.	ft.-lb.
Front axle	80	–	59
Front axle			
holder nuts	12	106	–
Front brake caliper			
mounting bolt	32	–	24
Rear axle nut	100	–	74
Brake disc bolts			
front and rear	12	106	–
Drive sprocket nut	100	–	74

Table 2 TIRE INFLATION PRESSURE (COLD)*

Model	kPa	PSI
Front wheels		
Rider only	186	27
Full load	228	33
Rear wheels		
Rider only		
F 650, Funduro, Strada, SE	196	28.5
F 650 ST	228	33
Full load	245	35.5

*Tire pressure for original equipment tires. Aftermarket tires may require different inflation pressure.

CHAPTER TWELVE

FRONT SUSPENSION AND STEERING

This chapter covers the handlebar, steering head and front fork assembly.

Refer to **Table 1** and **Table 2** at the end of the chapter for specifications.

HANDLEBAR

Removal/Installation

Refer to **Figure 1**.

1. Cover the fuel tank cover with a blanket or towels to protect the finish.

2. Support the motorcycle with the front wheel off the ground. See *Bike Stands* in Chapter Nine.

> *NOTE*
> *Before removing the handlebar, make a drawing of the clutch and throttle cable routing from the handlebar and through the frame. This information will prove helpful when reinstalling the handlebar and connecting the cables.*

3. On the right side of the handlebar, refer to **Figure 2** and perform the following:

    a. Unscrew and remove the mirror (A, **Figure 3**).

    b. Remove the screws securing the master cylinder clamp (B, **Figure 3**). Do not disconnect the hydraulic brake line. Tie the master cylinder assembly to the frame, keeping the reservoir in the upright position to prevent air from entering the system.

    c. Remove the mounting bolt and remove the weight (C, **Figure 3**).

    d. Remove the screws securing the right side switch assembly (D, **Figure 3**) together and separate the housing halves.

    e. Remove the tie wrap securing the cables to the handlebar.

    f. Slide the throttle housing and cable assembly (E, **Figure 3**) off the handlebar.

4. On the left side of the handlebar, refer to **Figure 4** and perform the following:

12

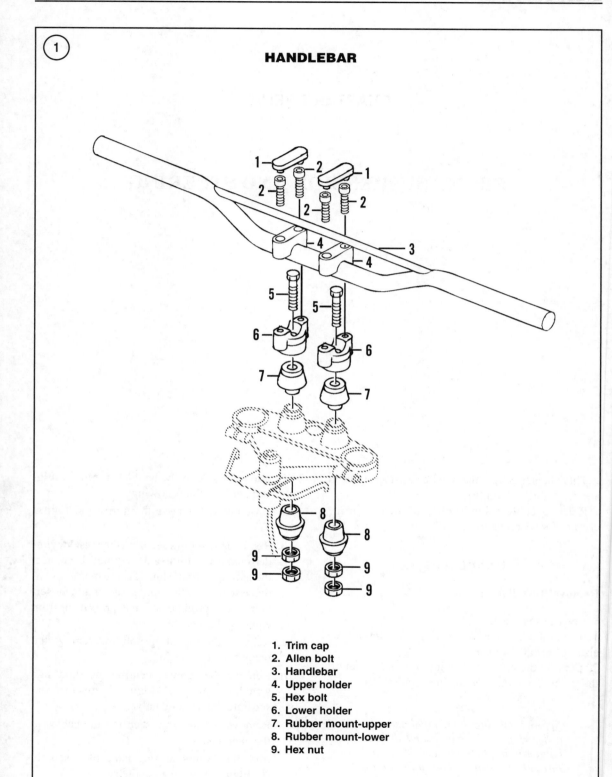

HANDLEBAR

1. Trim cap
2. Allen bolt
3. Handlebar
4. Upper holder
5. Hex bolt
6. Lower holder
7. Rubber mount-upper
8. Rubber mount-lower
9. Hex nut

② **RIGHT SIDE HANDLEBAR CONTROLS**

1
2
3
4
5
6
6
9
7
8
10
11
12 — 6 — 6
13
14
15

1. Bolt
2. Weigt
3. Rubber grip
4. Switch-upper half
5. Rear view mirror
6. Bolt
7. Ring
8. Throttle grip
9. Handlebar
10. Front brake master cylinder
11. Switch-lower half
12. Nut
13. Throttle cable
14. Boot
15. Throttle cable sheath

12

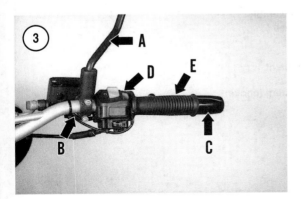

③

a. Unscrew and remove the mirror (A, **Figure 5**).

b. Remove the tie wrap securing the cables to the handlebar.

c. Remove the screws securing the left side switch assembly (B, **Figure 5**) together and separate the housing halves.

d. Remove the clutch lever clamp (C, **Figure 5**) mounting screws and washers and separate the clamp halves.

④

LEFT SIDE HANDLEBAR CONTROLS

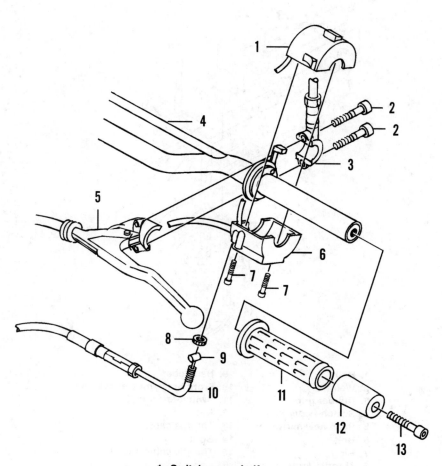

1. Switch-upper half
2. Bolt
3. Rear view mirror
4. Handlebar
5. Clutch lever assembly
6. Switch-lower half
7. Screw
8. Nut
9. Starter enrichment
   (choke) cable
10. Starter enrichment (choke)
    cable sheath
11. Rubber grip
12. Weight
13. Bolt

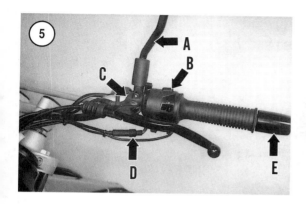

e. Disconnect the starting enrichment valve (choke) cable from the control lever (D, **Figure 5**).

f. Remove the mounting bolt and remove the weight (E, **Figure 5**).

5. Remove the trim caps (**Figure 6**).

6. Remove the four handlebar clamp Allen bolts (A, **Figure 7**), then remove the holders and handlebar (B).

7. To remove the lower holders, perform the following:

a. Secure the upper hex bolts, then remove the locknut and nuts securing the lower holders to the upper fork bridge.

b. Remove the lower rubber mounts from the bolts.

c. Pull straight up and remove the lower holders and upper rubber mounts.

8. Install the handlebar by reversing these steps while noting the following:

a. Check the knurled rings on the handlebar for galling and bits of aluminum. Clean the knurled section with a wire brush.

b. Check the handlebar for cracks, bends or other damage. Replace the handlebar if necessary. Do not attempt to repair it.

c. Thoroughly clean all residue from the clamp halves.

d. Position the upper holders with the arrows (**Figure 8**) pointing toward the front.

e. After installing the handlebar, reposition the handlebar while sitting on the motorcycle.

f. Tighten all mounting bolts to the specifications in **Table 2**. Tighten the forward Allen bolts. Secure the upper mounts first, then the rear, leaving a gap (**Figure 9**) at the rear.

g. Adjust the mirrors.

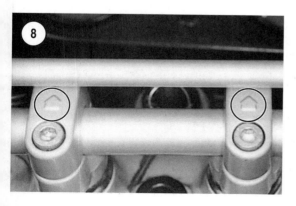

12

⑩   **STEERING STEM**

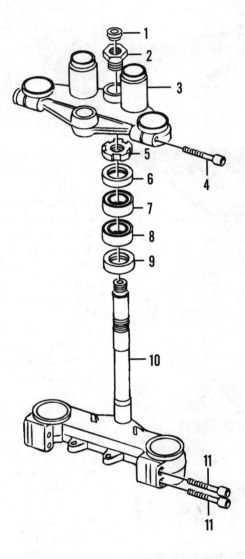

1. Trim cap
2. Steering stem locknut
3. Upper fork bridge
4. Bolt
5. Slotted adjust nut
6. Bearing cap
7. Roller bearing-upper
8. Roller bearing-lower
9. Dust seal
10. Steering stem/lower fork bridge
11. Bolt

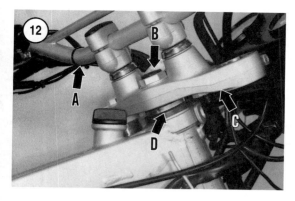

STEERING HEAD

The steering head uses tapered roller bearings at the top and bottom pivot positions. The tapered roller bearing inner races, mounted in the frame, and the lower bearing, mounted on the steering stem, (**Figure 10**) should *not* be removed unless they require replacement.

Remove the steering stem and lubricate the bearings at the intervals specified in Chapter Three.

Disassembly

1. Remove the front fairing as described in Chapter Fifteen.
2. Remove the instrument cluster as described in Chapter Nine.
3. Remove the front fairing mount bracket as described in Chapter Fifteen.
4. Disconnect the front brake hose holder from the lower fork bridge.
5. Remove the bolts securing the lower fork bridge cover and remove the cover (**Figure 11**).
6. Disconnect the electrical connector from the horn.
7. Remove the front wheel as described in Chapter Eleven.
8. Remove the front fork as described in this chapter.
9. Remove the handlebar (A, **Figure 12**) as described in this chapter.
10. Loosen and remove the steering stem locknut (B, **Figure 12**).
11. Remove the upper fork bridge (C, **Figure 12**).
12. Loosen the steering stem adjust nut (D, **Figure 12**) with a spanner wrench. (**Figure 13**, typical).

> *CAUTION*
> *Support the weight of the steering stem while removing the steering stem adjust nut, or else the assembly will drop out of the steering head.*

13. Hold onto the steering stem and remove the adjust nut.
14. Gently lower the steering stem/lower fork bridge assembly out of the frame.
15. Remove the bearing cap.
16. Remove the upper bearing from the steering stem.

> *CAUTION*
> *Do not attempt to remove the lower roller bearing from the steering stem unless the bearing is going to be replaced. The bearing is pressed onto the steering stem and will be damaged during removal.*

Inspection

Replace worn or damaged parts.

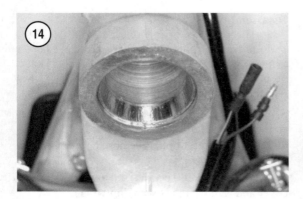

1. Wipe the bearing races with a solvent-soaked rag and then dry with compressed air or a lint-free cloth. Check the races in the steering head for pitting, scratches, galling or excessive wear. If any of these conditions exist, replace the races as described in this chapter. If the races are in good condition, wipe each race with grease.

2. Clean the bearings with solvent to remove all of the old grease. Dry the bearings with compressed air, making sure not to allow the air jet to spin the bearings. Do not remove the lower bearing from the stem unless it is to be replaced. Clean the bearing while installed on the steering stem.

3. After the bearings are dry, turn the bearings slowly. The bearings must turn smoothly. Visually check the bearings for pitting, scratches or visible damage. If the bearings are worn, check the dust covers for wear or damage or for improper bearing lubrication. Replace the bearings if necessary. If a bearing is going to be reused, pack it with grease and wrap it with waxed paper or some other type of lint-free material until it is reinstalled. To prevent rust, do not store the bearings for any length of time without lubricating them.

4. Check the steering stem for cracks or damage. Check the threads at the top of the stem for damage. Check the steering stem nut for damage. Thread it into the steering stem; make sure the nut threads easily with no roughness.

5. Check the steering head frame welds for cracks and fractures. If any are found, have them repaired by a competent frame shop or welding service familiar with motorcycle frame repair.

6. Check the steering stem locknut and slotted adjust nut for damage.

7. Check the steering stem/lower fork bridge assembly for cracks and damage.

8. Check the bearing races in the frame (**Figure 14** and **Figure 15**, typical) for pitting, galling and corrosion. If a race is worn or damaged, replace both races and bearings as described in this section.

9. Check the tapered roller bearings (**Figure 16**) for pitting, scratches or discoloration that indicate wear or corrosion damage.

10. When reusing bearings, clean them thoroughly with a bearing degreaser. After cleaning and thoroughly drying the bearings, pack them with Shell Retinax EP2 or a waterproof bearing grease.

Outer Bearing Race Replacement

Do *not* remove the upper and lower outer bearing races unless they are going to be replaced. If a bearing race is removed, the tapered bearing must be also replaced.

1. Insert an aluminum drift into the frame tube (**Figure 17**) and carefully drive the race out from the inside (**Figure 18**). Strike at different spots around the race to prevent it from binding in the mounting bore. Repeat for the other race.

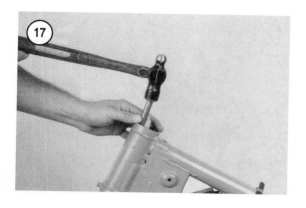

17

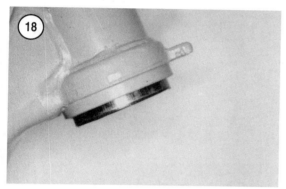

18

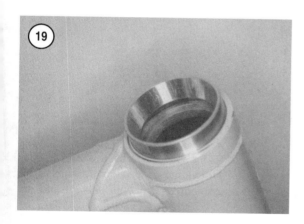

19

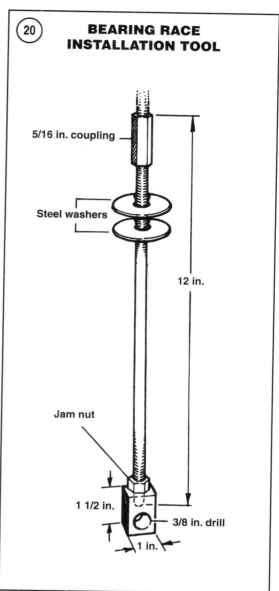

20 **BEARING RACE INSTALLATION TOOL**

5/16 in. coupling

Steel washers

12 in.

Jam nut

1 1/2 in.

3/8 in. drill

1 in.

12

2. Clean the race bore and check for cracks or other damage.

3. Place the new race squarely into the mounting bore opening with its tapered side facing out (**Figure 19**).

4. To prevent damaging the races or frame mounting bore, install the races as follows:

   a. Assemble the tool shown in **Figure 20**. The block mounted at the bottom of the threaded rod is used as a T-handle to hold the rod sta-

tionary while installing the race from the opposite end. The hole drilled horizontally through the block must be large enough to accept a suitable rod for the T-handle.

CAUTION
When using the threaded rod or a similar tool to install the bearing races in the following steps, do not allow the rod or tool to contact the face of the bearing race, as any contact could damage the bearing race.

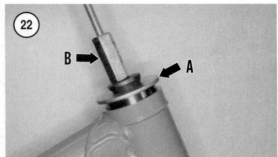

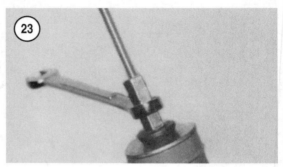

b. To install the upper race, insert the through the bottom of the frame tube (**Figure 21**, typical). Seat the lower washer or plate against the frame.

c. At the top of the puller, slide the large washer down and seat it squarely on top of the bearing race (A, **Figure 22**). Then install the required washers and coupling nut (B) that will work with the puller.

d. Hand-tighten the coupling nut, checking that the washer is centered on the bearing race.

e. Hold the threaded rod to prevent it from turning and tighten the coupling nut with a wrench (**Figure 23**). Continue until the race is drawn into the frame tube and the washer seats against the frame tube. Remove the puller assembly and inspect the bearing race. It must bottom out in the frame tube as shown in **Figure 24**.

f. Repeat to install the bottom race.

5. Lubricate the upper and lower bearing races with Shell Retinax EP2 or an equivalent waterproof bearing grease.

Steering Stem Bearing Replacement

Perform the following steps to replace the steering stem bearing (**Figure 25**).

1. Thread the steering stem locknut onto the steering stem to protect the threads.

WARNING
Wear safety glasses when removing
the steering stem bearing in Step 2.

2. Remove the steering stem bearing and dust seal with a hammer and chisel, as shown in **Figure 26**.

Strike at different spots underneath the bearing to prevent it from binding on the steering stem.

3. Clean the steering stem with solvent and dry thoroughly.

4. Inspect the steering stem and replace if damaged.

5. Pack the new bearing with Shell Retinax EP2 or an equivalent waterproof bearing grease.

6. Slide the new dust seal and bearing onto the steering stem until it stops.

7A. To install the new steering stem bearing with a press, perform the following:

a. Install the steering stem and the new bearing in a press and support it with two bearing drivers, as shown in **Figure 27**. Make sure the lower bearing driver seats against the inner

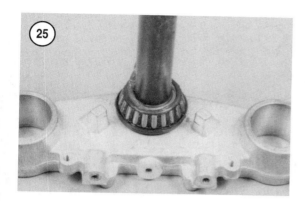

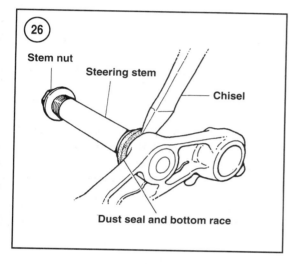

Stem nut
Steering stem
Chisel

Dust seal and bottom race

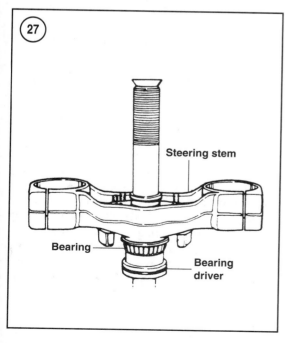

Steering stem
Bearing
Bearing driver

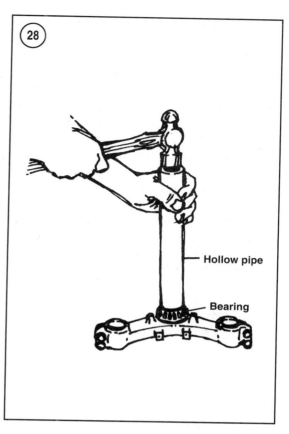

Hollow pipe

Bearing

bearing race and does not contact the bearing rollers.

b. Press the bearing onto the steering stem until it bottoms (**Figure 25**).

7B. To install the new steering stem bearing with a bearing driver, perform the following:

a. Slide a bearing driver or long hollow pipe over the steering stem until it seats against the bearing's inner race (**Figure 28**).

b. Drive the bearing onto the steering stem until it bottoms (**Figure 25**).

Assembly and Steering Stem Adjustment

Refer to **Figure 10** when assembling the steering stem assembly.

1. Make sure the upper (**Figure 24**) and lower (**Figure 18**) bearing races are properly seated in the frame tube.

2. Lubricate the bearings and races with Shell Retinax EP2 or an equivalent waterproof bearing grease.

12

3. Install the upper bearing and seat it into its race.

4. Install the steering stem/lower fork bridge through the bottom of the frame and hold it in place.

5. Install the bearing race cover.

6. Install the steering stem slotted adjust nut and tighten with a spanner wrench (**Figure 29**) until there is zero play both horizontal and vertical (**Figure 30**).

7. Tighten the steering stem slotted adjust nut to seat the bearings. Then loosen the adjust nut completely. Use a spanner wrench or punch and hammer to tighten and loosen the nut.

8. Slowly tighten the steering adjust nut while checking bearing play. The adjust nut must be tight enough to remove play, both horizontal and vertical, yet loose enough so the assembly will turn to both lock positions under its own weight after an assist.

9. Install the upper fork bridge (C, **Figure 12**).

10. Install the steering stem locknut (B, **Figure 12**). Install the nut finger-tight.

11. Install the front fork as described in this chapter and tighten the upper and lower fork bridge clamp bolts as specified in **Table 1**.

> *NOTE*
> *Because tightening the steering stem nut effects the steering bearing preload, it may be necessary to repeat these steps a few times until the steering adjustment is correct.*

12. Check bearing play by turning the steering stem from side to side. The steering stem must pivot smoothly. If the steering stem does not turn freely, readjust the bearing play as follows:

    a. Loosen the steering stem locknut (B, **Figure 12**), then slightly loosen the slotted adjust nut.

    b. Retighten the steering stem locknut (B, **Figure 12**) to the torque specification in **Table 1**.

    c. Recheck bearing play by turning the steering stem from side-to-side. If the play feels correct, turn the steering stem so the front fork is facing straight ahead. While an assistant steadies the motorcycle, grasp the fork tubes and try to move them front to back. If there is play and the bearing adjustment feels correct, the bearings and races are probably worn and require replacement. It helps to have someone steady the bike when checking steering head play.

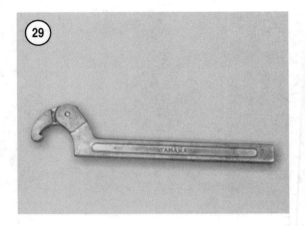

13. Install the handlebar (A, **Figure 12**) as described in this chapter.

14. Install the front wheel as described in this chapter.

15. Install the front fender as described in Chapter Fifteen.

16. Connect the electrical connector onto the horn.

17. Install the lower fork bridge cover (**Figure 11**) and tighten the bolts securely.

18. Connect the front brake hose holder onto the lower fork bridge.

19. Install the front fairing mount bracket as described in Chapter Fifteen.

20. Install the instrument cluster as described in Chapter Nine.

21. Install the upper section of the front fairing as described in Chapter Fifteen.

22. After 30 minutes to 1 hour of riding time, check the steering adjustment and adjust if necessary as described under *Steering Play Check and Adjustment* in this chapter.

Steering Play Check and Adjustment

Steering adjustment takes up any slack in the steering stem and bearings and allows the steering stem to operate with free rotation. Any excessive play or roughness in the steering stem will make the steering imprecise and difficult, causing bearing damage. Improper bearing lubrication or an incorrect steering adjustment (too loose or tight) usually causes these conditions. An incorrectly routed clutch or throttle cable can also affect steering operation.

1. Support the motorcycle with the front wheel off the ground.

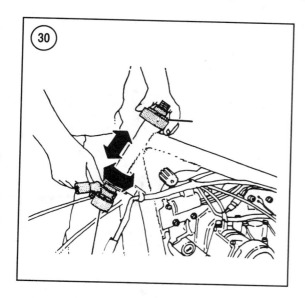

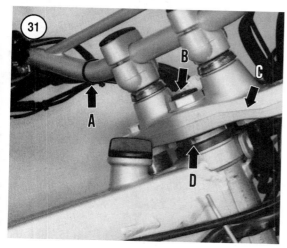

c. If the steering stem moved from side to side correctly, perform Step 4 to check for excessive looseness.

NOTE
When checking for excessive steering play in Step 4, have an assistant steady the motorcycle.

4. Grasp the fork tubes firmly (near the axle) and attempt to move the wheel front to back. Note the following:

a. If movement can be felt at the steering stem, the steering adjustment is probably loose. Go to Step 5 to adjust the steering.

b. If there is no excessive movement and the front end turns correctly as described in Steps 2-4, the steering adjustment is correct.

5. Remove the handlebar (A, **Figure 31**) as described in this chapter.

6. Loosen the steering stem locknut (B, **Figure 31**) securing the upper fork bridge (C).

7. Adjust the steering slotted adjust nut (D, **Figure 31**) as follows:

a. If the steering is too loose, tighten the steering slotted adjust nut.

b. If the steering is too tight, loosen the steering slotted adjust nut.

8. Tighten the steering stem locknut (B, **Figure 31**) to the torque specification in **Table 1**.

9. Recheck the steering adjustment as described in this procedure. When the steering adjustment is correct, continue with Step 10.

NOTE
Because tightening the steering stem nut affects the steering bearing preload, it may be necessary to repeat Steps 7-9 a few times until the steering adjustment is correct. If the steering adjustment cannot be corrected, the steering bearings may require lubrication or be damaged. Remove the steering stem and inspect the bearings as described in this chapter.

2. Turn the handlebar from side to side. The steering stem should move freely and without any binding or roughness.
3. Turn the handlebar so the front wheel points straight ahead. Then alternately push (slightly) one end of the handlebar and then the other. The front end must turn to each side from center under its own weight. Note the following:

a. If the steering stem moved roughly or stopped before hitting the frame stop, check the clutch and throttle cable routing. Reroute the cable(s) if necessary.

b. If the cable routing is correct and the steering is tight, the steering adjustment is too tight or the bearings require lubrication or replacement.

10. Install the handlebar (A, **Figure 31**) as described in this chapter. Then recheck the steering adjustment.

FRONT FORK

Front Fork Service

Before assuming that a fork is internally malfunctioning, drain the front fork oil and refill with the proper type and quantity fork oil as described in Chapter Three. If there is still a problem, such as poor damping, a tendency to bottom or top out or leakage around the oil seals, follow the service procedures in this section.

To simplify fork service and to prevent the mixing of parts, remove, service and install the fork legs individually.

Removal (Fork Not To Be Serviced)

1. Support the motorcycle with the front wheel off the ground. See *Bike Stands* in Chapter Eleven.
2. Refer to Chapter Fifteen and perform the following:
   a. Remove the front fairing.
   b. Remove the front fender.
3. Remove the front wheel as described in Chapter Eleven.
4. Remove the bolts securing the fork brace (**Figure 32**) and remove the fork brace.
5. If both fork tube assemblies are going to be removed, mark them with a R (right side) and L (left side) so the assemblies will be reinstalled on the correct side.
6. Loosen the upper (A, **Figure 33**) and lower (B) fork bridge clamp bolts.
7. Carefully lower the fork tube from the upper fork bridge, continue to slide the fork tube out of the lower fork bridge. It may be necessary to rotate the fork tube slightly while pulling it down and out. Remove the fork assembly and wrap it in a bath towel or blanket to protect the surface from damage.
8. Repeat for the other fork assembly.

Installation (Fork Was Not Serviced)

1. Refer to the marks made during Step 5 of *Removal* and install a fork assembly onto the correct side of the motorcycle. The brake caliper mounting bracket is on the left side.
2. Install the fork tube through the lower fork bridge.

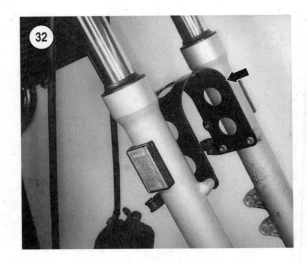

3. Continue to push the fork tube up through the upper fork bridge. Position the fork tube so the top surface is 3 mm (0.12 in.) above the top surface of the upper fork bridge (**Figure 34**).

4. Tighten the upper (A, **Figure 33**) and lower (B) fork bridge clamp bolts to the specification in **Table 1**.

5. Install the fork brace (**Figure 32**) and tighten the bolts securely.

6. Install the front wheel as described in Chapter Eleven. Turn the front wheel several times and apply the front brake several times to reposition the pistons in the caliper. If the brake feels spongy, bleed the front brake as described in Chapter Fourteen.

7. Refer to Chapter Fifteen and perform the following:

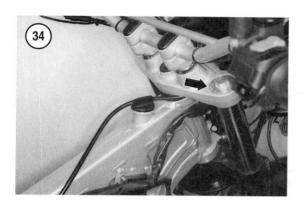

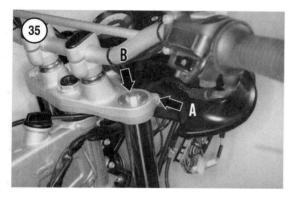

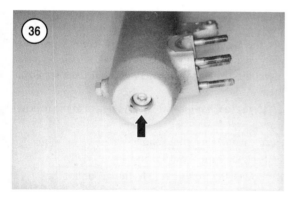

a. Install the front fender.
b. Install the front fairing.
8. Lower the motorcycle to the ground.

Removal (Fork To Be Serviced)

1. Support the motorcycle with the front wheel off the ground. See *Bike Stands* in Chapter Eleven.
2. Refer to Chapter Fifteen and perform the following:
a. Remove the front fairing.

b. Remove the front fender.
3. Remove the front wheel as described in Chapter Eleven.
4. Remove the bolts securing the fork brace (**Figure 32**) and remove the fork brace.
5. If both fork tube assemblies are going to be removed, mark them with a R (right side) and L (left side) so the assemblies will be reinstalled on the correct side.
6. Loosen the upper fork bridge bolt (A, **Figure 35**).
7. Loosen, but do not remove, the fork top cap (B, **Figure 35**). The fork top cap must remain in place until the Allen bolt is loosened in Step 8. Tighten the upper fork bridge bolt.
8. Apply coarse grit valve lapping compound to the end of the Allen wrench. This will create a better bond between the wrench and the Allen bolt head.

CAUTION
Press very hard on the impact wrench in the next step to ensure the wrench is completely seated within the Allen bolt head. If the Allen wrench starts to rotate within the socket, it will damage the Allen bolt head.

NOTE
Figure 36 *is shown with the fork assembly removed to better illustrate the step.*

9. Use an electric or air-driven impact wrench to loosen the Allen bolt (**Figure 36**) at the bottom of the slider. Do not remove the Allen bolt and gasket washer from the slider at this time, as the fork oil will start to drain out.

WARNING
Be careful when removing the fork cap bolt because the spring is under pressure. Protect yourself accordingly.

10. Remove the fork cap bolt, spacer and support ring.
11. Place a drain pan under the fork slider to catch the fork oil.
12. Remove the Allen bolt and gasket washer, then drain the fork oil.
13. Wrap a shop cloth around the top of the fork tube to catch residual fork oil, then remove the spring.

12

14. Pump the slider by hand several times to expel most of the fork oil. Reinstall the Allen bolt and washer gasket to keep residual oil in the fork.

15. Slide the dust seal up on the fork tube (A, **Figure 37**).

16. Remove the retaining ring from the fork slider (B, **Figure 37**).

NOTE
It may be necessary to slightly heat the area on the slider around the oil seal prior to removal. Use a rag soaked in hot water; do not apply a flame directly to the fork slider.

17. There is an interference fit between the bushing in the fork slider and the bushing on the fork tube. In order to remove the fork tube from the slider, pull hard on the fork tube using quick up and down strokes (**Figure 38**). Doing so will withdraw the bushing and the oil seal from the slider.

18. Remove the slider from the fork tube. If still in place, remove the oil lock piece from the damper rod.

19. Loosen the upper (A, **Figure 33**) and lower (B) fork bridge clamp bolts.

20. Carefully lower the fork tube from the upper fork bridge, continue to slide the fork tube out of the lower fork bridge. It may be necessary to rotate the fork tube slightly while pulling it down and out. Remove the fork assembly and take it to the workbench for service.

21. Repeat for the other fork assembly.

Installation (Fork Was Serviced)

1. Refer to the marks made during Step 5 of *Removal* and install a fork assembly onto the correct side of the motorcycle. The brake caliper mounting bracket is on the left side.

2. Install the fork tube through the lower fork bridge.

3. Continue to push the fork tube up through the upper fork bridge. Position the fork tube so the top surface is 3 mm (0.12 in.) above the top surface of the upper fork bridge (**Figure 34**).

4. Tighten the upper (A, **Figure 33**) and lower (B) fork bridge clamp bolts to the specification in **Table 1**.

5. Install the fork brace (**Figure 32**) and tighten the bolts securely.

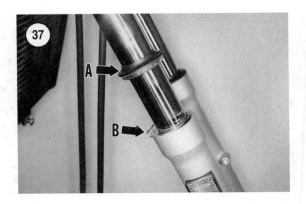

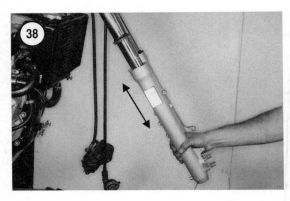

6. Install the front wheel as described in Chapter Eleven. Turn the front wheel several times and apply the front brake several times to reposition the pistons in the caliper. If the brake feels spongy, bleed the front brake as described in Chapter Fourteen.

7. Refer to Chapter Fifteen and perform the following:
   a. Install the front fender.
   b. Install the front fairing.

8. Lower the motorcycle to the ground.

Disassembly

Refer to **Figure 39**.

1. If still in place, remove the oil lock piece from the damper rod.

2. If the fork spring is still in place, perform the following:
   a. Hold the fork tube in a vise with soft jaws.

WARNING
Be careful when removing the fork cap bolt because the spring is under

FRONT FORK

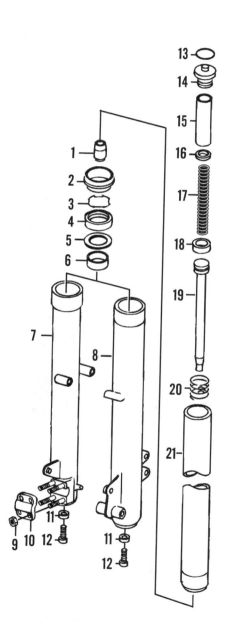

1. Oil lock piece
2. Dust seal
3. Retaining ring
4. Oil seal
5. Washer
6. Slider bushing
7. Slider-right side
8. Slider-left side
9. Nut
10. Front axle holder
11. Gasket washer
12. Allen bolt
13. O-ring
14. Fork cap bolt
15. Spacer
16. Support ring
17. Spring
18. Piston ring
19. Damper rod
20. Rebound spring
21. Fork tube

12

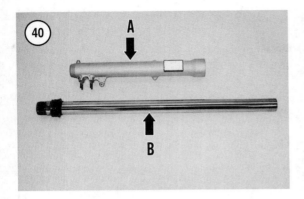

pressure. Protect yourself accordingly.

   b. Remove the fork cap bolt and withdraw the spacer, support ring and the spring.

   c. Remove the fork tube from the vise and drain out any residual fork oil. Dispose of the fork oil properly.

3. Turn the fork tube upside down to remove the damper rod and rebound spring.

4. Remove the slider bushing, washer, retaining ring and dust seal from the fork tube.

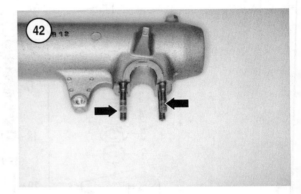

Inspection

Replace any worn or damaged parts.

1. Thoroughly clean all parts in solvent and dry them.

2. Check the slider (A, **Figure 40**) for dents or other exterior damage. Check the retaining ring groove (**Figure 41**) in the top of the slider for cracks or other damage.

3. Check the threaded studs (**Figure 42**) at the base of the right side slider for damage. Repair if necessary.

4. Check the left side slider caliper mount bosses for cracks or damage.

5. Check the fork tube (B, **Figure 40**) for bending, nicks, rust or other damage. Place the fork tube on a set of V-blocks and check runout with a dial indicator. If the special tools are not available, roll the fork tube on a large piece of plate glass or other flat surface. BMW does not provide service specifications for runout.

6. Check the internal threads in the top of the fork tube (**Figure 43**) for stripping or cross threading. Use a tap to true up the threads.

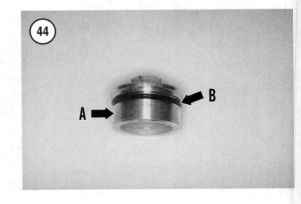

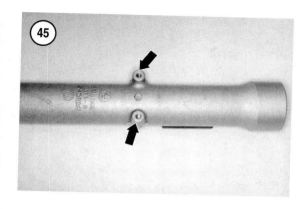

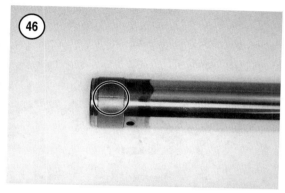

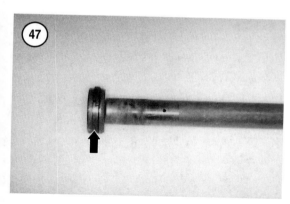

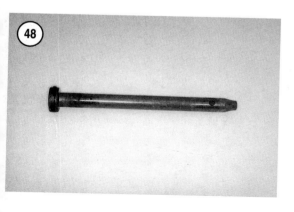

7. Check the external threads (A, **Figure 44**) on the fork cap bolt for stripping or cross threading. Use a die to true up the threads.

8. Check the front fender brace bosses (**Figure 45**) for cracks or damage.

9. Check the slider and fork tube bushings for excessive wear, cracks or damage.

10. To remove the fork tube bushing, perform the following:

    a. Expand the bushing slit (**Figure 46**) with a screwdriver, then slide the bushing off the fork tube.

    b. Coat the new bushing with new fork oil.

    c. Install the new bushing by expanding the slit with a screwdriver.

    d. Seat the new bushing into the fork tube groove.

11. Check the damper rod piston ring (**Figure 47**) for excessive wear, cracks or other damage. Replace as necessary.

12. Check the damper rod (**Figure 48**) for straightness with a set of V-blocks and a dial indicator (**Figure 49**) or by rolling it on a piece of plate glass. Specifications for runout are not available. If the damper rod is not straight, replace it.

13. Make sure the oil passage hole in the damper rod (A, **Figure 50**) is open. If it is clogged, flush it with solvent and dry with compressed air.

14. Check the internal threads (B, **Figure 50**) in the bottom of the damper rod for stripping, cross-threading or sealer residue. Use a tap to true up the threads and to remove sealer deposits.

12

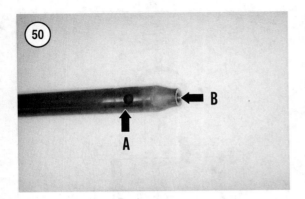

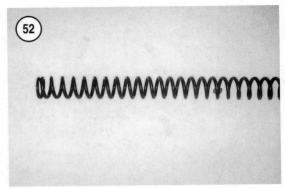

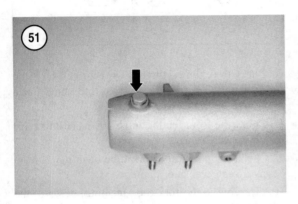

15. Remove the drain screw (**Figure 51**) and check for thread damage. Replace the gasket washer if there are signs of fluid leakage.

16. Check the damper rod rebound spring and the fork spring (**Figure 52**) for wear or damage. Service limit specifications for spring free length are not available.

17. Replace the oil seal whenever it is removed. Always replace both oil seals as a set.

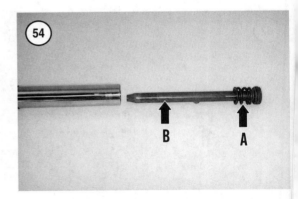

Assembly

1. Install a *new* O-ring (B, **Figure 44**) onto the fork cap bolt.

2. Coat all parts with BMW Special Performance Grade 7.5 fork oil (**Figure 53**), or an equivalent fork oil, before assembly.

3. Install the rebound spring (A, **Figure 54**) onto the damper rod and slide the damper rod (B) into the fork tube until it extends out the end of the fork tube (**Figure 55**).

4. Install the oil lock piece (**Figure 56**) onto the end of the damper rod.

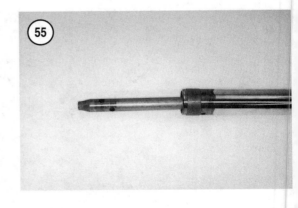

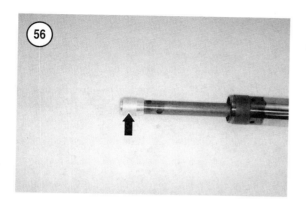

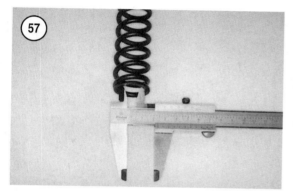

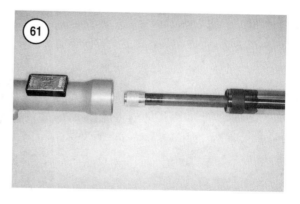

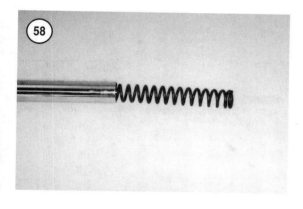

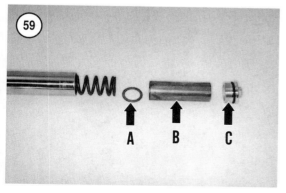

NOTE
*The spring taper is minimal. Measure the inner diameter of the coil with a vernier caliper (**Figure 57**) to establish the taper.*

5. Position the fork spring with the tapered end coils going in first and install the fork spring into the fork tube (**Figure 58**).

6. Install the support ring (A, **Figure 59**) and spacer (B) onto the top of the fork spring.

7. Make sure the O-ring (**Figure 60**) is in place on the fork cap bolt and temporarily install the fork cap bolt (C, **Figure 59**). Tighten securely.

8. Install the upper fork assembly into the slider (**Figure 61**). Using a Phillips screwdriver, guide the damper rod end into the receptacle in the base of the slider.

9. Install a *new* gasket washer (**Figure 62**) onto the Allen bolt.

10. Apply a non-permanent threadlocking compound to the damper rod Allen bolt threads prior to installation. Insert the Allen bolt (**Figure 63**) through the lower end of the slider and thread it into

12

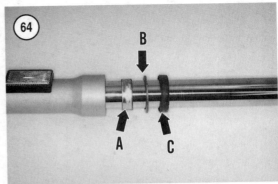

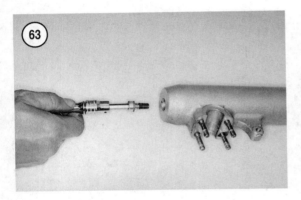

the damper rod. Tighten the bolt to the specification in **Table 1**.

> *NOTE*
> *To protect the oil seal lips, place a thin plastic bag on top of the fork tube. Before installing the seal in the following steps, lightly coat the bag and the seal lips with fork oil.*

11. Slide the fork slider bushing (A, **Figure 64**), washer (B) and oil seal (C) (with the letters facing up) down into the fork tube receptacle.

> *NOTE*
> *A fork seal driver (Figure 65), is required to install the fork tube bushing and seal into the fork tube. A number of different aftermarket fork seal drivers are available that can be used for this purpose. Another method is to use a piece of pipe or metal collar with correct dimensions to slide over the fork tube and seat against the seal. The tool must not contact and damage the inner surface of the slider area. When selecting or fabricating a driver*

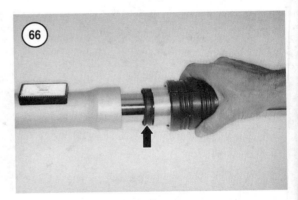

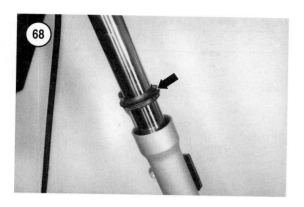

tool, it must have sufficient weight to drive the bushing and oil seal into the fork slider.

12. Slide the fork seal driver down the fork tube and seat it against the oil seal (**Figure 66**).

13. Operate the driver and drive the fork slider bushing, washer and new seal into the fork slider. Continue to operate the driver until the retaining ring groove in the tube is visible above the fork seal. Remove the fork seal driver tool.

14. Install the retaining ring into the slider groove. Make sure the retaining ring seats in the groove (**Figure 67**).

15. Slide the dust seal (**Figure 68**) down and tap into place (**Figure 69**).

16. Install the fork assembly as described in this chapter.

17. Loosen and remove the fork top cap (**Figure 70**), spacer and support ring.

18. Fill the fork assembly with the BMW Special Performance Grade 7.5 fork oil (**Figure 71**). Refer to **Table 2** for oil capacity.

19. Install the support ring, spacer and fork top cap. Tighten the fork top cap to the specification in **Table 1**.

12

Table 1 and Table 2 are on the following page.

Table 1 FRONT SUSPENSION TORQUE SPECIFICATIONS

Item	N•m	in.-lb.	ft.-lb.
Front fork			
Cap bolt	25	–	18
Drain plug	6	53	–
Damper rod Allen bolt	20	–	15
Fork bridge clamp bolts			
Upper and lower	25	–	18
Cover shoulder screw	12	106	–
Steering stem locknut	100	–	74
Mudguard reinforcement			
bolt	8	71	–
Handlebar			
Upper holder bolts	25	–	18
Lower holder nuts	10	88	–
Lower holder locknuts	40	–	29
Clutch lever clamp screw	12	106	–
Master cylinder			
clamp screw	12	106	–
Switch housing screws	5	44	–

Table 2 FRONT FORK OIL CAPACITY

	cc	U.S. oz.	Imp. oz.
Regular suspension	600	20	16.8
Lowered suspension	650	22	18

CHAPTER THIRTEEN

REAR SUSPENSION

This chapter describes repair and replacement procedures for the rear suspension components. **Table 1** is located at the end of this chapter.

> *NOTE*
> *All rear suspension fasteners must be replaced with parts of the same type. Do not use a replacement part of lesser quality or substitute design, as it may affect the performance of the rear suspension or it may fail, leading*

to loss of control of the motorcycle. Refer to the torque specifications in **Table 1** *during installation to ensure proper retention of these components.*

SHOCK ABSORBER

Shock Rebound Adjustment

The shock absorber can be adjusted with the adjuster at the base of the unit (**Figure 1**) to either a soft or hard setting. Turning the adjuster clockwise stiffens the suspension and turning it counterclockwise results in a softer setting.

1. Place the motorcycle on the center stand with the rear wheel off the ground.

> *NOTE*
> **Figure 2** *is shown with the rear wheel removed to better illustrate the step.*

2. Use a slotted screwdriver to turn the adjuster (A, **Figure 2**) at the base of the shock absorber. Make

13

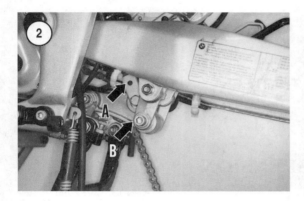

sure to place the adjuster on one of the settings, not in between settings. If left between settings, it will set the shock to the firmer setting.

Shock Spring Preload Adjustment

The spring preload can be adjusted from soft to hard in increments of ten.

1. Place the motorcycle on the center stand with the rear wheel off the ground.

2. On the left side, rotate the knob (**Figure 3**) on the remote adjuster to the desired setting.

Removal/Installation

1. Refer to Chapter Fifteen and perform the following:

    a. Remove the seat.

    b. Remove both frame side covers.

2. Remove the rear wheel as described in Chapter Eleven.

3. Remove the bolt and nut (B, **Figure 2**) securing the tension struts to the idler lever.

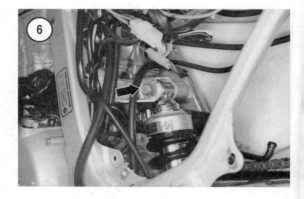

4. Slightly raise the swing arm to release any load on the shock absorber. Block it in this position.

5. Remove the bolt, washer, lockwasher and nut (**Figure 4**) securing the shock absorber to the idler lever.

6. On the left side, remove the bolt (A, **Figure 5**) securing the remote reservoir (B) to the frame.

7. Remove the bolt and nut (**Figure 6**) securing the upper portion of the shock absorber to the frame.

8. Completely raise the swing arm and block it in this position.

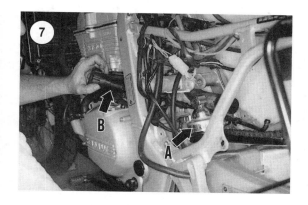

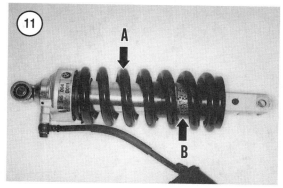

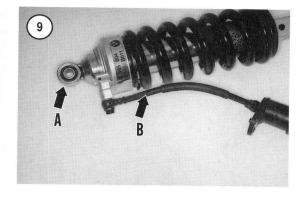

9. Carefully lower the shock absorber (A, **Figure 7**) and remote reservoir (B) out from the frame and swing arm, then remove it (**Figure 8**).

10. Inspect the shock absorber as described in this chapter.

11. Install the shock by reversing these removal steps while noting the following:

a. Apply a non-permanent threadlocking compound to the mounting bolt threads prior to installation. Tighten the bolts to the specification in **Table 1**.

b. Lower the motorcycle and test ride it to make the rear suspension is working properly.

Inspection

There are no shock replacement parts available for the shock absorber. If any part other than the mounting hardware is defective, replace the shock assembly.

1. Remove the shock absorber as described in this chapter.

2. Inspect the shock upper bushing (A, **Figure 9**) for wear and deterioration.

3. Inspect the shock lower mounting for hole (**Figure 10**) elongation and thread damage.

4. Check the interconnecting hose (B, **Figure 9**) between the remote reservoir to the shock body for cracks or deterioration.

5. Inspect the spring (A, **Figure 11**) for cracks or sagging.

6. Check the damper unit (B, **Figure 11**) for leakage.

13

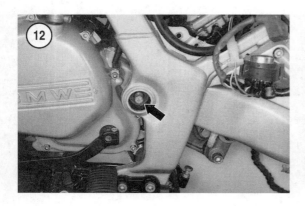

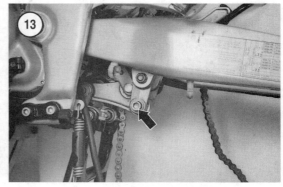

REAR SWING ARM

Rear Swing Arm Bearing Check

Worn or damaged bearings can greatly affect handling performance. If these worn parts are not replaced, they can produce erratic and dangerous handling. Common symptoms are wheel hop, pulling to one side during acceleration and pulling to the other side during braking.

1. Remove the rear wheel as described in Chapter Eleven.

2. Remove the trim caps on both sides of the pivot shaft.

3. Check that the swing arm pivot shaft nut (**Figure 12**) is tight.

4. Remove the bolt, lockwasher and washer (**Figure 13**) securing both tension struts to the idler lever. Move them away from the swing arm.

5. Have an assistant hold the motorcycle securely.

6. Grasp the back of the swing arm and try to move it from side to side. Any play (movement) between the swing arm and the frame and transmission may suggest worn or damaged swing arm bushings. If there is any play, remove the swing arm and inspect the needle bearings.

7. Install all components removed.

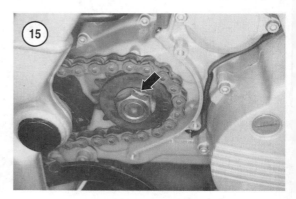

Removal

1. Refer to Chapter Fifteen and perform the following:

    a. Remove the seat.

    b. Remove both frame side covers.

2. Support the motorcycle with the rear wheel off the ground. See *Bike Stands* in this chapter.

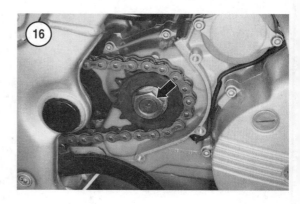

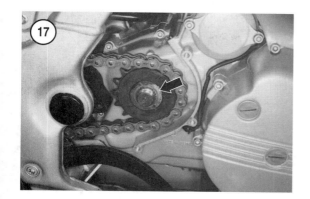

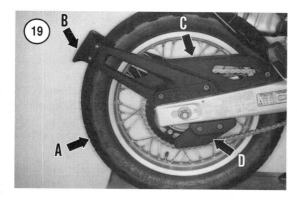

3. Remove the screws securing the drive sprocket cover (**Figure 14**) and remove the cover. Depress the rear brake pedal to access the lower screw.

4A. On models equipped with a snap ring, remove the snap ring from the transmission countershaft.

4B. On models equipped with a nut, perform the following:

    a. Straighten the tab on the lockwasher (**Figure 15**).

    b. Have an assistant hold the rear brake and loosen the drive sprocket nut (**Figure 16**).

    c. Remove the drive sprocket nut and lockwasher (**Figure 17**).

5. Remove the drive sprocket and drive chain (**Figure 18**) from the transmission countershaft . Remove the O-ring from the countershaft.

6. Remove the rear wheel (A, **Figure 19**) as described in Chapter Eleven.

7. Remove the bolts on each side and remove the mudguard (B, **Figure 19**).

8. Remove the screws securing the drive chain guard (C, **Figure 19**) and remove the guard.

9. Remove the screws securing the driven sprocket guard (D, **Figure 19**) and remove the guard.

10. Remove the bolt, lockwasher and washer (**Figure 13**) securing both tension struts to the idler lever.

11. Move the idler lever and shock absorber away from the swing arm.

12. Place a suitable size floor jack under the engine to support it when the swing arm pivot shaft is removed. Place a piece of wood between the jack and the engine. Apply jack pressure to the engine.

13. Remove the bearing trim cap (**Figure 20**) on each side covering the swing arm pivot bolt and nut.

14. On the right side, have an assistant hold the swing arm pivot bolt with a socket.

15. On the left side, remove the nut and washer (**Figure 21**) from the swing arm pivot bolt.

16. Place a box under the swing arm to support it securely.

17. On the left side, carefully tap the pivot shaft part way out of the frame.

18. On the right side, slowly withdraw the pivot shaft from the frame and engine crankcase. If necessary, adjust jack pressure under the engine to ease removal of the pivot shaft from the crankcase.

19. Release the drive chain from the engine drive sprocket area of the crankcase (A, **Figure 22**).

13

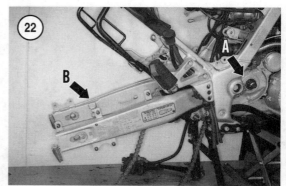

20. Remove the swing arm (B, **Figure 22**) and drive chain from the frame and engine crankcase.
21. Remove the drive chain from the swing arm.
22. Reinstall the pivot shaft into the frame and crankcase to secure the engine in the frame.
23. If the swing arm is not going to be serviced, place a strip of duct tape over each pivot area to protect the bearing assemblies and prevent the loss of small parts.
24. Inspect the swing arm as described in this chapter.

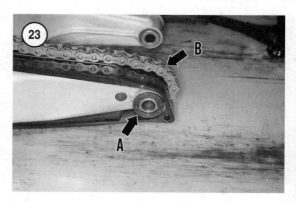

Installation

1. If used, remove the duct tape from the pivot areas. Make sure the grease seals (A, **Figure 23**) are in place on both sides of both pivot areas of the swing arm.

> *NOTE*
> *Do not forget to loop the drive chain over the end of the swing arm. The original drive chain is an endless loop-type with no master link.*

2. Position the drive chain (B, **Figure 23**) over the end of the swing arm prior to installation.
3. Withdraw the pivot shaft from the frame and crankcase.
4. Lubricate the swing arm and shock linkage with Shell Retinax EP2, or an equivalent water-resistant grease prior to installation.
5. Position the swing arm onto the pivot area of the frame.

> *NOTE*
> *It may be necessary to slightly reposition the swing arm to accept the pivot shaft. Also it may be necessary to ad-*

just the jack under the engine assembly.

6. Make sure the pivot shaft holes in both sides of the frame, the swing arm and the crankcase are correctly aligned prior to inserting the pivot shaft. Insert a long drift punch into one side of the frame to align the parts on one side. Insert another drift punch into the other side and align those parts. Remove both drift punches.
7. On the right side, slowly install the pivot shaft into the frame and engine crankcase. If necessary, adjust jack pressure under the engine to ease installation of the pivot shaft through the crankcase.
8. Install the washers and nut (**Figure 21**) onto the pivot shaft.
9. Have an assistant secure the pivot shaft with a wrench and tighten the nut to the specification in **Table 1**.
10. After the pivot shaft nut is tightened to the correct torque, move the swing arm up and down to check for smooth movement. If the swing arm is tight or loose, then the pivot shaft nut was tightened to the incorrect specification. Repeat Step 9 if necessary.

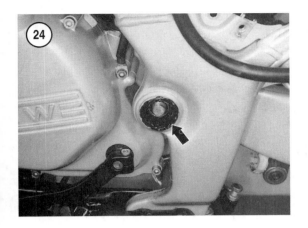

18. Install the mudguard (B, **Figure 19**) and tighten the bolts securely.

19. Install the drive chain guard (C, **Figure 19**) and tighten the screws securely.

20. Install the driven sprocket guard (D, **Figure 19**) and tighten the screws securely.

21. Install a *new* O-ring onto the countershaft.

22. Install the drive sprocket and drive chain onto the transmission countershaft (**Figure 18**).

23A. On models equipped with a snap ring, install a *new* snap ring onto the transmission shaft and make sure it is properly seated.

23B. On models equipped with a nut, perform the following:

    a. Install the lockwasher and the drive sprocket nut (**Figure 17**).

    b. Have an assistant hold the rear brake on and tighten the drive sprocket nut (**Figure 16**).

    c. Bend down the lockwasher onto one side of the sprocket nut (**Figure 15**).

24. Install the drive sprocket cover (**Figure 14**) and screws. Tighten the screws securely.

25. Refer to Chapter Fifteen and perform the following:

    a. Install both frame side covers.

    b. Install the seat.

26. Have an assistant sit on the seat, push down on the rear to make sure the swing arm is moving freely with no interference.

11. Apply a light coat of ThreeBond 1209 sealant to the outer perimeter of the bearing trim cap areas (**Figure 24**) prior to installation. Install both bearing trim caps (**Figure 20**) and tap them into place.

12. Release the floor jack pressure and remove it from under the engine.

13. Install the bolt and nut (**Figure 13**) securing the tension struts to the idler lever. Tighten to the specification in **Table 1**.

14. Install the rear caliper onto the swing arm and install the rear wheel as described in Chapter Eleven.

15. Move the rear brake caliper brake line into position on the swing arm. Secure it with the plastic clip.

16. Correctly position the drain tubes through the swing arm opening and the crankcase as shown in **Figure 25**.

17. Install the rear wheel (A, **Figure 19**) as described in Chapter Eleven.

SWING ARM SERVICE

Disassembly

Refer to **Figure 26**.

1. Remove the grease seal (A, **Figure 27**) from the outer surface on each side.

2. Remove the pivot bushing (B, **Figure 27**) from the inside surface on each side.

3. Repeat for the other side.

4. Slide out and remove the drive chain adjuster assembly (**Figure 28**) from each side.

Inspection

Replace the swing arm and/or parts that show excessive wear or damage as described in this section.

1. Thoroughly clean the swing arm and its components in solvent. Dry with compressed air.

13

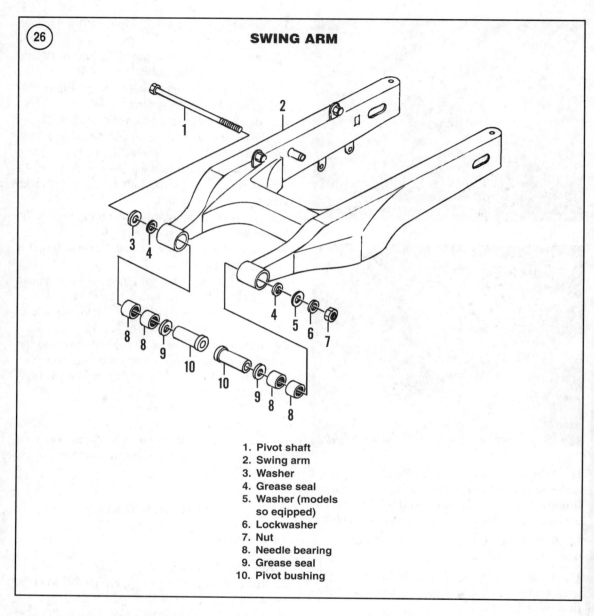

1. Pivot shaft
2. Swing arm
3. Washer
4. Grease seal
5. Washer (models so eqipped)
6. Lockwasher
7. Nut
8. Needle bearing
9. Grease seal
10. Pivot bushing

2. Inspect the pivot bushings (B, **Figure 27**) and grease seals (A).

NOTE
If the pivot bushing is excessively worn or damaged, its mating needle bearing(s) is probably worn also. Inspect the bearings carefully in Step 3.

3. Inspect the needle bearings (**Figure 29**) for cracks, flat spots, rust or other damage. If there is no visible damage, lubricate the pivot bushing with grease and install it into the swing arm. Turn the pivot bushing and check the bearing for any roughness. To replace the bearings, refer to *Swing Arm Needle Bearing Replacement* in this chapter.

4. Inspect the pivot bushing (B, **Figure 27**) for cracks, flat spots, rust or other damage. Turn the pivot bushing by hand and check for any roughness.

5. Check the swing arm (**Figure 30**) for cracks, bending or other damage. Check the bearing mounting bore for cracks and other damage.

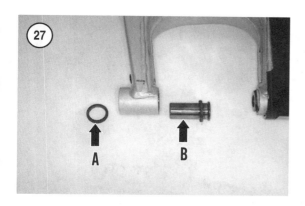

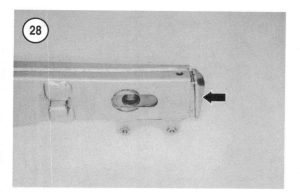

6. Inspect the drive chain slider (**Figure 31**) for severe wear or missing fasteners.

CAUTION
The chain slider protects the swing arm from chain contact damage. Replace the chain slider before the chain wears completely through and damages the swing arm.

7. Inspect the drive chain adjuster assembly (**Figure 32**) for wear or damage.

8. Check the areas where the rear axle and drive chain adjuster ride (A, **Figure 33**) for wear or damage.

9. Check the mounting tabs (B, **Figure 33**) for the drive chain guard and driven sprocket guard for cracks or damage.

10. Inspect the tension strut bolt mounting area (**Figure 34**) on the lower surface of the swing arm for wear, damage or elongation.

11. Inspect the swing arm pivot bolt for cracks, rust, bending and other damage. Install one of the swing arm pivot bushings onto the swing arm and

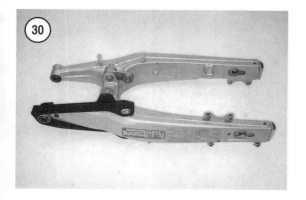

13

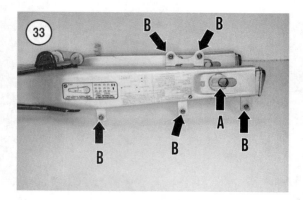

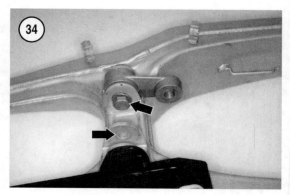

slide it back and forth by hand. There must be no binding or roughness.

Assembly

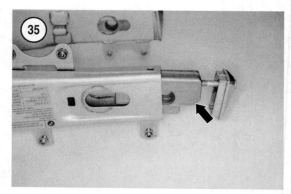

NOTE
Use a waterproof bearing grease in the following steps.

1. If removed, install the chain slider (**Figure 31**) and the tighten the screws securely.

2. Assemble and install the drive chain adjuster assembly (**Figure 35**) onto each side.

3. Lubricate the needle bearings and grease seals with grease. Force grease between the bearing rollers by hand.

4. Install the pivot bushing and grease seal (B, **Figure 27**) from the inside surface to the pivot area. Push it in until it bottoms.

5. Install the grease seal (**Figure 36**) on the outside surface and press it into place.

6. Repeat for the opposite side.

7. Install the swing arm as described in this chapter.

SHOCK LINKAGE

Removal/Installation

1. Remove the rear wheel as described in Chapter Eleven.

2. Remove the bolt and nut (**Figure 37**) securing the tension struts to the idler lever.

NOTE
The right side tension strut is secured only with a bolt and washer.

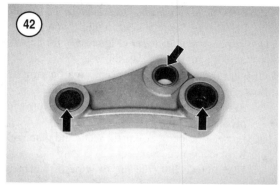

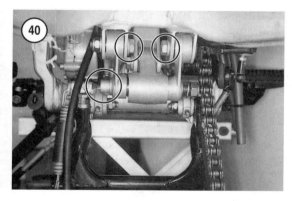

3. Remove the bolts, washers and nut (A, **Figure 38**) securing the tension struts (B) to the swing arm.

4. Remove the shock absorber as described in this chapter.

5. Remove the bolt, washers and nut (A, **Figure 39**) securing the idler lever (B) to the frame. Remove the idler lever.

6. Inspect the linkage as described in this chapter.

7. Install the shock linkage by reversing these removal steps while noting the following:

    a. Apply grease to the pivot points on the linkage and to the frame mount bosses.

    b. Install all three components and install the mounting bolts and washers. Refer to **Figure 40** for the correct direction for bolt installation.

    c. Tighten the bolts and nuts to the specification in **Table 1**.

Inspection

1. Inspect the idler lever pivot area bearings as follows:

    a. Remove the pivot collars (**Figure 41**) from the pivot areas.

    b. Inspect the pivot collars for wear and damage. Replace as necessary.

    c. Use a clean lint-free rag to wipe off surface grease from the pivot area needle bearings (**Figure 42**).

    d. Turn each bearing by hand; the bearing should turn smoothly. Check the rollers for evidence of wear, pitting or rust

    e. Reinstall the pivot collars (**Figure 41**) into the bearings and slowly rotate each pivot collar. The collars must turn smoothly.

13

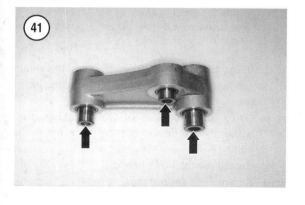

f. If the needle bearings must be replaced, refer to *Bearing Replacement* in this chapter.

g. Inspect the idler lever (**Figure 43**) for cracks or damage. Replace as necessary.

2. Inspect the tension struts pivot area bearing as follows:

a. Remove the pivot collar (**Figure 44**) from the pivot area.

b. Inspect the pivot collar for wear and damage. Replace as necessary.

c. Use a clean lint-free rag to wipe off surface grease from the pivot area needle bearing (**Figure 45**).

d. Turn the bearing by hand; the bearing should turn smoothly. Check the rollers for evidence of wear, pitting or rust

e. Reinstall the pivot collar (**Figure 44**) into the bearing and slowly rotate the pivot collar. The collars must turn smoothly.

f. If the needle bearing must be replaced, refer to *Bearing Replacement* in this chapter.

g. Inspect the idler lever (**Figure 46**) for cracks or damage. Replace as necessary.

h. Repeat for the other tension strut.

3. Clean the pivot bolts and nuts in solvent. Check the bolts for straightness; if the bolt is bent, it will restrict the movement of the rocker arm.

4. Prior to installing the pivot collars, coat the inner surface of the bearings with Shell Retinax EP2, or an equivalent waterproof grease.

BEARING REPLACEMENT

Swing Arm Needle Bearing Replacement

Refer to **Figure 26**.

Do not remove the swing arm needle bearings unless replacing them. The needle bearings are pressed onto the swing arm. The needle bearings can be replaced with a blind puller, suitable size socket or the BMW special tools.

NOTE
If the needle bearings are replaced, replace the pivot bushings at the same time. Always replace these parts as a set.

1. If still installed, remove the grease seals (A, **Figure 27**) and the pivot bushing (B) from the needle bearings.

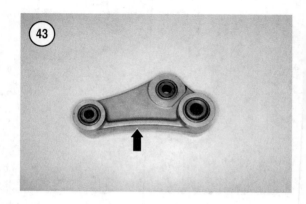

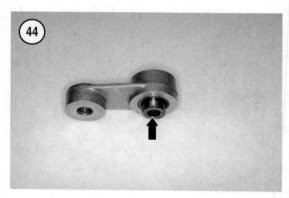

2A. If using the BMW special tools, perform the following:

a. Support the inner portion of the swing arm pivot point.

b. On the outer surface of the pivot point, install the drift (BMW part No. 33 6 600) into the pivot point and drive out both needle bearings.

c. Repeat for the pivot point on the other side.

2B. If using the blind puller, perform the following:

NOTE
In the following steps, the special tool grabs the inner surface of the bearing and withdraws it from the pivot points of the swing arm.

a. Insert the bearing puller through the outer needle bearing and expand it behind the bearing.

b. Using sharp strokes of the slide hammer, withdraw the needle bearing from the pivot point.

c. Repeat for the inner bearing.

d. Remove the special tool.

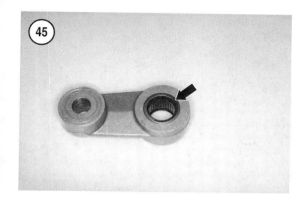

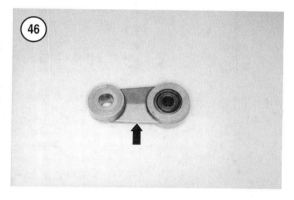

2C. If the BMW tools are not available, perform the following:

a. Support the inner portion of the swing arm pivot point.

b. On the outer surface of the pivot point, install an appropriate size socket into the pivot point and drive out both needle bearings.

c. Repeat for the pivot point on the other side.

3. Thoroughly clean out the inside of the pivot bearing areas with solvent and dry with compressed air.

4. Apply a light coat of grease to the exterior of the new bearings and to the inner pivot holes.

> *NOTE*
> *Install one needle bearing at a time. Make sure the bearing is entering the pivot hole squarely, otherwise the bearing and the pivot hole may be damaged.*

5. Use an industrial-type heat gun, capable of 100° C (212° F), to heat the swing arm pivot point to this temperature.

6A. If using the BMW tools, perform the following:

a. Support the inner portion of the swing arm pivot point.

b. Position the bearing with the manufacturer's marks facing out.

c. Locate and square the new inner bearing in the pivot hole.

d. Use the drift (BMW part No. 33 6 611) to tap the inner bearing in until the bearing's outer surface is 26 mm (1.02 in.) from the outer surface of the pivot point. Remove the drift.

e. Add the adapter (BMW part No. 33 6 612) to the drift.

f. Locate and square the new outer bearing in the pivot hole.

g. Use the drift and adapter to tap the outer bearing in until the bearing's outer surface is 4 mm (0.16 in.) from the outer surface of the pivot point. Remove the tools.

6B. If the BMW tools are not used, perform the following:

a. Support the inner portion of the pivot point.

b. Position the bearing with the manufacturer's marks facing out.

c. Locate and square the new inner bearing in the pivot hole.

d. Install an appropriate size socket into the inner bearing and drive the inner bearing squarely into the pivot hole until the bearings outer surface is 26 mm (1.02 in.) from the outer surface of the pivot point.

e. Locate and square the new outer bearing in the pivot hole.

f. Install an appropriate size socket into the outer bearing and drive the outer bearing squarely into the pivot hole until the bearing's outer surface is 4 mm (0.16 in.) from the outer surface of the pivot point.

Idler Lever Needle Bearings

Removal

Refer to **Figure 47**.

Do not remove the idler lever needle bearings unless they are to be replaced. The needle bearings are pressed onto the idler lever. The needle bearings can be removed with a blind puller, suitable size socket or the BMW special tools.

There are three pivot points on the idler lever and the bearings must be installed at different locations

13

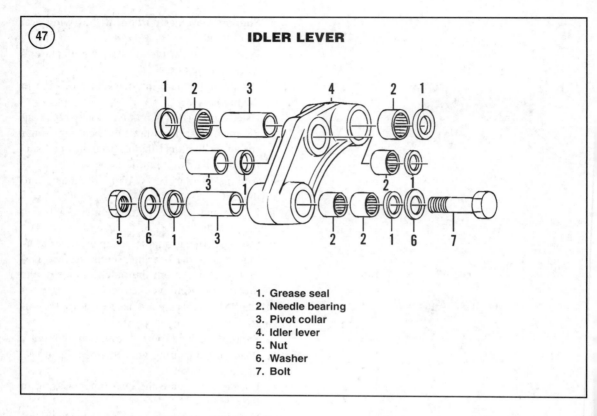

47

IDLER LEVER

1. Grease seal
2. Needle bearing
3. Pivot collar
4. Idler lever
5. Nut
6. Washer
7. Bolt

from the outer surface. Refer to locations A, B and C in **Figure 48** in the following procedure.

> *NOTE*
> *If the needle bearings are replaced, replace the pivot bushings at the same time. Always replace these parts as a set.*

1. If still installed, remove the grease seals and the pivot bushing (**Figure 41**) from the needle bearings.

2A. If using the BMW tools, perform the following:

  a. Support the idler lever next to one of the outer pivot points.

  b. At locations A and B, install the drift (BMW part No. 33 6 620) into the pivot point and drive out the needle bearing(s). Two bearings are at location A and one bearing is at location B.

  c. At location C, install the drift (BMW part No. 33 6 600) into the pivot point and drive out the two needle bearings.

2B. If BMW tools are not available, perform the following:

  a. Support the idler lever next to one of the outer pivot points.

  b. On the outer surface of the pivot point, install an appropriate size outer diameter socket into the pivot point and drive out the needle bearing(s) (**Figure 42**). There are two bearings at locations A and C and one bearing at location B.

  c. Repeat for all three pivot points.

3. Thoroughly clean out the inside of the pivot bearing areas with solvent and dry with compressed air.

4. Apply a light coat of grease to the exterior of the new bearings and to the inner pivot holes.

> *NOTE*
> *Install one needle bearing at a time. Make sure the bearing is entering the pivot hole squarely, otherwise the bearing and the pivot hole may be damaged.*

Installation at location A

Refer to **Figure 47**.

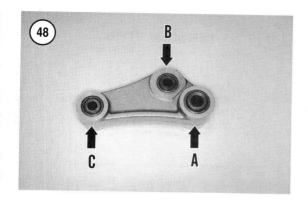

1. Use an industrial-type heat gun, capable of 100° C (212° F), to heat each pivot point area of the idler lever to this temperature.

2A. If using the BMW tools, perform the following at pivot point location A:

a. Support the idler lever next to the location A pivot point.

b. Position the bearing with the manufacturer's marks facing out.

c. Locate and square the new bearing in the pivot hole.

d. Use the drift (BMW part No. 33 6 611) and adapter (BMW part No. 33 6 613) to tap this bearing in until the bearing's outer surface is 4.5 mm (0.18 in.) from the outer surface of the pivot point. Remove the tools.

e. Turn the idler lever over and support it next to the location A pivot point.

f. Locate and square the other new bearing in the pivot hole.

g. Use the drift and adapter to tap the other bearing in until the bearing's outer surface is 4.5 mm (0.18 in.) from the outer surface of the pivot point. Remove the tools.

2B. If the BMW tools are not available, perform the following at pivot point A:

a. Support the idler lever next to the location A pivot point.

b. Position the bearing with the manufacturer's marks facing out.

c. Locate and square the new bearing in the pivot hole.

d. Install an appropriate size outside diameter socket into the bearing and drive the bearing squarely into the pivot hole until the bearing's outer surface is 4.5 mm (0.18 in.) from the

outer surface of the pivot point. Remove the socket.

e. Turn the idler lever over and support it next to the location A pivot point.

f. Locate and square the other new bearing in the pivot hole.

g. Use the same socket and tap the other bearing in until the bearing's outer surface is 4.5 mm (0.18 in.) from the outer surface of the pivot point. Remove the socket.

Installation at location B

Refer to **Figure 47**.

1. Use an industrial-type heat gun, capable of 100° C (212° F), to heat the each pivot point area of the idler lever to this temperature.

2A. If using the BMW tools, perform the following at pivot point location B:

a. Support the idler lever next to the location B pivot point.

b. Position the bearing with the manufacturer's marks facing out.

c. Locate and square the new bearing in the pivot hole.

d. Use the drift (BMW part No. 33 6 631) to tap this bearing in until the bearing's outer surface is 4.0 mm (0.16 in.) from the outer surface of the pivot point. Remove the special tool.

2B. If the BMW tools are not available, perform the following at pivot point B:

a. Support the idler lever next to the location B pivot point.

b. Position the bearing with the manufacturer's marks facing out.

c. Locate and square the new bearing in the pivot hole.

d. Install an appropriate size outside diameter socket into the bearing and drive the bearing squarely into the pivot hole until the bearing's outer surface is 4.0 mm (0.16 in.) from the outer surface of the pivot point. Remove the socket.

e. The bearing should be centered within the pivot hole. It should be 4.0 mm (0.16 in.) from the outer surface of each side of the pivot point.

13

Installation at location C

Refer to **Figure 47**.

1. Use an industrial-type heat gun, capable of 100° C (212° F), to heat the each pivot point area of the idler lever to this temperature.

2A. If using the BMW tools, perform the following at pivot point location C:

  a. Support the idler lever next to the location C pivot point.

  b. Position the bearing with the manufacturer's marks facing out.

  c. Locate and square the new bearing in the pivot hole.

  d. Use the drift (BMW part No. 33 6 631) to tap this bearing in until the bearing's outer surface is 4.0 mm (0.16 in.) from the outer surface of the pivot point. Remove the special tool.

  e. Turn the idler lever over and support it next to the location C pivot point.

  f. Locate and square the other new bearing in the pivot hole.

  g. Use the drift and adapter to tap the other bearing in until the bearing's outer surface is 4.0 mm (0.16 in.) from the outer surface of the pivot point. Remove the special tools.

2B. If the BMW tools are not used, perform the following at pivot point C:

  a. Support the idler lever next to the location C pivot point.

  b. Position the bearing with the manufacturer's marks facing out.

  c. Locate and square the new bearing in the pivot hole.

  d. Install an appropriate size outside diameter socket into the bearing and drive the bearing squarely into the pivot hole until the bearings outer surface is 4.0 mm (0.16 in.) from the outer surface of the pivot point. Remove the socket.

  e. Turn the idler lever over and support it next to the location C pivot point.

  f. Locate and square the other new bearing in the pivot hole.

  g. Use the same socket to tap the other bearing in until the bearings outer surface is 4.0 mm (0.16 in.) from the outer surface of the pivot point. Remove the socket.

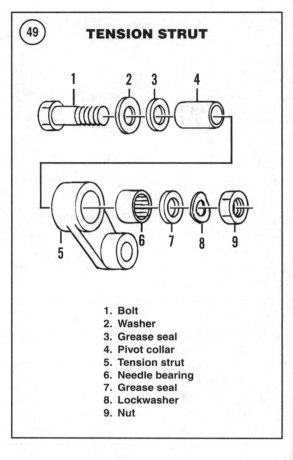

TENSION STRUT

1. Bolt
2. Washer
3. Grease seal
4. Pivot collar
5. Tension strut
6. Needle bearing
7. Grease seal
8. Lockwasher
9. Nut

Tension Strut Bearing Replacement

Refer to **Figure 49**.

Do not remove the tension strut needle bearing unless it is to be replaced. The needle bearing is pressed onto the tension strut. The needle bearing can also be removed with a blind puller, suitable size socket or the BMW special tools.

NOTE
If the needle bearing is replaced, replace the pivot bushing at the same time. Always replace these parts as a set.

1. If still installed, remove the grease seals and the pivot bushing (**Figure 44**) from the needle bearing.

2A. If using the BMW tools, perform the following:

  a. Support the inner portion of the tension strut pivot point.

b. On the outer surface of the pivot point, install the drift (BMW part No. 33 6 620) into the pivot point and drive out the needle bearing.

2B. If using the blind puller, perform the following:

NOTE
In the following steps, the special tool grabs the inner surface of the bearing and then withdraws it from the pivot point of the tension strut.

a. Insert the bearing puller through the needle bearing and expand it behind the bearing.
b. Using sharp strokes of the slide hammer portion of the bearing remover tool, withdraw the needle bearing from the pivot point.
c. Remove the tool.

2C. If the BMW tools are not available, perform the following:

a. Support the inner portion of the tension strut pivot point.
b. On the outer surface of the pivot point, install an appropriate size outside diameter socket into the pivot point and drive out the needle bearing (**Figure 45**).

3. Thoroughly clean out the inside of the pivot bearing area with solvent and dry with compressed air.

4. Apply a light coat of grease to the exterior of the new bearing and to the inner pivot hole. This will make bearing installation easier.

5. Use an industrial-type heat gun, capable of 100° C (212° F), to heat the pivot point area of the tension strut arm to this temperature.

6A. If using the BMW special tool, perform the following:

a. Support the inner portion of the tension strut pivot point.
b. Position the bearing with the manufacturer's marks facing out.
c. Locate and square the new bearing in the pivot hole.
d. Use the drift (BMW part No. 33 6 631) to tap the bearing in until the bearing's outer surface is 4.0 mm (0.16 in.) from the outer surface of the pivot point. Remove the tool.

6B. If the BMW tools are not available, perform the following:

a. Support the inner portion of the pivot point.
b. Position the bearing with the manufacturer's marks facing out.
c. Locate and square the new inner bearing in the pivot hole.
d. Install an appropriate size outside diameter socket into the inner bearing and drive the inner bearing squarely into the pivot hole until the bearing's outer surface is 4.0 mm (0.16 in.) from the outer surface of the pivot point. Remove the socket.

13

Table 1 REAR SUSPENSION TORQUE SPECIFICATIONS

Item	N•m	in.-lb.	ft.-lb.
Shock absorber			
Upper bolt to frame	50	–	37
Lower bolt to idler			
lever bolt	30	–	22
Remote adjuster to			
frame bolt	25	–	18
Tension strut-to-idler arm	80	–	59
Idler arm-to-frame	50	–	37
Swing arm pivot bolt nut	100	–	74

CHAPTER FOURTEEN

BRAKES

This chapter describes repair and replacement procedures for all brake components.

Table 1 contains brake system specifications and **Table 2** contains the brake system torque specifications. **Table 1** and **Table 2** are located at the end of this chapter.

NOTE
If the master cylinder(s) or brake caliper(s) are faulty, they must be replaced with new assemblies. Replacement parts for these assemblies are not available.

BRAKE FLUID SELECTION

Use DOT 4 brake fluid from a sealed container.

BRAKE SERVICE

WARNING
*When working on the brake system, do **not** inhale brake dust. It may contain asbestos, which is a known carcinogen. Do **not** use compressed air to blow off brake dust. Use an aerosol brake cleaner. Wear a face mask and wash thoroughly after completing the work.*

The disc brake system transmits hydraulic pressure from the master cylinders to the brake calipers. This pressure is transmitted from the calipers to the brake pads, which grip both sides of the brake discs and slow the motorcycle. As the pads wear, the pistons move out of the caliper bores to automatically compensate for wear. As this occurs, the fluid level in the master cylinder reservoir goes down. This must be compensated for by occasionally adding fluid.

The proper operation of this system depends on a supply of clean brake fluid (DOT 4) and a clean work environment when any service is being performed. Any tiny particle of debris that enters the system can damage the components and cause poor brake performance.

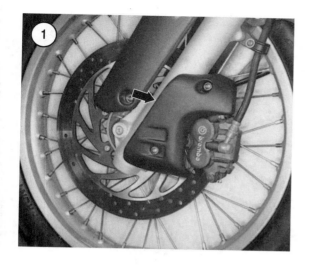

Brake fluid is hygroscopic (easily absorbs moisture) and moisture in the system will reduce brake performance. Purchase new brake fluid in small containers and properly discard any small quantities that remain. Small quantities of fluid will quickly absorb the moisture in the container. Use only fluid clearly marked DOT 4. If possible, use the same brand of fluid. Do not replace the fluid with a silicone-based brake fluid, as it is not compatible with DOT 4. Do not reuse drained fluid and discard old fluid properly. Do not combine brake fluid with other fluids for recycling.

Proper service also includes carefully performed procedures. Do not use any sharp tools inside the master cylinders or calipers or on the pistons. Any damage to these components could cause a loss in the system's ability to maintain hydraulic pressure. If there is any doubt about having the ability to correctly and safely service the brake system, have a professional technician perform the task.

Consider the following when servicing the brake system:

1. The hydraulic components rarely require disassembly. Make sure it is necessary.

2. Keep the reservoir covers in place to prevent the entry of moisture and debris.

3. Clean parts with an aerosol brake part cleaner or isopropyl alcohol. Never use petroleum-based solvents on internal brake system components. They will cause seals to swell and distort.

4. Do not allow brake fluid to contact plastic, painted or plated parts. It will damage the surface.

5. Dispose of brake fluid properly.

6. If the hydraulic system has been opened (not including the reservoir cover) the system must be bled to remove air from the system. Refer to *Bleeding the System* in this chapter.

7. The manufacturer does not provide wear limit specifications for the caliper and master cylinder assemblies. Use good judgment when inspecting these components or consult a professional technician for advice.

FRONT BRAKE PAD REPLACEMENT

There is no recommended mileage interval for changing the friction pads in the disc brake. Pad wear depends greatly on riding habits and conditions. Frequently check the brake pads for wear. Increase the inspection interval when the backing plate reaches the edge of the brake disc. After removal, measure the thickness of each brake pad with a vernier caliper or ruler and compare to the specifications in **Table 1**.

Always replace both pads in the caliper at the same time to maintain an even brake pressure on the disc. Do not disconnect the hydraulic brake hose from the brake caliper for brake pad replacement. Disconnect the hose only if the caliper assembly is going to be removed.

CAUTION
Check the pads more frequently when the lining approaches the pad metal backing plate. If pad wear happens to be uneven for some reason, the backing plate may come in contact with the disc and cause damage.

1. Read the information under *Brake Service* in this chapter.

2. Park the motorcycle on a level surface on the centerstand.

3. Remove the screws that secure the front air guide (**Figure 1**) to the fork slider and remove it.

4. To prevent the front brake lever from being applied, place a spacer between the brake lever and the throttle grip and secure it in place. If the brake lever is inadvertently squeezed, the piston will not be forced out of the cylinder.

5. Remove the Allen bolts (**Figure 2**) and bracket securing the front caliper to the fork slider.

6. Carefully slide the caliper off the brake disc.

14

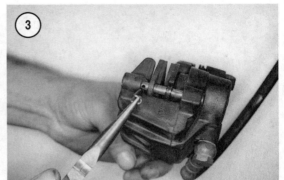

7. Remove the split pin (**Figure 3**) and carefully tap the keeper (**Figure 4**) toward the open side of the caliper. Remove the keeper from the caliper.

> *NOTE*
> *If the brake pads are going to be re-used, mark them so they can be rein-stalled into their original location.*

8. Remove the inboard pad (A, **Figure 5**) and the outboard pad (B).

9. Check the brake pads (**Figure 6**) for wear or damage. Measure the thickness of the brake pad friction material. Replace the brake pads if they are worn to the service limit in **Table 1**. Replace the pads as a set.

10. Check the friction surface of the new pads for any debris or manufacturing residue. If necessary, clean off with an aerosol brake cleaner.

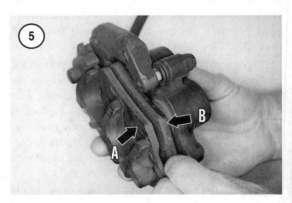

> *NOTE*
> *When purchasing new pads, check with the dealership to make sure the friction compound of the new pad is compatible with the disc material. Re-move any roughness from the backs of the new pads with a fine-cut file, then thoroughly clean off with brake cleaner.*

11. Check the keeper and split pin (**Figure 7**) for wear or damage. Clean all brake pad residue from the keeper.

12. Make sure the pad retainer (**Figure 8**) and anti-rattle spring (**Figure 9**) are in place.

13. Inspect the caliper as described in this chapter.

14. Remove all corrosion from the brake disc and clean off with an aerosol brake cleaner.

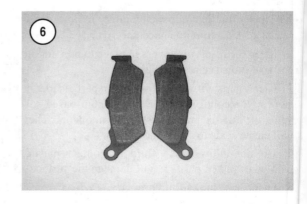

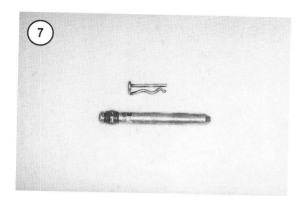

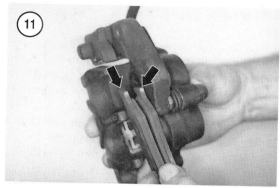

15. Check the brake disc for wear as described under *Brake Disc* in this chapter. Service the brake disc if necessary.

16. After installing new brake pads, the caliper piston must be relocated into the caliper before installing the caliper over the brake disc. Doing so forces brake fluid back up into the reservoir. To prevent the reservoir from overflowing, perform the following:

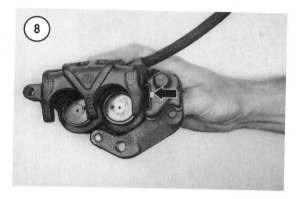

    a. Remove the screws securing the cover (**Figure 10**) and remove the cover and diaphragm.

    b. Use a shop syringe to remove about 50 percent of the brake fluid from the reservoir. This will prevent the master cylinder from overflowing when the piston is pushed back into the caliper bore. Do *not* drain more than 50 percent of the brake fluid, or air will enter the system. Discard the brake fluid properly.

> *CAUTION*
> *Do not allow the master cylinder to overflow when performing this step. Wash brake fluid off any painted, plated or plastic surfaces immediately, as it will damage most surfaces it contacts. Use soapy water and rinse it completely.*

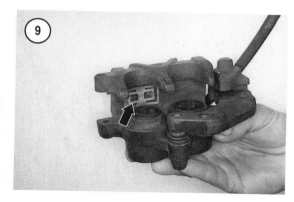

    c. Install the old outer brake pad into the caliper and against the piston.

    d. Slowly push the outer brake pad and piston back into the caliper and watch the brake fluid level in the master cylinder reservoir. If necessary, siphon off fluid prior to it overflowing.

    e. Remove the old brake pad.

    f. Temporarily install the diaphragm and cover. Install the screws finger-tight at this time.

17. Install the inner and outer brake pads into the caliper (**Figure 11**). Hook the end under the caliper

14

boss and push the pads in until they bottom (**Figure 12**).

18. Install the keeper (**Figure 13**) from the open side of the caliper and carefully tap it into place until the split pin hole is visible (**Figure 4**). Install the split pin (**Figure 3**) and make sure it is correctly seated (**Figure 14**).

19. Refill the master cylinder reservoir with DOT 4 brake fluid, if necessary, to maintain the correct fluid level. Install the diaphragm, top cover (**Figure 10**) and tighten the screws securely.

20. Carefully install the caliper over the brake disc, making sure the friction surface on each pad faces against the disc.

21. Install the caliper mounting bolts and bracket (**Figure 2**) and tighten to the specification in **Table 2**.

22. Apply the front brake lever several times to seat the pads against the disc.

> *WARNING*
> *Do not ride the motorcycle until the front brake operates correctly with full hydraulic advantage. If necessary, bleed the brake as described in this chapter.*

23. Install the air guide (**Figure 1**) onto the fork slider and tighten the screws securely,

FRONT BRAKE CALIPER

Removal

1. Read the information under *Brake Service* in this chapter.

2. Park the motorcycle on a level surface on the centerstand.

3. Remove the screws that secure the front air guide (**Figure 1**) to the fork slider and remove it.

4. Remove the front brake hose banjo bolt (A, **Figure 15**) and sealing washers.

5. Place the loose end of the brake hose in a reclosable plastic bag to prevent the entry of debris and to prevent any residual brake fluid from leaking out.

6. Remove the Allen bolts (B, **Figure 15**) and bracket securing the front caliper to the fork slider.

7. Slide the brake caliper off the brake disc and remove it.

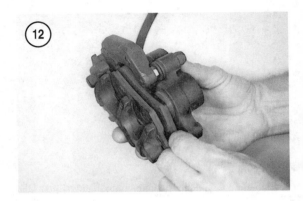

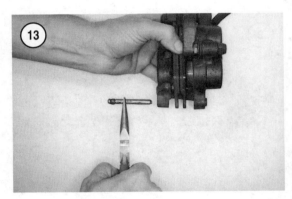

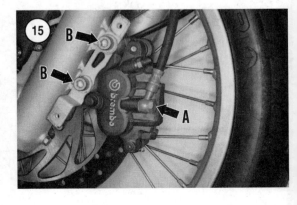

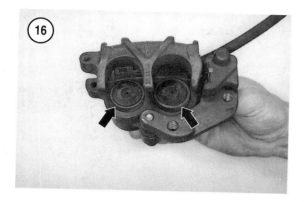

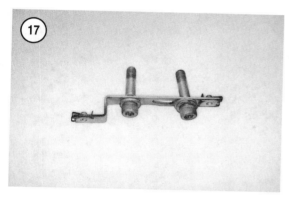

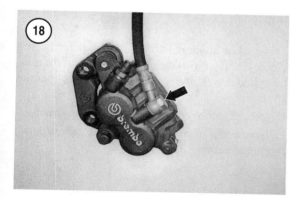

8. If the caliper is not going to be replaced, place it in a reclosable plastic bag to keep it clean.

9. Inspect the caliper as described in this chapter.

Inspection

The front brake caliper *cannot* be serviced. The only serviceable portion of the caliper is the brake pads. If brake fluid leakage is evident or if the caliper is faulty in any other respect, replace the caliper as an assembly.

1. Check the area surrounding the caliper pistons (**Figure 16**) for brake fluid leakage. If the piston seal(s) is leaking, replace the caliper assembly.

2. Inspect the upper and the lower mounting bolt holes for elongation and damage.

3. Inspect the mounting bolts and bracket (**Figure 17**) for wear or damage.

Installation

1. If removed, install the brake pads as described in this chapter.

2. Install the brake hose onto the caliper with a *new* sealing washer on both sides of the brake hose fitting, then secure the fitting to the caliper with the banjo bolt (**Figure 18**). Tighten the banjo bolt to the specification in **Table 2**.

3. Carefully install the caliper over the brake disc, making sure the friction surface on each pad faces against the disc.

4. Install the caliper mounting bolts (**Figure 19**) and tighten to the specification in **Table 2**.

5. Refill the master cylinder reservoir with DOT 4 brake fluid, if necessary, to maintain the correct fluid level. Install the diaphragm, top cover (**Figure 10**) and tighten the screws securely.

6. Apply the front brake lever several times to seat the pads against the disc.

> *WARNING*
> *Do not ride the motorcycle until the front brakes operate correctly with full hydraulic advantage. If necessary, bleed the brake as described in this chapter.*

7. Install the front air guide (**Figure 1**) onto the fork slide and tighten the screws securely.

14

FRONT MASTER CYLINDER

Removal

> *CAUTION*
> *Cover the fuel tank and front fairing with a heavy cloth or plastic tarp to protect them from accidental brake fluid spills. Wash brake fluid off any painted, plated or plastic surfaces immediately, as it will damage most surfaces it contacts. Use soapy water and rinse completely.*

1. Read the information under *Brake Service* in this chapter.

2. Park the motorcycle on a level surface on the centerstand.

3. Unscrew and remove the mirror (A, **Figure 20**).

4. Clean the top of the master cylinder of all dirt and debris.

5. Remove the screws securing the top cover (B, **Figure 20**).

6. Remove the top cover and diaphragm from the master cylinder reservoir.

7. Use a shop syringe to draw all of the brake fluid out of the master cylinder reservoir. Temporarily reinstall the diaphragm and the cover. Tighten the screws finger-tight.

8. Remove the banjo bolt and sealing washers (C, **Figure 20**) securing the brake hose to the master cylinder.

9. Place the loose end of the brake hose in a reclosable plastic bag to prevent the entry of moisture and debris. Tie the loose end of the line up to the handlebar.

10. Remove the small screws securing the brake light switch to the master cylinder. Reinstall the screws onto the switch to prevent misplacing them.

11. Remove the bolts and washers securing the clamp (D, **Figure 20**) and master cylinder to the handlebar.

12. Remove the master cylinder assembly from the handlebar.

13. Drain any residual brake fluid from the master cylinder and dispose of it properly.

14. If the master cylinder assembly is not going to be replaced, place the assembly in a reclosable plastic bag to protect it from debris.

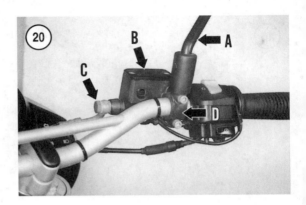

Inspection

The front brake master cylinder *cannot* be serviced. If brake fluid leakage is evident or if the master cylinder is faulty, replace the master cylinder as an assembly.

1. Check the top cover and diaphragm for damage.

2. Inspect the clamp and the mounting bolt holes for thread damage.

Installation

1. Position the front master cylinder onto the handlebar and place it in a comfortable position.

2. Position the clamp (D, **Figure 20**) and install the clamp bolts and washers. Tighten the upper mounting bolt first, then the lower bolt. Tighten the bolts to the specification in **Table 2**.

3. Install the brake hose onto the master cylinder with a *new* sealing washer on both sides of the brake hose fitting, then secure the fitting to the master cylinder with the banjo bolt (C, **Figure 20**). Tighten the banjo bolt to the specification in **Table 2**.

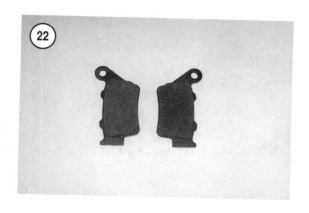

4. Install the brake light switch onto the master cylinder and tighten the small screws and nuts securely.

5. Install the mirror (A, **Figure 20**) onto the master cylinder. Correctly adjust the mirror.

6. Temporarily install the diaphragm and top cover (B, **Figure 20**) onto the reservoir. Tighten the screws finger-tight at this time.

7. Refill the master cylinder reservoir and bleed the brake system as described under *Bleeding the System* in this chapter.

REAR BRAKE PAD REPLACEMENT

There is no recommended mileage interval for changing the brake pads. Pad wear depends greatly on riding habits and conditions. Frequently check the pads for wear. Increase the inspection interval when the wear indicator reaches the edge of the brake disc. After removal, measure the thickness of each brake pad with a vernier caliper or ruler and compare it to the specifications in **Table 1**.

Always replace both pads in the caliper at the same time to maintain an even brake pressure on the disc. Do not disconnect the hydraulic brake hose from the brake caliper for brake pad replacement; disconnect the hose only if the caliper assembly is going to be removed.

> *CAUTION*
> *Check the pads more frequently when the lining approaches the pad metal backing plate. If pad wear happens to be uneven for some reason, the backing plate may come in contact with the disc and cause damage.*

1. Read *Brake Service* in this chapter.

2. Park the motorcycle on a level surface on the centerstand.

3. Remove the mudguard as described in Chapter Fifteen.

4. On models so equipped, remove both saddlebags as described in Chapter Fifteen.

5. Tie the end of the brake pedal up to the frame. If the brake pedal is inadvertently applied, this will prevent the piston from being forced out of the cylinder.

6. Remove the split pin (**Figure 21**) and carefully tap the keeper in toward the wheel. Remove the keeper from the caliper.

> *NOTE*
> *If the brake pads are going to be reused, mark them so they can be reinstalled into their original location.*

7. Remove the inboard and the outboard pads.

8. Check the brake pads (**Figure 22**) for wear or damage. Measure the thickness of the brake pad friction material. Replace the brake pads if they are worn to the service limit in **Table 1**. Replace the pad sets in both calipers at the same time.

9. Check the friction surface of the new pads for any debris or manufacturing residue. If necessary, clean off with an aerosol brake cleaner.

> *NOTE*
> *When purchasing new pads, check with the dealership to make sure the friction compound of the new pad is compatible with the disc material. Remove any roughness from the backs of the new pads with a fine-cut file, then thoroughly clean them off with brake cleaner.*

> *NOTE*
> *The following photographs show the caliper assembly removed to better illustrate the steps.*

10. Make sure the pad retainer (**Figure 23**) and anti-rattle spring (**Figure 24**) are in place.

11. Inspect the caliper as described in this chapter.

12. Remove all corrosion from the brake disc and clean off with an aerosol brake cleaner.

13. Check the brake disc for wear as described under *Brake Disc* in this chapter. Service the brake disc if necessary.

14

14. After installing new brake pads, the caliper piston must be relocated into the caliper before installing the caliper over the brake disc. Doing so will force brake fluid back up into the reservoir. To prevent the reservoir from overflowing, perform the following:

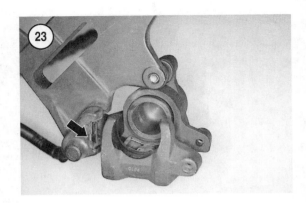

   a. Remove the frame right side cover as described in Chapter Fifteen.
   b. Unscrew and remove the remote reservoir cover (**Figure 25**). Remove the diaphragm.
   c. Use a shop syringe to remove about 50 percent of the brake fluid from the remote reservoir. This will prevent the master cylinder from overflowing when the piston is pushed back into the caliper bore. Do *not* drain more than 50 percent of the brake fluid or air will enter the system. Discard the brake fluid properly.

> *CAUTION*
> *Do not allow the master cylinder remote reservoir to overflow when performing this step. Wash brake fluid off any painted, plated or plastic surfaces immediately, as it will damage most surfaces it contacts. Use soapy water and rinse completely.*

   d. Install the old outer brake pad into the caliper and against the piston.
   e. Slowly push the outer brake pad and piston back into the caliper and watch the brake fluid level in the master cylinder reservoir. If necessary, siphon off fluid prior to it overflowing.
   f. Remove the old brake pad.
   g. Temporarily install the diaphragm and cover, and tighten the cover securely.

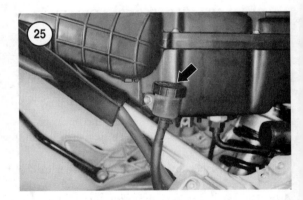

15. Install the inboard brake pad into the caliper (**Figure 26**) from the inside surface. Push the pad into place.

16. Partially install the keeper from the inside and through the inner pad (**Figure 27**).

17. Install the outboard brake pad into the caliper (**Figure 28**) from the outside surface. Push the pad into place.

18. Push the keeper through the outboard pad (**Figure 29**).

19. Carefully tap the keeper into place (**Figure 30**) until the split pin hole is visible.

20. Install the split pin and make sure it is correctly seated (**Figure 31**).

> *NOTE*
> *To control the flow of hydraulic fluid, punch a small hole into the seal of a new container of brake fluid next to the edge of the pour spout. This will help eliminate fluid spillage, especially while adding fluid to the very small reservoir.*

21. Refill the master cylinder remote reservoir with DOT 4 brake fluid, if necessary, to maintain the correct fluid level as indicated on the side of the remote reservoir. Install the diaphragm, top cover (**Figure 25**) and tighten securely.

22. Untie the brake pedal from the frame and pump the rear brake pedal to reposition the brake pads against the brake disc. Roll the motorcycle back and forth and continue to pump the brake pedal as many times as it takes to correctly locate the brake pads against the disc.

> *WARNING*
> *Do not ride the motorcycle until the rear brake is operating correctly with full hydraulic advantage. If necessary, bleed the brake as described in this chapter.*

23. Install the mudguard and, on models so equipped, both saddlebags.

REAR BRAKE CALIPER

Removal

1. Read *Brake Service* in this chapter.

14

2. Park the motorcycle on a level surface on the centerstand.

3. Remove the mudguard as described in Chapter Fifteen.

4. On models so equipped, remove both saddlebags as described in Chapter Fifteen.

5. Tie the end of the brake pedal up to the frame. If the brake pedal is inadvertently applied, this will prevent brake fluid from being expelled from the brake line after the caliper is removed.

6. Remove the rear wheel as described in Chapter Eleven.

7. Remove the rear brake caliper (**Figure 32**) from the swing arm.

8. If the caliper is going to be replaced, remove the banjo bolt and washers (**Figure 33**) securing the brake hose to the rear caliper.

9. Place the loose end of the brake hose in a resealable plastic bag to prevent the entry of debris and prevent any residual brake fluid from leaking out.

10. If the caliper is not going to be replaced, place it in a resealable plastic bag to keep it clean.

11. Inspect the caliper as described in this chapter.

Inspection

The rear brake caliper *cannot* be serviced. The only serviceable portion of the caliper is the brake pads. If brake fluid leakage is evident or if the caliper is faulty in any other respect, replace the caliper as an assembly.

1. Check the area surrounding the caliper piston (**Figure 34**) for brake fluid leakage. If the piston seal is leaking, replace the caliper assembly.

2. Inspect the sliding pin rubber boots for deterioration or damage.

Installation

1. If removed, install the brake pads as described in this chapter.

2. If removed, install the brake hose onto the caliper with a *new* sealing washer on both sides of the brake hose fitting, then secure the fitting to the caliper with the banjo bolt (**Figure 33**). Tighten the banjo bolt to the specification in **Table 2**.

3. Install the rear brake caliper (**Figure 32**) onto the swing arm.

4. Install the rear wheel as described in Chapter Eleven.

5. Refill the master cylinder reservoir and bleed the brake system as described under *Bleeding the System* in this chapter.

6. Install the mudguard and, on models so equipped, the left side saddlebag.

c. Remove the right side passenger footpeg assembly.

d. On models so equipped, remove both saddlebags.

e. Remove the mudguard.

4. At the rear brake caliper, perform the following:

a. Insert a hose onto the end of the bleed valve (**Figure 35**). Insert the open end of the hose into a container.

b. Open the bleed valve and operate the rear brake pedal to drain the brake fluid. Remove the hose and close the bleed valve after draining the assembly. Discard the brake fluid properly.

5. Remove the keeper securing the master cylinder pushrod ball end (**Figure 36**) and disconnect it from the rear brake pedal.

6. Disconnect the banjo bolt and sealing washers (A, **Figure 37**) securing the rear caliper brake hose to the master cylinder.

7. Place the loose end of the brake hose in a resealable plastic bag to prevent the entry of debris and any residual brake fluid from leaking out.

8. Disconnect the remote reservoir brake hose (B, **Figure 37**) from the master cylinder.

9. Remove the bolts (C, **Figure 37**) securing the master cylinder to the frame and remove it.

10. Remove the master cylinder from the frame.

11. If the master cylinder is not going to be replaced, place the master cylinder in a resealsable plastic bag to keep it clean.

12. Inspect the caliper as described in this chapter.

Inspection

The rear master cylinder *cannot* be serviced. If brake fluid leakage is evident, or if the master cylinder is faulty in any other respect, replace it as an assembly.

1. Check the body for brake fluid leakage. If the piston is leaking, replace the master cylinder assembly.

2. Inspect the pushrod rubber boot for hardness or deterioration.

3. Inspect the mounting bolt holes for elongation and damage.

REAR MASTER CYLINDER

Removal

1. Read *Brake Service* in this chapter.

2. Park the motorcycle on a level surface on the centerstand.

3. Refer to Chapter Fifteen and perform the following:

a. Remove the seat.

b. Remove the frame right side cover.

14

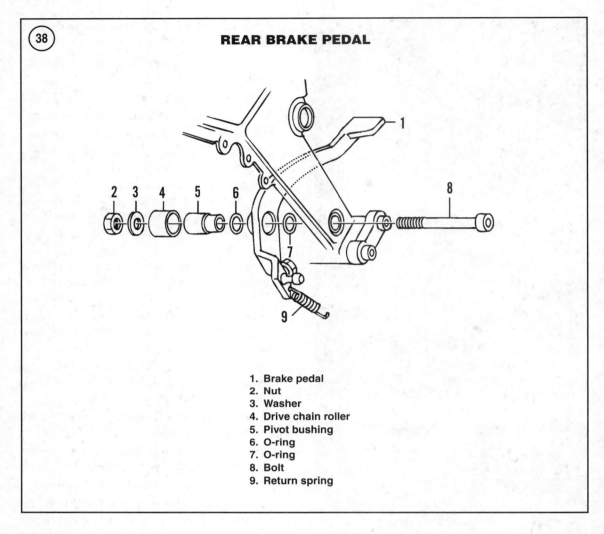

38   **REAR BRAKE PEDAL**

1. Brake pedal
2. Nut
3. Washer
4. Drive chain roller
5. Pivot bushing
6. O-ring
7. O-ring
8. Bolt
9. Return spring

Installation

1. Install the master cylinder onto the frame and tighten the bolts (C, **Figure 37**) to the specification in **Table 2**.

2. Connect the master cylinder pushrod ball end (**Figure 36**) onto the rear brake pedal and install the keeper.

3. Connect the remote reservoir brake hose (B, **Figure 37**) onto the master cylinder.

4. Install the rear caliper brake hose onto the caliper with a *new* sealing washer on both sides of the brake line fitting, then secure the fitting to the caliper with the banjo bolt (A, **Figure 37**). Tighten the banjo bolt to the specification in **Table 2**.

5. Bleed the brake as described under *Bleeding the System* in this chapter.

6. Refer to Chapter Fifteen and perform the following:

   a. Install the mudguard.

   b. On models so equipped, install both saddle-bags.

   c. Install the right side passenger footpeg assembly.

   d. Install the frame right side cover.

   e. Install the seat.

WARNING
Do not ride the motorcycle until the rear brake is operating correctly with full hydraulic advantage.

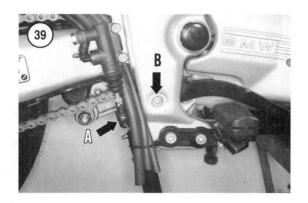

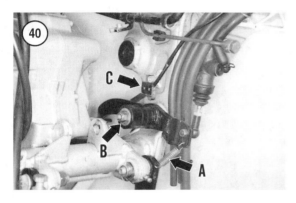

8. Withdraw the bolt, and carefully move the brake pedal down and away from the brake light switch (C, **Figure 40**). Remove the brake pedal.

9. Inspect the components as described in this chapter.

10. Install by reversing these removal steps. Tighten the pivot bolt and nut to the torque specification in **Table 2**.

Inspection

Replace any worn or damaged parts.

1. Thoroughly clean all parts in solvent and dry.

NOTE
If the drive chain roller requires replacement, inspect the swing arm drive chain guide. It may also require replacement.

2. Inspect the drive chain roller for wear or damage.

3. Check the return spring for sagging.

4. Check the brake pedal for bending or cracks.

REAR BRAKE PEDAL

Removal/Installation

Refer to **Figure 38**.

1. Read the *Brake Service* in this chapter.

2. Remove the rear wheel as described in Chapter Eleven.

3. Remove the keeper securing the master cylinder pushrod ball end (A, **Figure 39**) and disconnect it from the rear brake pedal.

NOTE
The following photographs are shown with the rear swing arm removed to better illustrate the steps.

4. Use Vise Grip pliers to disconnect the return spring (A, **Figure 40**) from the frame hook.

5. Working inside the frame area, place a wrench on the pivot bolt nut (B, **Figure 40**).

6. While holding onto the nut, loosen the Allen bolt (B, **Figure 39**) securing the brake pedal to the frame.

7. Remove the nut, washer and drive chain roller from the bolt.

BRAKE HOSE REPLACEMENT

A combination of flexible brake hoses and metal lines connect the master cylinder to the brake caliper. Banjo fittings and bolts connect brake hoses to the master cylinder and brake calipers. Washers seal the banjo fittings. The rear brake remote reservoir is connected to the master cylinder with a brake hose and clamps.

Replace a brake hose(s) and/or brake line if it shows swelling, cracking or other damage.

Front Brake Hose Removal/Installation

A flexible brake hose (A, **Figure 41**) connects the front master cylinder to the front brake caliper. When purchasing a new hose, compare it to the old hose to make sure that the length is correct. Install new banjo bolt washers at both ends.

CAUTION
Do not spill any brake fluid on the front fork or front wheel. Wash brake fluid off any painted, plated or plastic surfaces, as it will damage most sur-

14

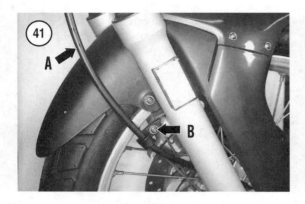

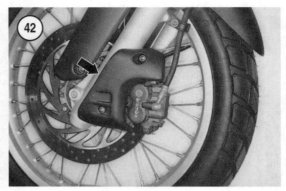

*faces it contacts. Use soapy water and
rinse completely.*

1. Read *Brake Service* in this chapter.

2. Park the motorcycle on a level surface on the
centerstand.

3. Remove the screws that secure the front air
guide (**Figure 42**) and remove it.

4. Remove the fuel tank as described in Chapter
Eight.

5. Refer to Chapter Fifteen and perform the following:

    a. Remove the front fender.

    b. Remove the front fairing.

6. Remove the bolts securing the lower fork bridge
cover and remove the cover (**Figure 43**).

7. Disconnect the brake hose from the cover grommet.

8. Drain the front brake system as follows:

    a. Remove the bleed valve cap (A, **Figure 44**)
and connect a hose over the bleed valve .

    b. Insert the loose end of the hose in a container
to catch the brake fluid.

    c. Open the bleed valve and apply the front
brake lever to pump the fluid out of the master
cylinder and brake line. Continue until the
fluid is removed.

    d. Close the bleed valve and disconnect the
hose.

    e. Dispose of this brake fluid—never reuse
brake fluid. Contaminated brake fluid could
cause brake failure.

9. Before removing the brake hose assembly, note
the brake hose routing from the master cylinder to
the caliper. In addition, note the number and position of any metal hose clamps (B, **Figure 41**) and/or
plastic ties used to hold the brake hose in place. In-

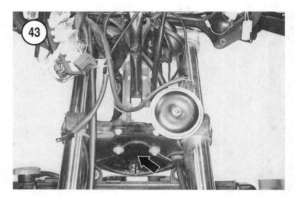

stall the brake hose assembly along its original path.
The metal clamps can be reused.

10. Cut any plastic ties and discard them.

11. Remove the banjo bolt (B, **Figure 44**) and
washers securing the hose to the brake caliper.

12. Remove the banjo bolt (**Figure 45**) and washers securing the hose to the front master cylinder.

13. Cover the ends of the brake hose to prevent
brake fluid from leaking out.

14. Remove the brake hose assembly from the motorcycle.

15. If the existing brake hose assembly is going to
be reinstalled, inspect it as follows:

    a. Check the flexible hose portions for swelling,
cracks or other damage.

    b. If any wear or damage is found, replace the
brake hose assembly.

16. Install the brake hose, washers and banjo bolts
in the reverse order of removal while noting the following:

    a. Install *new* sealing washers on each side of
the hose fittings.

    b. Carefully install the clips and guides to hold
the brake hose in place.

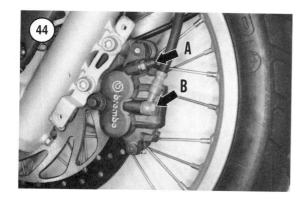

c. Tighten the banjo bolts to the specification in **Table 2**.

d. Refill the front master cylinder with clean brake fluid clearly marked DOT 4. Bleed the front brake system as described in this chapter.

WARNING
Do not ride the motorcycle until the front brakes operate correctly with full hydraulic advantage.

Rear Brake Line and Hose Removal/Installation

A single combination steel line and rubber brake hose connects the rear master cylinder to the rear brake caliper. When buying a new hose, compare it to the old hose. Make sure the length and angle of the steel hose portion is correct. Install new banjo bolt washers at both hose ends.

CAUTION
Do not spill any brake fluid on the swing arm, frame or rear wheel. Wash brake fluid off any painted, plated or plastic surfaces immediately, as it will damage most surfaces it contacts. Use soapy water and rinse completely.

1. Read the information under *Brake Service* in this chapter.
2. Park the motorcycle on a level surface on the centerstand.
3. Refer to Chapter Fifteen and perform the following:
    a. On models so equipped, remove both saddlebags.
    b. Remove the rear mudguard.
    c. Remove the passenger right side footpeg assembly.
4. At the rear brake caliper, perform the following:
    a. Remove the bleed valve cap (**Figure 46**) and connect a hose onto the end of the bleed valve. Insert the open end of the hose into a container.
    b. Open the bleed valve and operate the rear brake pedal to drain the brake fluid. Remove the hose and close the bleed valve after draining the assembly. Discard the brake fluid properly.
5. Before removing the brake line and hose assembly, note the brake line and hose routing from the master cylinder to the caliper. In addition, note the number and position of the metal hose clamps, plastic clips and plastic ties used to hold the brake line in place. Install the brake hose assembly along its original path. The metal clamp and plastic clips can be reused. However, new plastic ties must be installed.
6. Disconnect the banjo bolt (A, **Figure 47**) and sealing washers securing the rear caliper brake hose to the master cylinder.
7. Remove the rear wheel as described in Chapter Eleven.

14

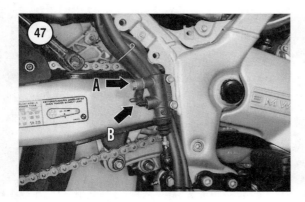

8. Remove the banjo bolt and (**Figure 48**) washers securing the hose to the brake caliper.

NOTE
The following photograph shows the rear swing arm removed to better illustrate the step.

9. Remove the brake line from the frame clip (A, **Figure 49**).

10. Disconnect the brake hose from the hose clamp on the left side of the swing arm.

11. Carefully move the rear brake line and brake hose assembly (B, **Figure 49**) toward the rear and away from the rear swing arm. Remove the brake line and brake hose assembly from the motorcycle.

12. If the existing brake line and brake hose assembly is going to be reinstalled , inspect it as follows:
   a. Check the metal pipe where it enters and exits the flexible hose. Check the crimped clamp for looseness or damage.
   b. Check the flexible hose portion for swelling, cracks or other damage.
   c. If any wear or damage is found, replace the brake hose.

13. To replace the remote reservoir, perform the following:
   a. Disconnect the remote reservoir brake hose (B, **Figure 47**) from the master cylinder.
   b. Unhook the brake hose from the frame clip (A, **Figure 50**).
   c. Remove the bolt (B, **Figure 50**) securing the remote reservoir to the air box.
   d. Remove the hose (C, **Figure 50**) and remote reservoir from the frame.

14. Install the brake line and brake hose in the reverse order of removal while noting the following:

   a. Install *new* sealing washers on each side of the hose fittings.
   b. Carefully install the clips and guides to hold the brake line and brake hose in place.
   c. Tighten the banjo bolts to the specification in **Table 2**.
   d. Refill the master cylinder with clean brake fluid clearly marked DOT 4. Bleed the rear brake system as described in this chapter.

WARNING
Do not ride the motorcycle until the rear brake is operating correctly with full hydraulic advantage.

BRAKE DISC

The brake discs are separate from the wheel hubs and can be removed once the wheel is removed from the motorcycle.

Inspection

It is not necessary to remove the disc from the wheel to inspect it. Small nicks and marks on the

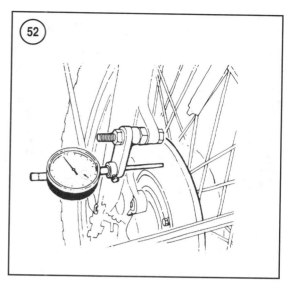

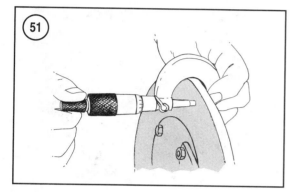

NOTE
It is not necessary to remove the wheel to measure the disc thickness. The measurement can be performed with the wheel installed on the motorcycle.

1. Measure the thickness of the disc at several locations around the disc with a vernier caliper or a micrometer (**Figure 51**). The disc must be replaced if the thickness in any area is less than that specified in **Table 1** (or the marked MIN dimension on the disc).

2. Make sure the disc mounting bolts are tightened to the specification in **Table 1** prior to measuring disc runout as shown in **Figure 52**.

NOTE
When checking the front disc, turn the handlebar all the way to one side, then to the other side.

3. Slowly rotate the wheel and watch the dial indicator. If the runout exceeds that listed in **Table 1**, replace the disc(s).

4. Clean rust or corrosion from the disc and wipe it clean with an aerosol brake parts cleaner. Never use an oil-based solvent that may leave an oil residue on the disc.

Removal/Installation

1. Remove the front or rear wheel as described in Chapter Eleven.

disc are not important, but radial scratches deep enough to snag a fingernail reduce braking effectiveness and increase brake pad wear. If these grooves are evident, and the brake pads are wearing rapidly, replace the disc.

The specifications for the standard and wear limits are in **Table 1**. Each disc is also marked with the minimum (MIN) thickness. If the specification marked on the disc differs from that in **Table 1**, refer to the specification marks on the disc.

When servicing the brake discs, do not have the discs surfaced to compensate for warp. The discs are thin, and grinding will only reduce their thickness and cause them to warp quite rapidly. If the disc is warped, the brake pads may be dragging on the disc due to a faulty caliper and causing the disc to overheat. Overheating can also be caused when there is unequal pad pressure on the disc.

Worn or damaged piston seals, a plugged master cylinder relief port, or a worn or damaged master cylinder primary cup can cause unequal brake pad pressure.

14

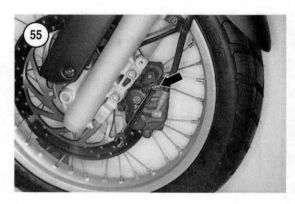

2. Remove the Torx bolts (**Figure 53**) that secure the brake disc to the hub, then remove the disc.

3. Check the brake disc bolts for thread damage. Replace worn or damaged fasteners.

4. Check the mounting brake disc holes in the wheel hub for thread damage. Clean out with a tap if necessary.

5. Clean the disc and the disc mounting surface thoroughly with brake cleaner. Allow the surfaces to dry before installation.

6. Install the disc onto the correct side of the wheel hub.

7. Apply a drop of ThreeBond TB1342 or an equivalent to each bolt threads prior to installation.

8. Install new Torx bolts and tighten to the specification in **Table 2**.

BLEEDING THE SYSTEM

If air enters the brake system, the brake will feel soft or spongy, greatly reducing braking pressure. If this happens, the system must be bled to remove the air. Air can enter the system if there is a leak in the system, the brake fluid level in a master cylinder runs low, a brake line is opened, or if the brake fluid is replaced.

When bleeding the brakes, two different methods can be used—with a brake bleeder or manually. This section describes both procedures separately.

Before bleeding the brake system, observe the following conditions:

1. Check the brake lines and hoses to make sure that all fittings are tight.

2. Check that the caliper piston does not stick or bind in its bore.

3. Check piston movement in each master cylinder. Operate the lever or brake pedal, making sure there is no binding or other abnormal conditions present.

Brake Bleeder Process

This procedure uses the Mityvac hydraulic brake bleeding kit (**Figure 54**) that is available from automotive or motorcycle supply stores.

NOTE
Before bleeding the brake, check that all brake line and brake hose connections are tight.

NOTE
This procedure is shown on the front wheel and relates to the rear wheel as well.

1A. On the front wheel, remove the screws securing the front air guide (**Figure 42**) and remove it.

1B. On the rear wheel, remove the mudguard and the frame right side cover as described in Chapter Fifteen.

7A. On the front wheel, remove the screws securing the master cylinder top cover (**Figure 57**) and remove the cover and diaphragm.

7B. On the rear wheel, unscrew and remove the remote reservoir top cover (**Figure 58**) and remove the cover and diaphragm.

8. Fill the reservoir almost to the top with DOT 4 brake fluid and reinstall the diaphragm and cover. Leave the cover in place during this procedure to prevent the entry of dirt.

WARNING
Use brake fluid from a sealed container marked DOT 4. Do not intermix a silicone-based DOT 5 brake fluid, as this can cause brake failure.

9. Operate the pump several times to create a vacuum in the line. Brake fluid will quickly flow from the caliper into the pump's reservoir. Tighten the caliper bleed valve before the fluid stops flowing through the hose. To prevent air from being drawn through the master cylinder, add fluid to maintain its level at the top of the reservoir.

NOTE
Do not allow the master cylinder reservoir to empty during the bleeding operation, or more air will enter the system. If this occurs, the procedure must be repeated.

10. Continue the bleeding process until the fluid drawn from the caliper is bubble-free. If bubbles are withdrawn with the brake fluid, more air is trapped in the line. Repeat Step 8, making sure to refill the master cylinder to prevent air from being drawn into the system.

11. When the brake fluid is free of bubbles, tighten the bleed valve and remove the brake bleeder assembly. Reinstall the bleed valve dust cap.

NOTE
Dispose of the brake fluid expelled during the bleeding process. Do not reuse the brake fluid.

12. If necessary, add fluid to correct the level in the master cylinder reservoir. When topping off the front master cylinder, turn the handlebar until the reservoir is level; add fluid until it is level with the reservoir gasket surface. The fluid level in the rear

2. Remove the cap from the caliper bleed valve (**Figure 55**).

3. Place a clean shop cloth over the caliper to protect it from accidental brake fluid spills.

4. Using a wrench, open the bleed screw approximately 1/2 turn.

5. Assemble the brake bleeder according to its manufacturer's instructions. Secure it to the caliper bleed valve (**Figure 56**).

6. Clean the top of the master cylinder of all debris.

14

master cylinder must be slightly below the upper gasket surface.

13A. On the front wheel, install the reservoir diaphragm and cover (**Figure 57**). Install the screws and tighten securely

13B. On the rear wheel, install the diaphragm and remote reservoir top cover (**Figure 58**). Tighten the cover securely.

14. Test the feel of the brake lever or pedal. It must be firm and offer the same resistance each time it is operated. If it feels spongy, it is likely that there is still air in the system and it must be bleed again. After bleeding the system, check for leaks and tighten all fittings and connections as necessary.

> *WARNING*
> *Do not ride the motorcycle until the front and/or rear brakes are operating correctly with full hydraulic advantage.*

15. Test ride the motorcycle slowly at first to make sure that the brakes are operating properly.

Without a Brake Bleeder

This procedure uses a small jar, clear plastic tubing and a brake bleeder wrench (**Figure 59**).

> *NOTE*
> *Before bleeding the brake, check that all brake line and brake hose connections are tight.*

> *NOTE*
> *This procedure is shown on the front wheel and relates to the rear wheel as well.*

1A. On the front wheel, remove the screws that secure the front air guide (**Figure 42**) and remove it.

1B. On the rear wheel, remove the mudguard and the frame right side cover as described in Chapter Fifteen.

2. Remove the dust cap from the caliper bleed valve (**Figure 55**).

3. Place a clean shop cloth over the caliper to protect it from accidental brake fluid spills.

4. Using a wrench, open the bleed screw approximately 1/2 turn.

5. Connect a length of clear tubing to the bleed valve on the caliper. Place the other end of the tube

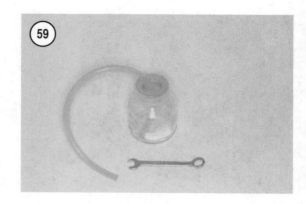

into a clean container (**Figure 60**). Fill the container with enough clean DOT 4 brake fluid to keep the end of the tube submerged. The tube must be long enough so that a loop can be made higher than the bleeder valve to prevent air from being drawn into the caliper during bleeding.

6. Clean the top of the master cylinder of all debris.

7A. On the front wheel, remove the screws securing the master cylinder top cover (**Figure 57**) and remove the cover and diaphragm.

7B. On the rear wheel, unscrew and remove the remote reservoir top cover (**Figure 58**) and remove the cover and diaphragm.

8. Fill the reservoir almost to the top with DOT 4 brake fluid and reinstall the diaphragm and cover. Leave the cover in place during this procedure to prevent the entry of dirt.

> *WARNING*
> *Use brake fluid from a sealed container marked DOT 4. Do not intermix a silicone-based DOT 5 brake fluid, as this can cause brake failure.*

> *NOTE*
> *During this procedure, it is important to check the fluid level in the master cylinder reservoir often. If the reservoir runs dry, air will enter the system.*

9. Slowly apply the brake lever several times. Hold the lever in the applied position and open the bleed valve about 1/2 turn. Allow the lever to travel to its limit. When the limit is reached, tighten the bleed valve, then release the brake lever. As the brake fluid enters the system, the level will drop in the master cylinder reservoir. Maintain the level at the

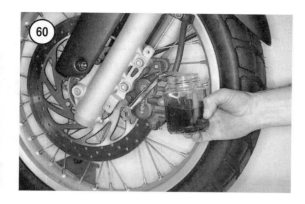

top of the reservoir to prevent air from being drawn into the system.

10. Continue the bleeding process until the fluid emerging from the hose is completely free of air bubbles. If the fluid is being replaced, continue until the fluid emerging from the hose is clean.

NOTE
If bleeding is difficult, allow the fluid to stabilize for a few hours. Repeat the bleeding procedure when the tiny bubbles in the system settle out.

11. Hold the lever in the applied position and tighten the bleed valve. Remove the bleed tube and install the bleed valve cap.

NOTE
Dispose of the brake fluid expelled during the bleeding process. Do not reuse the brake fluid.

12. If necessary, add fluid to correct the level in the master cylinder reservoir. When topping off the front master cylinder, turn the handlebar until the reservoir is level; add fluid until it is level with the reservoir gasket surface. The fluid level in the rear master cylinder must be slightly below the upper gasket surface.

13A. On the front wheel, install the reservoir diaphragm and cover (**Figure 57**). Install the screws and tighten securely

13B. On the rear wheel, install the diaphragm and remote reservoir top cover (**Figure 58**). Tighten the cover securely.

14. Test the feel of the brake lever or pedal. It must be firm and offer the same resistance each time it is operated. If it feels spongy, it is likely that there is still air in the system and it must be bled again. After bleeding the system, check for leaks and tighten all fittings and connections as necessary.

WARNING
Do not ride the motorcycle until the front and/or rear brake are operating correctly with full hydraulic advantage.

15. Test ride the motorcycle slowly at first to make sure that the brakes are operating properly.

14

Table 1 BRAKE SYSTEM SPECIFICATIONS

Item	Specification
Brake fluid	DOT 4
Brake pad minimum thickness	
Front and rear	1.5 mm (0.06 in.)
Brake disc outside diameter	
Front	300 mm (11.81 in.)
Rear	240 mm (9.45 in.)
Brake disc thickness (front and rear)	
New	5 mm (0.20 in.)
Wear limit	4.5 mm (0.18 in.)
Brake disc lateral runout (maximum)	0.25 mm (0.010 in.)

Table 2 BRAKE SYSTEM TORQUE SPECIFICATIONS

Item	N•m	in.-lb.	ft.-lb.
Bleed valves	2	18	–
Brake disc bolts (front and rear)	12	106	–
Front brake caliper mounting bolts	50	–	37
Front master cylinder clamp bolts	12	106	–
Rear master cylinder mounting bolts	12	106	–
Rear brake pedal pivot bolt and nut	25	–	18
Brake line banjo bolts	7	62	–

CHAPTER FIFTEEN

BODY

This chapter describes the removal and installation of the body components. Most of these components are fragile and must be handled carefully. Protect the finish when handling them. If a component is going to be removed for a period of time, wrap it with a blanket or towels and place it in a safe location.

SEAT

Removal/Installation

1. Place the motorcycle on level ground on the centerstand.
2. On the right side, insert the ignition key (**Figure 1**) and turn it to unlock the seat.
3. Raise the rear of the seat (A, **Figure 2**), pull toward the rear to disengage the front locating tab from the frame mount.
4. Remove the seat.
5. Inspect the seat front mounting tab for damage.

6. Install the seat.
7. Pull up on the front of the seat (B, **Figure 2**) to ensure the seat front hook is secured in place in the frame backbone slot.

FRONT FENDER

Removal/Installation (F650 ST and Funduro F650 Models)

1. Place the motorcycle on level ground on the centerstand.
2. Remove the screws securing the front fender to the mounting bracket.
3. Be careful not scratch the paint. Carefully rotate the front fender forward and away from the fork assembly and front wheel.
4. Install by reversing these removal steps. Tighten the screws securely.

15

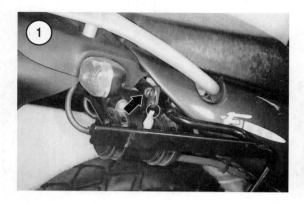

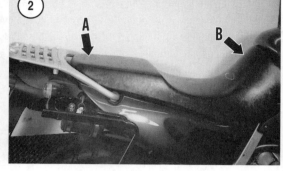

Removal/Installation (F650 Funduro, Strada SE Models)

1. Place the motorcycle on level ground on the centerstand.

2. Remove the screw (**Figure 3**) securing the lower section of the front fender to the slider.

3. Remove the screw (**Figure 4**) securing the upper section of the front fender to the slider.

4. Be careful not scratch the paint. Carefully rotate the front fender forward (**Figure 5**) and away from the fork assembly and front wheel.

5. Install by reversing these removal steps. Tighten the screws securely.

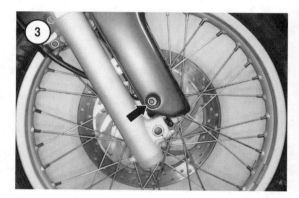

REAR MUDGUARD

Removal/Installation

1. Place the motorcycle on level ground on the centerstand.

2. Remove the screws (A, **Figure 6**) securing the mudguard to the swing arm mounting tabs.

3. Pull the mudguard (B, **Figure 6**) toward the rear and off the swing arm and rear wheel.

4. Install by reversing these removal steps. Tighten the screws securely.

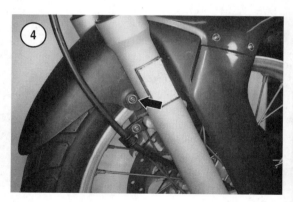

CYLINDER HEAD SIDE COVER

Removal/Installation

> *NOTE*
> *This procedure is shown on a F650 model. The procedure is the same for all other models; only the shape of the side cover is different.*

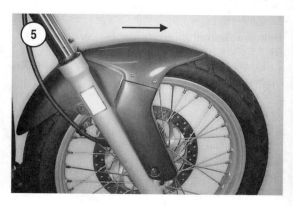

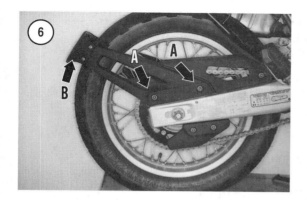

1. Place the motorcycle on level ground on the centerstand.

2. Remove the seat as described in this chapter.

3. Remove the screws (**Figure 7**) securing the cylinder head side cover to the front fairing, the frame and the mounting bracket.

4. Remove the cylinder head side cover and store it in a safe place.

5. Repeat for the other side, if necessary.

6. Install by reversing these removal steps. Tighten the screws securely. Do not overtighten, as the plastic surrounding the screw hole may fracture.

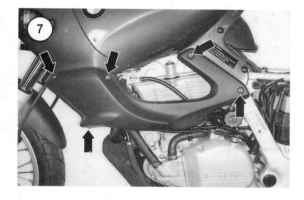

SIDE COVER

Removal/Installation

1. Place the motorcycle on level ground on the centerstand.

2. Remove the seat as described in this chapter.

3. Remove the lower screw (A, **Figure 8**) securing the frame side cover to the frame.

4. Carefully pull out on the cover and disengage the two cover posts from the rubber grommets on the frame in the locations shown in B, **Figure 8**.

5. Install by reversing these removal steps. Tighten the screw securely. Do not overtighten, as the plastic surrounding the screw hole may fracture.

ENGINE LOWER COVER

Removal/Installation

NOTE
This procedure is shown on a F650 model. The procedure is the same for all other models, only the shape of the lower cover is different.

1. Place the motorcycle on level ground on the centerstand.

2. Remove the lower screw (A, **Figure 9**) and front screw (B) on each side securing the cover to the frame.

3. Remove the engine lower cover.

4. Install by reversing these removal steps. Tighten the screws securely. Do not overtighten, as the plastic surrounding the screw hole may fracture.

15

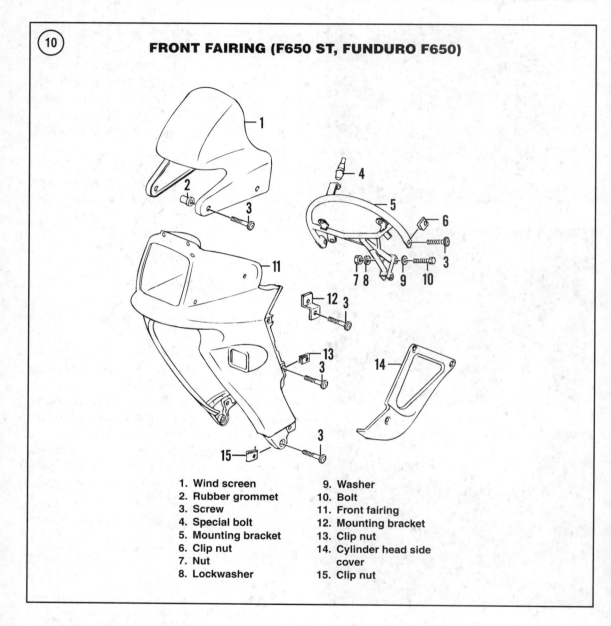

FRONT FAIRING (F650 ST, FUNDURO F650)

1. Wind screen
2. Rubber grommet
3. Screw
4. Special bolt
5. Mounting bracket
6. Clip nut
7. Nut
8. Lockwasher
9. Washer
10. Bolt
11. Front fairing
12. Mounting bracket
13. Clip nut
14. Cylinder head side cover
15. Clip nut

WINDSHIELD AND FRONT FAIRING

Windshield Only Removal/Installation (F650 ST, Funduro F650 Models)

Refer to **Figure 10**.

1. Place the motorcycle on level ground on the centerstand.

2. Remove the screws on each side that secure the windshield to the front fairing.

3. Remove the windshield.

4. Install by reversing these removal steps. Tighten the screws securely. Do not overtighten as the plastic surrounding the screw hole may fracture.

Windshield Only Removal/Installation (F650, F650 Strada, F650 Strada/SE Models)

Refer to **Figure 11**.

NOTE
The screws securing the windshield and inner panel thread into the rubber

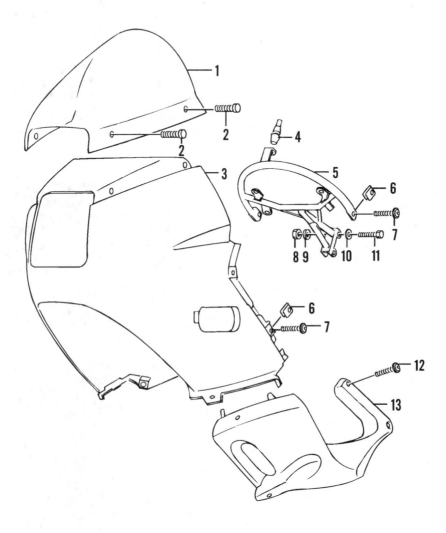

11

FRONT FAIRING
(F650, F650 STRADA, F650 STRADA SE)

1. Windshield
2. Screw
3. Front fairing
4. Special bolt
5. Mounting bracket
6. Clip nut
7. Bolt
8. Nut
9. Lockwasher
10. Washer
11. Bolt
12. Screw
13. Cylinder head side
    cover

grommets in the front fairing. There is no metal attachment at any of these locations.

1. Place the motorcycle on level ground on the centerstand.

2. Remove the screws (A, **Figure 12**) on each side securing the windshield and inner panel.

3. Remove the windshield (B, **Figure 12**).

4. Remove the inner panel (A, **Figure 13**).

5. If removed, insert the rubber grommets (**Figure 14**) into front fairing mounting holes prior to installation.

6. Install the inner panel and align the mounting holes (B, **Figure 13**).

7. Install the windshield onto the inner panel and align the mounting holes.

8. Install the screws (A, **Figure 12**) through both parts and into the rubber grommets in the front fairing. Tighten the screws into the rubber grommets. Do not overtighten, as the rubber grommets will be destroyed.

Front Fairing Removal/Installation

Refer to **Figure 10** and **Figure 11**.

NOTE
This procedure is shown on a F650 model. The procedure is the same for all other models; only the shape of the front fairing is different.

1. Place the motorcycle on level ground on the centerstand.

2. Disconnect the negative battery cable as described in Chapter Eight

3. Remove the seat and the cylinder head cover on both sides.

4. Cover the front fender with towels or a blanket to protect the painted finish.

5. Remove the three screws (**Figure 15**) on each side securing the front fairing to the fuel tank cover.

6. Remove the two screws (**Figure 16**) on each side securing the front fairing to the fairing inner panel.

NOTE
The following step requires the aid of an assistant.

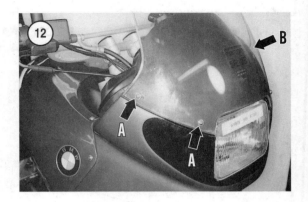

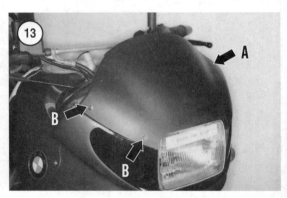

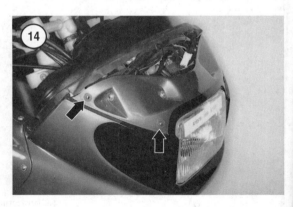

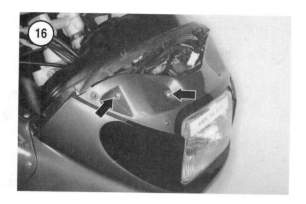

7. Slowly pull the front fairing forward and have the assistant disconnect the electrical connectors from the headlight and both front turn signals.

8. Remove the front fairing and store it in a safe place.

9. Install by reversing these removal steps while noting the following:

    a. Make sure to connect the electrical connectors to the headlight and turn signals.

    b. Tighten the screws securely. Do not overtighten, as the plastic surrounding the screw hole may fracture.

FUEL TANK COVER

Removal/Installation

NOTE
This procedure is shown on a F650 model. The procedure is the same for all other models, only the shape of the fuel tank cover is different.

1. Place the motorcycle on level ground on the centerstand.

2. Disconnect the negative battery cable as described in Chapter Eight.

3. Refer to the procedures in this chapter and perform the following:

    a. Remove the seat.

    b. Remove the cylinder head cover from each side.

    c. Remove the front fairing.

4. Remove the fuel filler cap (**Figure 17**) as follows:

    a. Using the ignition key, open the fuel filler cap.

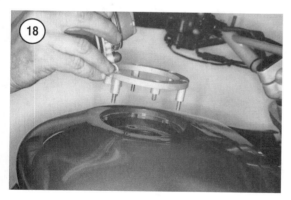

NOTE
*It is not necessary to remove the following screws. Loosen and leave them in place on the flange (**Figure 18**). This will lessen the chance of dropping the screws into the fuel tank opening.*

    b. Loosen the Torx screws (A, **Figure 19**) securing the fuel filler cap to the fuel tank. Be careful not to drop the single inner Torx screw (B) into the fuel tank opening.

    c. Pull the filler cap assembly straight up and off the fuel tank and cover.

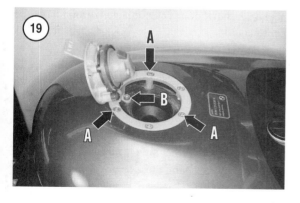

15

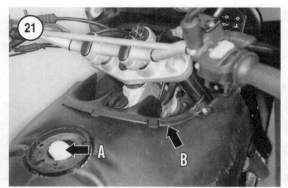

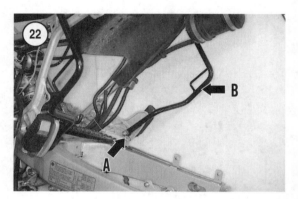

5. Remove the single screw (**Figure 20**) on each side securing the fuel tank cover to the frame.

6. Carefully pull the fuel tank cover up and toward the rear. Remove it from the fuel tank and frame. Store it in a safe place.

7. Place a clean shop cloth into the fuel tank opening (A, **Figure 21**) to keep out debris.

8. Install by reversing these removal steps while noting the following:

    a. Make sure the rubber skirt (B, **Figure 21**) is in place on the fuel tank.

    b. Tighten the screw securely. Do not overtighten, as the plastic surrounding the screw hole may fracture.

SADDLEBAGS

Saddlebags Removal/Installation

1. Place the motorcycle on level ground on the centerstand.

2. Use the ignition key and unlock the saddlebag lock in the handle.

3. Open the saddlebag lid.

4. Release the saddlebag from the mounting bracket and remove the saddlebag.

5. Install by reversing these removal steps. Make sure the saddlebag is secured to the mounting bracket.

Saddlebag Mounting Bracket Removal/Installation

NOTE
The following photographs show the rear wheel removed to better illustrate the procedure.

1. Place the motorcycle on level ground on the centerstand.

2. Remove the saddlebag.

3. Remove the lower bolt (A, **Figure 22**) securing the bracket to the footrest bracket.

4. Remove the upper bolts (**Figure 23**) securing the bracket to the frame.

5. Remove the mounting bracket (B, **Figure 22**).

6. Repeat for the other side if necessary.

7. Install by reversing these removal steps. Tighten all bolts securely.

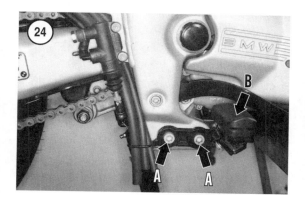

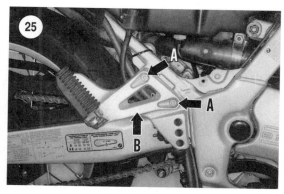

FOOTPEGS

Front Footpeg Removal/Installation

1. Place the motorcycle on level ground on the centerstand.
2. Remove the bolts (A, **Figure 24**) securing the footpeg bracket to the frame.
3. Remove the footpeg assembly (B, **Figure 24**) from the frame.
4. Repeat for the other side if necessary.
5. Install by reversing these removal steps. Tighten all bolts securely.

Rear Footpeg Removal/Installation

1. Place the motorcycle on level ground on the centerstand.
2. Remove the bolts (A, **Figure 25**) securing the footpeg bracket to the frame.
3. Remove the footpeg assembly (B, **Figure 25**) from the frame.
4. Repeat for the other side if necessary.
5. Install by reversing these removal steps. Tighten all bolts securely.

15

INDEX

A

Air filter 60
  air box 218-219
Alternator 230-234

B

Balancer shaft 147-166
  cleaning and inspection 159
  disassembly/assembly 159-160
Battery 49-53
  box 228
  state of charge 80
Bearing replacement 324-329
Bike stands 265
Bleeding the system, brakes 348-351
Body
  cylinder head side cover 354-355
  engine lower cover 355
  fender, front 353-354
  footpegs 361
  fuel tank cover 359-360
  mudguard, rear 354
  saddlebags 360
  seat 353
  side cover 355
  windshield and front fairing 356-359
Brakes 61-62
  bleeding the system 348-351

disc 346-348
fluid selection 330
front
  caliper 334-335
  master cylinder 336-337
  pad replacement 331-334
hose replacement 343-346
rear
  caliper 339-340
  master cylinder 341-342
  pad replacement 337-339
  pedal 343
service 330-331
system specifications 351
  torque 352
troubleshooting 45-46
Bulbs
  replacement 254

C

Cable
  starter enrichment valve (choke)
    replacement 212-213
  throttle 211-212
Caliper
  front 334-335

rear 339-340
Camshafts 85-94
  drive chain 98-100
    and primary drive gear 141-143
  chain tensioner and guide rails 94-98
Capacitor discharge ignition 235-238
Carburetor. 201-211
  operation 200-201
  specifications 224-225
Charging system 228-229
  troubleshooting 40-41
Clutch 170
  cable replacement 180-181
  release lever and bearings 169-170
  service. 170-180
  specifications 181-182
    torque. 182
  starter and gears 143-147
  troubleshooting. 44
Control cables 57-59
Conversion tables 32-33
Cooling system 65-68
  fan 259
    and radiator 257-258
  hoses and clamps 256
  inspection 256-257
  safety precautions 255
  specifications. 264
  thermostat 259-262
  water pump 262-264
Cover, side 355
Crankcase. 147-166
  assembly 160-166
  bearing replacement
    ball 154-155
    main 152-154
  breather system. 223
  cleaning and inspection 150-152
  cover
    left side 133-134
    right side 133
  disassembly 147-150
Crankshaft
  and connecting rod
  cleaning and inspection 155-156
  end float inspection and adjustment . . . 157-159
Cylinder 117-119
  head 100-105
    cover 84-85
    side cover 354-355

master
  front 336-337
  rear. 341-342

D

Disc, brakes 346-348
Drive chain
  and sprockets. 62-65
  drive sprocket and chain. 284-288
  driven sprocket and driven flange 271-273
Drive gear, primary and camshaft
  drive chain 141-143
Driven
  sprocket 271-273
  and flange 271-273

E

Electrical system
  alternator. 230-234
  battery box 228
  capacitor discharge ignition 235-238
  charging system 228-229
  fundamentals. 22-24
  fuses 253-254
  horn 252-253
  instruments 253
  lighting system 244-247
  preliminary inspections 226-228
  replacement bulbs 254
  specifications. 254
    torque. 254
  starter relay replacement 244
  starting system. 238-244
  switches 247-252
  voltage regulator 234
  wiring diagram 254, 368-369
Emission control system
  crankcase breather system 223
  evaporative control system
  California models 223-224
  evaporative system service 224
  secondary air system, U.S. and
  Switzerland models 224

16

Engine
  lower cover 355
  lower end 130-133
    balancer shaft system 147
      cleaning and inspection 159
      disassembly/assembly 159-160
    bearing replacement
      ball 154-155
      main 152-154
    break-in 167
    crankcase
      assembly 160-166
      cleaning and inspection 150-152
      disassembly 147-150
      left side cover 133-134
      right side cover 133
    crankshaft
      and connecting rod
        cleaning and inspection 155-156
      end float inspection
        and adjustment 157-159
    oil
      circuit bleeding 166-167
      pumps 136-141
    primary drive gear and
      camshaft drive chain 141-143
    servicing in frame 129-130
    specifications
      service 167
      torque 168
    starter clutch and gears 143-147
    tachometer drive mechanism 134-136
  lubrication 53-56
    troubleshooting 44
  noises, troubleshooting 43-44
  performance, troubleshooting 38-39
  starting, troubleshooting 37-38
  top end
    camshafts 85-94
      chain tensioner and guide rails 94-98
      drive chain 98-100
    cylinder 117-119
    head 100-105
      cover 84-85
    pistons, and rings 119-125
  service precautions 82-84

  specifications
    general engine 125-126
    service 126-127
    torque 127-128
  valves
    and components 107-117
    lifters and shims 105-107
Evaporative emission control
  system service 224
Excessive vibration
  troubleshooting 45
Exhaust system 219-223
  specifications, torque 225

                          F
Fan, cooling 259
  and radiator 257-258
Fasteners 4-6, 69
Fender, front 353-354
Footpegs 361
Fork
  front
    oil capacity 312
    oil 56-57
Front fairing and windshield 356-359
Front fork 302-311
Fuel system
  air filter air box 218-219
  carburetor 201-211
    operation 200-201
    specifications 224-225
  shutoff valve 217-218
  starting enrichment valve (choke)
  cable replacment 212-213
  tank 213-217
    cover 359-360
  throttle cable 211-212
  troubleshooting 42-43
Fuses 253-254

                          G

Gears and starter clutch 143-147
Gearshift mechanism
  internal shift 195-198

General information
  basic service methods 24-30
  conversion tables. 32-33
  decimal and metric equivalents 35
  electrical system fundamentals. 22-24
  fasteners 4-6
  general specifications 31
    torque 33
  metric tap and drill sizes 34
  model year coverage. 31
  serial numbers 3-4
  shop supplies 6-9
  storage 30-31
  technical abbreviations. 33-34
  tools
    basic 9-14
    precision measuring 14-22
    special 24
  vehicle weight 32
Guide rails and camshaft chain tensioner . . 94-98

H
Handlebar 289-293
Horn 252-253
Hoses
  and clamps 256
  replacement 343-346
Hubs
  front and rear 273-278

I
Ignition system, troubleshooting 41-42
Instruments 253

L
Lighting system 244-247
  troubleshooting 44-45
Lubrication
  and maintenance schedule 78-79
  control cables 57-59
  engine 53-56
  fork oil 56-57
  periodic 59-60
  recommended lubricants and fluids 80

M
Maintenance
  air filter 60

and lubrication schedule 78-79
and tune-up
  specifications 81
  torque 81
battery 49-53
  state of charge 80
brakes 61-62
cooling system 65-68
drive chain and sprockets. 62-65
fasteners 69
periodic lubrication 59-60
pre-ride checklist 47-48
rear suspenion 68-69
recommended lubricants and fluids 80
tire inflation pressure, cold 79-80
tires and wheels 48
Master cylinder
  front 336-337
  rear 341-342
Mudguard, rear 354

O
Oil
  circuit bleeding, engine 166-167
  pumps 136-141
Operating requirements
  troubleshooting 37

P
Pad replacement
  front 331-334
  rear 337-339
Pedal, rear 343
Pistons, and rings 119-125
Pre-ride checklist 47-48

R
Radiator and cooling fan 257-258
Rear suspenion 68-69
Rear swing arm 316-319
  service 319-322

S
Saddlebags 360
Seat 353
Secondary air system
  U.S. and Switzerland models 224

16

Serial numbers 3-4
Service
  basic 24-30
  precautions 82-84
Servicing engine in frame
  lower end 129-130
Shift mechanism, internal 195-198
Shock
  absorber 313-315
  linkage 322-324
Specifications
  general 31
  engine 125-126
  torque 33
Sprockets and drive chain 62-65
Starter
  clutch and gears 143-147
  relay replacement 244
Starting 238-244
  enrichment valve (choke)
    cable replacment 212-213
  troubleshooting 39-40
  engine, troubleshooting 37-38
Steering
  handlebar 289-293
  head 295-301
Storage 30-31
Supplies, shop 6-9
Suspension
  front
    and steering, troulbeshooting 45
    fork 302-311
      oil capacity 312
      specifications, torque 312
  rear
    shock absorber 313-315
    shock linkage 322-324
    specifications, torque 329
    swing arm 316-319
    service 319-322
Swing arm
  rear 316-319
  service 319-322
Switches 247-252

T

Tachometer drive mechanism 134-136
Thermostat 259-262
Throttle cable 211-212
Tires 281

and wheels 48
bike stands 265
changing 281-284
inflation pressure, cold 79-80, 288
wheel
  front 265-268
  rear 268-271
Tools
  basic 9-14
  precision measuring 14-22
  special 24
Torque specifications, general 33
Transmission 184-185
  inspection 193-195
  internal shift mechanism 195-198
  operation 183-184
  overhaul 185-192
  specifications
    general 198
    service 199
  troubleshooting 44
Troubleshooting
  brake system 45-46
  charging system 40-41
  clutch 44
  engine
    lubrication 44
    noises 43-44
    performance 38-39
    starting the 37-38
    excessive vibration 45
  front suspension and steering 45
  fuel system 42-43
  ignition system 41-42
  lighting system 44-45
  operating requirements 37
  starting system 39-40
  transmission 44
Tune-up 69-78
  air filter 60
  and maintenance specifications 81
  torque 81

V

Valve
  and components 107-111
  lifters and shims 105-107
Voltage regulator 234

W

Water pump 262-264
Weight, vehicle 32
Wheels
  balance 280-281
  bike stands 265
  front 265-268
  rear 268-271

runout 278
service 278-280
specifications 288
  torque 288
tires 48
Windshield and front fairing 356-359
Wiring diagram 254, 368-369

16

ALL MODELS 1994-2000

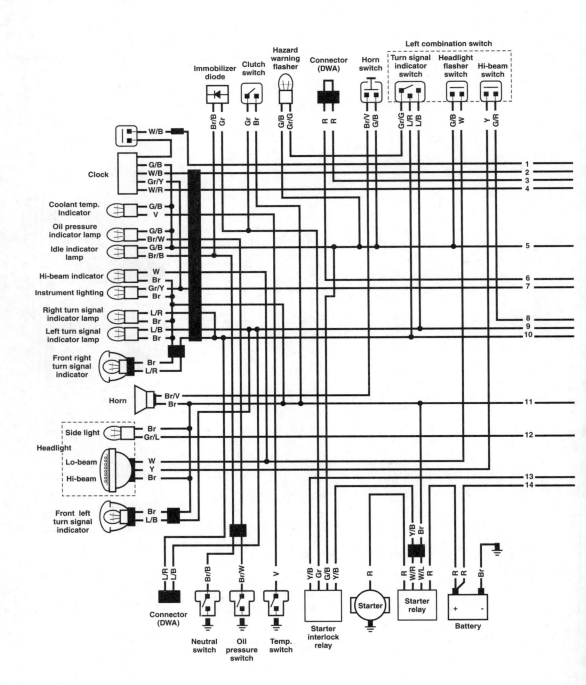

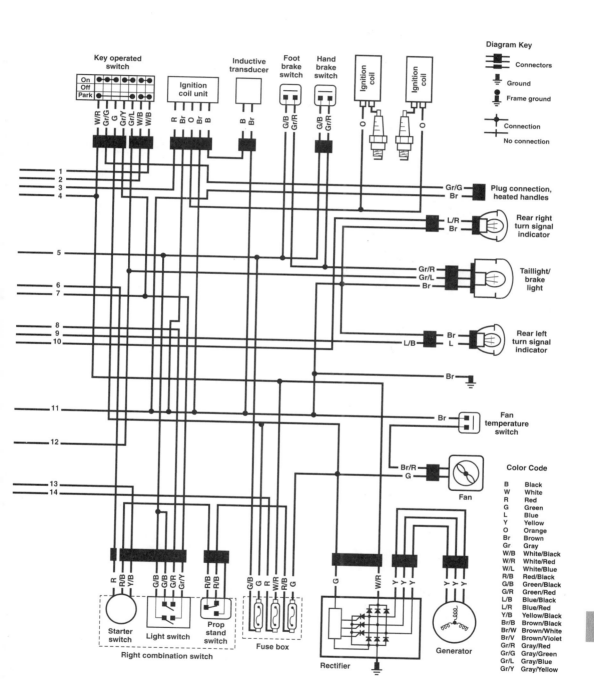

Diagram Key

Connectors

Ground

Frame ground

Connection

No connection

Key operated switch

On	●	●	●	●	●	●
Off						
Park	●			●	●	●

W/R
Gr/G
G
Gr/Y
Gr/L
W/B
W/B

Ignition coil unit

R
Br
O
Br
B

Inductive transducer

B
Br

Foot brake switch

G/B
Gr/R

Hand brake switch

G/B
Gr/R

Ignition coil

O

Ignition coil

O

1
2
3
4

Gr/G
Br

Plug connection, heated handles

L/R
Br

Rear right turn signal indicator

5

Gr/R
Gr/L
Br

Taillight/ brake light

6
7

8
9
10

L/B

Br
L

Rear left turn signal indicator

Br

11

Br

Fan temperature switch

12

13
14

Br/R
G

Fan

Color Code

B Black
W White
R Red
G Green
L Blue
Y Yellow
O Orange
Br Brown
Gr Gray
W/B White/Black
W/R White/Red
W/L White/Blue
R/B Red/Black
G/B Green/Black
G/R Green/Red
L/B Blue/Black
L/R Blue/Red
Y/B Yellow/Black
Br/B Brown/Black
Br/W Brown/White
Br/V Brown/Violet
Gr/R Gray/Red
Gr/G Gray/Green
Gr/L Gray/Blue
Gr/Y Gray/Yellow

R
R/B
Y/B

Starter switch

G/B
G/B
G/R
Gr/Y

Light switch

R/B
R/B

Prop stand switch

Right combination switch

G/B
G
R
W/R
R/B
G

Fuse box

G

W/R

Y Y Y

Rectifier

Y Y Y

Generator

17

NOTES

MAINTENANCE LOG

Date	Miles	Type of Service

Check out *clymer.com* for our full line of powersport repair manuals.

BMW

M308	500 & 600 CC twins, 55-69
M502	BMW R-Series, 70-94
M500	BMW K-Series, 85-95
M503	R-850 & R-1100, 93-98

HARLEY-DAVIDSON

M419	Sportsters, 59-85
M428	Sportster Evolution, 86-90
M429-3	Sportster Evolution, 91-02
M418	Panheads, 48-65
M420	Shovelheads, 66-84
M421	FX/FL Softail Big-Twin Evolution, 84-94
M422	FLT/FXR Big-Twin Evolution, 84-94
M424	Dyna Glide, 91-95
M425	Dyna Glide Twin Cam, 99-01
M430	FLH/FLT 1999-2002

HONDA

ATVs

M316	Odyssey FL250, 77-84
M311	ATC, TRX & Fourtrax 70-125, 70-87
M433	Fourtrax 90 ATV, 93-00
M326	ATC185 & 200, 80-86
M347	ATC200X & Fourtrax 200SX, 86-88
M455	ATC250 & Fourtrax 200/250, 84-87
M342	ATC250R, 81-84
M348	TRX250R/Fourtrax 250R & ATC250R, 85-89
M456	TRX250X 1987-1988, 91-92; TRX300EX 93-96
M446	TRX250 Recon 1997-02
M346-3	TRX300/Fourtrax 300 & TRX300FW/Fourtrax 4x4, 88-00
M459	Fourtrax Foreman 95-98
M454	TRX400EX 1999-02

Singles

M310-13	50-110cc OHC Singles, 65-99
M315	100-350cc OHC, 69-82
M317	Elsinore, 125-250cc, 73-80
M442	CR60-125R Pro-Link, 81-88
M431-2	CR80R, 89-95, CR125R, 89-91
M435	CR80, 96-02
M457-2	CR125R & CR250R, 92-97
M443	CR250R-500R Pro-Link, 81-87
M432	CR250R & CR500R, 88-96
M437	CR250R, 97-01
M312-12	XL/XR75-100, 75-02
M318	XL/XR/TLR 125-200, 79-87
M328-2	XL/XR250, 78-00; XL/XR350R 83-85; XR200R, 84-85; XR250L, 91-96
M320	XR400R, 96-00
M339-6	XL/XR 500-650, 79-02

Twins

M321	125-200cc, 64-77
M322	250-350cc, 64-74
M323	250-360cc Twins, 74-77
M324-4	Rebel 250 & Twinstar, 78-87; Nighthawk 250, 91-97; Rebel 250, 96-97
M334	400-450cc, 78-87
M333	450 & 500cc, 65-76
M335	CX & GL500/650 Twins, 78-83
M344	VT500, 83-88
M313	VT700 & 750, 83-87
M460	VT1100C2 A.C.E. Shadow, 95-97
M440	Shadow 1100cc V-Twin, 85-96

Fours

M332	350-550cc 71-78
M345	CB550 & 650, 83-85
M336	CB650, 79-82
M341	CB750 SOHC, 69-78
M337	CB750 DOHC, 79-82
M436	CB750 Nighthawk, 91-93 & 95-99
M325	CB900, 1000 & 1100, 80-83
M439	Hurricane 600, 87-90
M441-2	CBR600, 91-98
M434	CBR900RR Fireblade, 93-98
M329	500cc V-Fours, 84-86
M438	Honda VFR800, 98-00
M349	700-1000 Interceptor, 83-85
M458-2	VFR700F-750F, 86-97
M327	700-1100cc V-Fours, 82-88
M340	GL1000 & 1100, 75-83
M504	GL1200, 84-87

Sixes

M505	GL1500 Gold Wing, 88-92
M506	GL1500 Gold Wing, 93-95
M462	GL1500C Valkyrie, 97-00

KAWASAKI

ATVs

M465	KLF220 Bayou, 88-95
M466-2	KLF300 Bayou, 86-98
M467	KLF400 Bayou, 93-99
M470	KEF300 Lakota, 95-99
M385	KSF250 Mojave, 87-00

Singles

M350-9	Rotary Valve 80-350cc, 66-01
M444	KX60-80, 83-90
M351	KDX200, 83-88
M447	KX125 & KX250, 82-91 KX500, 83-93
M472	KX125, 92-98
M473	KX250, 92-98

Twins

M355	KZ400, KZ/Z440, EN450 & EN500, 74-95
M360	EX500/GPZ500S, 87-93
M356-2	700-750 Vulcan, 85-01
M354	VN800 Vulcan 95-98
M357	VN1500 Vulcan 87-98
M471	VN1500 Vulcan Classic, 96-98

Fours

M449	KZ500/550 & ZX550, 79-85
M450	KZ, Z & ZX750, 80-85
M358	KZ650, 77-83
M359	900-1000cc Fours, 73-80
M451	1000 &1100cc Fours, 81-85
M452-3	ZX500 & 600 Ninja, 85-97
M453-3	Ninja ZX900-1100 84-01
M468	ZX6 Ninja, 90-97
M469	ZX7 Ninja, 91-98
M453	900-1100 Ninja, 84-93

POLARIS

ATVs

M496	Polaris ATV, 85-95
M362	Polaris Magnum ATV, 96-98
M363	Scrambler 500, 4X4 97-00
M365	Sportsman/Xplorer, 96-00

SUZUKI

ATVs

M381	ALT/LT 125 & 185, 83-87
M475	LT230 & LT250, 85-90
M380	LT250R Quad Racer, 85-88
M343	LTF500F Quadrunner, 98-00
M483	Suzuki King Quad/ Quad Runner 250, 87-95

Singles

M371	RM50-400 Twin Shock, 75-81
M369	125-400cc 64-81
M379	RM125-500 Single Shock, 81-88
M476	DR250-350, 90-94
M384	LS650 Savage Single, 86-88
M386	RM80-250, 89-95

Twins

M372	GS400-450 Twins, 77-87
M481-3	VS700-800 Intruder, 85-02
M482	VS1400 Intruder, 87-98
M484-2	GS500E Twins, 89-00

Triple

M368	380-750cc, 72-77

Fours

M373	GS550, 77-86
M364	GS650, 81-83
M370	GS750 Fours, 77-82
M376	GS850-1100 Shaft Drive, 79-84
M378	GS1100 Chain Drive, 80-81
M383-3	Katana 600, 88-96
M331	GSX-R600, 97-00
M478-2	GSX-R750, 88-92 GSX750F Katana, 89-96
M485	GSX-R750, 96-99
M338	GSF600 Bandit, 95-00

YAMAHA

ATVs

M394	YTM/YFM200 & 225, 83-86
M487-3	YFM350 Warrior, 87-02
M486-3	YFZ350 Banshee, 87-02
M488-3	Blaster ATV, 88-01
M489-2	Timberwolf ATV, 89-00
M490-2	YFM350 Moto-4 & Big Bear, 87-98
M493	YFM400FW Kodiak, 93-98

Singles

M492-2	PW50 & PW80, BW80 Big Wheel 80, 81-02
M410	80-175 Piston Port, 68-76
M415	250-400cc Piston Port, 68-76
M412	DT & MX 100-400, 77-83
M414	IT125-490, 76-86
M393	YZ50-80 Monoshock, 78-90
M413	YZ100-490 Monoshock, 76-84
M390	YZ125-250, 85-87 YZ490, 85-90
M391	YZ125-250, 88-93 WR250Z, 91-93
M497	YZ125, 94-99
M498	YZ250, 94-98 and WR250Z, 94-97
M491	YZ400F, YZ426F & WR400F, 98-00
M417	XT125-250, 80-84
M480-2	XT/TT 350, 85-96
M405	XT500 & TT500, 76-81
M416	XT/TT 600, 83-89

Twins

M403	650cc, 70-82
M395-9	XV535-1100 Virago, 81-99
M495	XVS650 V-Star, 98-00

Triple

M404	XS750 & 850, 77-81

Fours

M387	XJ550, XJ600 & FJ600, 81-92
M494	XJ600 Seca II, 92-98
M388	YX600 Radian & FZ600, 86-90
M396	FZR600, 89-93
M392	FZ700-750 & Fazer, 85-87
M411	XS1100 Fours, 78-81
M397	FJ1100 & 1200, 84-93

VINTAGE MOTORCYCLES

Clymer® Collection Series

M330	Vintage British Street Bikes, BSA, 500 & 650cc Unit Twins; Norton, 750 & 850cc Commandos; Triumph, 500-750cc Twins
M300	Vintage Dirt Bikes, V. 1 Bultaco, 125-370cc Singles; Montesa, 123-360cc Singles; Ossa, 125-250cc Singles
M301	Vintage Dirt Bikes, V. 2 CZ, 125-400cc Singles; Husqvarna, 125-450cc Singles; Maico, 250-501cc Singles; Hodaka, 90-125cc Singles
M305	Vintage Japanese Street Bikes Honda, 250 & 305cc Twins; Kawasaki, 250-750cc Triples; Kawasaki, 900 & 1000cc Fours